cleo,

❦ ❦ ❦ POSSESSION ❦ ❦ ❦

POSSESSION

A NOVEL

by LOUIS BROMFIELD

Author of

"THE GREEN BAY TREE"

GROSSET & DUNLAP, *Publishers*

by arrangement with

FREDERICK A. STOKES COMPANY

Copyright, 1925, by
FREDERICK A. STOKES COMPANY

Published - - - - - - - September 30, 1925
Second Printing (before Publication), Sept. 26, 1925
Third Printing - - - - - - October 20, 1925
Fourth Printing - - - - - November 14, 1925
Fifth Printing - - - - - - November 25, 1925
Sixth Printing - - - - - - December 9, 1925
Seventh Printing - - - - - January 25, 1926
Eighth Printing - - - - - February 15, 1926
Ninth Printing - - - - - - - May 1, 1926
Tenth Printing - - - - - December 14, 1926
Eleventh Printing - - - - - - July 11, 1927
Twelfth Printing - - - - - - August 18, 1927
Thirteenth Printing - - - - - October 26, 1927

Printed in the United States of America

To
MARY

"Life is hard for our children. It isn't as simple as it was for us. Their grandfathers were pioneers and the same blood runs in their veins, only they haven't a frontier any longer. They stand—these children of ours—with their backs toward this rough-hewn middle west and their faces set toward Europe and the East and they belong to neither. They are lost somewhere between."

◆　　◆　　◆　　◆

"Wherever she goes, trouble will follow. She's born like most people with a touch of genius, under a curse. She is certain to affect the lives of every one about her . . . because, well, because the threads of our lives are hopelessly tangled. . . . Marry her if you will, but don't expect happiness to come of it. She would doubtless bear you a son . . . a fine strong son, because she's a fine cold animal. But don't expect satisfaction from her. She knows too well exactly where she is bound."

"Life is hard for our children. It isn't as simple as it was for us. Their grandfathers were pioneers and the same blood runs in their veins, only they haven't a frontier any longer. They stand—these children of ours—with their backs toward the rough hewn middle-west and their faces set toward Europe and the East and they belong to neither. They are lost somewhere between."

"Whatever she, the poor trouble will follow. She's born like most people, with a touch of genius under a curse. She is certain to affect the lives of every one about her . . . because, well, because the threads of our lives are hopelessly tangled. . . . Marry her if you will, but don't expect happiness to come of it. She would doubtless bear you a son . . . a fine strong son, because she's a fine cold animal. But don't expect satisfaction from her. She knows, too, will exactly where she is bound."

FOREWORD

"Possession" is in no sense a sequel to "The Green Bay Tree." The second novel does not carry the fortunes of the characters which appeared in the first; it reveals, speaking chronologically, little beyond the final page of the earlier book. On the contrary both novels cover virtually the same period of time, from the waning years of the nineteenth century up to the present time. The two are what might be called panel novels in a screen which, when complete, will consist of at least a half-dozen panels all interrelated and each giving a certain phase of the ungainly, swarming, glittering spectacle of American Life.

Those who read "The Green Bay Tree" must have felt that one character—that of Ellen Tolliver—was thrust aside in order to make way for the progress of Lily Shane. With the publication of the present novel, it is possible to say that the energetic Miss Tolliver was neglected for two reasons; first, because she was a character of such violence that, once given her way, she would soon have dominated all the others; second, because the author kept her purposely in restraint, as he desired to tell her story in proportions worthy of her.

In Ellen's story, the author, knowing that much which pertains to the life of a musician is boring and of little interest to any one outside the realm of music, has endeavored to eliminate all the technical side of her education. He does this not because he lacks knowledge of the facts but because they are in themselves uninteresting. Ellen Tolliver might have been a sculptor, a painter, an actress, a writer; the interest in her lies not in the calling she chose but in the character of the woman herself. She would, doubtless, have been successful in any direction she saw fit to direct her boundless energy.

✸ ✸ ✸ FOREWORD ✸ ✸ ✸

"Possession" is the second of several novels in which familiar characters will reappear and new ones will make their entrance.

L. B.

Cold Spring Harbor
May 1, 1925
Long Island.

❦ ❦ ❦ POSSESSION ❦ ❦ ❦

POSSESSION

I

IN the fading October twilight Grandpa Tolliver sat eating an apple and reading The Decline and Fall of the Roman Empire. The ponderous book (volume III) lay spread open upon his bony knees, for it was too heavy to be supported in any other way, and he read by leaning far over and peering at the pages through steel rimmed spectacles which were not quite clear, as they never were. The dimness of lens, however, did not appear to annoy him; undisturbed he read on as if the spectacles sharpened his vision instead of dimming it. Things were, after all, what you believed them to be; therefore the spectacles served their purpose. He was not one to be bothered by such small things. . . .

The room in which he sat was square and not too large. On two sides there were windows and in one corner an enormous and funereal bed of black walnut (the nuptial bed of three generations in the Tolliver family) which bore at the moment the imprint of the perverse and angular old body. He had lain there to think. Sometimes he lay thus for hours at a time in a sort of coma, ruminating the extraordinary and imbecile diversity of life. But it was the number of books which contributed the dominating characteristic of the room. There was row upon row of them rising from floor to ceiling, rows added year by year out of Grandpa's infinitesimal income until at last they had walled him in. There were books bound in fine leather and books in cheap leather, worn and frayed at the corners, books in cheap boards and an immense number of books bound in yellow paper.

Pressed close against the books on the north wall of the room there stood an enormous desk of the same funereal black walnut—a desk filled with innumerable pigeonholes into which had been stuffed without order or sequence bits of paper scribbled over with a handwriting that was fine and erratic like the tracks of a tiny bird strayed into an inkpot. The papers ranged through every variety of shade from the yellowish bisque of ancient documents to the gray white of comparatively new ones. Of all the room it was the desk alone that had an appearance of untidiness; it lay under a pall of dust save for two small spots rubbed clean by the sharp elbows of Grandpa Tolliver.

What did he write? What was contained in this immense collection of documents? No one knew that; not even the curiosity of his daughter-in-law Hattie, who entered the room each morning to throw open the windows (an action he detested) and force the old man out into the chill air of the streets, had been able to penetrate the mysteries of the extraordinary bird tracks. A word with luck, here or there . . . Nothing more. And she had examined them often enough in a fierce effort to penetrate the secret of his strength. From years of breathless, headlong writing the words had lost all resemblance to combinations of letters. The letters themselves were obscured; they flowed into one another until each one, in the fashion of the Chinese, had become a symbol, a mystery to which the old man alone held the key. It was the writing of a man whose pen had never been able to keep pace with the lightning speed of his thoughts. It may have been that the old man himself could not have deciphered the writing on those sheets which long since had turned to a yellow bisque. So far as any one could discover, he never took them from the pigeonholes and read them a second time. They were simply thrust away to turn yellow and gather dust, for Grandpa Tolliver had suffered for years from a sense of the immense futility of everything.

As he sat in the fading light in his decrepit rocking chair the appearance of the old man struck faintly a note of the sinister.

Something in the shape of his great, bony head, in the appearance of his unkempt gray beard, in the remarkable angularity of his lean body gave him the appearance of one in alliance with the powers of darkness. The peculiar gray green of his glittering eyes had a way of piercing through pretense, through barriers of reserve and secrecy. They were the eyes of one who knew far too much. They were the eyes that got somehow at the core of things, so that a person—even his bitterest enemy, the vigorous and unsubtle Hattie—winced before the shattering light that gathered in their depths. They looked out from under shaggy brows with a knowledge bred of solitude that was something more than human. And he had a terrible way of using them, of watching people, of silently and powerfully prying open their shells. For Grandpa Tolliver there were no longer any illusions; he was therefore a horrid and intolerable old man.

At length when the light grew too dim even for the unearthly eyes of the old man, he closed The Decline and Fall and devoted himself to finishing his apple, absorbed for the time being in reflecting triumphantly upon passages in the ponderous work which proved without any doubt that the human race lay beyond the possibility of improvement.

When his strong pointed teeth had finished with the apple, he cast it aside for Hattie to sweep out in the morning and, lifting The Decline and Fall as high as possible, he dropped it to the floor with a resounding crash. As the echo died there rose from belowstairs the sound of clattering pans shaken by the crash from the startled hands of Hattie, and then an inarticulate rumble of exasperation at this latest bit of minute deviltry.

The old man leaned back in his chair and chuckled, wickedly. It was one more skirmish in the state of war which had existed between him and his daughter-in-law over a period of years.

Through the closed window the homely sounds of a dozen backyards filtered into the room . . . the sharp slam of a refrigerator door, the sudden mad barking of a dog playing with a child, the faint whicker of a horse in one of the stables and then the sound of Hattie's vigorous voice, still carrying a persistent, unmistakable note of irritation, summoning her small sons from the far reaches of the neighborhood.

The sound of the voice rose and hung in the autumn night, rich, full-blooded, vigorous, redolent of energy, beautiful in its primitive strength. At the faint note of irritation Grandpa Tolliver, rubbing his teeth with a skinny finger, chuckled again.

The voice wavered, penetrating the remote distances of the back yards, and presently there came an answering cry in the shrill, high treble of a boy of twelve arrested suddenly in the midst of his play.

"Yay-*us!* Yay-*us!* We're coming!"

Primitive it was, like a ewe calling to her lambs, or more perhaps (thought the old man) like a lioness summoning her cubs. It was Robert who answered, the younger of the two. It was difficult for Fergus to yell in the same lusty fashion; his voice had reached the stage where it trembled perilously between a treble and a bass. The sounds he made shamed him. Fergus, like his father, disliked making a spectacle of himself. (Too sensitive, thought Grandpa Tolliver. Like his father he would be a failure in life, because he had no indifference.)

The room grew darker and after a time the sweet, acrid odor of smoldering leaves, stirred into flame by the children who played beneath the window, drifted through the cracks in the glass. As if the scent, the soft twilight, the sound of Hattie's voice, had set fire to a train of memories, Grandpa Tolliver began to rock gently. The chair made a faint squeaking sound which filled the room as if it had been invaded by a flock of bats which, circling wildly above the old man's head, uttered a chorus of faint shrill cries. . . . The old man chuckled again. It was a bitter, unearthly sound. . . .

The room in which Grandpa Tolliver sat had been added to

the Tolliver house during one of those rare intervals, years ago, when his son had prospered for a time. The house itself stood back from the street in the older part of a town which within a generation had changed from a frontier settlement into a bustling city whose prosperity centered about the black mills and the flaming furnaces of a marshy district known as The Flats, a district black and unsightly and inhabited by hordes of Italians, Poles, Slovaks and Russians who never emerged from its sooty environs into the clear air of the Hill where the old citizens had their homes. Among these houses the Tollivers' was marked by the need of paint, though this shameful fault was concealed somewhat by masses of vines—roses, honeysuckle, ivy—which overran all the dwelling and in summer threw a cloud of beauty over the horrid, imaginative trimmings conceived by some side-whiskered small town architect of the eighties. There was in the appearance of the house nothing of opulence. It was gray, commonplace and ornamented with extravagant jig-saw decorations. Also it suffered from a slate roof of a depressing shade of blue gray. But it was roomy and comfortable.

Houses occupied for a long period by the same family have a way of taking on imperceptibly but surely the characteristics of their owners. The Tollivers, Hattie and Charles, had come into the house as bride and bridegroom, in the days when Charles Tolliver had before him a bright future, years before he gave up, at the urging of his powerful wife, a commonplace adequate salary for a more reckless and extravagant career in the politics of the growing county. By now, twenty years after, the house, the lawn and the garden expressed the essence of the Tolliver family. The grass sometimes went in grave need of cutting. The paint had peeled here and there where it lay exposed to the middle-western winter. At the eaves there were streaks of black made by soot which drifted from the roaring Mills in the distant Flats. The shrubs were unpruned and the climbing roses would have been improved by a little cutting; yet these things, taken all in all, produced an effect of charm far greater than any to be found in the other neat, painted, monotonous houses that stood in unspectacular rows on either side of Sycamore Street. In the careless growth of the shrubs and vines there was a certain wildness and inspiring vigor, something full-blooded and lush which elsewhere in the block was absent. There was nothing ordered, pruned or clipped into a state of patterned mediocrity. Here, within the hedge that enclosed the Tolliver property there reigned a marked abandon, a sense of life lived recklessly with a shameless disregard for smug security. The Tollivers clearly had no time for those things which lay outside the main current.

Yet there was no rubbish in evidence. The whole was spotlessly clean from the linden trees which stood by the curb to the magenta-colored stable at the end of the garden. You might have walked the length of the block without consciousness of the other houses; but in front of the Tollivers' you would have halted, thinking, "Here is a difference indeed. Some careless householder without proper pride in his grounds!"

Yet you would have stopped to notice it. At least it would have interested you by the wild, vigorous, disheveled character of its difference.

In the beginning the room which Gramp occupied had been built for a servant and through its doors, in the spasmodic periods of Tolliver prosperity, had passed a procession of weird and striking "hired girls" . . . country maidens come to town in search of excitement, Bohemian and Russian girls, the offspring of the Flat-dwellers; one or two who had been, to Hattie's shocked amazement, simply daughters of joy. With the passing of Myrtle, the last of these, who was retired in order to bear a child of uncertain paternity, the Tollivers' ship of fortune had slipped into one of the periodical doldrums and the stormy, unsatisfactory era of the hired girl came to an end forever. Almost as if he had divined the event, Grandpa Tolliver appeared on the same day seated beside the driver on a wagon laden with books, to announce that he had come to take up his abode with the family of his son. There was nothing to be done. The books were moved into the room above the kitchen and there the old man settled himself. He had been there now for ten years, a gadfly to torment the virtuous, bustling existence of his daughter-in-law. He seldom stirred from his room. He had, indeed, done nothing in all his life which might be scored under the name of accomplishment. As a young man he had been trained for the church, but when his education had been completed, he discovered that he had learned too much and so believed nothing. He bothered no one. His crime was inertia. He possessed an indifference of colossal proportions.

As the room fell into a thick blackness, the rocking chair, under the urge of flooding memories, acquired a greater animation. It may have been that there was something in the homely sounds of the backyard vista and the pleasant smell of burning leaves that pierced by way of his senses the wall of the old man's impregnable solitude. Presently he chuckled again in a triumphant fashion, as if the memory of Hattie Tolliver's irritation still rang in his ears.

Ah, how she hated him! How they all scorned him! Even on his rare and solitary ramblings along the sidewalks of the Town, prosperous citizens regarded him with hostile looks. "Old Man Tolliver . . . The Failure!" They pointed him out to their children as the awful example of a man without ambition, a man who drifted into a lonely and desolate old age, abhorred and unwanted, a burden to his own children and grandchildren. That's what came of not having energy and push!

Old Man Tolliver . . . The Failure! At the thought, the wicked old man chortled more loudly than ever. Failure! Failure! What did they know of whether he was a failure or not. Failure! That was where he had the joke on the lot of them. He alone had fixed his ambition, captured his ideal; he had done always exactly what he wanted to do.

In sudden satisfaction over his secret triumph the old man was very nearly overcome by his own chuckling.

Old? Yes, he felt very old to-night. Perhaps he hadn't many years before him. Maybe it was only a matter of months. Then he would die. What was it like to die? Just a passing out probably, into something vast and dark. Oblivion! That was it. Why wasn't that the ideal end? Oblivion, where you were nothing and had no mind and no memory and no books, where you simply did not exist. Just nothingness and eternal peace. Aratu, that kingdom where reigned mere oblivion. He wasn't looking forward to Heaven and harps. (Imagine Hattie strumming a harp!) He was filled with a sense of great completeness, of having done everything there was to do, of having known all of life that it was possible for one man to know. Sin? What was sin? He didn't regret anything he had done. He had no remorse, no regrets. On the contrary he was glad of all the things he had done which people called sin. It gave him a satisfactory feeling of completeness. Now when he was so old, he needn't wish he had done this or done that. He had. To be sure, he hadn't murdered any one! He hadn't been guilty of theft. It was very satisfactory . . . that feeling of completeness.

Nothing remained. Death . . . Deadness . . . Why he was dead already. Death must be like this room, blank, dark, negative, neither one thing nor the other. He had been dead for weeks, for months, for years; and here he was walled up in a tomb of books. "La Pucelle" (a rare edition). What would become of it? Like as not Hattie would burn it, never knowing its value. Think how she would suffer if ever she discovered she had burned up a great pile of banknotes! Candide, The Critique of Pure Reason, Spinoza, Montaigne, Darwin, Huxley. (What a a row they'd caused! How well he remembered the chatter.) Plato. And there was Verlaine and George Sand and all of Thackeray. Colonel Newcome and Rebecca Sharp with her pointed nose and green eyes. What an amusing creature she was! Amelia Sedley, that tiresome, uninteresting, virtuous bore! And Charles Honeyman. (Ah! He knew things they didn't dream of in this town!) And there in the corner by the old desk, Emma Bovary tearing voluptuously at her bodice.

But they were not all ghosts of books. There were ghosts too of reality, ghosts born of memories, which came dimly out of the past, out of a youth that, dried now at its source, had been hot-blooded and romantic and restless; such ghosts as one called Celeste (in a poke bonnet with a camelia pinned just above the brim) who seemed forever peeping round the corner of a staircase as she had once peeped, in a glowing reality round the corner of a staircase in the Rue de Clichy. Nina who was more alive now than she had ever been. . . . And they thought him a failure!

Yes, they were amusing ghosts. He had lived with them so many years. Lonely? How was it possible to be lonely among such fascinating companions? He had lived with them too long. He knew them too well, inside and out. They kept him company in this tomb of books. He seldom left it. Once a week, perhaps, to walk around the block; and then the children ran from him as if they saw the Devil himself.

Grandpa Tolliver began to rock more gently now. Yes, he'd been wicked enough. He'd known everything there was to know and didn't regret it. They shut him up in this room and didn't address him for days at a time, but he had Emma Bovary and Becky Sharp to amuse him; and Celeste who belonged to him alone. Grandpa Barr didn't even have them. His children had left him—all but his daughter Hattie—to go to Iowa, to Oregon, to Wyoming, always toward the open country. Your friends might die and your children might go away, but your memories couldn't desert you, nor such friends as Emma and Becky.

Outside it began presently to rain, at first slowly with isolate, hesitating drops, and then more and more steadily until at last the whole parched earth drank up the autumn downpour.

2·

IN the sound of rain falling through soft darkness there is a
healing quality of peace. Its persistence—the very effort-
less unswerving rhythm of the downpour—have the power
of engulfing the spirit in a kind of sensuous oblivion. Even upon
one of so violent and unreflective a nature as Ellen Tolliver, one
so young, so impatient and so moody, the sound of the autumn
rain falling on the roof and in the parched garden had its effect.
It created a music of its own, delicate yet primitive, abundant
of the richness of earth and air, so that presently in a room a
dozen feet from her grandfather, Ellen stopped sobbing and
buried her face in the pillow of her great oak bed, soothed,
peaceful; and presently in the darkness of her room she lay at
last silent and still, her dark hair tossed and disheveled against
the white of the pillowcase. She lay thus in a solitude of her
own, separated only by the thinness of a single wall from the
solitude in which her grandfather sat enveloped. If the sound
of her sobbing had been audible, there was another wall that
would have stopped it . . . the wall of warm autumn rain that
beat upon the earth and shut her away from all the world.

She knew no reason for this outburst of weeping. If there had
been a reason she would not have locked herself in her room to
weep until she had no more tears. She could not say, "I weep
because some one has been unkind to me," or "I weep because I
have suffered a sudden disappointment." She wept because she
could not help herself; because she had been overcome by a
mood that was at once melancholy and heroic, sad yet luxuriously
sensuous. After a fashion, her weeping gave her pleasure. Now
that the sound of the rain had quieted her, she lay bathing her
soul in the darkness. Somehow it protected her. Here in a
locked room where no splinter of light penetrated, she was for
a little time completely herself. That was the great thing. . . .
She was *herself*. . . . There was no one about her. . . . Some-

times this same triumphant aloofness came to her from music. . . .
It too was able to set her apart where she was forced to share
nothing of herself with any one. In the darkness people couldn't
pry their way into your soul. All this she understood but vaguely,
with the understanding of a sensitive girl who has not learned
to search her own soul. And this understanding she kept to
herself. None knew of it. The face she showed to the world
betrayed nothing of loneliness, of wild and turbulent moods, of
fierce exasperation. To the world she was a girl very like other
girls, rather more hasty and bad-tempered perhaps, but not
vastly different—a girl driven alone by a wild vague impulse
hidden far back in the harassed regions of her impatient soul.
It is one of the tragedies of youth that it feels and suffers without understanding.

For an hour she lay quite still listening to the rain; and at
the end of that time, hearing sounds from below stairs which
forecast the arrival of supper, she rose and lighted the gas
bracket above her dressing table.

At the first pin point of flame, the world of darkness and rain
vanished and in its place, as if by some abracadabra, there sprang
into existence the hard, definite walls of a room, square and
commonplace, touched with quaint efforts to create an illusion
of beauty. The walls were covered with wall paper bearing a
florid design of lattices heavily laden with red roses on anemic
stalks. Two Gibson pictures, faithfully copied by an admirer,
hung on either side of the oak dresser. They were "The Eternal
Question" and "The Queen of Hearts." The bed, vast and
ugly, and still bearing in the white counterpane the imprint of
Ellen's slim young body, fitted the room as neatly as a canal
barge fits a lock. The chairs varied in type from an old arm
chair of curly maple, brought across the mountains into the middle-
west by Ellen's great-grandfather and now relegated to the
bedroom, to a damaged patent rocker upholstered in red plush
with yellow tassels. On the top of the dressing table lay a
cover made elaborately of imitation Valenciennes and fine cam-

bric, profusely ornamented by bow knots of pink baby ribbon. By the flickering light, the girl arranged her hair before the mirror. It was dark, heavy, lustrous hair with deep blue lights. Hastily tossing it into a pompadour over a wire rat, she washed her eyes with cold water to destroy the redness. She was preparing the face she showed the world. It was not a beautiful face though it had its points. It was too long perhaps and the nose was a trifle prominent; otherwise it was a pleasant face, with large dark eyes, fine straight lips and a really beautiful chin. It held the beginnings of a beauty that was fine and proud. The way the chin and throat leapt from her shoulders was a thing at which to marvel. The line was clear, triumphant, determined. Even Ellen was forced to admire it. What she lacked in beauty was amply compensated by the interest which her face inspired. The pompadour, to be sure, was ridiculous. It was but a week or two old, the sign of her emancipation from the estate of a little girl.

For a long time she studied the reflection in the mirror. This way and that she turned her proud head, admiring all the while the line of the throat and tilted chin. It delighted her as music sometimes delighted her, with a strange leaping sensation of triumph over people about her.

She thought, "Am I to be great one day? Am I to be famous? Is it written in my face? I will be or die . . . I must be!"

Early in the afternoon, before the long rain settled in for the night, she had walked out of Miss Ogilvie's little house down the brick path under the elms with a heart singing in triumph. Before she arrived home, the sense of triumph had faded a little, and by the time she reached her room it was gone altogether, submerged by a wave of despair. It seemed that her triumph only made life more difficult; instead of being an end it was only a beginning. It created the most insuperable difficulties, the most perilous and agitating problems.

Miss Ogilvie lived in a weathered old house that withdrew

from the street behind a verdant bulwark of lilacs, syringas, and old apple trees abounding in birds,—wrens, blackbirds, finches and robins. In the warm season, as if the wild birds were not enough, a canary or two and a pair of love-birds hung suspended from the roof of the narrow piazza high above the scroll-work of the jig-saw rail. There were those who believed that Miss Ogilvie, in some earlier incarnation, was herself a bird . . . a wren perhaps, or a song sparrow flitting in and out of hedges and tufts of grass, shaking its immaculate tail briskly in defiance of a changing world.

When she sat in her big rocker listening to the horrible exercises of her pupils, she resembled a linnet on a swaying bough. She rocked gently as if she found the motion soothing to some wildness inside her correct and spinsterish little body. Always she rocked, perhaps because it helped her to endure the horrible renderings of Schumann and Mendelssohn by the simpering daughters and the sullen sons of the baker, the butcher, the candlestick maker. For Miss Ogilvie understood music and she was sensitive enough. In her youth, before her father failed in the deluge that followed the Civil War, she had been abroad. She had heard music, real music, in her day. In all the Town she and Grandpa Tolliver alone knew what real music could be. She had even studied for a time in Munich where she lived in her birdlike way in a well chaperoned *pension*. The other girls fluttered too, for in her day women were all a little birdlike; it was a part of their training.

In the early afternoon when Ellen Tolliver came for her weekly lesson, Miss Ogilvie, dressed in a tight-fitting basque of purple poplin ornamented with pins of coral and cameo, received her formally into the little drawing-room where she lived in a nest of pampas grass, conch shells, raffia baskets, and spotless bits of bric-a-brac. There was in the reception nothing unusual; Miss Ogilvie permitted herself no relaxation, even in the privacy of her own bed-chamber. She remained a lady, elegantly so, who supported herself in a genteel fashion by giving music lessons. But with Ellen a certain warmth and kindliness, seldom to be found in her contact with other pupils, occasionally tempered the formality. To-day her manner carried even a hint of respect.

Ellen sat at the upright piano and played. She played with a wild emotionalism unhampered by problems of technique. She poured her young, rebellious soul into the music until the ebony piano rocked and the ball-fringe of the brocade piano-cover swayed. Miss Ogilvie sat in her big rocking chair in a spot of sunlight and listened. It was significant that she did not rock. She sat quite still, her tiny feet barely touching the floor, her thin blue-veined hands lying quietly like little birds at rest in her purple poplin lap. The canaries too became still and listened. A hush fell upon the garden.

"And now," said Miss Ogilvie, when Ellen paused for a moment, "some Bach," and the girl set off into the tortuous, architectural beauties of a fugue. She played without notes, her eyes closed a little, her body swaying with a passionate rhythm which arose from something far more profound than the genteel precepts of Miss Ogilvie. It was savage. It must have terrified the gentle little old woman, for she knew that to play Bach savagely was sacrilege. And yet . . . somehow it didn't matter, when Ellen did it. There was in the music a smoldering, disturbing magnificence.

Then she played some Chopin, delicately, poetically; and at last she finished and turned about on the piano stool to await the criticism of her teacher.

Miss Ogilvie said nothing. Her blue eyes winked a bit in embarrassment and down one withered cheek ran a tear which had escaped her dignity and self-possession. The sunlight flickered across her thin hands, and presently she stirred.

"My child," she said, "there is nothing for me to say."

And Ellen's heart leapt so suddenly that she grew faint with joy.

"I no longer count for anything," said Miss Ogilvie gently. "You are beyond me. . . ." She smiled suddenly and dabbed her eyes politely. "Who am I to instruct you? My child, you are an artist. You frighten me!" She leaned forward a little, confidingly, and whispered. "It happens like that . . . in the most unexpected places, in villages, in ugly towns . . . why, even in a dirty mill town like this."

Between the two there was a bond, a thing which neither ever mentioned but which, in the silence that followed Miss Ogilvie's undignified outburst, took possession of both and drew them together. Both scorned the Town, a treason which none had discovered; and now when Miss Ogilvie spoke again she dragged the secret bond into the glaring light of day.

"Artists occur," she said, "without respect for places." And then after a little pause . . . "But you must never let any one here suspect you're an artist. It would make you unhappy." Recovering herself a little she began again to rock gently. "For a long time I've known you were escaping me. . . . It was no use hiding it from myself. . . . I know it now. . . ."

She smiled triumphantly a withered, rosy smile, a bit like the smile one might see on the bright face of a lady apple, and began pulling at the lace on her handkerchief. "It's wonderful," she said, "to think I have discovered it. . . . Poor me! But you must work, Ellen, there are hard days ahead . . . harder than you guess.

"D'you know?" she continued, in her excitement leaning forward once more, "when I was a girl, I played well . . . I was like you . . . not so independent, not so strong, because I was always a little woman . . . even then," she added as if she were conscious that age had shriveled her. "Sometimes I thought I would like to be a great pianist . . . a great artist. . . . But women didn't do such things in my day. My father would never have listened to it for a moment. It wasn't a ladylike thing to do. It was like being a circus rider. He let me take lessons so that I could play in the drawing-room and accompany my young men when they sang. My father even let me study in Munich, but when he found out I was more interested in music than in young men . . . he brought me home. I never got very interested in young men . . . I always liked music better."

Ellen listened respectfully, moved as much by her feeling for Miss Ogilvie in the rôle of a friend as by her respect for older people in general. She was carefully brought up and had good manners. But, secretly, the tale bored her a little. There was nothing interesting in it, nothing to seize one's imagination, nothing to soothe her impatience, nothing which fed that wild ambition. All that Miss Ogilvie told her had happened so long ago.

"I suppose I ought to have got married," continued Miss Ogilvie. "But I waited too long. . . . I had chances!" she added proudly, "good ones. . . . Maybe I would have been happier today. . . . I don't know, though," she added doubtfully, puckering her withered lips as if she could come to no decision in the matter. "There's so much to be said on both sides. But what I mean to say is, that you must go ahead. . . . You mustn't let anything stop you. . . . It's easier now than it was in my day. At least there's no one to oppose you. . . . It's a gift that doesn't come to every one. . . . You see I didn't marry and I didn't become an artist." And a note of wistfulness entered her voice. "So now I'm just an old spinster who gives music lessons. Maybe," she said, "you can manage both. I don't know . . . and you don't. . . . But don't let anything stop you. . . . Don't die without having done what you wanted to do. There's no more for me to tell you. . . . I can teach you nothing, but I hope you'll come sometimes and play for me. . . . I'd like it."

By the time she finished Miss Ogilvie's eyes were again bright with tears, as much from pity of herself as in a benevolent envy of the impetuous Ellen's youth and independence.

"It won't be easy. . . ." the girl said presently. "There's my mother. . . . She thinks I ought to get married. . . . She had me take music lessons because she thought it would make me more marriageable if I could play the piano. . . . Of course she's proud that I play so well. She's proud of anything I can do."

"Perhaps she'll come round," suggested Miss Ogilvie. "But it'll be a struggle. . . . I know your mother, Ellen. . . . She's made you ambitious. . . . That's where she made a mistake." She coughed suddenly with embarrassment. "But I don't want to interfere. She's your own mother. . . . It's for her to decide." And Miss Ogilvie abased herself and her high hopes for Ellen before the altar of her generation's respect for the position of a mother.

"And there's no money. . . ." said Ellen sullenly. "There never is."

"Perhaps we could work that out . . . I could let you take some of the pupils . . . I have too many now . . . I'd be willing to help . . . to sacrifice if necessary." It was clear that Miss Ogilvie meant to say nothing directly; she had no desire to be responsible for the actions of the impetuous girl. Yet she continued to hint, to imply that she would do her part if a crisis arose.

"I want to," said Ellen, "I want to more than anything in the world. . . . I want to be great and famous. . . . I've got to be." She became so savage, so intense that in her great rocking chair Miss Ogilvie trembled.

At last Ellen put on her hat, which perched well up on the absurd pompadour, bade Miss Ogilvie good-by, and went out to the piazza where her bicycle rested against the fancy railing under the cages of the canaries and love-birds. As she turned down the brick path, the voice of Miss Ogilvie followed her.

"If the chance comes," she said, "look to me. I'll do what I can to help you." The words came out in little gasps as if she were unable to keep them—bold though they were—imprisoned any longer. Ellen smiled back at her over her shoulder and the old lady retired into the weathered house.

As Ellen pedaled over the brick streets between rows of maple trees, her delight faded slowly before the assaults of her com-

mon sense. In these skirmishes, wild hope and inspiration went
down in defeat. There were too many obstacles . . . poverty,
prejudice, even her own sense of provinciality. Yet underneath a
little voice kept saying, "You'll do it . . . you'll do it. . . .
Nothing can stop you. You'll be able to get what you want
if you want it hard enough."

And by the time she turned into the block where the Tolliver family lived, clinging like grim death to a respectability
which demanded a brave face turned toward the world, her mind
began once more to work in its secret way, planning how it would
be possible.

Miss Ogilvie's timid, frightened offer of help she had quite
forgotten. Miss Ogilvie was so old, so gentle, so ineffec-
tual . . . like her own caged canaries. Ellen's mind had begun
already to turn toward her cousin Lily. The glamorous Lily
must know some way out.

3

IT was Lily who still dominated her thoughts when she
descended at last to find her mother setting the table for
the family supper. This was an operation into which Mrs.
Tolliver threw all the great energy and force of her character.
It was impossible for her to do things easily; the placing of
each fork involved as much precision, as much thoroughness and
intensity as the building of a bridge or a skyscraper. It was the
gesture of an ardent housekeeper burning incense before the Gods
of Domesticity, the abandoned devotion of an artist striving for
perfection.

For an instant Ellen stood in the doorway watching her mother
as if somewhere in the recesses of her clever brain she considered
this parent as she might consider a stranger, marking the woman's
strong face, her vigorous black hair, the rosiness of her healthy

cheeks. Ellen, her mother said, had a disconcerting way of study-
ing people, of prying into their lives, even of imagining things
about them that could not possibly have been true. This was
exactly what Ellen did as she waited in the doorway. She
regarded silently the figure that stood before her, swathed in
durable serge and ornamented with a gold chain and a tiny Swiss
watch out of all proportion with the size and vigor of her body.

Then suddenly Mrs. Tolliver became aware of her daughter's
presence. She straightened her back and stood with the knives
and forks poised in her hand beneath the glare of the ornate chandelier.

"Well," she said. "You might speak when you come into a
room." Then after a slight pause, "You can finish the table.
I've got to watch the pies."

Listlessly the daughter took the silverware and absently she
began laying it at the places to be occupied by her father, by Fergus, by Robert. There was no place for Gramp Tolliver. He
ate in the solitude of his own room meals which were placed
on the bottom step of the "back way" to be carried up by him in
response to a loud knock on the door of his hermitage. For eight
years he had eaten thus in exile.

"Ma," began Ellen, "when does Lily arrive?"

The mother continued to pour water into the shining glasses.
"In a week or two . . . I don't know exactly," she said, and
then raised her blue eyes to regard her daughter with a long and
penetrating look. Between the two there was a sort of constant
and secret warfare which went on perpetually as if, failing to
understand each other, there could be no grounds between them
for trust. Now Mrs. Tolliver saw nothing but the top of Ellen's
dark head, secretive, silent, as she bent over the table.

"Why do you want to know?" she asked with an air of
suspicion. "You've been talking a great deal about Lily
lately. . . ."

"I don't know," came the evasive answer. "I like her. . . . I'd
like to be like Lily some day."

Mrs. Tolliver resumed her task in silence but with an air of thoughtfulness. Again it was Ellen who broke the silence.

"I suppose there's no money . . . now that everything is settled." She put this forward tentatively, as if the matter was of no great interest to her.

"There's nothing over. . . ." replied her mother. "You knew there wouldn't be. . . . If Papa is elected, things will be all right again . . . for a time at least." This last she added with a profound sigh—a signal that at any moment consideration of the trials brought upon her by an easy-going husband might loose all the torrent of an emotional, primitive nature. "Why do you ask?"

"I just wondered," said Ellen. "I'd hoped things might be a little better."

"They won't be . . . for a time. . . ."

The significance of this conversation lay not so much in what was said as in what was not said. Neither the mother nor the daughter approached the real subject of the conversation openly. They hovered about it, descending for a time on the edge of it, flitting away again coyly, with backward glances. The fault may have been Ellen's. Certainly the ways of the honest, emotional Mrs. Tolliver were neither dark nor devious. Presently the mother made an effort to strike at the heart of the situation.

"I wish," she said, "that you would settle down and be content, Ellen. . . . I thought you were better for a time. . . . What is it you want? Is it to go away just when you're old enough to be a comfort to me? Is that the reward a mother has for her care and sacrifices? That she loses her only daughter as soon as she is old enough to think she is grown up?"

She was slipping into one of the most unbearable of her emotional moods, a mood of self-pity, when she threw herself as the Pope before the Visigoths upon the mercy of her husband and children. All the signs of its approach were at hand—the pathos, the slightly theatrical tone. The mood was aggravating because fundamentally it was reasonable. You could not argue the right-ness of her position. She had sacrificed everything for her husband and her children. Day by day she continued to sacrifice every-thing. She would go on sacrificing herself until she died. She would have given her life for them without a regret. To wait upon her amiable unsuccessful husband and her three superlatively wonderful children was her idea of love, of perfect service. They were her world, her life, the beginning, the very core, the end of her passionate existence. The only reward she asked was possession; they must belong to her always.

And then it struck Ellen suddenly that the position of the mother was pitiable. It was pitiable because she knew so little of what was in her daughter's heart . . . so precious little of all the things stirring there so wildly, so savagely. She could never know, at least until after it was done—whatever it was that was to be done. Even then she could not understand that there were stronger things than love, things which were more profound and more important.

"And why are you so interested in Lily?" began her mother. "Why do you say you want to be like her?"

"I don't know," replied Ellen in a low voice. "I don't know except that I don't want to be like the others."

Her mother considered her for a moment and then shook her head, as if silently she had reached a decision.

"I can't understand your restlessness," she said. "I don't know where you get it."

Ellen stood now leaning against the mantelpiece above the gas log. Outside the rain still fell heavily.

"Well," she said, "it's not my fault that one grandfather ran away from home as a boy and went to California to dig gold. . . . And it's not my fault that the other left his wife and ran away to live in Europe for thirteen years."

Mrs. Tolliver turned sharply. "Who told you that? I mean about your grandfather Tolliver. . . ."

Ellen smiled in her silent, proud way. "I'm not deaf, Mama, nor blind. . . . I've been about the house now for nearly nineteen years. I know about Gramp Tolliver."

Again Ellen was smitten by amazement at her mother's ignorance of how much she knew, at how little the older woman understood of the shrewd knowledge she had hoarded away.

"I'm sorry you know it," said Mrs. Tolliver. "It would have been just as well if you hadn't known." Again she nodded her head with that same air of reaching a secret decision. "But now that you know it, you might as well know some other things. . . . You're old enough now, I guess." She sat down on one of the stiff-backed chairs and beckoned to her daughter. "Come here," she said, "and sit on my lap. . . . I'll tell you other things."

Ellen came to her and sat upon her lap, rather awkwardly, for to her it seemed a silly thing. She had not the faintest understanding of all that this small gesture meant to her mother. And secretly she hardened herself against a treacherous attack upon her affections. It was the habit of her mother to attack her through love. Always it had been a sure method of reducing Ellen's fortress of secrecy and hardness.

"It's about Lily," began Mrs. Tolliver. "I know Lily is beautiful. She's very kind and pleasant . . . but there are things about her that aren't nice. In some ways Lily is a loose woman. . . . She's laid herself open to talk. . . . People smirch her good name. . . . Perhaps she isn't really bad. . . . Nobody really *knows* anything against her, but she is free with men. . . . There's been talk, Ellen, and when there's smoke, there's fire."

Here Ellen interrupted her. "I don't believe it. . . . I don't believe any of it," she exclaimed stubbornly. "It's the way people talk. I know how they do. . . . I've heard. . . . It's one reason why I hate the Town."

And then Ellen saw her mother assume a great calmness, deliberately and with a certain ostentation, in order to impress Ellen with her sense of justice. It was like taking a cloak from a closet and putting it gravely about her. "I've never mentioned it to any one," she said (never once guessing the thoughts in her daughter's mind), "not to a soul. . . . Nothing could induce me to. . . . After all, Lily is my first cousin, the daughter of Aunt Julia, my own mother's sister. . . . I wouldn't permit any one to befoul her name in my presence. . . . But here we are alone, together, you and I. . . . It's in the family. That makes a difference. . . . Sometimes, in the family, one has to face the facts. And the facts are that Lily hasn't behaved well. . . . She's lived in Paris for years, alone in the wickedest city in the world. . . . There's even talk about her having had a baby . . . and she's never been married. . . . Nobody knows . . . and Aunt Julia wouldn't tell me. . . . You can't get a word out of her. . . . You wouldn't want to be like that, now would you?"

Ellen fell to pleating the folds of her cheap dress. Her dark brows drew closer together. She was sullen, awkward.

"I don't see that it makes any difference . . . not to Lily. She's free. . . . She's happy."

"But she's rich," said her mother. "That's why she's free . . . and only God knows whether she's happy. . . . A woman like that can't be happy. . . . I don't want my daughter, my pure, lovely little daughter to be contaminated."

The tide of Mrs. Tolliver's emotions displayed all the signs of bursting the dam of her restraint. Ellen knew these signs. Her mother was beginning to drag in God. She was beginning to use words like "pure," and "lovely." And for the first time in her life, Ellen found herself instead of softening, growing harder and harder. Strangely enough, it was the words of the gentle, birdlike Miss Ogilvie which gave her a new power. This time, she was not to be defeated.

"Well, it doesn't make any difference," she said, rising from her mother's lap. "I like Lily better than any one in this town . . . I always will . . . and nothing can change me." The fine line of her young chin grew stubborn and there rose between mother and daughter the old impregnable wall.

It is impossible to imagine what ruse Mrs. Tolliver would have used next, impossible to calculate the depths of emotion into which she might have plunged, had she not been halted by so small a thing as the ringing of a doorbell. The sound jangled noisily through the house and Ellen, finding in it the opportunity for escape, sped away to open the door.

Outside on the doorstep, drenched, tow-headed and grinning, stood Jimmy Seton, the little brother of May Seton. In one grubby hand he held a note.

"It's from May," he grinned. "I guess it's an invitation to a party."

And without another word, he vanished like an imp into the dark wall of pouring rain.

4

THE father of May Seton was rich according to standards. He was not so wealthy as the Harrison family which owned the Mills, or as Julia Shane, Mrs. Tolliver's Aunt Julia, a great and proud lady who lived in Shane's Castle, a gloomy house, relic of a past day, which stood isolated now upon a low hill in the midst of the clamorous and ascendant Mills. There were some who said that Harvey Seton was richer than Julia Shane, but it was impossible to know. The Seton wealth was public property. The wealth of Julia Shane, except for the land which she owned, lay concealed in the vaults of banks in Paris, in New York, in Pittsburgh, in Chicago. No one could gage it; and from the old woman's mode of living, it was impossible to make any estimate. There had been a day when Shane's Castle was the great house of the Town, even of the state. Great people stopped there, politicians, artists, musicians, even a President or two. But for years now, ever since Lily went to live in Paris, the famous drawing-room, glittering with crystal and silver and glowing with tapestries and paintings, had been closed and muffled in cheese-cloth. In the big house, beneath the unceasing fall of soot from the furnaces, Julia Shane with her spinster daughter, Irene, lived in three rooms. It was this state of affairs which led people in the Town to believe that her fortune had decreased in some mysterious way. The old woman alone knew that she could have bought up Harvey Seton, tossed his corset factory into the midst of the Atlantic Ocean and never missed the money. She lived upon the income of her income. The Town, so far as she was concerned, no longer existed.

These things played an important part in the life of the Town. No one ever tired of discussing them. It was by these standards that citizens were judged; and there were no better standards in a town which had emerged less than a century before from a complete wilderness. There was nothing unusual in them, for it is the man of property after all whom most people, in their heart of hearts, honor most profoundly.

The success of Harvey Seton was, in itself, not especially interesting. It paralleled very closely the tale of any successful middle-western manufacturer. The interest lay in what he manufactured and in his character. He was born and brought up in what people call straitened circumstances. At twenty-one he entered a pharmaceutical school and upon being graduated, started life as a clerk in a pharmacy of the Town. For eight years he lived rigorously and saved his money. He was a Methodist and attended church regularly, despising card-playing and the theater as implements of the devil. In this there is nothing unusual. It is here that the bizarre makes its appearance.

There came a day when he learned that Samuel Barr, a brother of Julia Shane and of Mrs. Tolliver's father, had invented a combination of gutta percha and steel which served as an admirable substitute for whalebone. Now Samuel Barr was always inventing something. He invented a cash-carrier, a patent rocker, and had even meddled with the idea of perpetual motion. He had invented a machine which he set up in a field on the farm of his brother-in-law, because he said the contrivance. once it was started, would not stop until it flew into pieces of its own velocity; therefore one must have an open space about it so that no one might be injured by the flying fragments. With his brother-in-law, Colonel John Shane, he waited behind a tree for the machine to fly to bits. It revolved a few times and presently came to an abrupt halt. No fragments flew through space. The machine was a failure.

It is standing there to-day, in the midst of a field now culti-vated by Bohemian immigrants. It is too bulky to be moved. It remains, like a gigantic rock, in the midst of waving corn, the single monument to Samuel Barr's inventive genius. The other things,—the cash-carrier, the patent rocker, the synthetic whale-bone have survived. With a few variations they whiz coins through gigantic department stores in a hundred cities; they sup-port the tired backs of a million exhausted housewives; and they enclose the swelling forms of even more millions of too plump women. But Samuel Barr made no money out of these things. Others made the money and stole the credit. It was the perpetual motion machine which was the apple of his eye, the great creative effort of his soul. No one wanted that, so no one stole it from him. It remained, the single possession of his trusting soul. The weather is eating it slowly away. Sometimes people stop along the road and walk into the field to regard the strange Gargantuan engine. "Sam Barr's Perpetual Motion Machine" exists, the only monument to his name.

Samuel Barr is important to this tale because it was he who founded Harvey Seton's fortune, and because it was his machine which stands as a superb symbol for the taint which ran through all his family. It was the taint of a family of great energy which had fantastic visions, which gambled high, staking everything to win or lose. It was a curious taint, rare and unhappy, but out of it there sometimes rose a sudden genius—an artist, an adven-turer, a philosopher, an inventor. The taint was in all of them. His sister Julia risked her fortune a dozen times and, winning, increased it a dozen times. His niece Hattie Tolliver never ceased

to plan great undertakings which would make her husband rich.
She risked her fortune a dozen times and, losing, saw it vanish
into a mass of debts. His great-niece Ellen Tolliver had it
strongly, though few would have suspected it. She was subtle like
old Julia Shane. She told her affairs to no one.

When Harvey Seton, twenty-nine, rather pallid and ambitious
in a cold-blooded fashion, heard of Samuel Barr's invention, he
set about to gain possession of it. This he accomplished in time,
by methods not entirely honest, at the cost of one hundred and
fifty dollars. Then he secured a partner and the Eureka Reinforced Corset Factory came to raise its walls in the factory
district under the windows of Shane's Castle.

In justice to Harvey Seton, it must be said that he struggled
for a time with his conscience. He was not a bad man. His
fault lay in a too great desire for wealth; that is to say, wealth
in the abstract, for its own sake alone, and not for what it could
bring to him of this world's pleasures. He had some pangs over
his treatment of Samuel Barr, but they were as nothing to the
pangs he endured from the nature of his enterprise. . . . A
Methodist corset manufacturer might seem a contradiction in
terms, a combination of two elements which are in no way soluble,
the one in the other; but somehow, Harvey Seton—perhaps
because he was really shrewd—managed to unite them. He
continued to sing in the church choir; and, on the left hand, he
manufactured corsets. He knew, no doubt, that some of the most
devout of his Methodist sisters wore stays beneath their clothes.
Perhaps if they had been forced to wear them on the outside, the
corset business would have suffered. The world being what it
is, Harvey Seton prospered. His corsets became known in remote
lands for their durability and their restrictive values. Eureka
Reinforced Corsets came to be worn by the great ladies of New
York and London, by the housewives of the Middle West, by the
demi-mondaines of Paris and Brussels, by professors' fat wives in

Germany. They were introduced at length even among the bisque ladies of Polynesia and the black ladies of brothels in Mozambique. In 1897 Harvey Seton opened a branch factory at St. Denis on the outskirts of Paris. It brought him nearer to his continental markets.

Meanwhile Harvey Seton's life followed a narrow path to and from the corset factory, and presently he married one of the plumpest of Methodist sisters who presented him after a hesitation of three years with a daughter, May. Then followed an hiatus of ten years and there appeared a thin anemic little boy. These are the facts of Harvey Seton's life. There was nothing more and nothing less. It was the thin sickly little boy, now grown precocious and somewhat spiteful, who brought the note through the pouring autumn rain to Ellen's doorstep and thus played his tiny, anemic part in the drama of her life.

But May and Ellen were friends, or as near friends as it was possible for any one to be with such a girl as Ellen. May frankly adored her. She admired her straight, slim figure, so different from her own vague softness, and her handsome dark hair. She envied her ability to play the piano. What Ellen said or believed, to May was gospel. And in this there was nothing extraordinary. It was the worship of a weak, good-natured soul for a strong, self-willed one. May was pretty in a plump, blonde, pale fashion. She giggled a great deal and liked the companionship of the Town boys. Ellen did neither of these things. In fact she hated the boys with a kind of savage resentment, as if it were presumptuous of them even to fancy they might interest her. She permitted May to worship her, since there seemed nothing to be done about it; yet the adoration annoyed her at times so profoundly that she wanted to strike the blonde, silly girl, to really hurt her, to destroy her as she might destroy some pale, stupid worm. She hated her because May had those things which would have made her own way easy. But her pride kept her silent. She smiled at May in her cold, aloof fashion and permitted her to continue worship.

5

WHEN Ellen arrived at the Setons' on the night following the visit of Jimmy, she found that the family had not yet finished supper. They sat about the table, Seton *père* at the head, thin, bloodless, bearded, looking like one of the more austere of the saints, rather than a corset manufacturer. Seton *mère,* fat, fleshy, good-natured, occupied a seat at the far end. Between them sat disposed little Jimmy, anemic and insignificant, May plump and pale, and last of all, a stranger.

"This," said May Seton, giggling and indicating the young man at her left, "is Mr. Clarence Murdock. I've been wanting you to meet him, Ellen. I'm sure you'll like each other. He's from New York . . . here to see Papa on business."

The young man rose and bowed a little stiffly but with a flattering deference.

"May has told me so much about you . . . I'm delighted to know you."

"Sit down until we finish," said May. "We're just eating the last of our dessert."

Now May's introduction of Mr. Clarence Murdock was not altogether straightforward. From the phrases she chose, it could be gathered that it was the first time she had ever seen Mr. Murdock and that Ellen had never heard of him before. In this there was no truth for he had seen May many times. They even called each other by their Christian names. And May had given Ellen elaborately detailed descriptions of the young man, having gone even so far as to hint that there was more between them than mere friendship. But May could not resist doing things of this sort where a man was concerned. It was impossible for her to be honest. The mere shadow of a man upon the horizon goaded her into a display of dimples and coquetry. She bridled, grew arch and mysterious. She was taught by an aspiring mother that these things were a part of a game. Ellen might have replied, "Yes. I've heard a great deal concerning you, Mr. Murdock," but she did not. She said, "I'm so glad to know you," gave him a faint smile and a look which seemed not so much concerned with Mr. Murdock as with the dead fish and boiled lobsters in the ornamental print on the wall behind him. All the same she began quietly examining the points of the stranger.

He was not bad looking and he had nice manners. To be sure he might have been taller. He was not quite so tall as Ellen. He had nice brown hair sleekly brushed back from a high forehead, and he wore a starched collar of the high, ungainly sort which was the fashion in those days. His eyes were brown and gentle and near-sighted, his face well-shaped and his nose straight, though a trifle thin so that it gave his countenance a look of insignificance which one might expect in a perpetual clerk. He was not, Ellen decided, the sort of romantic figure which could sweep her off her feet. Still, he came from New York. That was something. He had lived in the world.

"My, what a rain we've been having," observed Mrs. Seton. "I suppose it's what you'd call the equinoctial storms."

Yes, her spouse replied, it was just that. And he launched into a dissertation upon equinoctial storms, their origin, their effect, their endurance, their manifestations in various quarters of the globe,—in short all about them. Fifteen precious minutes passed beyond recall into eternity while Harvey Seton discussed equinoctial storms. No one else spoke, for it was the edict of this father that no one should interrupt him until he had exhausted his subject. He was indeed a King among Bores. And when he had finished, his wife, instead of going further with this topic or one of similar profundity, struck out in the exasperating fashion of women upon some new and trivial tangent.

"Herman Biggs is coming in, Ellen," she observed brightly. "Right after supper." And she beamed on Ellen with the air of a great benefactress. Her thoughts were not uttered, yet to one of Ellen's shrewdness they were clear. The smile said, "Of course a poor girl like you could not aspire to a New Yorker like Mr. Murdock, but I am doing my best to see that you get a good husband. Herman Biggs is respectable and honest. He'll make a good husband. We must look higher for May. She must have something like Mr. Murdock."

And even as she spoke the doorbell rang and the anemic Jimmy sped away to open it as if on the doorstep outside stood not the freckled Herman Biggs but some wild adventure in the form of a romantic stranger.

It *was* Herman Biggs. He came in as he had come in a thousand times before, and stood with his dripping hat in his hand, awkwardly, while he was introduced to Mr. Clarence Murdock. But he did not sit down. The lecture upon equinoctial storms had claimed the remainder of the time allotted to dessert. The little group rose and distributed itself through the house. Mr. Seton went into a room known as his den. Mrs. Seton went into the kitchen and the young people disappeared into the cavernous parlor, followed by Jimmy, still filled with the same expectancy of stupendous adventure, intent upon harassing the little party for the rest of the evening by the sort of guerilla warfare in which he excelled.

It was a gaunt house constructed in a bad period when houses broke out into cupolas, unusual bay windows and variations of the mansard roof. Outside it was painted a liverish brown; inside the effect was the same. In the parlor there was an enormous bronze chandelier with burners constructed in imitation of the lamps found during the excavation of Pompeii, an event which considerably agitated the world of the eighties. The walls were covered with deep red paper of a very complicated design of arabesques upon which was superimposed a second design in very elegant gold, even more complicated. Against this hung engravings of Dignity and Impudence, The Monarch of the Forest, and The Trial of Effie Deans. Pampas grass in vases ornamented with realistic pink porcelain roses, waved its dusty plumes above a bronze clock surmounted by a bronze chariot driver and horses which rushed headlong toward a collision with a porcelain rosebud. By the side of the clock stood a large conch shell bearing in gilt lettering the legend, "Souvenir of Los Angeles, Cal."

"Shall we play hearts?" asked May, with appropriate glances, "or shall we just talk? . . . There's no moon and the piazza is all wet."

Ellen said nothing; she continued to regard Mr. Murdock with a curious, speculative air.

"Let's play hearts," said the anemic Jimmy, fidgeting and climbing over the sofa. "I kin play, Mr. Murdock," he added proudly.

Upon the pride of the Seton family, Ellen turned a withering glance, charged with homicidal meaning. It said, "What are you doing here? . . . If you were my brother you'd be in bed where you belong."

"Ellen wants to play hearts! . . . Ellen wants to play hearts!" sang out Jimmy, pulling awry the shade of the imitation bronze lamp.

Herman Biggs blushed and stammered that it made no difference to him. Mr. Murdock was gentle and polite. "Let's talk," he suggested mildly, "we might as well get acquainted." As the oldest by nearly ten years and the most sophisticated by virtue of his residence in New York, he took the lead.

"I think so too," replied Ellen and a curious flash of understanding passed between them, a glance which implied a mutual superiority founded upon something deep in Ellen's nature and upon Mr. Murdock's superior age and metropolitan bearing.

So they talked, rather stupid talk, punctuated by May's giggles, the guffaws of Herman Biggs, and the pinches of the anemic Jimmy, who was never still. Now this pale pest swung himself from the curtains, now he climbed the back of a chair, now he sought the top of the oak piano, menacing lamps and vases and pictures. And after a while Ellen was induced to sit at the piano and play for the party. It was ragtime they wanted, so she played "I'm afraid to go home in the dark" and "Bon-bon Buddy" and other favorites which Mr. Murdock sang in a pleasant baritone voice. After that he gave imitations of various vaudeville artists singing these same ballads.

At length May and Herman Biggs retired, accompanied by Jimmy, to bring in the refreshments, and Ellen was left alone with the stranger.

"I suppose," she began, "you find it dull here after New York."

Mr. Murdock coughed. "No, it's pleasant enough. . . . Mr. Seton has been very kind to me. . . . I'll be here another week or two installing the electrical equipment."

Ellen raised her head proudly. "I'm going to New York myself soon . . . probably this winter. . . . I'm going to study music."

Mr. Murdock was very ready. "Well, we must meet again there. . . . It's a lonely place for a girl without family or friends."

"But I don't get homesick," said Ellen, with the sophisticated air of an experienced traveler. "I certainly wouldn't be homesick in New York."

From that moment Mr. Murdock began to regard her with a deeper interest. Perhaps he saw that by her side May had no points to be compared with Ellen's air of quiet assurance, her youthful dignity, her curiously apparent respect for herself as an individual. She sat in the plush rocker within the glow from the bronze lamp. At the moment she was not awkward at all; she was tall, graceful, dark, even a little imposing. The essence of her individuality rose triumphant above the plush rocker, the engravings that hung against the elaborate wall paper, above even the cheap dress which concealed her young slenderness. She stirred the imagination. Certainly her face was interesting.

"I didn't know," began Mr. Murdock, "that you were a professional musician. . . . I don't suppose you like playing ragtime. . . . Maybe you'd play me something good . . . something classical, really good, I mean like Nevin or MacDowell."

And Mr. Murdock, growing communicative, went on to say that his sister played too. She lived in Ogdensburg, New York. He had come from Ogdensburg to make his fortune in the city. That was the reason, he said, that he understood how lonely a person could be.

"Of course, it's different now," he continued, "I have lots of friends. . . . Homer Bunce and Herbert Wyck. . . . But you'll meet them when you come to New York."

He was very pleasant, Mr. Murdock. And he was nice looking in a rather spiritless way. His eyes were kind and his hands nice. To Ellen hands were important features. Shrewd beyond her years, she saw people by their hands and their mouths. Mr. Murdock's mouth was a trifle small and compressed, but otherwise all right. He might be a prig, but underneath the priggishness there lay a character nice enough.

"And now won't you play for me?" he persisted, "something of Nevin or MacDowell?"

Ellen went to the piano and played a Venetian Sketch and To a Waterlily. She and Miss Ogilvie considered such music pap. From choice she would not have played it, but she understood at once that Mr. Murdock would like this music. Indeed he had asked for it. She knew he would like what the people in the Town liked. Mr. Murdock listened with his eyes closed and when she had finished he said, "My, that's fine. . . . I like soft, sweet music."

She was still playing when May and Herman returned bearing the hot chocolate and plates of cakes, followed closely by the simian Jimmy, his mouth stuffed to overflowing. Mr. Murdock still listened, lying back in his chair with closed eyes.

It was Mr. Murdock who outmaneuvered the *gauche* Herman Biggs and escorted her home. They talked stiffly, walking very close to each other through the pouring rain beneath the Tolliver family umbrella.

On the steps of the porch, Ellen bade him good-night.

"We must meet again before I go away."

"Certainly," said Ellen; but in her heart she had resolved against it, for she considered Mr. Murdock slightly boring. It was possible, she could see now, for people to live in a city and still never leave their home towns.

It was like Mr. Seton, thought Ellen. Every two years he went to Europe to visit the Junoform Reinforced Corset branch factory at St. Denis near Paris, but he really never left the Town at all. He carried it with him.

If only she could go to Paris. . . .

6

MR. MURDOCK stayed a week longer than he had planned, and before he left he managed to see Ellen not once, but many times. Always May was present, giggling and admiring, though toward the end, under the prodding of a shrewd mother who saw a concealed menace in the situation, she betrayed a slight and refreshing coldness toward her friend. Before he left, Ellen called him Mr. Murdock no longer, but Clarence.

In the weeks that followed she received from him two post cards, one a colored picture of lower New York photographed from Brooklyn Bridge against the sunset and the other a view of the Reservoir at Forty-Second street which, he wrote, had been demolished a little while before. On them he recalled her promise to let him know when she came to New York. May, however, received a dozen post cards and a half-dozen letters, so his correspondence with Ellen must have signified nothing at all. Certainly it did not excite her deeply.

"Clarence writes me," said May one day, "that you are going to New York. Why didn't you tell me? . . . I should think you'd tell your best friend a thing like that."

And Ellen slipped into a cloud of evasions. "I may have told him that," she replied airily. "I don't know how he could have found out. . . . It was a secret, I haven't mentioned it to anyone." And she made a number of vague excuses, which seemed neither logical nor founded upon fact. It was as if she considered May too stupid to understand such things or thought her too unimportant to consider at all.

" It's funny," said May, "that you'd tell such a thing to a stranger like Clarence. . . ." For a moment the suspicions planted in her complacent mind by an aspiring mother stirred with life and raised their heads. But she succumbed again quickly to the domination of her companion and thrust an arm about Ellen's waist.

"It's only because I'm interested," she said. "I know that you're going to be great and famous some day. . . . We're all going to be proud of you."

At which Ellen sniffed, not without an air of scorn, as if she cared not a fig whether the Town was proud of her or not.

At home, however, May received another warning from her mother. "Mr. Murdock," said the plump Mrs. Seaton, "is not a young man to be passed up lightly. . . . There aren't many like him. . . . He suits your father to a T, and he would fit in fine at the factory. Your father needs some one like that to help him out, until Jimmy is big enough to take hold. . . . Don't trust Ellen too far. . . . She's too quiet to be trusted."

At which May only laughed. "Why, Ellen wouldn't think of marrying him," she said, "she won't marry anybody in this town. . . . It isn't likely she'll ever marry . . . at least for a long time. Besides, she doesn't think he's good enough."

Mrs. Seton snorted angrily and put down the Ladies' Home Journal. "Good enough for her. . . ! Who is she to be so choosey? . . . Why, the Tollivers can't pay their bills. . . . They're just out of bankruptcy. . . . Good enough for her. . . ! If she ever gets as fine and upstanding a young man as Mr. Murdock . . . a man so industrious and hardworking and well-behaved, she can thank her stars. . . ." For a moment Mrs. Seton paused to recover her breath, greatly dissipated by this indignant outburst. That Ellen should scorn Mr. Clarence Murdock was not a thing to be borne lightly. Then she continued, "And this talk about going to New York. . . . How's she going to get to New York? Who's to put up the money, I'd like to know? Old Julia Shane, I suppose. . . . It's not likely the old woman would part with a cent even if she could."

It was, in the Seton family, a cherished fiction that Julia Shane was stricken by an overwhelming poverty: it was a fiction that increased the confidence of a fortune founded upon reinforced corsets.

"Julia Shane!" continued the ambitious mother, "Julia Shane! What's she got to be proud about? . . . With a daughter as fast and loose as Lily? . . . I suppose she's proud of living in that filthy old house in the midst of the Flats."

And so the ashes of the feud between the Setons and the Barr-Shane-Tolliver clan, lighted accidentally by the chance appearance of the guiltless and model Mr. Murdock, showed signs of flaming up again after a peace of twenty years.

7

THE Christmas holidays arrived; the Tollivers sold the last of their horses, and went on showing brave and indifferent faces to the world. Ellen, going her secret way, awaited the arrival of her cousin Lily, still certain that Lily would have a solution. She no longer argued with her mother. Instead she took refuge in silence and if she spoke at all it was in a docile and pleasant fashion. She permitted herself to be petted and admired, so that Mrs. Tolliver in the eternal optimism of her nature believed that Ellen had forgotten or out-grown her restlessness, and was content.

But the girl spent hours at her piano, playing wildly, as if the sound of her music in some way eased the fierce restlessness of her spirit. At times she attacked a polonaise with such violence and fire that the spangled notes soared through the air and pene-trated even the stillness of Gramp Tolliver's solitary chamber. At such moments the old man paused in his reading, permitted his book to slip to the floor and sat in his rocking chair motionless, listening with his lean old head cocked a little on one side, a wild and dancing light in his eye. For hours at a time he listened thus, muttering occasionally to himself.

(That granddaughter of his had something which none of them suspected, something that was rare and precious in this world.) When the music at last died away, losing itself in the maze of walls which shut him into exile, it was his habit to sink back with a clucking sound and begin to rock, gently at first and then more and more savagely, until at last he became submerged by the stream of shrewd, malicious thoughts which swept through his old brain.

"She's got something none of them understand. . . . And I'm the only one who knows it. But they'll kill it in her. They'll pull her down until she's on the level with the rest of them. I know. . . . I know. . . . Haven't I heard Liszt himself, in Paris

in the heyday of his fame? And Rubinstein? They'll destroy
her if they can with all their little tricks and deceits. . . . Mean
they are, meaner than dirt, trying to drag her down to the rest
of them. . . . The girl doesn't know it herself. . . . How good
she is no one has ever told her. . . . She doesn't know the power
that's in her. They'll never let her free. They'll clip her wings.
They've clipped the wings of greater ones. . . ."

And then with a cascade of wicked chuckles the old man settled
back to his reading. "They've never clipped my wings. They
can't because I don't live in their world. They can't come close
enough to catch me. They can't fly high enough. . . ."

And slowly the rocking decreased in violence until at last the
chair became quite still and the skinny arm reached down to
recover the heavy book. Belowstairs the last echoes of the turbulent music died away until the silence was broken only by the
distant cries of children playing in the streets and the faint
muttering of the old man. . . .

"It's best that she doesn't know. . . . It wouldn't help her . . .
only make her miserable . . . only give them a chance to tear
her to pieces, nerve by nerve. . . ."

Again the persistent rocking until at last the room grew
dark, and the old man rose in response to a loud knock on the
door of the stairs, stirred himself and lighted an oil lamp so that
he might find his way to the tray of food that Mrs. Tolliver
thrust in at the door of his cell. There was no gas in this room
beneath the roof; Gramp Tolliver had been an expense for too
many years. It would have cost twenty dollars to fit his room
with gas lights. And in ten years he had produced nothing
save the scraps of paper covered with bird track handwriting
that were stowed away in the pigeonholes of the desk.

In those days there came to Grandpa Tolliver, more by some
obscure instinct than by any communication with those outside

his cell, the certainty that his granddaughter's behavior was a source of irritation to the people of the Town. True, he occasionally overheard from the kitchen below snatches of reproachful conversation which drifted upward by way of the ventilator . . . strange remarks which appeared to come out of the blue, yet when pieced together they provided a coherent story. Reproaches of sulkiness, of silence, of secrecy, cast by a mother, who desired nothing so much as confidences, against a daughter who was incapable of anything but secrecy. They were an ill-matched pair. This the old man understood, with a sort of wicked satisfaction, because the things which in Ellen were incomprehensible to her mother were the things which had come down to the girl from himself. It was another mark in the long score between Grandpa Tolliver and his daughter-in-law; another, in which nature herself took a hand, in the long battle between two fiercely antagonistic temperaments.

He could not have known that the people in the Town likewise had reproaches for Ellen. He could not have known that they said it was her duty to begin giving music lessons in order to prop up the fortunes of a proud and bankrupt family. Yet in his unearthly way, he did know; and in some vague way he was pleased. Even in his isolation so impregnable, so defiant, his heart was warmed by the thought of an ally. The enemy was driving Ellen, a neutral, into his camp; and into his icy heart there came drop by drop a warm trickle of unaccustomed sympathy. Not that Gramp Tolliver planned active aid; that would have been too much to expect, for Gramp Tolliver had discovered half a century earlier the idiocy of mixing in the affairs of other people.

Instead he chuckled and read in triumph and vindication The Decline and Fall.

8

ON the morning of the third day before Christmas, Clarence Murdock, bearing a neat handbag packed with those things which he would need during a journey of three weeks through the middle-western country, turned his back on the Babylon Arms and made his way toward the railway station and the transcontinental express. Behind him he left the two young men whom, in the fashion of bachelors who have migrated without root or connection from the provinces into a great city, he had picked up as companions somewhere amid the flotsam and jetsam of Manhattan life. They had come to him separately, each drawn perhaps in his own way by the smug neatness which marked the life and character of Clarence. Yet the two men were in no way alike. Their difference was manifested in the very reasons for their attachment to Clarence. The one, an adventurous boisterous soul, had fastened upon Clarence because Clarence had a talent for keeping things in order, a perfect genius indeed for pigeonholing the very emotions of his own life. Out of the mighty chaos which was the essence of the wholehearted Homer .Bunce, there emerged a pathetic need for order and comfort; and this Clarence supplied to superb satisfaction. Even the books and pillows of their tiny apartment were kept in scrupulous order. Disorder made Clarence nervous.

Mr. Wyck, on the other hand, had found strength in Clarence, a thing which Bunce himself never even thought of finding in the orderly depths of Clarence's soul. For Mr. Wyck's family was old and Mr. Wyck himself lacked vitality. There was in the lower Manhattan in those days a street named for the Wycks, a street renamed long since, in the hasty fashion of a great city, for a Tammany politician. His family was so old (as age went in New York) that there remained only himself and two spinster aunts who lived at Yonkers. It was this antiquity of blood which the pale Mr. Wyck counted upon as the very rod and staff of his existence. At his first meeting with Clarence, at an annual outing on Staten Island of the employees of the Superba Electrical Company, Inc., Mr. Wyck had sensed in Clarence a certain un-American and shameful respect for an old family name, the strange yearning in a man with no tradition for a name which carried with it memories, even though they were very distant and virtually obsolete, of coaches and country estates. They *were* distant, for seventy years had gone the way of eternity since there had been money in the Wyck family, and the descendant of the patroons, the last of the Wycks, now followed his fortune as a clerk in the accounting department of the Superba Electrical Company, Inc.

On the rock of this respect for tradition, Wyck had fastened his hope. At length, he discovered in Clarence a man who was impressed; and the self-respect of Mr. Wyck, for all the insignificance of his world, increased in direct proportion with the awe produced in Clarence Murdock by the awful sound of the name Wyck.

Thus the three had come together, living in a fashion contented enough, in a tiny apartment filled with beaded portières bought at a Seventh Avenue emporium and leather cushions decorated with pyrographic Indian heads by loving sisters and aunts. Yet a spirit of unrest hovered over the place, an uneasiness which none save Mr. Wyck discerned with any degree of clarity. He alone knew that the day would come when, one after the other with fatal precision, his two companions would find their present mode of life unendurable. In turn each was certain to choose, from among the hordes of girls that swarmed the streets of New York, a mate. Only the gods knew who these two women might be or where they were at that moment. There was only one certainty, and that Mr. Wyck, with the sensitiveness of an effeminate man of low vitality, admitted to himself. Clarence and Bunce would marry, Bunce no doubt for love because his animal spirits were high, Clarence perhaps because he would be trapped by the glamour of a tradition.

Oh, Mr. Wyck understood this. It troubled him in the moments when he was left in solitude. It disturbed his digestion of the greasy meals which he ate alone each day in some hole-in-the-wall restaurant far downtown near the offices of the Superba Electrical Company, Inc. It was impossible that he should ever marry. Women had never interested him; the very idea filled him with a faint disgust. He would not only be left alone in the world; he would no longer possess even Clarence who respected his name. He knew that any woman was stronger than himself.

The Babylon Arms raised its twelve stories in one of the Eighties just east of Riverside Drive. Among the brownstone fronts of the early part of this century its gaunt sides gave it an overpowering appearance of height, loneliness, even grandeur. In those days great apartments were rare in that part of New York, and the Babylon Arms stood as a solitary outpost of the army of apartment houses which since have ranged their extravagant bulks in a solid face along the North River and eastward to the Park. The Babylon Arms is still there, rather shabby and *démodé,* a belle of the early nineteen hundreds, out of fashion, overpainted, with electric bulbs fitted into gas brackets and the once somber red walls of its hallways painted over in grotesque imitation of the more ostentatious marble of its newer sisters. But its pride is gone. It stands jostled now and a little battered, like the bedizened women who came in from the streets to flit through its gloomy corridors. It is shabby genteel, like the two old ladies who live in the parlor bed-room of the first floor. It is jolly and good-natured, like the clerk and his family who climb the two flights of worn stairs above the point where the antiquated elevator rocks uncertainly to its final stop. It is comic, respectable, quaint, vulgar, tragic, common and happy . . . all these things;

and so after a fashion, in the way of old houses, it is like life itself.

But it was new and elegant in the early nineteen hundreds. The Babylon Arms! It was a name known throughout the growing Upper West Side! It was the first of the skyscraping apartment houses. And among the pioneer cliff dwellers were Clarence Murdock and two companions who shared among them the expenses of the apartment two floors above where the elevator jolted uncertainly to a final stop. It was not so expensive—living two floors above the elevator; and the name "Babylon Arms" looked impressive, even a little flamboyant, on one's card. To Bunce the name signified opulence, a certain grandiose triumph of success; to Clarence it meant that people would say, "Ah, the Babylon Arms! He must have a good background to live there!" To Mr. Wyck, it meant simply that he was keeping up one of the traditions of his name; yet there were times too when he was a little ashamed of the Babylon Arms as an institution touched by vulgarity.

As Clarence on the third day before Christmas closed the door behind him on the bead portières and burnt leather cushions, he left Bunce singing lustily as he rubbed his great healthy body in the chilly air of the bathroom, and Mr. Wyck, still lying in bed, his thin, slightly yellow nose peeping above the blankets against the hour when it would be painfully necessary for him to rise. As the door closed, Bunce's rendition of "I'm afraid to go home in the dark" was interrupted for an instant while he shouted after Clarence, "Look out now and don't come home married to that fat, pretty Seton girl!"

At the shout Clarence hastened away, shocked a little by the vulgarity of Bunce. As for Mr. Wyck the words struck terror into his heart. He saw the breaking up of his home. He saw himself, a timid, frightened little man, lost once more among the obscenities of a cheap boarding house.

9

A NUMBER of things made necessary this trip of Clarence; there were the usual customers to be visited; the new equipment of the Junoform Corset Factory was in need of inspection, and finally there was an engagement to spend Christmas and several days of the holiday season as the guest of the Seton family; and this he looked upon with relief because life in hotels had come to weary him inexpressibly. He longed for a home, with a wife who would put by his slippers for him and sit by his fireside. The prospect of one dreary hotel after another burdened his soul; so the acceptance of Mr. Seton's invitation had been even colored by a subdued enthusiasm.

It was, after all, ambition which had betrayed him into city life and the wretched, fly-by-night existence of a drummer. He was ambitious to be wealthy, to be admired, to be honored in a community.

There were times, but these were rare and isolated moments, when his ambitions rose for an instant beyond even these things, times when, in an ecstasy of intoxication, they soared dizzily among the pinnacles of hope far beyond the reach of one whose place in the structure of life was clearly somewhere in the foundations. It was then that he caught for an instant glimpses of a life in which he saw himself not only wealthy and respectable but distinguished and glamorous, one whose character captured the imagination, who gave himself and his life to the great world.

All this was perhaps not clearly thought out in his mind; yet he sensed its presence a little way beyond his reach as a small boy searches in the darkness of a jam closet for something which he knows is there but cannot see.

In these lurid, almost ecstatic moments, he saw his future wife not so much in the rôle of a domestic paragon, as a brilliant and beautiful creature. fit to walk through the avenues of the great world by the side of a clever and worldly man. To be sure, such things were never mentioned to fellow-drummers, yet they were there, shut up in his heart, quiet save for rare moments. His companions in the smoking car may have had their secrets too. It is impossible to say. If such secrets existed, they were too well hidden beneath their suspicions of each other.

It was in one of his placid, normal moods that he boarded the train for the west. He took off his brown overcoat with the half-belt at the back, his brown fedora hat, adjusted his eyeglasses, and settled himself in his chair. At the moment he permitted his thoughts to hover about the picture of May Seton, pale, blonde, good-natured and pretty in her plump way. There was nothing in the least carnal in these thoughts, for he was a young man who might have served as a model for those institutions which concern themselves with the morals of young men and preach the doctrine that complete purity of mind is possible by sheer perseverance alone. He was innocent of women. He had worked hard and had no time for them. Indeed the very thought of them in that way gave him a faintly squeamish feeling. He was one of those in whom desire follows in the wake of timid experience, who cannot in the beginning conceive passion otherwise than abstractly. So now he conceived May Seton more as an idea, a sort of stepping stone to comfort and warmth, than as a woman to be desired. That he might be a sensual man had never occurred to him.

As the train moved across the Jersey Flats he fell to considering his prospects as a son-in-law of Harvey Seton and the certainty of an interest in the Junoform Reinforced Corset Company, a thing already hinted at by his suppositious mother-in-law. He thought of the Town. He pictured, quite clearly and placidly, a small and pleasant house surrounded by shrubs and trees, a comfortable front porch. He even pictured Mrs. May Seton Murdock in a rocking chair, far more attractive than she was in the flesh, darning his socks. In fact, he saw his future bounded on four sides by Junoform Reinforced Corsets, by May Seton, by the Town and by hard work. It was this placid and uneventful path that his feet were to follow.

The car in which Clarence sat, like all cars bound from the East across the mountains into the fertile and prosperous Midlands, was crowded. He was not a man gifted with great curiosity and rarely indulged himself in speculation concerning his fellow travelers. Indeed, from his manner one soon understood that he observed very little about him. And now as the wheels clicked along the smooth track he settled himself to reading. He had brought with him against the monotonous agony of the trip a book by Richard Harding Davis and a copy of the *Saturday Evening Post,* and these absorbed his attention until the train had passed Philadelphia and turned northward a bit in the direction of Altoona. Presently his interest flagged and he fell to watching the scenery; but before long this too wearied him and he fell asleep. Slumber was a state which he welcomed, for there were long periods when his mind grew exhausted with turning over the same frayed thoughts. There were times when it might have been said that he existed in a state of suspended animation.

So between slumber and a bored wakefulness, the hours passed in a succession of dreary towns and monotonous winter-dead farms, punctuated by signs advertising patent medicines and cheap hotels. As the train swept through Johnstown, he was for a moment diverted by the sight of so much smoke and desolation, by the gigantic slag heaps and the flaming furnaces. The spectacle was not a new one. He must have seen it twenty times, by day when it was sordid, and by night when it became wild and fantastically magnificent. Yet it interested him as it always interested him, tugging at some part of his soul which failed to fit the neat pattern of his universal conformity.

"What a great country!" he reflected. "By George! It's a

privilege to be a citizen of a country so energetic and prosperous!"

A curious light came suddenly into his nice brown eyes, and for a time the corset factory and May Seton were forgotten in the face of a new emotion, so much more profound and stirring. Even the rawness, the barren crudity of the picture exalted him. For a moment his ambitions threatened to gain the upper hand— those wild unruly ambitions which sometimes bore him beyond the round of thoughts which wearied him.

"To own mills like these!" he thought. "To be a power in industry. To go to Europe every year. To have a great house and one of these new automobiles."

And Johnstown disappeared behind the train, lost in a gigantic and all-enveloping cloud of smoke and soot through which the flames of the furnaces flashed dimly.

The monotonous mountains, seamed with black rivers flowing between crags of blue ice, succeeded the smutty town, and Clarence settled back in his chair. But he did not read. He sat staring out of the window, thinking, thinking, thinking. Perhaps he tried to nurse his sense of importance, to persuade himself that he possessed the stuff which went into the accomplishments of great ambitions.

The roaring train sped on and on, and presently he went into the smoking compartment where he fell into conversation with other traveling salesmen. They exchanged stories of a broad nature, until Clarence, by nature a nice young man, found the flavor growing too strong and returned to his seat.

Then it was for the first time that he noticed his fellow passengers. He did not notice all of them, or even two or three. He noticed only one, a woman who sat in the chair beside him reading a novel with a yellow paper back called "Chèri" by a person with the queer name of Colette.

He sat down and tried to read but, for some obscure reason, the figure of the woman kept getting between him and the story of the great open spaces. He found himself reading paragraphs which meant nothing to him. He read an entire page without knowing what had happened in the tale. Such a thing had never happened to him before.

The woman who kept thrusting herself between him and the story was dressed all in black, though she did not appear to be in mourning. Rather it seemed that she wore black because it became her. Across one shoulder was thrown a stole of black fox and from the brim of her small hat hung a froth of black lace which obscured her dark eyes and permitted her to regard her companions without receiving in return the force of their stares. From beneath the hat there escaped a bit of tawny hair, so dark that in some lights it appeared almost red. She appeared to take full advantage of the shield made by the lace, for from time to time she put down her yellow-backed novel and fell to observing the people about her . . . a middle-aged woman with a little boy in a sailor suit, a fat man who lay back in his seat and snored quietly, a pair of college girls, one reading ponderously the essays of Emerson and the other absorbed (self-consciously) in the pages of Boccacio; another traveling salesman and a pair of old women returning from a funeral who vied with each other in a talking race.

"And then I said to her . . ." "She said, 'Mabel, he'll never be well again . . . even if he didn't die, he'll never be well again'" . . . and "What do you think of such behavior? . . . Unpardonable, I thought. . . ." "I quite agree with you, unpardonable. . . ." "Well, that's what I told Mabel."

Snatches of the old women's talk, projected in voices pitched high enough to override the clamor of the train, were tossed about them like jagged fragments of glass.

The woman with the veil put down her book and, smiling quietly, listened to them. She turned away from Clarence a little so that he was able to shift his position and thus obtain a clearer view of her.

She was beautiful, and even to Clarence, unskilled in such fine distinctions, it was clear that she was a lady. This fact was conveyed beyond all doubt by the way she sat, poised with a neat and easy grace, in the way her slender hands clasping her book lay against the black of her dress, the way she carried her head and wore her fine clothes, even by the veil which somehow stood as a symbol of all that was gently bred in her character. There seemed between her and the others in the car an invisible veil which shielded her while she looked out upon them from a different world.

At her feet stood a smart black handbag, covered with bright labels. Clarence read them one after another in a kind of intoxication—Sorrento, Cannes, Dieppe, Hotel Ruhl, Hotel Royal Splendide, Hotel Ritz-Carlton. And, surely yet imperceptibly, just as an hour or two earlier the sight of the Johnstown furnaces had captivated his moderate imagination, the woman began to take possession of him. Somehow these two impressions became blended, and out of them there came to Clarence glimpses of a brilliant world which he never before penetrated, even in the wildest flights of ambition.

Presently the stranger, wearied of listening to her companions, resumed her reading and Clarence, still fascinated, continued to watch her until, becoming conscious of his gaze, she turned suddenly and dismissed him by the faintest movement of her shoulder. At the gesture, which from her seemed a command, he turned quickly away and blushed as if she had spoken to him in rebuke. Yet it seemed to him that as she glanced in his direction, her lovely mouth was arched for an instant by the faintest of smiles— a smile which said: "Staring does not disturb me. It is nothing new to me." It may even have been that she mocked him. It was impossible to say. Only one thing remained certain; Clarence had been disturbed by something entirely new in his experience.

In his own way he tried to discover what it was that suddenly shattered all his peace. The woman was beautiful, yet he in no sense desired her. Indeed, in the dull purity of his mind, it is probable that no such unclean thought even occurred to him.

Beyond all doubt she fascinated him, yet it was not this which destroyed his ease. Rather it was something in her manner, something in her very bearing and personality which overwhelmed him . . . that sudden glimpse of another world, in which people lived lives as different from his as day is different from night, a sudden terror at her self-possession, at the unseen, impregnable barrier by which she protected herself from those others in the car. There was in her manner too a certain veiled but terrifying recklessness.

With an air of infinite absorption, she continued to read the yellow-backed novel, as if she had forgotten that the man in the seat beside her existed. Beyond her, the two old women continued, "And I said to her when she rang me up the next morning . . ." "It's shameful what some women will do!" . . . "Since that day he's been an invalid, unable to stir!" And they clucked and wagged their crêpe-clad heads like a pair of crows on a fence.

The train roared on through the blue-white mountains, into the west toward Pittsburgh. Upon the hills the early winter darkness had already begun to descend.

Still Clarence did not read. The novel and the *Saturday Evening Post* slipped to the floor and lay there unnoticed. The characters in his book failed to hold their own against the woman in the adjoining seat. He even had a faint sense of being on the edge of the romantic and exciting.

And at the same moment, the thoughts of May Seton and a comfortable house in the Town were swept away like so much rubbish into oblivion, carrying with them the sense of peace and certainty which a little time before made the future so pleasant and comfortable.

Presently he rose and went into the smoking compartment where he remained for a time. When he emerged, it was quite dark, and high up on the barren mountains an occasional warm yellow light indicated the existence of a lonely house. Returning to his chair he found the mysterious woman had vanished. Only the somber handbag covered with bright labels remained. The names glittered . . . Sorrento, Cannes, Firenze, Beau Rivage, Royal Splendide, Claridge's, Berkeley. . . .

He glanced at his gold watch (the gift of Uncle Henry) and decided to dine. Making his way toward the dining car, he found the passageway blocked by other passengers, college girls and boys, drummers like himself, old women, children, all swaying with the motion of the speeding train. It was a bad time to travel, on the eve of a holiday; yet the crowd was pleasant enough, good-natured, laughing, on the whole gay with the holiday spirit.

Slowly the door of the dining car devoured the thin line, casting out others who fought their way back in an opposing column, until at last Clarence stood at the entrance of the bright car, surveying the groups of heads bent over swaying soup and underdone chops.

Still harassed and unaccountably miserable, he stood first on one foot and then the other, surveying the crowd until at length he discovered far down the aisle his friend of the paper-backed novel. She sat at a table for two opposite an elderly man in a black frock coat who, quite properly, did not address her although he seemed not unconscious of her presence, for he stole from time to time glances at her tawny hair and fine throat until she dismissed him suddenly with a frank stare in which there was a great deal more than a hint of amusement. After that a wall, invisible as it was impenetrable, separated them, as was proper between two victims of a system which threw harassed travelers arbitrarily into each other's company. As she ate the woman continued to look about her as if she were profoundly amused by the friendly spectacle of the rocking car. Still she appeared to use the film of lace as a perpetual shield.

He had been watching her thus for a long time when, to his

sudden horror, he saw the elderly man wipe his thin mouth with his napkin, pay his check and, followed by the steward, move fatally toward the end of the car. At the sight Clarence was tempted suddenly to run. Yet it was impossible to run. The best one could do was to turn back and squeeze slowly and painfully past the fat encumbrances of the corridor. Besides, how could one make a spectacle of one's self? What would people think? He stood frozen with horror, filled with the sensations of one about to be dragged forward to torture. As in a nightmare he felt himself borne forward by a steward who grinned maliciously and said, "Place for one? Certainly! Right this way."

Without effort he floated through space until suddenly, with a tormented and unuttered groan, he sank into the seat opposite the woman with the delicate black veil.

He felt the pulses beating in his throat. He bent over the menu card, but even this did not protect him. Again the unreality of a nightmare smote him. This time he was naked and horribly embarrassed at his improper predicament. He sensed the woman examining him as she examined the others, with a detached and curious smile of appraisal.

These were his sensations, various, confused, terrifying. As though there were eyes in the top of his neatly brushed head, he saw all this happening. What he did not see, what he could not have known were the thoughts of the woman—that she watched him, that she saw the throbbing vein in his throat stand out suddenly and knew well enough its meaning. By the aid of that agitated vein she saw, with a sophistication beyond his wildest imaginings, in this mild little drummer a man of a sensual, passionate nature. The thing which amused her was a speculation, absurd to be sure, but none the less clear. She wondered whether this little man knew himself, whether he had ever been aroused.

"Chops," Clarence found himself writing on the check. "Chops. Mashed potatoes. Lima beans. Coffee."

Then the sound of a voice reached him, warm, low, insinuating. "I advise you against the chops. They are atrocious. I was forced to send them back and order something else."

The woman had spoken to him of her own accord and his suspicions arose in sudden array, bristling and fully armed. Yet he knew that he must answer. Heroically he looked up and asked, "What do you advise?"

"The roast beef is very good. . . ."

Though he detested it, he wrote down roast beef and then straightened in his chair, pulling at his collar and cravat. For the life of him, he could find nothing to say. It was impossible to overcome that fragile, invisible barrier.

"Don't think me impertinent," she said, "for speaking . . . but I'm almost bored to death. . . . I hate traveling. . . . I'd like always to stay in one spot."

For an instant he suspected the faintest trace of a foreign accent in her voice, though he could not be certain.

"I know," he said politely, "I hate it too. . . ."

She laughed softly.

"It's the first time I've traveled any distance in years. . . . I couldn't talk to the old crow who sat there before you. . . . It would have frightened him to death."

It was impossible for Clarence to say that it also frightened him to death, so he coughed and buttered a bit of roll.

"You don't mind my speaking, do you?" she pursued.

For a moment Clarence fancied he had lost his mind. It was queer enough that a strange woman should speak to him, but even queerer that she should sweep past all the procedure of good manners and ask him directly whether he minded it. And she was neither brazen nor embarrassed.

"No, of course not," he managed to say, "I mean I'm awfully glad. I hate traveling alone."

Then it occurred to him that he had made an indelicate, perhaps a suggestive remark, and the blushes once more swept his face.

After hours the waiter arrived with the roast beef and lima beans.

"I haven't much farther to go," continued the woman. "Thank God, I'm not bound for Chicago."

Clarence found it impossible to eat beneath her gaze.

"I get off at eleven something . . ." he said, "I've forgotten exactly. . . ."

The woman laughed. "Why, so do I! We must be bound for the same place."

For an instant he succumbed to a terrifying suspicion that, in truth, she had marked him for her own. But this idea he dismissed quickly, as utterly improbable. The woman was clearly a lady. She was terribly sure of herself, of keeping things just where she wanted them. She might be a spy, an adventuress. (Ghosts of a thousand cheap magazine stories danced through his brain.) Yet a woman like that, if she were bad, wouldn't be bothering herself with insignificant game like himself. He began to believe that she had been speaking the truth, that she had been driven to address him only out of a vast boredom.

"Perhaps we are," he said, and told her that he was bound for the Town.

"So am I," she replied. "It's the first time I've been back there in years. . . . Maybe you come from the Town?" she continued.

The discovery of this bond helped matters a little. It furnished at least some ground for the stumbling feet of Clarence.

"No, I'm going on business. . . . I've been there before. . . . It's a nice progressive Town, full of booming factories . . . a place to be proud of."

But he found abruptly that he had taken the wrong turning. The stranger was not proud of the Town. "I suppose you might be proud of it, if you like that sort of thing. . . . I find it abominable." For a moment, the bantering, charming, humorous look went out of the eyes behind the veil, supplanted by a sudden sadness. "No," she continued, "I don't like it, though I've no doubt it's very prosperous."

For a moment Clarence was baffled. He understood suddenly that this new strange world was more remote, more unfamiliar than he had imagined. It was not perhaps made out of factories and roaring furnaces. The discovery increased his awkwardness and in some strange way distended the glamour with which he surrounded her. He struggled for words.

"I'm going to spend Christmas with the Setons," he said. "Probably you know them. They've always lived in the Town."

The woman frowned slightly. "Seton?" she repeated, "Seton?" Then it appeared that the light dawned upon her. "To be sure. . . . I know. . . . They own a corset factory. . . . But they're new people. Yes, I know who they are although I don't know them."

She made the statement simply and without a trace of condescension. She made it as a simple observation. If she had said, "I know who the King of England is . . . but I don't know him," the intonation, the inflection would have been identical. She had answered his question, but she had answered it more profoundly than she knew, more profoundly, more tragically than even Clarence knew until years afterward. *"I know who they are although I don't know them."*

Before the eyes of Clarence there rose suddenly the image of May Seton, good-natured, trivial, blonde, commonplace. It was almost as if she had entered the train by some obscure miracle and stood there beside the mysterious stranger, awkward, silly, ungainly.

The woman was rising now. "I must go back to my seat," she said. "It isn't fair to keep the others waiting." She pulled the stole of black fox about her handsome shoulders and lowered the veil. "Thank you," she said, "for saving a poor helpless traveler from boredom."

And with that she closed the adventure.

When he returned to his seat, he found her sitting absorbed in her yellow-backed novel. Greeting him with a faint smile, she returned to her reading. After an hour she rested her head against the back of the chair and appeared to fall asleep. It was not until the train roared into the Town that she again addressed him.

Snow filled the air as they got down from the train at midnight. The big flakes, tormented by a rising wind, fell heavily, obscuring the yellow lights of the dirty brick station. They were the only passengers to descend and Clarence offered to take charge of her luggage. There were two large trunks and another handbag. The trunks she left at the station. She would send for them. The two handbags she would take with her.

The great train, spouting steam, got under way with a vast uproar. The brightly lighted cars moved away into the snowstorm and the pair of them were left alone beneath the yellow glare of the station lamps. A little way off two horse drawn cabs stood by the curb, the heads of the beasts hanging, their backs bent against the storm. From the warm station emerged a pair of drivers, muffled to the ears. To one of them, the lady called out.

"Oh, Jerry," she said, "I'm glad you're here. . . . There's no one to meet me. . . . I didn't send word ahead."

The plumper of the two old men took off his hat and peered at her for a moment while the snow fell on his bald head. Slowly recognition came to him. "Sure, Miss Lily. . . . It's a pleasure. . . . Back again, after so many years . . . and not a day older, if you'll let me say so."

At this the stranger laughed softly. The cabby took the bags from Clarence, who had bestirred himself briskly to do the proper thing.

"It's late," he said. "Perhaps I'd better go with you to see that nothing happens."

"Thank you," replied his companion, "but I'll be safe. . . . I haven't far to go . . . and I've known Jerry all my life. . . ."

He has driven me ever since I was a little girl. . . . You see I only live a little way off." She laughed again, "Right in the midst of the Mills." She made a little gesture with her big muff to indicate the direction of the Mills. There, above the encircling flames of the furnaces, rose dimly the silhouette of a great house crowning the top of a low hill. But for the flames of the furnaces it would have remained invisible. Now it stood out against the red, snow-dimmed glare, black, mysterious.

The woman stepped into the swaying, moth-eaten cab and the driver climbed to the seat. Suddenly she leaned out of the window and addressed Clarence. "Before we part," she said, "I suppose we ought to know each other's names, *pour sauver les convenances.* I'm Miss Shane," she added, "Miss Lily Shane."

Clarence took off his hat and bowed. "I'm Mr. Murdock. . . . Mr. Clarence Murdock."

"And you won't think me wicked, I know," she added, "for speaking to a strange man. . . . I'm careful who I speak to. . . . I knew I would be safe with you."

And the cab drove off through the snowstorm in the direction of Shane's Castle, leaving Clarence on the platform mumbling a polite answer, his face scarlet, his pulses beating faster than they had ever beaten before.

After a moment he climbed into the other cab and bade the driver take him to the residence of Mr. Harvey Seton. The contentment, the holiday spirit had oozed out of him. He was no longer glad to be spending Christmas with the Setons. Reflecting upon his recent encounter, it occurred to him suddenly what it was that was familiar about the woman. Lily Shane! To be sure, she was the cousin of Ellen Tolliver! The rich cousin . . . ! There was something about her that reminded him of Ellen as she sat talking to him in the Setons' parlor, something withdrawn and contained, rather distinguished and proud. In one of those moments of insight, so rare to him, he saw all at once that there was

in the girl and her cousin something which set them aside from
the others.

This thought he turned over and over in his mind as the musty
cab, smelling faintly of ammonia, bore him through the blowing
storm further and further into the smug future that lay spread
out before him in a suburban panorama of little white houses
with "artistic" piazzas and shutters ornamented by cut-out hearts
and diamonds; and after a time he became once more almost content. The wild disturbance caused by the sudden encounter with
the stranger appeared to have quieted, when another thought, entering suddenly his tired brain, made him miserable once more.
He fell to considering the final speech of Miss Lily Shane. . . .
*"I'm careful who I speak to. I knew I should be safe with
you."* . . .

He could not make out whether or not the speech was meant as a
tribute to him. Something in the memory of the stranger's manner implied that he was a poor thing.

And then it occurred to him that at this very moment he must
be passing the Tollivers' house, and poking his head out of the
cab window, he saw that there was still a light in the windows.
For an instant he fancied that the wind bore toward him the
strains of wild music, surging and passionate; but of this he could
not be certain, for the wind howled wildly and snow fell in a
thick blanket. It may have been, after all, only his imagination;
it had been playing him queer tricks since the very moment he
raised his eyes and saw Miss Lily Shane sitting there beside him.

10

THE same evening was for Mrs. Tolliver one of rare peace
and happiness—an evening when, warmed by the glow
from the open fire, she sat surrounded by her family
while the blizzard howled and tore at the eaves, setting the limbs
of the gnarled old apple tree to scratch against the frozen panes.

At such times there was in her appearance something grand and majestic; she sat in her ample chair like a triumphant Niobe, a sort of enthroned maternity the borders of whose narrow kingdom ended with the walls of the Tolliver living room.

It was a large square room, infinitely clean, although shabby and worn, for the dominant rules of the Tolliver household were cleanliness and comfort. It was this room which was the core of the Tolliver existence, the shrine of the sacred Lares and Penates, such a room as has existed rarely in each generation of the world since the beginning of time. With her family assembled about her, the cares and worries of the day slipped from her shoulders softly, beautifully into oblivion. She rested herself by darning the family stockings.

Near her Ellen sat at the piano playing, playing endlessly, in the wild and passionate fashion which sometimes overwhelmed them all, causing the mother to cease her darning for an instant, young Fergus to look up from his book, and even Charles Tolliver to stir himself sleepily and forget in the surge of her music the cares which he sought to drown each evening in sleep. The great shabby sofa was his. There it was that he lay for hours every night, until at length and after much effort, he was shepherded off to bed by his energetic wife. Perhaps he slept because in sleep he found a solace for the complacent failure of his life.

Robert, the younger brother, lay on his stomach beside the fire, his short nose wrinkled in an effort to decipher the mysteries of a picture puzzle. He had a passion for problems, and a persistence which had come to him from his mother.

Ah! They were a family in which to take pride! What was money compared to such a good husband and such fine children? So ran the thoughts of Mrs. Tolliver; and presently her face became wreathed in smiles, but she did not know she was smiling. If she had looked at that moment into a mirror, she would have been astounded. Her happiness at such moments ceased to be a conscious emotion.

Outside the windows the wind howled and the snow, falling

in the first real blizzard of the winter, whished against the rattling panes.

The fire crackled and presently beneath the great blanket her husband stirred slowly and murmured, "Ellen, play the one I like so much. . . . I don't know the 'name but you know what I mean."

And slowly Ellen turned into the melodies of one of Liebesträume—the one which is written about the lovers lost on a lake during a black storm.

In her strange way the girl loved her father best, perhaps because in his gentle impersonal way he made upon her none of those savage demands which her mother, in all the ferocity of her affection, constantly exacted. With Mrs. Tolliver love implied endearments, constant manifestations of affection. To her love between people separated by hundreds of miles was inconceivable. It was a thing to be touched, to be fondled and treasured. Those whom she loved must always be at hand, under her eye, full of protesting affection. Perhaps in this she was right; she was, after all, a primitive woman who trusted her instincts. There was no reason in her. Perhaps love *is* only fanned into life by close and breathless contacts.

Mr. Tolliver was so different. There was in him something of his father, a touch of the terrible philosophic aloofness of the gaunt old man who lived above the kitchen in another part of the house. But he lacked Gramp Tolliver's strength, as well as that implacable resistance of the old man to all the assaults of emotion. Where the old man was aloof, powerful, and independent through the very quality of his indifference, the son had failed by some weakness of character. There was in him too much of humanity. People liked him. Farmers in their fields stopped their horses and abandoned their plows to talk with Charlie Tolliver. At the elections they had supported him to a man; but there were not enough of them. The Town was too powerful.

In the world Charles Tolliver failed because of his very gentleness. He had a way of regarding life with a fine sense of proportion, of seeing things in their proper relation. It was as if he stood already at the end of his own existence and looked back through it as through a long tunnel, seeing that those things which others labeled as mountains were after all but mole-hills, and those things which others would have called trivial possessed the most uncanny importance. And this was a weakness, for it led one into the paths of philosophic acceptance; and it was a weakness which none recognized more shrewdly than his own direct and vigorous wife.

Ah (she thought) if only he would see things in the proper light. If only I could make him fight as I would fight in his place! He's innocent, like a little child; but it's not his fault. That old man abovestairs is to blame; that old devil who never cared for his own children. And, goaded by these thoughts, a kind of baffled rage at Gramp Tolliver swept the honest woman. She had no subtle way of combating his deviltries, because to a woman of so violent a nature, indifference was an unconquerable barrier. Gramp Tolliver lived, in his sinister fashion, in a world which she not only failed to understand but even to imagine.

Suddenly Ellen ceased her music; it died away in a faint, diminishing breath, disappearing slowly into silence beneath the strong beautiful fingers. The girl leaned forward on the piano and buried her face silently in her hands. She did not sob, and yet one could be sure that she was miserable. In her silence there was something far more terrible than weeping. It rose up and filled all the room, so that Mrs. Tolliver, lost in her angry thoughts of the old man in the lonely room overhead, sensed it suddenly and ceased her darning. This thing had come so often of late to break in upon the happiness of their lives. It was a monster, savage, insatiable. Something more powerful than all of them.

For a time she watched her daughter and slowly there spread over her face a look of trouble and bewilderment. It was an expression which of late had come to Mrs. Tolliver so often that it had begun already to leave its mark in the fine lines about her eyes and at the corners of her mouth. It was at times like this that her heart ceased all at once to beat and a coldness swept through her body; for love with her was really an intense and physical thing.

On the sofa her husband slept peacefully, quieted at last by the Liebestraum; and again she resented his indifference, all his willingness to accept life, his refusal to struggle against fate. "Things come out right in the end," he always said when she assailed him. "There is no use in struggling."

Ah, she thought bitterly, but there *is* use in struggling. There is a satisfaction to the spirit. But this, of course, her husband could never have known.

"Ellen," she murmured, "Ellen." And the girl raised her head with a look in her eyes so terrible that it appalled her mother. "Are you tired?"

"No."

Again a little pause. "Why are you unhappy?"

For an instant the face of the girl softened. There were signs of a sudden collapse, of sobbing, of yielding utterly. Perhaps if it had come in that moment—a sudden abrupt bursting of all restraint—the lives of all the people in that warm and comfortable room would have been changed. But it did not come, for one so young does not yield so easily. The girl sighed, stiffened her body and sat upright.

"I don't know," she answered dully. And yet she lied, because she did know, perfectly. In that moment life for her was an awful thing, baffling, suffocating, overwhelming. It was impossible to say so, because her mother would not have understood. It would have been the same as when Mrs. Tolliver said, "It is beautiful, your music . . . lovely," when she did not understand it at all, when she said such things simply because she loved her daughter and was proud of her cleverness.

Outside the storm persisted, increasing steadily in fury. And presently, Ellen said, "To-night Cousin Lily arrives, doesn't she?"

At which her mother regarded her sharply and paused in her darning to say, "Yes. But why do you ask? You talk of nothing but Lily."

And again Ellen answered, "I don't know. I simply want to see her."

Into the proud reflections of Mrs. Tolliver there entered from time to time thoughts of the most profound satisfaction over the part she had played in the existence of her children. In the beginning, even before they were born, she had determined for them careers which were to follow clearly demarcated lines. As a bride, after she had brought up her eight brothers and sisters and married at last the patient Charles Tolliver, she went, driven by eager duty, to a lecture given by a bearded man upon the things every mother should know. This doctor had told her that it was possible to begin even before birth to influence the characters of one's children, and so she had begun on that very night to plan their lives.

The first, she had decided, was to be a musician. It was a story which went back a long way into the days of Hattie Tolliver's own youth when she had longed in her passionate way to be a musician. But always there had been something to intervene— an invalid mother; and after her death the cares of a family of brothers and sisters and the management of her father's household, no easy task in those early days of great farms and broad lands. Yet in spite of these things she had managed to learn by sheer persistence something of the mysteries of the keyboard, and out of these she had woven on the melodeon of the old farmhouse the tunes of a few hymns, the Ninety and Nine, and snatches of The Blue Danube. So before Ellen was born, these fragments were revived and brought into service once more to be played over and over again on the upright piano purchased in the early years of her husband's prosperity. Thus, with the support of a vast energy and an overwhelming optimism, she had begun to plan the future of Ellen long before the girl was born.

Long before midnight the two boys, under the gentle urgence of their mother, had drifted sleepily to bed. Ellen remained, still playing, almost mournfully now with a kind of moving and tragic despair. Beyond the frozen windows the wind howled wildly and the snow piled against the wall of the house. Mrs. Tolliver darned savagely, with short, passionate stitches, because the thing of which she lived in constant terror had returned to come between her soul and that of Ellen.

On the great sofa, her husband snored gently.

At midnight she rose and, poking the ashes of the fire, she said to Ellen, "It's time we were all asleep. Lock up and I'll get papa to bed."

The transference of Mr. Tolliver from the sofa to his bed was nightly an operation lasting many minutes. When Ellen returned, her mother still stood by the sofa urging her husband gently to stir himself.

"Please, papa," she said, "come along to bed. It's after midnight."

There was a series of final plaints and slowly the gentle Mr. Tolliver sat up, placed his feet on the floor, yawned and made his way sleepily to the stairway. The mother turned off the gas and the room suddenly was bathed in the warm, mellow glow of the dying fire. Ellen, breathing against the frozen window pane, cleared a tiny space to look out upon the world. It stretched before her, white and mysterious, beckoning and inscrutable. And suddenly she saw far down the street the figure of a cab drawn by a skinny horse which leaned black against the slanting snow within the halo of a distant street lamp.

The mother joined her, watching the cab for an instant and murmuring at length, "I wonder who it could be at this time of night."

"I know," said Ellen softly. "It's Mr. Murdock. He was

coming to-night on the express to stay with the Setons. He must
have come on the same train with Lily."

At the mention of Lily, her mother turned away. Ellen followed her and in the doorway Mrs. Tolliver halted abruptly and
embraced her child, fiercely as if she would hold her thus forever.
For an instant they clung together in the warm darkness and
presently Mrs. Tolliver murmured, "Tell me, darling. . . . If
you have any secrets, tell them to me. I'm your mother. Whatever happens to you happens to me."

Ellen did not reply at once. For an instant she was silent,
thoughtful. When at last she spoke, it was to say dully, "I
haven't any." But the tears came suddenly into her blue eyes.
She was lying, for she had her secrets. They were the secrets
which youth finds it impossible to reveal because they are too
precious. All the evening she had not been in the comfortable,
firelit room. She had been far away in some vague and gigantic
concert hall where people listened breathlessly while she made
music that was moving and exquisite. The faces stretched out before her dimly in a half-light until in the farthest rows they were
blurred and no longer distinguishable. And when she finished
they cheered her and she had gone proudly off to return again and
again as they crowded nearer to the great stage.

After the mother and daughter had climbed the creaking stairs,
both lay awake for a long time, the one entangled in her wild and
glowing dreams, the other terrified by the unseen thing which in
her primitive way she divined with such certainty. It was not to
be seen; she could not understand it, yet it was there menacing,
impregnable.

And in a distant part of the house, a light was put out suddenly
and Gramp Tolliver thrust his skinny legs between the blankets.
All this time he had remained awake listening to the beauty of
the music which came to him distantly above the wild howling
of the storm. He was sure now of his secret. He could have

told Hattie Tolliver what it was that shut her out from the soul of her precious daughter. It was something that would keep the girl lonely so long as she lived. Gramp Tolliver knew about such things.

So at last all the house fell into sleep. Outside there lay a vast desert of white which, it seemed, began at the very walls of the warm shabby house and extended thence to the very ends of the world. Even the tracks, left a little while before by the passing of the cab which brought Clarence Murdock through the blizzard, were obliterated now. One might have said that he had not passed that way at all.

I I

WHEN the cab bearing Clarence drew up at length before the heavy portals of the Seton house, there was a light still burning in the room with the filigreed wallpaper. Leaving the bony horse and the smelly vehicle behind him, Clarence stumbled through the storm and pulled the bell. Far away, deep inside the house, it tinkled dismally in response, and presently there arose from within the sound of bodies sleepily setting themselves in motion to prepare a welcome. Mr. Seton himself opened the door, tall, bony, forbidding behind his thin whiskers, cold as the storm yet not so fresh or so dry. There was always a distinct dampness hanging about him, even in the touch of his hand.

"Well, well," he said in his hollow voice, "you're almost a stranger."

Behind him in a row stood Mrs. Seton, fat and obviously sleepy, and May who interspersed her giggles with yawns which she attempted to conceal with a refined hand. And last of all there was the anemic Jimmy, not at all sleepy, and fidgeting as usual, this time with the cord of the red plush portières which he kept pulling to and fro until halted in this pastime by his mother, who said, "Come, dear, you mustn't do that just when Mr. Murdock is arriving. Step forward and shake Mr. Murdock's hand like a little gentleman."

So Jimmy shook hands in a fashion which he had been taught was the very peak of gentility.

As for Clarence, the whole scene proved much less warm, much less vivid than he had pictured it. Somehow those dreams with which his day had begun were now dissipated, indeed almost lost in all that had happened since then. In the greeting there was a certain barrenness, intangible yet apparent. It may have been the dimness of the hall that depressed him, for Mr. Seton never permitted more than a faint flicker of gas in the red glass chalice which hung suspended by Moorish chains from the ceiling.

"Yes," said Mrs. Seton, "you're almost one of the family with us. May has talked of nothing else but your coming."

May wriggled a little and added, "Yes, we're glad you've come."

And Clarence, dropping his bag, shook the snow from his coat. He could find no answer that seemed appropriate. How could one answer such greetings? Somehow he had expected, after his journey through the wild storm, something of warmth; and there was only this strange, damp confusion, strained and inexplicable. In the room with the filigreed wall-paper there burned the remnants of a fire; it was clear that Mr. Seton had permitted it to die down for the night.

They asked him about his trip, whether the train had been delayed by the blizzard, which of the cab drivers he had engaged. He did not know the name of his driver, yet he was able to identify him because he had heard the name of the other one. (*"I've known Jerry all my life. . . . He has driven me ever since I was a little girl."*)

"Jerry. . . . Jerry was the name of the other driver," Clarence announced suddenly, as if, not having heard their talk, he had brought his mind by some heroic effort back from a great distance.

Mrs. Seton said, "I can see Mr. Murdock is very tired. We mustn't keep him up. . . . Mr. Seton will show you your room."

So Clarence bade them good night and, led by his soft-footed host, made his way through the dark halls until the corset manufacturer opened a door and admitted him to a room that was damp with the chill of a tomb. The sudden flicker of the gas revealed an enormous bed with the cotton sheets turned back.

"Here," said Mr. Seton, with a contracted gesture of the hand intended clearly to be hospitable. "You will find it a little chilly in the spare room, but it is a cold night. Once you're in bed it'll be warm enough."

Clarence murmured polite protests and Mr. Seton withdrew, closing the door behind him. The sound of its closing had a curious effect upon Clarence. For a moment he was tempted to turn suddenly, fling it open and run for his life. Why he should have experienced this impulse he did not know. The whole sensation was confused, disturbing, a part of the wretchedness which had overcome him as he saw the stranger enter her cab and drive off in the direction of the great black house among the flaming mills. He had visited this house before . . . many times. He knew the habits of its owners. They had not changed. It was clear that the trouble lay hidden in himself. Something had happened to him, something quite outside his neat and pigeon-holed calculations. He had come prepared to win success and a comfortable wife, and now . . . instead of that there was fear of something vague and indefinable, a curious instinct to escape from some dreadful trap.

For a time he sat quietly on a stiff chair, his overcoat thrown across his knees, trying to discover the cause of his uneasiness. It was entangled in some strange way with the woman of the veil. *The Setons. . . . I know who they are although I don't know them.* And then, *I'm careful who I speak to. . . . I knew I should be safe with you.*

Certainly he was not in love with her. Such a thing had never occurred to him. She was too remote, too far beyond even the wildest flights of his rarely erratic imagination.

And presently, shivering, he began to undress. With the routine of this daily act, he began at once to grow more calm and more assured. One by one, as he took each article from his pocket—a pen, a pencil, a pocketknife, the watch Uncle Henry had given him on his twenty-first birthday for never having touched tobacco, a few coins—the disturbing sensations seemed to loose their subtle hold. As he laid these things in turn on the mantelpiece beneath the chromo of Watts' Hope, it seemed that he deposited with each of them a fear, an uneasiness, a premonition; the breath-taking sense of grand adventure oozed out of his finger tips.

At length he hung his coat and waistcoat over the back of the chair, placed his shoes beneath the bed and his trousers, carefully folded (to preserve the neat creases that meant so much in the world of himself and Mr. Bruce) beneath the mattress. In the flickering gaslight his body looked pinched and cold, as if he suffered from a lack of warm blood. He was a muscular little man, but his muscles were hard and tight and knotty, the muscles of a man whose only exercise was taken each morning beside the bath tub.

At last after turning out the flickering gas flame, he slipped, shivering and gasping, into his nightshirt and sprang courageously into the monumental bed. Seldom used, it was like the room, dampish and chilly, but before long the warmth of his body permeated the cotton sheets and, coupled with the sound of the wild storm outside, it filled him with a certain comfort which lulled him presently to sleep. In the air-tight room he slept with his mouth opened a little, his teeth exposed, so that in breathing he made a faint wheezing noise.

12

THE snow lingered for days, blackening slowly under a downpour of soot from the Mills that penetrated even the distant reaches of the old Town where the Tollivers and the Setons had their houses. Throughout the Flats where the aliens lived and in the park of Shane's Castle it lay soft and thick as if a great and infernal blizzard had passed that way in a thick downfall of sable flakes. With the return of Lily, the old house set in the midst of the furnaces took on a new aspect. Lights glowed once more behind the diamond-shaped panes and the sound of music sometimes penetrated the tottering walls of the filthy houses where the steel workers dwelt. It was gay, triumphant music, for Lily was one whom the Town had never conquered. Any passer-by could have told that she had returned. . . .

The days passed slowly and meanwhile Ellen made no effort to see her cousin. This Mrs. Tolliver observed with astonishment, setting it down in her hopeful way as proof that the restlessness was passing out of her stormy Ellen; but she did not remark upon it because she feared the mere sound of Lily's name. There was something about Lily which made even Mrs. Tolliver uneasy; it was impossible to understand this woman who denied the existence of the Town, who could return to it when she chose out of a life which it was whispered was none too respectable, to dominate the townspeople again and again in her own disarming, pleasant fashion. In a vague way Lily stood for that vast land beyond the Mills which held such terror for the soul of the simple woman. It was as if Lily were a menace, as if there could be no peace, no contentment until she had gone back again into that vague and distant world from which she came. And here once more Mrs. Tolliver failed to understand. She did not see that Ellen, for all her stiff-necked pride, was shy and held by the same uncertain fear. It was a fear that Clarence Murdock knew.

Somehow it had touched him and changed alike himself and the world about him. It was the fear of naïve souls for one that was perhaps not good but one that was experienced, that moved through life with a sure step, without fear for those things which would have terrified the less courageous. The soul of Mrs. Tolliver was simple. The soul of Clarence was small, and that of Ellen had not begun to grow; until now, save as a bundle of wild desires and feverish unrest, it had not been born.

At length came Christmas day when it was no longer possible for Ellen to avoid her cousin. For seventy years this day had been set aside in the clan composed of the Barrs, the Tollivers and the Shanes as a day given over to feasting, an occasion which brought the most remote members of the great family from every part of the county to the black house among the Mills. But the seventy years had wrought changes. The great house that once raised its bulk, proud and aloof on its hill amid the marsh land, now stood surrounded and blackened by the great mills and factories. Of the family only nine gathered about a table which once had seated forty. The old ones were dying off, slowly; the younger ones had gone away, all save Hattie Tolliver and her children, Irene Shane, and a spinster cousin, the daughter of the Samuel Barr who died after inventing the celebrated and useless perpetual motion machine.

Of the older generation only two remained . . . the proud old Julia Shane and her brother-in-law Jacob Barr, the father of Mrs. Tolliver. This old man was an extraordinary character who at eighty still had a powerful stalwart figure and a great rosy face framed in white hair and a white beard which once had been red. In his youth the people of the county had called him The Red Scot and marveled at the superb strength of his great body. There were tales of his having moved his log barn alone and unaided when the men who were to have helped him failed to arrive at the appointed time. When at last they came, so the story ran, they found Jacob Barr mopping his great, handsome face by the side of the windlass and the barn moved a full hundred yards from the spot it once occupied. At eighty he still managed his farm and scorned his daughter's offer of care. He was the last of the pioneers.

There were times when this grandfather seemed even more remote to Ellen than old Gramp Tolliver in his cell lined with musty books; for the remoteness of Grandpa Barr was the remoteness of one who dwelt in a tower of unbending virtue. In the county he had been the first abolitionist, the first prohibitionist, the first advocate of woman suffrage. He had organized the Underground Railroad which aided slaves to escape to Canada. He was a Presbyterian without sympathy for those who were weak. His wife had died in bearing him child after child. For Gramp Tolliver his scorn was so profound that it was beyond all expression in words. He never spoke of Gramp Tolliver at all.

Jacob Barr was a citizen. He had what people called "backbone," and Ellen was not his granddaughter for nothing.

There was in this annual dinner a pomp, a circumstance that approached the medieval; it was a rite which symbolized the pride, the greatness of a family which admitted no weakness, no failure, no poverty; the persistence of a family which, because it lived sometimes in dreams when the reality became insupportable, knew no such thing as failure. What one does not admit, does not exist. This one sentence might indeed have stood above the crest of the clan. If Hattie Tolliver knew in her heart that Lily was a feeble reed, she ignored it. In her presence none would have dared to hint at such frailty; for Lily existed within the sacred barrier of the family.

On Christmas day, the guests arrived in a procession . . . first Grandpa Barr, rugged, handsome, defiant of his years, yet yielding through bitter necessity to the stout stick of cherry wood which he carried; Mrs. Tolliver, large, powerful, vigorous in a shabby astrakhan jacket, a beaver tippet and a small hat covered with ostrich plumes slightly frayed by age; Charles Tolliver, gentle, handsome, pleasant in his neat and faintly threadbare clothes; Ellen, stiff-necked, awkward, yet somehow handsome and over-powering and, last of all, the two brothers, Fergus, gentle, charming like his father and Robert, stocky and for all the world like the fierce, blue-eyed old Scot with his cherry stick. A vigorous family. And in the midst marched Mrs. Tolliver, erect and with a strange dignity, her plumes nodding a little as if she were a field marshal surrounded by a glorious army.

But Gramp Tolliver was nowhere to be seen. He had been left behind to have his Christmas meal alone in the room walled in by books. Gramp Tolliver, who never worked, who had wrought nothing in this world, was a disgrace which one did not air in public. He took his place among the things which one did not admit.

Before the wrought iron portico of Shane's Castle, the little family defiled across the blackened snow to the heavy door. Mrs. Tolliver pulled the bell as Hennery, the black servant, drove off the sleigh drawn by horses which the Tollivers had for their keep since the latest débâcle in family fortunes. Ellen, trembling a little, perhaps at the thought of the cousin who awaited her in-side the long, beautiful drawing-room, perhaps at the fear of the thing she had to ask of Lily, stood leaning against the iron rail-ing, gazing out across the furnaces that flamed even on Christmas day below the eminence of the dying park.

Inside the house there was a distant tinkle and the door swung open presently to reveal Sarah, the mulatto housekeeper, and be-hind her a long hallway, hung with silver mounted mirrors and a chandelier of crystal that reflected its dull light against the long, polished stairway. For in the Flats, where the Mills reigned, the darkness was so great that lights burned even at midday in Shane's Castle.

Once inside, there was the rustle of descending coats. Before the mirror Mrs. Tolliver frizzed her hair and Ellen patted the newborn pompadour. Beneath her coat she wore a starched white shirtwaist and a skirt of blue voile, with a tight belt and a contrivance known as a chatelaine dangling and jingling at one side. The Town called her well-dressed. It marveled that she could afford such clothes, although it knew well enough that they came from Hattie Tolliver's sewing machine. Yet she was ridiculous and in the next moment she knew it.

For as she turned there moved toward her out of the old drawing-room, that glittered softly in the reflected light of the candles upon mirror and bits of crystal and silver, the figure of Lily, whom she had not seen in seven years. Her cousin wore a gown of black stuff, exquisitely cut by the hand of some artist in the establishment of Worth, a gown which came from the other side of the earth, from a street known to every corner of the world. Her fine bronze hair she wore drawn back over her ears in a knot at the back of her beautiful head; about her throat close against the soft skin hung a string of pearls. As she moved there came from her the faint scent of mimosa, which smote the quivering nostrils of Ellen as some force strange and exotic yet almost recognizable. It was a perfume which she was never able to forget and one which so long as she lived exerted upon her a curious softening power. Years afterward as she passed the flower carts behind the Madeleine or moved along the Corniche above the unreal terraces of Nice the faint scent of mimosa still had the power of making her suddenly sad, even wistful . . . and those were the years when she had conquered the world, when she was hard.

Now she only trembled a little and offered her hand awkwardly to the smiling cousin.

"Well," said Lily, "and now, Ellen, you're a woman. To think of it! When I last saw you, you were a little girl with pigtails."

Her voice carried that thin trace of accent which Clarence had noticed. Somehow it made her strangeness, her glamour, overpowering; and thus it strengthened the very barrier which to Ellen seemed so impossible ever to pass. In that moment there rushed through the confused brain of the awkward girl a multitude of thoughts, but out of them only one emerged clearly defined. "Ah, if I could be like that, I would not care what people thought of me! To be so free, so certain, so gracious, to overcome every one so easily!"

For all Lily's warmth the talk was not easy between them. Yet for the first time it seemed to Ellen that the door stood open a little way. It was as if already she looked out upon the world.

And then Lily turned away to speak to the others, smiling, disarming them, even Grandpa Barr, who in the isolation of his virtue glared secretly at her from beneath his shaggy brows, suspecting her as that which was too pleasant to be good.

And Ellen, with a wildly beating heart, turned to gaunt Aunt Julia Shane, who, leaning on her ebony stick and dressed all in black with amethysts, shook her hand harshly and disapproved of her pompadour.

"It is a silly thing the way girls disfigure themselves nowadays," she said. But Ellen did not mind.

The old woman was handsome in a fierce, cold fashion and had the Barr nose, slightly curved, and intolerably proud, which had appeared again in this awkward great-niece of hers.

Then there was Irene to greet . . . Aunt Julia Shane's other daughter, given to charity and good works, thin, anemic, slightly withered, so different from the radiant, selfish Lily. Irene Ellen ignored, because Irene stood for a life which, it seemed to Ellen, it was best to forget. And beyond Irene there was the horse-faced Eva Barr, daughter of the perpetual motion machine, a terrifying spinster of forty-five who regarded Lily as obscene and spoke of Ellen as a "chit." Both of them she hated passionately for their freedom, because to her it was a thing forever lost. She, like Miss Ogilvie, had been trapped by another tradition. It was too late now. . . .

In the dark lovely room, all these figures passed before Ellen, but of them all, she saw only Lily who stood now before the fire of cannel coal beneath the glowing Venice painted by Mr. Turner. She was like the picture, and shared its warmth, its graciousness, its unreal, extravagant beauty.

Ellen in her dark corner savagely bit her lip. She would escape same day and herself see Venice. Lily should help her. Every one should help her. And into her handsome young face, beneath the absurd, ratted pompadour, there stole a look of determination so fierce that Irene, seeing it, was frightened, and old Julia Shane, seeing it, exulted in the spirit of this great-niece of hers.

13

In another part of the Town far on the Hill above the Flats, the Setons and their guest sat down to Christmas dinner at an hour somewhat earlier than that kept at Shane's Castle, for Harvey Seton, in the manner of many men who have made their own success, created social laws for himself, as if in some way he could thus place himself above the rules. Certainly he could not have brought himself to follow the fashions set by Shane's Castle. He was, he said, a simple man and hoped to remain so until he died.

The shadow of this unspoken defiance appeared to cloud the cheer of Christmas Day at the Setons. There was in the air a certain conscious tension, a vague uneasiness which manifested itself in a dozen ways . . . in the unflinching frown of the father, in the extreme politeness of the mother, in the nervous and concentrated giggles of May herself. The most uneasy of them all was the guest himself. Alone of all the group the simian Jimmy appeared to enjoy himself; and in this there was nothing strange or unusual, for it was an atmosphere in which he flourished and one to which he was highly sensitized. With the sharpness of a sickly, precocious nature, he understood that the air about him

was heavy with foreboding. He knew that it required but a spark
to precipitate a crisis with all the suddenness of an explosion. He
waited now, joyful, expectant, watching the others with an impish
satisfaction.

There was in the dampish atmosphere of the room an odor of
unwonted richness . . . the smell of a roast goose, strange and
exotic in this household. But Christmas was a season which
caused even Harvey Seton to unbend a little. It was the only
occasion when the Christianity of the man was tempered even for
an instant by anything faintly suggestive of warmth. His manner
as he carved was touched, despite the thinness of the slices which
fell from the breast of the bird, by a majestic air, which suggested
more than ever his likeness to a grotesque Gothic saint; (he might
have been one of those early fathers who battled and gave up
their lives for some minute point of dogma.)

As he stood whetting the knife coldly against the steel, a sense
of awe penetrated slowly one by one the hearts of those about
the table . . . all save Jimmy. With his small pointed head
barely visible above the table's edge, he waited. And presently,
as if he could restrain his impatience no longer, he banged his knife
sharply against the edge of his plate.

The effect was instantaneous. It brought from the harassed
mother a sharp scream and a violent slap on the wrist.

"Don't do that again or you'll be sent to bed without any
goose!"

But Jimmy, knowing his safety, only grinned and varied the
method of torture by scratching the fork against the cold surface of
the plate so that it produced a dreadful whining sound.

There were, to be sure, reasons for this strange condition of
nerves. Since the night when Clarence arrived out of the blizzard, things had not progressed. Indeed, it appeared that, on the
contrary, they were moving backwards. By now, everything
should have been settled, and yet nothing was done; there had
been no declaration, no hint. The wooer remained wary, suspi-

cious; and the consciousness of his failure penetrated even the sluggish workings of May's brain and hurt her pride. Mrs. Seton it baffled. She was conscious that some event, some obstacle, some peril which she was unable to divine had raised itself during these past few days full in the middle of her path.

"My," said May presently, "it's much warmer. I expect it's the January thaw."

Then the silence descended and again there was only the whine of Jimmy's fork and the metallic click of the carving knife against the plated dish which bore the goose.

As for Clarence, he managed to conceal that wavering sense of uncertainty and terror which had assailed him with increasing force as the visit progressed. It was a terror which, strangely enough, centered itself in the father, for Clarence, in his chivalrous fashion, regarded women as creatures whom one could put aside. Never having been assailed, he had no fear of them. But the face of the Methodist elder, slightly green and intensely forbidding, filled him with uneasiness. When the corset manufacturer turned to address him, the fishy eyes accused him of unspeakable things.

In all those days in the dampish house there had been no mention of the encounter aboard the transcontinental express. If Lily Shane had been a light woman with whom (Heaven forbid!) Clarence had spent the night, he could have been no more silent concerning the adventure. Somehow he understood that the very name of Lily Shane had no place in the household of the Setons. And the longer he kept silent, the more glamorous and wicked the secret had become, until now it had attained the proportions of a monstrous thing. Each time the Elder looked at him the offense increased a degree or two in magnitude.

Yet in the end he betrayed himself. Perhaps it was the strained silence, perhaps the unbearable whine of Jimmy's fork against the cold plate. In any case there came a moment when even Clarence could bear the strained silence no longer. He knew that something must be said. What he chose to say was calamitous and no sooner had the words passed his lips than he knew his error.

He said, "Do you know a woman called Lily Shane? I met her on the train."

It was purely an effort at conversation; he knew well enough that they knew her, but the effect was terrific. Mr. Seton's carving halted in mid-air. The mouth of Mrs. Seton went down at the corners. May giggled nervously and Jimmy, sensing triumph, raised himself until he displayed several inches of skinny neck above the table's edge.

"Yes," said Mr. Seton in a hollow voice, "we know about her. She is not a good woman." What he said was mild enough, yet it carried overtones of the unspeakable, of bacchanalian orgies, of debauchery. And the mother, seeing her chance, took it.

"She is not nice, you know. There are things about her . . ." She would have gone on but a look from her husband halted her. It was a look which said, "We do not discuss such women before May and Mr. Murdock." So Mrs. Seton coughed and suppressed her revelations. Instead she made a conversational step aside. "I suppose she looks old and worn now. A woman leading that sort of life always pays in the end."

At this point Clarence, like a plumed knight, went to the defense of the damozel. "No, I wouldn't say that. She seemed quite young and beautiful." And then as if he had gone too far, he added mildly, "Of course, I don't know her well."

"It's better to avoid women like her," rejoined the father. "Take a word of advice from an older man. Women like that can ruin men . . . just by talking to them. They are creatures of the Devil."

Somewhere within the mind of Clarence a great light broke, and he saw everything clearly. He understood then that all the visit differed from his expectations not because the Setons had changed but because he had encountered Lily Shane. . . . She lay at the root of the trouble. Yes, women like her were powerful. There was no denying it.

The talk came easily enough now. Mrs. Seton, following her instincts, saw an opportunity to destroy the single menace which she fancied stood between her and her success. "She is a cousin, you know, of Ellen . . . that Tolliver girl. They all have bad blood in 'em."

But she had taken a false turning and, though she never knew it, her implications were in their effect fatal. Without understanding it she brought into the room both Ellen and her cousin Lily Shane, and Clarence saw them there, aloof and proud, more clearly than he had ever seen them in the flesh. He saw in them the same qualities, the assurance, the subtle, bedeviling reckless-ness, the outward indifference that concealed beneath it things un-dreamed of.

And then May giggled, nervously, as if she were smirking at the veiled improprieties which her mother kept concealed. The sound was more terrible than the scraping of the fork against the cold plate, for suddenly May stood revealed, and Clarence, in the nicety of his soul, was horrified.

"I couldn't tell you the whole story," continued Mrs. Seton. "Perhaps Mr. Seton could. I think you ought to know."

But the thoughts of Clarence had wandered away from the little group, away from the goose and cranberry sauce on his plate. Indeed they had wandered a long way, for they were centered now on the great black house he had seen for an instant high above the flames of the furnaces, so distant, so unattainable. In his mind he had created a picture of the house, of what sort of a din-ner must be in progress within its sooty, decaying walls. It was a picture, to be sure, far more magnificent than the reality and therefore more fatal to his happiness. The old ambitions began to stir once more, ponderously and terribly.

And far away he heard May saying, "She doesn't stay much in the Town. She thinks it isn't good enough for her." And then following the cue of so bad a campaigner as her mother, "Neither does Ellen. They're both stuck up. They think there's nothing good enough for them in the Town."

"You'd think," rejoined Mrs. Seton, "to see Ellen in her home-made clothes that she was a princess!"

A fierce resentment, bordering upon savagery, colored her voice. In the course of the conversation the fat, complacent woman became transformed into a spiteful, witch-like creature. And in the brain of Clarence there echoed a soft voice which said, *"Ah, the Setons! To be sure, I know who they are but I don't know them,"* dismissing them all quite easily, without resentment, without savagery, even without thought, forgetting in the next moment their very existence.

And then the lightning struck.

The shrill voice of Jimmy, impatient of results, suddenly cut the dampish air like a knife. "I know what it is! She's had a baby and she was never married! . . . She's had a baby and she was never married!"

14

DUSK had already fallen and the black servants had placed silver candlesticks among the wreckage of the Christmas feast before the first chair was drawn back with a scraping sound in the paneled dining room of Shane's Castle.

Throughout the long dinner, Ellen sat silent and somewhat abashed, eating little, hearing nothing, not even the family talk which each year followed the same course, rambling backward into reminiscences of the Civil War and of Grandpa Barr's adventure to the Gold Coast in the Forties. Even when the old man, lost in a torrent of sweeping memories, described with flashing blue eyes and the resonant voice of youth the jungle tapestries of Panama and a terrible shipwreck off the Cocos Islands, Ellen did not raise her head. It was not these things which interested her;

they were too far away and she was still too young, too egoistic, to understand the burning romance that lay in them.

It was only Lily who interested her, and with Lily she had been able to make no progress. Her cousin was placed opposite her, between Charles Tolliver and his son Fergus; and between these two Lily divided her attention, save in those moments when the stentorian tones of the Red Old Scot drowned all conversation. Even the boy she addressed with as much charm and as much interest as if he had been the most fascinating of men; and Fergus, young though he was, had been affected. His clear blue eyes, half-hidden by dark lashes, glowed with a naïve pleasure. Ellen, watching the pair, understood suddenly that this brother, so fascinated by the woman beside him, would one day escape as Lily had escaped. It was easy for him; it was easy for any man. For a girl to escape was a different matter. Yet, sitting there wrapped in despair, she planned how she might help him if she were the first to make her way into the world.

For Fergus exerted upon her a strange effect of softening. His fanciful mind she alone understood, and there were times in the long winter evenings when it was to him alone that she played her savage music. His shyness, which, unlike hers, lacked all the quality of savagery, aroused in her a fierce instinct of protection. There were times when the sight of his clear eyes, his blond curly head and snub nose filled her with an unaccountable melancholy and foreboding.

Sometimes during the dinner Ellen turned at the sound of a loud, rasping voice to regard her cousin Eva Barr, who sat by the side of Irene discussing harshly their work among the poor. Something about the horse-faced spinster filled her with a vague terror. It was as if Eva Barr stood as a symbol of that which a courageous, strong-minded woman might become if kept too long imprisoned. To Ellen, turning these things over secretly in her mind, it seemed that the way of her own destiny lay before her, branching now into two paths. At the end of the one stood the glowing Lily and at the end of the other Eva Barr, baffled sour, dogmatic, driving herself with a fierce energy into good works.

In a sudden access of pity and sorrow, for herself as much as for Eva Barr and old Miss Ogilvie, the tears welled in her eyes and dropped to the starched front of her shirtwaist. But she dried them, quickly and proudly, before they were seen, with the handkerchief she kept in the jangling chatelaine at her waist.

Ah, she saw everything very clearly . . . even the tragedy of her mother, so contented at this moment, in the midst of all her family, talking in her rich, vigorous voice to bitter old Julia Shane. Yet there was no way of saving any one, of changing anything. By some profound and feminine instinct, the girl knew this and it made her weep silently. . . . Ellen, who people said was so proud and had no heart.

Thus all her plans for seeking help from Lily were dissipated. If she had been less proud, she might, by an heroic effort, have approached her cousin saying, "You must give me money . . . lend it to me. Some day I will pay you back, for I will be rich, powerful. You must help me to do what I know I must do." But she found herself incapable of speaking the words, because the pride of a poverty which has been trained to show an indifferent face was too deeply planted in her. She would ask anything else . . . anything. She could not ask for money.

It was Lily herself who, all unconsciously, closed the matter once and for all. As the family, much wrapped in coats and furs against the cold, stood in the dark hallway making their farewells, she drew Ellen aside and, placing a friendly arm about the waist of the girl, said, "You play superbly, Ellen. If you can play always as you have played to-day, you will be a great artist." And then in a whisper, almost furtive, she said, "You must not throw it away. It is too great a gift. And don't let them make you settle into the pattern of the Town. It's what they'll try to do, but don't let them. We only live once, Ellen. Don't waste your life. . . . And when the time comes, if you want to come

and study in Paris with the great Philippe, you can live with me."
For a moment, the girl blushed and regarded the floor silently.
"I won't let them," she managed to murmur presently. "Thank
you, cousin Lily." It was all that she was able to say.

And when she stepped through the doorway into the cold air,
the flames above the furnaces were blurred before her glistening
eyes. Lily had promised Paris. That was something; but
Paris was a long way off and the road between was certain to be
hard.

15

THE heavy snow lasted until the day before the New
Year when the weather, turning suddenly, sent it slith-
ering away down the gutters of the Town in streams
of black water to swell the volume of the Black Fork so that in
the Flats, where the stream meandered a tortuous course, it overflowed its banks and filled the cellars of the hovels with stinking
damp. It was through this malodorous area that the fastidious
carriages of the Town made their way on New Year's Eve to the
eminence crowned by Shane's Castle, aglow now with the lights
that had flashed into existence upon the arrival of Lily. Ken-
tucky thoroughbreds picked their way daintily through the streaming gutters, drawing behind them the old families of the Town
and one or two of the new, for the Shanes, the Barrs and the
Tollivers did not, save in cases of rare distinction, admit the existence of the new. Consequently there was no carriage bearing a
member of the Seton family. It was this circumstance, far more
perhaps than any other, which had precipitated the dinner table
crisis of Christmas Day. And its consequences had not ended
there; they were destined once more to enter into the existence of
Clarence Murdock.

On the same New Year's Eve at about the hour when the gaiety in the house among the mills, centering itself about the re-

turned prodigal, had reached its height, Mrs. Seton, with a rustling of her voile skirts, drew May off to bed. Even the persistent Jimmy was swept with them, so that Clarence, left conspicuously alone with the father, understood that some event of grave importance had been arranged. Indeed, the manner of the corset manufacturer made his divination doubly sure. The man poked the remnants of the fire to make certain that it was entirely consumed before he retired, and then faced his guest.

Clarence, opposite him in a stiff backed chair of mahogany veneer, stirred with a sense of impending doom. The green eyes of his host fastened upon him with the old implication of guilt. From one corner of his narrow mouth there hung, limply, an unlighted and rather worn cigar which had done service all the day.

"I've been thinking it over," he said presently in his cold, deliberate voice. "I thought perhaps we'd better talk over a few things before you go away for good." A cinder slipping in the grate disturbed the stillness of the room and he continued. "I don't want to hurry you about anything, but it's best to come to an understanding."

In his uncomfortable chair, Clarence, swayed by the cold deliberate manner of the Elder, shifted his position as if he were sitting on a bag of rocks.

"Yes," he managed to articulate, as if he knew what was coming. "It's always better."

"First of all," began his host, "there is this matter of the Shane woman. . . . Lily Shane." He coughed and looked into the fire for a long time. And then, "It's a matter I don't care to discuss before May. . . . She's innocent, you know, like a flower. . . . The way girls should be."

"Yes," said Clarence agreeably; but there rang in his ears the horrid memory of May's knowing giggle.

"I don't understand how Jimmy could have found out unless he overheard his mother discussing it," continued the father. "We've always kept such things from the children. My wife and

I are great believers in innocence . . . and purity. It's a fine protection."

A month ago, Clarence would have agreed. Now he murmured, "Yes," politely, but in his heart he felt stirring a faint desire to protest, to deny this assertion. Lately there had come into his mind a certainty that the greatest of all protections lay in knowledge. One could not know too much. Each bit of knowledge was a link in the armor.

"It's true . . . what Jimmy said."

And again there was a silence in which Clarence flushed slowly a deep red.

"We can speak of such things . . . man to man," continued the torturer and slowly there swept over Clarence a terrible sense of becoming involved. Life in the Babylon Arms in the midst of a great and teeming city was simple compared to the complications of these last few days.

"But it doesn't seem to make any difference," he said presently. "All the Town has gone to the ball. . . . I saw the carriages going there . . . a whole stream of them, and it's Lily Shane who is giving it."

For an instant, Harvey Seton remained silent, turning the worn cigar round and round in his thin lips, as if it might be the very thought he was turning over in much the same fashion in his own devious mind. "Yes," he replied, after a long time. "That's true. But it's because nobody really knows."

At this speech Clarence, moved perhaps by the memory of Lily leaning from the window of the cab as she drove off through the storm, asked, "But do *you* know?"

Slowly his host eyed him with suspicion. It was as if the veiled accusations contained in their depths had suddenly become defined, specific; as if he accused this model young man opposite him of being the father of the vague and suppositious child.

"I have no proofs . . . to be sure," he said. "But a woman like that. . . . Well, to look at her is enough. To look at her in her fine Paris clothes. A woman has no right to make herself a

lure to men. It's like the women of the streets." Then he added
gruffly with a sudden glance at the dying fire, "She's always been
bad. They're a bad lot . . . the whole family, unstable, not to
be relied upon. They go their crazy way . . . all of 'em. Why
there was Sam Barr, Lily Shane's uncle, who spent his whole life
inventing useless things . . . never making a cent out of 'em.
His daughter lives in a cheap boarding house now. . . . If he'd
made an honest living instead of mooning about." He laughed
scornfully. "Why, he even thought he could invent a perpetual
motion machine." Then he halted abruptly as if he realized that
he had protested too much, and returned to the main stream of
his discourse. "As for the Town going to the ball, all the Town
knows just what I know, and they talk about it, only they see fit
to ignore it to-night because there is music and good food and
champagne punch at Shane's Castle."

In the silence that followed Clarence bent his neatly brushed
head and slipped away into a world of philosophy new and strange
to him. "Yes," he found himself thinking, "the world is like
that and nobody can change it much. If Lily Shane had asked
you, you would have gone."

But in this he was unfair to his enemy; Skinflint Seton would
not have gone, because he would have taken too great a satisfaction in refusing. It was this satisfaction, undoubtedly, which he
now missed so bitterly.

But the turn things had taken exerted upon Clarence a curious
effect. It was as if he found himself for the first time on the offensive, as if he were placed now within the ranks of all the
others who were at the ball, laughing, dancing, forgetful (as Lily
Shane had been) that Harvey Seton even existed. He had begun
to lose the feeling of isolation, of being trapped. There appeared
in the offing a gleam of hope.

He knew vaguely that it was difficult to deal with this man

who sat opposite him; but he did not understand the reason—that it lay in the very positiveness of his opponent, in the fact that the world of Harvey Seton consisted entirely of blacks and whites. There were in between no soft, warm shades of gray. May was (despite that fatal giggle) innocent as a flower, just as Lily Shane was the apotheosis of sin; and they were so because he willed them to be so. Thus he had created them, knowing his own daughter perhaps no better than he knew Lily Shane.

Clarence looked at him and blushed slowly. The walls began once more to close about him; he was frozen into silence.

"It was about May," Seton repeated slowly. . . . "She's unhappy. . . . At least her mother says she is, and it's on account of you."

In response to this Clarence found nothing to say. He would have protested but there were no words with which to frame a protest. The corset manufacturer bore down upon his victim like a Juggernaut. Clarence could neither speak, nor scream, nor rise from its path.

"I've guessed for a long time that there was something between you two." And here he permitted himself to smirk suddenly with a frigid sentimentality. "I'm not sorry, you understand. . . . Nothing could please me more. I'll need some one to help me in the factory . . . until Jimmy's old enough to take hold."

In his chair before the chilly, dying fire Clarence sat motionless; betraying no sign of the tortured soul that writhed within him.

"But I don't . . ." he began. "I mean . . ."

The Juggernaut rolled on. "I understand your bashfulness," continued his host. "I once had the honor of speaking myself . . . to the fine woman who is now my wife. My boy, there is nothing like a wife. It's the finest step a man can take . . . to settle himself into honorable matrimony." Here he bit a piece from the badly worn cigar and spat it into the ashes of the fire. "I am only speaking to you because I wanted to know if your intentions are honorable. After all, you have been close to us now . . . for a long time, living as one of the family, and under such conditions it is not surprising that a young girl should . . . should have her interest aroused."

By now Clarence managed to speak. He sat upright and with superhuman effort turned upon his torturer.

"My intentions . . ." he began. "My intentions . . ." And then he ended weakly. "Of course they're honorable, sir. What did you think?" It was as if he were in some terrible nightmare in which there was no faint gleam of reality.

"Then," continued the Elder, "a declaration would clear up everything . . . everything. I wouldn't have hurried you except on the girl's account."

It was impossible to believe that this was happening to him— Clarence Murdock—that he was being forced slowly into a life of slavery, of horror, a world of damp cotton sheets and reinforced corsets, of cold piety and stewed mutton. He must fight for time, somehow.

"You know, sir," he heard himself saying from a great distance, "I am bashful. . . . I've meant to propose, but I can't screw up my courage. . . . I've . . . I've meant to all along . . . and then I thought I'd leave it until I went away."

"I have no intention," replied the Elder firmly, "of hurrying things. I only thought that it would make every one easier . . . yourself included."

"I'm going away to-morrow . . . for three days," said Clarence. "When I come back we're going on a skating party if it's cold enough. . . . I'll . . . I'll ask May then if she'll have me."

Harvey Seton rose and came over to him, placing one hand on his shoulder. "That's fine," he said. "May's a fine girl. She'll make you a fine wife." Then he withdrew his hand for an instant and regarded Clarence with his accusing green eyes. "I suppose," he began, "there's no reason why you shouldn't marry her? And at the look of astonishment in the eyes of his guest he continued, "I mean, there's been no other woman . . . you've led a clean, pure life. You are fit to marry such a pure, innocent girl."

By now Clarence had became quite still, with the stillness of one who cannot believe the sensations conveyed by his own nerves. His mouth opened. It closed. At last he stammered, "Why. . . . Why . . . of course there's been no other woman. . . . I don't know anything about women." (And in the back of his mind a still small voice said, "But I'm learning . . . I'm learning.")

Harvey Seton backed away and stood with his lean legs between Clarence and the dead fire. He shook himself suddenly as if the chill had penetrated even his spare frame. "Well, I'm glad to hear that . . . I'm glad to hear that . . . I didn't know. Things are different in a city like New York. . . . And then you talked to Lily Shane. . . ."

"But she spoke to me first. . . ."

"I know . . . I know. I've encountered temptations." And he squared his thin shoulders with the air of St. Anthony resisting all the forces of the Devil. "I know." Then he turned suddenly and raised his arm toward the flickering gas. "It's gettin' chilly in here. . . . We'd best go to bed."

On the way to the door, the father turned in the darkness. "Of course," he said, "you can leave your things here if you're only going to be gone three days. . . . There's no use in lugging all that stuff away with you. . . . You can get it when you come back. . . ." There was a little pause, during which Clarence shuddered silently. "When you come back to propose to May. My, it'll make her happy. You know, she's one of the marryin' kind."

In the mind of Clarence there lingered the memory of that obscene giggle. With this new turn of affairs, it filled him with actual terror.

After he had gone to his room, he stood for a time looking out of the window far across to the other side of the Town. The house stood on a hill so that it overlooked all the wide and flooded expanse of the Flats. It was impossible to have seen Shane's Castle but above the spot where it raised its gloomy pile there was a great glow that filled all the sky. To be sure, it was a glow caused by the flames from the furnaces but it might have come from a great house where there was a ball in progress with music and good food and champagne punch. . . . The glow appeared at length to spread over all the Town and penetrate the very blood of Clarence as he stood there silhouetted against the light. His bony legs shivered beneath his cotton nightshirt; it may have been the cold, or it may have been fright. Clarence himself could not have said which it was.

Presently he lifted the window a little way. Unmistakably it was growing colder. There would be skating in three days. Nothing could alter the course of nature.

16

It was about this time that Gramp Tolliver, as if he scented the imminence of stupendous happenings, began like a long dormant volcano to display signs of activity. Despite the bitter cold and the ice that lay thick upon the pavement, he left his cell and, clad in a beaver cap and a moth-eaten coonskin coat, took to wandering about the streets. This activity Hattie Tolliver observed with apprehension, not alone because of the risk which the glittering pavements placed upon his brittle old bones, but because from long experience she interpreted such behavior as an omen of disaster. Standing in the doorway she watched his daily departure with a hostile eye, knowing well enough that if he did not come to grief, he would return in time for meals; his appetite was the best and on the rare occasions when he undertook any exercise it suffered a consequent augmentation. All the signs were present at meal time when the noise in the room above the kitchen became more violent and assumed a variety of manifestations. On occasion there was an admirable directness in Gramp Tolliver, not distantly akin to the directness of an elderly tiger at the approach of the feeding hour.

The sight of his grotesque figure, wrapped in furs and perambulating with uncanny skill the slippery places of the street, provided the people of the neighborhood with a divertissement of rare quality. As he passed along the street they took their children to the windows and there pointed out with ominous fingers his figure, saying, "There goes old man Tolliver, a living example of what laziness comes to. A perfect failure in life! Let him be an example to you. . . . Just watch him! If it was a good hard working man like *your* grandfather, children, he would have fallen and broken his leg long ago. But not him! Not old man Tolliver! The devil looks out for him!"

And by that time Gramp Tolliver would have vanished around the next corner to draw new moralists to peer at him from behind the Boston fern that adorned each successive bay window.

Knowing these things, Hattie Tolliver in her respectable heart experienced a certain shame at this frank exposure of Gramp. She would have preferred some other person as a walking example of failure; but there was nothing to be done unless she locked him in his room, and then he might easily have climbed to freedom by way of the grape arbor, a proceeding even more perilous to his brittle limbs than these icy promenades.

Into the midst of Gramp Tolliver's unusual behavior, Ellen returned from Shane's Castle with her appearance altered almost beyond the realms of the imagination. She had stayed with Lily, at the request of her cousin, over the three days following the ball, and now, on her return, it was clear that something stupendous had taken place during the visit.

She came upon her mother without warning in the very midst of a busy morning, and at sight of her Mrs. Tolliver halted her work abruptly and stood staring quietly for a good three minutes, while Ellen took off her hat and laid aside her coat. It was then that the shock became so great that Mrs. Tolliver broke the silence. She went at once into the heart of things.

"What has Lily done to you? What ideas has she put into your head?"

There was reason for her astonishment; the girl had changed. She appeared older, more mature. The wire rat, that so recently had supported the pompadour which was her pride, had vanished, and her fine black hair lay smooth and close to her head, in a fashion created by a doubtful lady named Cléo de Merode and appropriated not long afterward by Lily Shane. Her corsets, instead of being laced to give her the hourglass figure and the slight stoop forward so cherished in those days, were now worn so indecently loose that the clasps of her flaring skirt no longer fulfilled their mission. She was, according to the standards of the Town, extremely unfashionable in appearance, but she was far more beautiful. She belonged now not to the world of fashion plates fed to small towns by gigantic women's papers, but to a world of her own which had little to do with fashion or convention. Even though there was something ridiculous in her appearance, she had a new dignity. Something of the provinciality had slipped away. It was this, perhaps, which alarmed her mother—as if suddenly the girl had escaped into that horrid world where Lily moved and had her being.

"To think," said Mrs. Tolliver mournfully, "that I sent away my little girl and now she comes back to me a grown woman. That's what Lily has done to you. You aren't my little girl any longer."

To this Ellen made no reply. She stood, somewhat sullenly, as if she implied that there was no answer to such a sentimental observation.

"I suppose it's Lily who had you change your hair."

"I have beautiful hair. Why should I spoil it with a rat?"

"Lily said that. I know she did. . . . I can hear her saying it.

But that doesn't make it right. . . . It's not the fashion, at least not in the Town.   And that's where you're living."

For the first time Ellen smiled, in her old secretive fashion, as if she and Lily had entered upon some dark compact.

"It *was* just what Lily said.   Rats are silly things, anyway."

"They'll laugh at you," continued her mother, with an air of feeling her way.   "Young men don't like girls to be different. It makes them seem eccentric."

Ellen must have known, in her shrewd way, that her mother was not speaking frankly.   She knew beyond all doubt that her mother was not concerned with what the young men would think. She was talking thus because she saw these things—the rat, the corsets, the new air—all as signs of something far deeper.   She was fighting against the escape of her child, battling to keep her always.

"Yes, they would laugh, wouldn't they?" remarked Ellen presently.   And then, quite suddenly, the timbre of her voice changed. "Well, let 'em," she added abruptly.

As if she saw the beginnings of a storm, her mother sighed, turned away and observed casually, "Gramp has started to wander about again.   It worries me."

But Ellen swept past her and placing her handbag on the dining room table, she opened it, saying, "Lily gave me some clothes."

"You shouldn't have taken them.   I don't want Lily making paupers of us."

"I thought about that," said Ellen with an air of reflection. "But you don't understand Lily. . . . It wasn't like that at all. She doesn't do things that way. . . . She gave them to me as a present, the way she might have given me a book."

For a time there was a silence during which Ellen proceeded with the unpacking of her bag.   Reverently, almost with an air of worship, she took out from among her own threadbare clothes three gowns of superb material and spread them across the table under the gray winter light.   One was of black, one of green—the color of deep jade—and the third was the color of flame, so brilliant that in the comfortable shabby room it destroyed all else.

"I'm sorry I let you stay at Shane's Castle," began her mother. "Lily . . . Lily . . ." she halted abruptly and regarded her daughter with suspicion.   "She didn't promise you anything, did she?"

Ellen laughed, but through the sound of her soft mirth there ran, like a taut singing wire, the echo of subdued bitterness. "No.   At least nothing very definite. . . . She said that when I came to Paris to study I could live with her.   We didn't get beyond that."

"But you don't want to go to Paris. . . . It's a wicked city. . . . I thought you'd given all that up long ago."

But Ellen only lifted the flame colored gown and said, "Look at it.   Feel it.   Isn't it beautiful?"   And she ran her hand over the soft brocade with a sensuous air that was new and alarming. "There's nothing like it in all the Town."

Dumbly the mother fingered the stuff; she felt of it tenderly, reverently, and after a long time she said, "But you couldn't wear such clothes here.   Nobody has ever seen anything like them . . . except on Lily, and she's different.   That's why people talk about her.   No, you couldn't wear them here.   People would laugh at you."

For an answer Ellen only held up the green gown and then the black one.   They were simply made and not dissimilar, the flame colored one girdled by a chain of glittering rhinestones, the others by cords of silver.   They were so scant there seemed to be nothing to them, so simply made that their lack of ornament conveyed to Hattie Tolliver a sense of nakedness.   People in the Town wore bows, rosebuds, festoons of lace—all save Lily.

"I don't see what Lily was thinking of," she observed presently. And she drew in her lower lip doubtfully with an air of meditation as if the gowns raised before her eyes a wild vista of foreign orgies.

"Yes, people *would* laugh at me," said Ellen, "not that it makes any difference."

And placing the gowns over her arm, she turned away and started up the stairs to her own room. Her mother, staring after her, made a clucking sound which was her invariable signal of alarm. She must have speculated upon what passed between Ellen and her mysterious cousin within the depths of the gloomy house among the Mills; but she said nothing. In such a mood, it was impossible to learn anything from the girl.

And as she turned at last to resume her duties in the kitchen, the shadow of a motheaten coonskin coat and beaver hat passed the window. It was the ominous shadow of Gramp Tolliver hungrily returning for his noon meal. Clearly there was calamity in the air. He had never been so active before. . . .

Ellen had a way of dealing with the truth which must have alarmed her mother. It was not that she lied; rather it was that by some selective process she withheld certain truths and brought forward others so that the resulting effect was one of distortion, complicated by the wildest variation of mood. At the moment the girl appeared to be elated, perhaps only by the possession of the three naked gowns—so elated that her high spirits carried into the afternoon when she announced her intention of going skating.

"Are you going with May?" questioned her mother as she left the house.

"No, I'm going alone. May has Clarence Murdock. I don't imagine she'll want to be disturbed." And then with a sort of grim malice she added, "Things aren't moving very fast for May. . . . Not fast enough to suit her mother. You see she spread the story months ago that she was already engaged, and now she has to make it work out."

And without another word she passed out of the door into the bright cold sunshine, her tall, fine figure moving briskly down the path between the shaggy, frozen lilacs that marked the path to that extraordinary house of the shabby and respectable Tollivers.

17

WALKER'S Pond lay on the outskirts of the Town, a long sinuous expanse of water, frozen now, which wound its length between two long low hills left behind by the melting of the second great glacier. It twisted its way among the convolutions of rock and earth in a multitude of small coves and inlets, fringed by tangled bushes and low willows that stood black and naked in the winter wind. At the lower end the pond expanded into a broad and circular lake on the borders of which stood a low shed. Here it was that the crowds from the Town did their skating and here it was that May, in ignorance of the promise exacted by her impatient father, had brought the reluctant Clarence.

Any one watching the course of Ellen as she neared the spot must have realized that she had no intention of joining the crowd; instead of approaching the pond by the road of frozen clay which ended near the shed, she turned off through the fields, and swinging her skates, struck out for the far end where it lengthened into a serpentine canal. As she walked her skirts struck the ice coated stalks of the dead weeds, causing them to break off and fall beneath her feet with a slight tinkling sound of distant, crystal music. Among the bushes that bordered the fields the berries of the dogwood showed crimson against the black of the bare branches with a color rivaled only by the dark flame of the plumed sumach. Something in the day's brilliance must have penetrated the soul of the girl, for she sang as she walked more and more quickly in the direction of the ice. There was in her manner, now that she was once more alone and unharassed, something wild and passionate, a sort of untamed fierceness of the spirit.

Before her from the crest of the low hill, the lower pond at last spread out its glittering oval, sprinkled now with the black figures of skaters moving round and round with a soft rhythmic motion. The crisp air rang with the distant sound of steel upon ice. It was a queer, muted sound, like the music of violins in a far-off orchestra. For a moment Ellen stood quietly among the trees contemplating the distant black figures, as if she stood, a goddess, upon some Olympian peak regarding the spectacle of Man; and then with a sudden bound, she ran down the long slope and in a little cove sheltered from the wind, fastened her skates, and sprang forward on to the glistening ice.

She skated superbly. The lines of her young body, so slender, so sinuous, so strong, despite all the awkwardness of her clothes, stood revealed in the triumphant swing of her strokes. Here in her own hidden cove, she gave full rein to the wild, secret ecstasy of a proud, shy soul. Now she flew ahead into the biting wind; now she halted, pirouetting in a wild freedom; now, with a careless grace, she skated backward for a time, and presently she fell to practising with the precision of an artist one intricate figure after another. In this lonely backwater, she must have skated thus, triumphing in her skill and grace, for more than an hour; and at length, when she had accomplished each figure with perfection, she glided to the bank and, removing her skates, set about gathering sticks. In another moment she had lighted a fire and sat down by the side of it, her hair streaming, her cheeks bright with the cold, to warm her hands and sit staring into the blaze. Drifting up the sinuous curves of the pond, the sound of skating still floated toward her, but of this she no longer appeared to take any notice. She sat thoughtfully, ignoring it, and presently the color began a little to recede from her cheek and the old expression of restlessness to steal back into her dark eyes. The hills shut her in now, as if they might imprison her in their brooding fashion forever.

She had been sitting thus for more than an hour, apparently in profound thought, when slowly she became aware that the soli-

tude of her retreat had been violated. In the gathering dusk
of the early winter evening she beheld, through the branches of
the thick willows which sheltered her, the figure of an intruder—
a man—who skated awkwardly and with an air of effort, as if the
act required the most profound concentration. Yet it was clear
that his mind wandered now and then to other things, for from
time to time in the stillness of the evening the sound of his muttering reached her. He failed even to notice the smoke of the dying
fire, and as he came nearer a sudden gust of wind carried his words
toward her so that in snatches they became audible.

"I won't do it. . . . I'll be damned if I do. (And then the
labored, steady ring of his skates on the glittering ice.) They
can't make me. . . ." (Then once more a painful labored concentration upon skates and ankles that were too weak.)

By now Ellen must have recognized him. The figure was
unmistakable—slight, rather stiff and incredibly neat, even to
the carefully pressed line of his trousers. In place of a warm
skating cap he wore a Fedora hat pulled over his ears to prevent
the wind, which had reddened his smooth face, from blowing it
astray. The man was Clarence Murdock. Ellen might have
permitted him to pass unnoticed, save that in the next moment
he came round the willows and, tottering upon his skates, stood
face to face with her.

For a moment he stared at her silently, with the air of one who
cannot believe his senses.

"Well?" said Ellen, rising to her feet slowly.

Clarence shook himself, balancing more and more perilously on
his skates. "I didn't know you were here," he began. "I didn't
see you."

"I wasn't *there*," replied Ellen, indicating the direction of the
round pond. "I've been skating here all afternoon. . . . You
look cold. Wait, I'll poke up the fire. I was going home, but
I'm in no hurry."

Once his astonishment had passed away, his manner assumed a

certain calm; it appeared even that he experienced a relief in finding her there among the willows. He began to rub his ears vigorously while the fire, beneath the proddings of Ellen and the addition of more fuel, sprang into a blaze. It crackled cheerily and sent a bright shower of sparks heavenward. Within its glow Clarence, extending his hands toward the warmth, seated himself. He was more calm now, as if the quiet, capable directness of the girl had quieted his anxiety.

There was a long silence and presently Ellen asked, "Where's May?" But all the answer she received was a nod of the head indicating the round pond that lay beyond the hill. Again the silence enveloped them.

"It's fine skating," said Ellen, in another attempt at conversation. "The best there has been this winter." (It was clear that she could not say she had heard him talking to himself.)

"It is," replied her companion, thoughtfully, "but I can't skate very well. It's been a long time. . . ."

The girl was slipping on her skates once more with an air which said, "If you won't talk then I'll skate, at least until you warm yourself." She slipped to the edge of the ice and glided away, but she did not go any great distance. She circled about, gracefully, with a sure strength which carried an air of defiance, as if she sought to show Mr. Murdock how well it could be done. She pirouetted and did difficult figures with all the grace of a soaring bird. Indeed, she should have been to Clarence Murdock an intolerable spectacle. But she was not insufferable; on the contrary she clearly inspired him with a profound wonder. He watched her with a concentration approached only by that which he had given to his own efforts in the same direction. To observe her more clearly, he had put on his nose glasses and, beneath their neatly polished surface, his near-sighted eyes grew bright with admiration. Presently as she approached the shore in a sudden graceful swoop, he stirred himself and said, "You skate beautifully. . . . I wonder if you could help me."

"To skate?" inquired Ellen.

Clarence coughed nervously. "I don't mean that," he said. "I mean in another way."

Ellen, halting abruptly, seated herself on a rock. "In what way?" she asked. "I'll help you if I can."

For a time Clarence did not reply. In the distance, the faint whirring sound of the other skaters had grown gradually less and less distinct as one by one they withdrew from the ice to turn their feet homeward toward the Town. At last he said, "I oughtn't to speak to you, but I thought you might understand . . . being a woman."

It was the first time any one had ever called her a woman, and, despite all her hard independence, it flattered her. She leaned forward a little and said, "Maybe I will . . . I don't know until you tell me what it is."

And then Clarence blurted out the truth. "It's about May. . . . I don't want to marry her!"

Ellen laughed suddenly in a mocking fashion. "Well," she said, "do you have to? Have you asked her to? There's no law to make you do it."

At this speech Clarence blushed, and to cover his embarrassment, he bent his head and started once more to rub his ears, so that when he spoke again it was without looking at her. "It isn't that . . . I haven't asked her. But I'm in a bad position. You see, I promised her father that I'd ask her to-day. . . . I didn't want to. I really didn't. I had meant to once, but I changed my mind. . . . I can't explain that. It was her father that forced the promise out of me."

There was no doubt of his misery. Even to Ellen it must have been clear that he felt cornered, trapped, like some mild and inoffensive animal. He was such a nice young man.

Again Ellen laughed scornfully. "It's what old man Seton would do . . . the old skinflint!"

In the darkness beyond the little ring of flame the shadows

danced on the black and naked bushes. There was in the lonely figures by the fire an air of infinite pathos. They were both so young, so ignorant, so perplexed by the business of living.

"You can always run away," suggested Ellen. "They couldn't arrest you for it. . . ."

At this Clarence looked up suddenly. "But don't you see, all my clothes are at the Setons'. . . everything I brought with me. I have to get them and if I go back I'll have to face her father."

"But is that the only reason?" asked his companion. "I should think you'd be glad enough to escape at the price of a few clothes." She laughed suddenly with a curious, scornful mockery that confused Clarence. "That is, if you really want to escape. I should think you wouldn't want to settle down in this nasty Town. . . . There's nothing here for you. There's nothing for any one. I'm going to run away before long myself," she added boldly.

She spoke with such passion that Clarence made no reply for a long time. He sat watching her across the circle of light, contemplating her clear blue eyes, the fine glow of her face, the superb line of the throat which she herself admired so passionately. Something was happening to him; it was the old thing once more at work, the thing which betrayed him when he least expected it. Presently he said, "You're still going to New York? To study?"

To which Ellen replied with the same intensity, "Of course I am. I don't want a little shut-in world. They can't smother me . . . none of them! Not all of them together!"

It may have been that Clarence gathered strength from her strength, that far down in his timid soul some chord of his nature responded to the defiance of the girl. Certainly she was admirable . . . the way she had come to this hidden spot to skate in solitude, to build a fire with her own hands, to ask him in a friendly way, so frank and so free from all coyness and giggling, to warm his anemic frozen body. She *was* like the woman on the train. She wasn't afraid. And she didn't giggle. . . .

"I've been wondering," he said after a little time. "I've been wondering . . ." and then he coughed suddenly. "Would you come with me to New York?"

At this speech Ellen looked at him with a sudden penetrating glance, as if she failed to understand his meaning. Then, with the caution of a proud nature, she said, "But you see, I haven't enough money yet. It takes money for a girl alone in a city." She did not expose herself to the peril of being hurt.

But Clarence, now that he was started, rushed on, "I don't mean that . . . I mean . . . would you marry me? Would you come as my wife?"

The sound of the distant skating had died away until by now only the faintest ring of steel singing upon the ice was borne by the rising wind into the little cove. In the darkness Ellen bowed her head and sat thus silently for a long time. Her thoughts, whatever they may have been, were interrupted presently by the sound of Clarence's voice, softer this time, and less frightened, though it still carried a timidity, almost the abjectness of an apology.

"I could help you. . . . I could make money and you could go on with your music. You see, this didn't come over me suddenly. I've thought about it before . . . ever since I saw you that first time."

There was nothing in the least dominating in his manner. He sat there at a proper distance from her, mild and gentle, pleading his case. It was clear that he was even a little frightened, as if he had spoken almost without willing it. But the little vein in his throat which Lily had noticed so long before began to throb, slowly at first and then with steadily mounting rapidity. If Lily had been there, she would have understood its significance as surely as a ship's captain watching his barometer in a storm. Lily understood such things.

When at last Ellen raised her head, it was to look at him directly and with a certain appraising frankness.

"Yes. . . . I'll marry you," she said at last. She spoke breathlessly, her voice clouded by a faint choking sound as if for the first time in her life she were really frightened.

"I'm glad," said Clarence. "You see, I want to be great and famous some day. I want to be rich, and I want some one to share it with me. I couldn't marry May. It would be like shutting myself up in a trap." The terrible ambitions were loose again, running wild, leaping all bounds, intoxicating him. "I want to be great and rich . . . if I can. I never told anybody this before, but I thought you might understand because you're different."

It was the longest speech he had ever made in her presence, and throughout its duration Ellen watched him with a growing wonder mirrored in her eyes.

"I didn't know you felt that way," she said almost with reverence. "You never mentioned it before. I thought you'd be content with May."

But all the same, her words lacked the ring of conviction. All at once she felt herself engulfed by a great and unaccustomed wave of pity that was quite beyond explanation. She felt that Mr. Murdock was pathetic. It was almost as if she could weep for him. It was not until long afterward that she understood this chaotic emotion. It passed quickly, and she said, "But you'd better go now and find May. . . . Don't wait for me . . . I'm all right. . . . She must be all alone by now, wondering where you are. I can look out for myself."

And a little later Clarence, treacherously shepherding May on their last walk together, saw in the far distance against the dying glow the black silhouette of Ellen. Alone she moved over the crest of the high hill, walking slowly now, her head bent in thought . . . remote, proud and somehow terrifying.

18

IT was not until ten o'clock that Mrs. Tolliver began to grow uneasy. There had been, after all, nothing to cause alarm. An hour before supper Ellen had come in from skating with a countenance fresh and almost happy. True, Gramp Tolliver had returned late from one of his expeditions—the second that day —and was noisier and more impatient than usual in his room above stairs. Indeed his uproar continued even after feeding time, until long after Ellen, saying that she was to spend the evening at the Setons', had gone out into the rising wind. If there was anything which alarmed Mrs. Tolliver it was the mutterings of the volcano overhead; so great was the variety of its manifestations that she remarked upon it to her husband.

"You know," she said, "Gramp is restless again . . . worse than ever . . . worse than he was at election time."

From his refuge on the great threadbare sofa her husband mumbled a reply, indistinct yet understandable because it was a speech he made so frequently when his wife insisted upon conversation.

"You're worrying again. . . . There's nothing to worry about."

But she knew that she was right. It was a feeling which was almost physical, an intuition, an instinct which her husband, in the way of fathers (which at best were but poor things), did not share. After all he came by his conclusions in a logical fashion, not without the aid of a peculiar and individual philosophy, and therefore, by omitting the human equation, he gave his wife the opportunity more than once of saying, "I told you so."

Though Mrs. Tolliver rocked and darned placidly enough, she was not, even out of respect for her husband's love of slumber and forgetfulness, to be kept silent. When Ellen was out and there was no flow of music to bind together the comfort of the evening, it was necessary to talk; otherwise the peace became mere stillness, and the contentment a barren boredom. For Mrs. Tolliver needed constant evidence of happiness or cordiality. It was a thing not to be taken easily and for granted; one must make a show of it.

"He behaved like this, only not as bad, when Judge Weissman —the dirty scoundrel—bought the last election."

This time the only reply from the sofa was an engulfing silence, broken now and then by the aggravating sound of heavy breathing.

"Why don't you say something?" she said at last in exasperation. "Why don't you talk to me? I work all day and then when evening comes, all you do is to sleep."

The blanket on the sofa heaved a little and Charles Tolliver changed his position, muttering at the same time, "What shall I say? What do you want me to say?" And then after a pregnant silence, "If Gramp is ranting around, I don't see what we can do about it."

He spoke thus of his father in the most natural fashion. It was as if the old man were something of a stranger to him, a vague figure entirely outside the circle of the family existence.

After another long silence, Mrs. Tolliver observed, "It's nearly eleven o'clock and Ellen hasn't come in yet." Then she leaned forward to address her sons who lay sprawled on the floor, the older one reading as usual, the other lying on his back staring in his sulky way at the ceiling. "You boys must go to bed now. I'll come up with you and see that you're tucked in properly. It's a cold night."

The three departed and after a time, during which the hall clock sounded the hour of eleven, she descended from the neat upper regions and went into the kitchen to see that the door was locked, that the dog was on his mat, that the tap was not dripping, indeed, to oversee all the minutiæ of the household that were the very breath of her existence. When at last she reëntered the living room there was in her manner every evidence of agitation. She approached her husband and shook him from his comfortable oblivion.

"I don't understand about Ellen," she said. "It's very late.

Maybe you'd better go over to the Setons' and see what has happened to her."

But her spouse only groaned and muttered. "Wait a while. . . . Like as not she's in bed asleep."

"That couldn't be . . . not without my knowing it."

What she would have done next was a matter for speculation, but before she had opportunity to act there rang through the silent house the sound of the doorbell being pushed violently and with annoying energy. It rang in a series of staccato periods, broken now and then with a single long and violent clamor. At the sound Mrs. Tolliver ran, and, as she approached the door, she cried out, "Yes! . . . Yes! . . . I'm coming. You needn't wear out the battery!"

On opening it she discovered on the outside that source of all evil, Jimmy Seton. Even at sight of her he was unable to relinquish the pleasure of ringing the bell. Indeed he kept his hand upon the button until she knocked it loose by a sudden slap on the wrist.

"What do you mean by ringing like that?"

Jimmy, unabashed, faced her. "Ma," he began, in his shrill voice, "wants to know if Mr. Murdock is over here. He ain't been at our house since before supper. He said he was going to the barber shop and he never came back."

For an instant, Mrs. Tolliver, wisely, held her tongue. The old instinct, working rapidly, told her that she must protect Ellen. It was clear then that the girl had not gone to the Setons'. Where could she be? Where was Mr. Murdock? Within the space of a second unspeakable catastrophes framed themselves in her mind. But she managed to answer. "He's not here. He hasn't been here. I don't know anything about him."

"All right," said Jimmy. "I'll tell her."

He made a faint gesture toward the button of the doorbell but Mrs. Tolliver thrust her powerful body between him and the object of his temptation, so that Jimmy, with a baffled air, turned and sped away into the darkness. When he had vanished she closed the door slowly, and stood for an instant leaning against it. Then, before she moved away, she raised her voice in a summons.

"Papa!" she called "Papa! Something *has* happened. Ellen wasn't at the Setons' and Mr. Murdock is missing."

In the moment or two while she stood thus with her hand resting on the knob of the door, there passed quickly through her mind in a series of isolated fragments all the events and the forebodings of the past few weeks. Gradually these fitted into a pattern. She understood well enough what had happened; she knew that Ellen had gone. Yet she refused to admit this, as if by refusing to acknowledge the fact it might come gradually to have no existence. She understood Gramp Tolliver's ominous outburst of restlessness, Ellen's strange look of triumph, the air almost of happiness which had come over the girl. Only one thing she could not understand. . . . Clarence Murdock! After all, Ellen had mocked him as something quite beneath her consideration. Why had she chosen him?

In that single brief moment she was hurt more deeply than she was ever hurt again. Those things which came afterward were not so cruel because she came in time to be used to them. But this . . . this was so sudden, so cruel. She had no defenses ready, not even the defense which the less primitive have—a capacity for putting themselves into the shoes of the other fellow, of understanding why he should have acted thus and so. No, there was nothing, save only a sudden sharp physical pain and that which was far greater—a fear for a child who was gone suddenly from her protection.

When she reëntered the warm living room, she found her husband sitting on the edge of his sofa. Because he was a man who enjoyed his sleep and was reluctant to shake it off, he was not altogether awake.

"You say," he murmured drowsily, "that Ellen has run off with that Murdock?"

"They are both gone. . . . They must have gone together."

This the husband considered for a moment. Foolishly exalting logic above intuition, he asked, "How do you know?" To which his wife retorted, "Know! Know! Because I do know! I'm sure of it. . . . What are we going to do?" Suddenly she leaned forward and shook him violently. "Why, they're not even married. They can't have been and they've gone off together. Anything might happen."

The husband, out of the depths of knowledge which arose not from instinct or profound love but from long speculation upon the human race answered, "Don't worry about that. Ellen's no fool! She's not in love with him!"

"When you talk like that, you're like your father!" Nothing could have signified in clearer fashion the gravity of the situation, for this was a retort which Mrs. Tolliver used only upon occasions of profound disaster. It was, she believed, the most cruel thing she could say. This time she did not wait for him to reply.

"What train have they taken? . . . They're bound to go east. Perhaps you can stop them. Come! Get up. . . . If you don't go I will!"

With exasperating slowness her husband gained his feet. "There's a train a little after eleven." He regarded his watch. "We might be able to catch them, though I don't think I can make it."

Already his wife stood before him with the coat she had taken from the living room closet. "Here!" she said. "And wrap your throat well. It's a bitter night." Then she herself helped him into his coat and fastened his muffler with great care. Before she had finished, he asked, "What sort of a person is this Murdock?"

"It's no time to ask that. . . . Go! Hurry!"

Barely had these speeding words fallen from her lips when from overhead there came with the suddenness of an explosion the sound of a terrific crash, as if some part of the house had suddenly collapsed. The sound distinctly came from the rear. The volcano at last had burst forth!

In a breathless instant, the pair faced each other. It was Mrs. Tolliver who spoke first.

"What has he done now?" And with a fierce emphasis she added, "I think the Devil himself has gotten into him." Then she recovered herself quickly. "Go! Go! Catch Ellen. I'll take care of Gramp."

He argued for a moment—one precious moment—and losing as usual, was sped on his way by his powerful wife.

When her husband had vanished sleepily into the darkness, Mrs. Tolliver made her way up the back stairs to the room under the tin roof. As she opened the door, there rose before her in the flickering light of the kerosene lamp a room which had the appearance of a place wrecked by a cyclone. One of the vast bookcases lay overturned, the worn leather volumes sprawled in a wild confusion about the floor. Bits of paper covered with bird track handwriting lay scattered like fallen leaves and at one side, a little removed from the path of the catastrophe, lay stretched at full length the brittle body of Gramp Tolliver, still and apparently unconscious. There was in its rigidity something ghastly. Only a miracle had saved him from being buried under his own books, battered and broken perhaps by his own beloved Decline and Fall.

Climbing over the wreckage, Mrs. Tolliver leaned down and took the body of the old man in her arms. Thus a truce was declared, and when the one enemy had made certain that the other was still alive, she went downstairs, wrapped a shawl about her and fetched a doctor.

19

IT was midnight when Charles Tolliver returned alone. Without removing his coat or the carefully bound muffler, he made his way through the house to the back stairs which he climbed slowly and with an air of sheepishness. His wife was, after all, no easy woman to face under conditions like this. The news he had for her was not the best. Indeed it is probable that he experienced a great relief when he found that his wife was not alone. In the dusty room thrown now into a wild disorder which Mrs. Tolliver was already vigorously engaged in clearing away, the doctor stood beside the bed. There was a quality of the grotesque in the battered figure of the old man and the fantastic shadow of the physician cast by the flickering light upon the wall. At the sound of his footsteps Mrs. Tolliver, still holding in her arms volumes three and four of the Decline and Fall, looked up from her task. She stared hard at him as if by concentration she might produce out of thin air the figure of her daughter. But there was no mistake. He was alone.

It was Charles Tolliver who spoke first. He found no pleasure in airing his troubles in public, so he said nothing of his errand. "What's the matter with Gramp?"

The doctor faced him. He was a short fat man with little mutton chop whiskers. "It seems he's had a stroke," he murmured. "And yet I don't know. It might be something else. The symptoms aren't right." And he took up once more the bony wrist, to count the pulse. Instantly Mrs. Tolliver stepped close to her husband.

"Did you find her?" she asked in a low voice.

"No. . . . The train was pulling out just as I reached the station. I was a minute too late."

"It was Gramp who let her get away. If you hadn't stayed to argue. You could have hurried. My God, who knows what will happen to her. . . . My little girl!"

"She isn't that. . . . Not any longer."

But before she could reply the doctor interrupted. "No, I don't know what it is. His pulse seems all right and he has no fever." And the little man fell to wagging his head, in the manner of a physician who was always secretly doubtful of his own opinion. "To-morrow I'll fetch another doctor. We'll have to have a consultation."

After that he packed his bag, wrapped himself up to the throat and bidding them good night in a mournful, bedside whisper, as if (thought Hattie sourly) Gramp had been an adored child cut off in the bloom of youth, made his way down the creaking stairs.

When he had gone, Mrs. Tolliver turned abruptly and said again, "You could have made it if Gramp hadn't thrown this fit. And now she's gone. . . ."

In the shadows that covered the vast bed, Gramp Tolliver's body lay stiff as a poker thrust beneath the sheets. But presently in the midst of the hushed talk that went on by his side, one eye opened slowly and surveyed the scene. For an instant there rose in the still cold air the echo—it could not have been more than that—of a far-off demoniacal chuckle. At the sound Mrs. Tolliver turned and approached the bed.

"He laughed," she said to her husband. "I'm sure of it . . ." and she shook the old man gently without gaining the faintest suspicion of a response. He lay rigid and still. At last she turned away.

"Go," she said, "and take the next train. You might catch them at Pittsburgh. If you haven't enough money there's some tied in a handkerchief under the mattress."

"But you. . . . What'll you do?"

"Never mind me . . . I'll sit here in the rocker and keep watch. . . ."

And until the gray winter dawn crept in at the windows she sat there, awake, with one eye on the old man, for the echo of that wicked chuckle had awakened in her mind the most amazing suspicions. In the single moment that she had stood listening to the sound of the catastrophe overhead, Ellen had made her escape.

. . . How could he have known what no one else knew? Yet she was certain that he had known.

Charles Tolliver did not overtake his daughter; indeed, on that night she escaped from him forever. He saw her afterward . . . long afterward, but he never recaptured her, even for one fleeting moment. Perhaps in the dismal solitude of a day coach filled with weary travelers rushing eastward through the winter night, he understood this in his own way. It was, after all, a way different from that of his father, Old Gramp, or his wife who sat patiently now in a kind of dumb, animal agony by the side of the old man. Of Charles Tolliver, it might have been said that he expected nothing of life, that from the very first he had accepted life as at best a matter of compromise. One took what came and was thankful that it was not worse. Because he was like this people called him a weak man.

And it is impossible to say that he regretted profoundly the flight of his daughter. In his gentleness, he understood that this thing which she had done was inevitable. Nothing could have prevented it. Even the pursuit was a futile thing. If Ellen were recaptured, it was vain to hope that she would remain so; yet the pursuit was in itself a symbol of action and therefore it satisfied his wife in at least a small way. It may even have been that in the rare wakeful moments of his lonely, fruitless journey he envied Ellen; that he saw in her escape a hope which had always eluded him. He had been known since childhood as a worthy man, the unfortunate son of a father who was worthless and a failure. He had existed always as a symbol of virtue, as one who had stood by his mother (dead now these many years) in the long periods of poverty and unhappiness. If he had been ruthless instead of dutiful, if he had escaped, if he had ventured into a new world . . . What might have happened? But even this thought could not have troubled him for long. He slipped easily back into the pleasant oblivion of sleep.

The passengers wakeful, uncomfortable, restless in the close air of the crowded car could never have guessed that the gray-haired, handsome man, who slept so peacefully, was a father in pursuit of an eloping daughter.

And in another train a hundred miles beyond, rushing faster and faster toward the rising dawn, sat Ellen and Clarence Murdock. They too rode in the common car, for the train was crowded. They sat bolt upright and rather far apart for lovers. From time to time Clarence reached out and touched her hand, gently, almost with deprecation, and to this she submitted quietly, as if she were unconscious of the humble gesture toward affection. It is true that they were both a little frightened; what had happened had happened so quickly. Even Clarence could not have explained it. To Ellen, though she came in the end to understand it all, it must have been a great mystery.

The romance—what little of it there had been—was all vanished now, gone cold before the glare of the flaring lights, beneath the staring, bleary eyes of their fellow passengers. Somehow everything had turned cold and stuffy, touched by the taste of soot and the accumulated dust of half a continent. The train rocked and swayed over the glittering rails, and presently Clarence, who had been frowning for a long time over something, said, "D'you think they'll ever send on my hand bags?"

Ellen laughed and regarded him suddenly with a curious glance of startled affection. For a moment one might have taken them for a mother and child . . . a mother who saw that her child must be protected and pitied a little.

"I wouldn't worry over that," she answered. "What difference does it make now?"

"And May . . ." began Clarence once more.

"It's done now," said Ellen gravely. "Besides in a little while she'll forget everything and marry some one else. Any man will suit May. It's only *a* man she wants, not *the* man."

But Clarence was not comforted; there was his conscience to

torment him, and worse than that there was a distrust, vague and undefined, of what lay ahead. He could not have described it. If he had been a strong man, he would have said, "All this is a mistake. We will not marry. It is wrong, everything about it." He could have turned back then and saved himself; but he did not. He sat quietly against the dusty plush, watching Ellen now and then out of the corner of his nice eyes with the manner of a man resting upon the rim of a volcano.

By dawn the train had come in sight of the furnaces on the outskirts of Pittsburgh and the color of the flames mingled with the cold gray of the January sky. He had come out on the train with Lily; he was going back on the train with her cousin. He stood there, timidly, upon the threshold of his new world—a world filled with people who haunted those rare flights of a treacherous imagination.

20

IT was not until noon of the following day that the amazing news percolated fully through the houses of the Town. Women congregated and discussed it, passionately; men greeted each other with the news, "Have you heard that Charlie Tolliver's girl has eloped with that young Murdock who was visiting Skinflint Seton?" They turned the news over and over, worrying it, adding details, filling in the gaps in a story which could have been known to no one. And always the conclusion was the same . . . that here was another evidence of the wildness and eccentricity of the Barr family. Old Julia Shane, in her youth, had done the same thing. And then there was Sam Barr and his crazy perpetual motion machine. The history of this spirited family was ransacked and a thousand odd, half-forgotten stories brought to light. There was, of course, that element which hinted that Ellen had eloped because the circumstances made it necessary. Women said this, not because they believed it, but because they hated Ellen and old Julia Shane.

In her sooty house among the Mills this grim old woman received the news, rather later than most (it was brought her by one of her negro servants) with a sort of wicked delight. This was a great-niece worthy of her blood, who took matters into her own hands and acted, quickly, sensationally! And before an hour had passed she seated herself with a quill pen and wrote the news triumphantly to Lily who, that morning, had started back to Paris. The letter finally overtook her daughter a month later when Lily, installed once more in her big house in the Rue Raynouard, sat awaiting the arrival of her friend the Baron. To him she read it aloud, creating for his pleasure a picture of the smoky Town, of the effect the news would have upon its residents. She described to him the fierce impetuous Ellen. She told him the Town was a town like Roubaix or Tourcoing or Lille, only more provincial.

Across the silver-laden tea table in her long drawing-room in Passy, she said, "You may see her one day yourself. I've told her to come here and live with me. She wants to be a great pianist. . . . A girl like that can accomplish anything she sets her mind to. . . . But I don't think you'll like her. . . . She's too powerful."

Nearer home, the news came to May Seton and her mother a little after midnight when Jimmy, sent a second time as messenger, brought back the suspicion of their elopement. In the beginning the situation was embarrassing, for May in her optimism had spread the story that the *fiançailles* of Clarence and herself had been accomplished. Once this had passed, she experienced a sort of inverted triumph, superior if possible even to that which might have arisen from the capture of a New York young man. She understood presently that people regarded her as a martyr, a virgin robbed of her lover, and once she got the full sense of this she played the rôle to perfection. Dressed in her most somber clothing, as if she mourned a lover worse than dead, she paid and received a great number of calls, always in company with her mother who now assumed the rôle of duenna and garnished May's account of the affair with appropriate and growing details. Old ladies swooped about and settled upon the tale to pick it over and contemplate the ruins with ghoulish satisfaction, until at length the event, now of proportions beyond the realms of the imagination, became an epic in the chronicles of the Town, a piece in which May Seton played the rôle of injured innocence and Ellen that of adventuress in the grand manner of East Lynne or Lady Audley's Secret. In short, what had appeared in the beginning to be a calamity, turned out to be a triumph. Husbands might be found at every turn, but public martyrdom comes rarely. Indeed before many weeks had passed, potential husbands began to loom upon the horizon and crowd into the middle distance. Because May in her bereavement had become what she had never been . . . a figure of interest.

But there was one part of the story which remained known to only one person in the Town. It was the space of time which elapsed between the hour that Clarence departed for the mythical barber shop and the hour the train left for the east. This was a matter of five hours, in which much might have taken place. No one seemed able to account for it. No one had seen either of them. They had, to all intents, disappeared for five hours . . . a thing which in the Town was incredible.

Yet there was one person who knew, and she was the last whom any one could suspect. It was impossible to believe that a creature so birdlike, so gentle, could have played a part in so scandalous an affair as the rape of May Seton's lover. Yet it was true; the guilty pair had spent the five hours in the room filled with conch shells and pampas grass and plush, for Miss Ogilvie had kept her rash promise to Ellen. Indeed, the whole affair had been planned under her very eyes. But in the little house surrounded by lilacs and syringa bushes, she kept her secret as faithfully as she had kept her promise, though it was the most exciting thing that had ever happened to her. It was almost as if she herself had escaped

into a great world where there were no neighbors and no sewing
circles.

But the two who suffered most were the two whose pride was
greatest . . . those born enemies Mrs. Tolliver and Skinflint
Seton. From the moment of the elopement the ancient feud over
the swindle of the synthetic corset stays emerged without shame or
pretense into the open, and the story became common property
that Harvey Seton had been seen on the Tollivers' piazza being
ordered into the street because he suggested that Ellen had eloped
because the circumstances made it necessary.

Scarcely less mysterious than the missing five hours was the
nature of Gramp's illness, a thing which had baffled the consul-
tations and head waggings of the Town's best medical talent.
Two days later he was up and about again perambulating once
more, in his coonskin coat, the icy pavement of the Town. And it
was with a new look of defiant malice that he regarded the faces
peering at him from behind the Boston ferns of Sycamore Street.
The sharp old eyes mocked the passers-by. They said, "My
Granddaughter has a good deal of the old man in her. She has
the courage to do as she sees fit. You'll hear from that girl!"
All this punctuated by the sharp tap! tap! tap! of his tough
hickory stick on icy pavements where an ordinary man would long
ago have slipped and broken his leg.

21

WEEKS passed before there came from Ellen any news
beyond the mere statement that she was alive, comfortable and well, and that although she was sorry for
her actions she could not have done otherwise. Some day, she
implied with romantic overtones, they would understand.

When at last a real letter came, it was turbulent, hard and
unrepentant. Nor was the spelling the best.

"I am sorry for May . . . a little," she wrote, "but it won't make any difference to her. She is in love with men and not one man. To have lost Clarence won't end her happiness. Any man will do as well. In a year she'll be married, like as not to Herman Biggs. It was different with me. Everything depended upon Clarence . . . everything, you understand. To me he made all the difference.

"And we are happy," she continued, as if this was, after all, a matter of secondary importance. "Clarence loves me. We have a nice apartment quite near to Riverside Drive that overlooks the river where the warships anchor. It is the top floor of an enormous apartment house . . . ten stories high, and the view is wonderful. You can see over half the city. It is called the Babylon Arms.

"You see, Clarence and two friends of his (a Mr. Bunce and a Mr. Wyck) shared it before I came and now we have it to ourselves, because his two friends kindly moved elsewhere. Mr. Bunce is nice but Mr. Wyck is a poor sport, always talking about his relatives. You see, he's what he calls an 'old New Yorker,' sort of run-down and pathetic, and awfully dependent. I think he hates me for having taken Clarence away from him, and for breaking up the apartment. But it doesn't matter. He's too insignificant to count.

"Mr. Bunce got married the other day. He says we drove him to it, chasing him out into the street with no place to live. That's the way he talks . . . hearty and pleasant but a bit noisy. The girl isn't much—a big, pleasant girl like himself whose father is a building contractor in Hoboken, which is really a suburb of New York."

And so she sketched briefly, and with the careless cynicism of youth, the downfall of Mr. Wyck; for it is true that the reverberations of the elopement made themselves felt in a place so far from the Town as the Magical City. With her appearance the whole world of Mr. Wyck toppled, hung for a moment in mid-air, and at last collapsed, leaving him in the backwater of a grimy boarding house on lower Lexington Avenue. No longer had he any one to admire or honor him for the sake of the ancient Wyck blood and the spinster aunts in Yonkers. On the very day of Ellen's arrival the name of Wyck Street was changed to Sullivan in honor of a Tammany politician. Night after night, a lonely little man, he sat, an outcast, on the edge of his narrow bed, waiting for his milk to heat over the gas jet in the fourth floor rear. He mourned Clarence who represented the only friendship he had ever known. He mourned the Babylon Arms where for a time he had been almost a man, independent and free. And as he mourned the hatred grew in the recesses of his timid, unhappy soul.

It is true that in her letter Ellen revealed a great deal, but it is true that she did not reveal everything, for there remained between her and a complete revelation the pride which would not allow her to admit disillusion. She did not, for example, say that the view from her windows included, besides the noble river, glimpses of wooden shacks and bleak factories, half-veiled in smoke and mist, on the distant Jersey shore. Nor did she say that beneath her window there were monotonous and hideous rows of brownstone houses, unrelieved in their ugliness even by tiny patches of mangy grass. And she said nothing of the railway tracks that lay between her and the river, crowded with cars that imprisoned lines of wretched cattle standing shoulder to shoulder, whose presence sometimes filled the lofty flat with the faint, dismal sounds and odors of the barnyard. These things she could not bring herself to set down on paper because they would have dimmed the splendor raised by such a name as The Babylon Arms.

Nor did she say that after all Mr. Bunce and Mr. Wyck and even perhaps Clarence were not so different from the people in the Town; because this might have given rise to a faint suspicion that, after all, she had not escaped. There were things and shades of things which the Town must never know. She understood, perhaps even then, the affair of building a career. There must be glory, only glory, and triumph.

And Mrs. Tolliver, reading the letter over and over in the long darkness of the winter evenings, stirred herself night after night to observe that "something had happened to Ellen."

"She's told me more in this letter than she has ever told me in all her life before. She must be happy or she couldn't write such a letter."

And for a time she consoled herself with this thought, only to utter after a long silence the eternal doubt. "I only hope he's good enough for her."

Then, when her husband had fallen into a final deep slumber from which he stubbornly refused to be roused, it was the habit of the woman to go to the piano and dissipate the terrible stillness of the lonely room with the strains of The Blue Danube and The Ninety and Nine played laboriously with fingers that were stained and a little stiff from hard work.

The faint, awkward sounds, arising so uncertainly from the depths of a piano accustomed now to silence, must have roused in her a long sequence of memories turning backward slowly as she played, into the days when she had struggled for time from household cares to learn those pitiful tunes. The hours spent at the old harmonium in her father's parlor were hours stolen from cooking and baking, from caring for her younger brothers and sisters, hours which, so long ago, had raised in her imagination sounds and scenes more glamorous than anything found in the borders of the country that was her home. They were not great, these two melodies—one born of Evangelism and the other out of the gaiety of an Austrian city—yet they were in a fashion the little parcel of glamour which life had dealt out to Hattie Tolliver. The rest was work and watchfulness, worries and cares.

There must have been in the woman something magnificent, for never, even in deep recesses of her heart, did she complain of the niggardliness of that tiny parcel. She sought only to wrest a larger share for her children, for her Ellen who was gone now a-seeking glamour on her own.

And, of course, the sound of the music made by her stiffened fingers may have brought back for a time something of her lost Ellen.

Because there was in Hattie no softness which would allow her to admit defeat, she set about, once the first shock of the affair had softened, to reconstruct all her existence upon a new plan, motivated by a single ideal. How this change came about, she would have been the last to understand. It came, in a sense, as a revelation. She awoke one morning and there it was, clear as the very winter landscape—a vision of the sort which guides people of passionate nature. True, there were circumstances which led her mind in that one direction; there was, to be sure, the look that had come into the blue eyes of her elder son since the day when Ellen had fled. Any one could have seen it, a look so eloquent and so intense, which said, "I too must have my chance. I too must go into the world." Perhaps he remembered the half-humorous promises to help him that Ellen had made so frequently. There was, she knew, a secret sympathy between the two in which she played no part. It was a look which came often enough into the eyes of Hattie Tolliver's family. If the boy had been old enough to reason and understand such things, he might have said, "My grandfathers set out into a wilderness to conquer and subdue it. It was a land filled with savages and adventure. I too must have my chance. I am of a race of pioneers but I no longer have any frontier. I must turn back again, as Ellen has turned, to the east!" In a little while—a few years more—the look was certain to come into the eyes of Robert, the youngest.

And doubtless the woman came to understand that it was impossible any longer to hope that her husband might realize any of the wild and gaudy dreams she had held so often before his philosophic and indifferent eyes. He was a gentleman, and no longer young; he had indeed turned the corner into middle age. What must be done rested with her alone.

And so, understanding that Ellen would never turn back, the plan of her existence ceased to find its being in the smoky Town; it became instead a pursuit of her children. If they would not remain in the home she had made for them then she must follow them, and, like a nomad, place her tent and build her fires where they saw fit to rest.

So she set about planning how it was possible to escape from the Town, to transport all her family and their belongings into a world which she had disliked and even feared but which now must be faced. Fantastical schemes were born, reared their heads and collapsed in a brain which considered nothing impossible. She would herself support them all if necessary, though she had not the faintest idea of how it was to be done. Surely in a great city like New York, there were ways of becoming rich, even fabulously so. She had read stories in the newspapers. . . .

But her first action was a direct one. Dressed in black merino and armed with an umbrella which she carried on important occasions as a general bears his baton, she assailed her enemy Judge Weissman in the sanctuary of his untidy office, and after a scene in which she accused him of thievery, bribery and a dozen other crimes, she bullied him, playing shrewdly upon a horsewhipping incident out of his own past, into using his influence to gain for her husband some new work—not mere work but a position worthy of him and of the dignity of her family.

She won the battle and in her triumph, which mounted higher and higher during the walk home, she gave rein in her unbounded optimism to even wilder and more fantastic schemes. There was relief in the knowledge that at last she had taken things into her own hands. No longer was she to be a power behind the throne urging forward an amiable and indifferent husband. Things must change now. She herself would act. She had achieved an opening wedge. In time she would secure an appointment for her husband in New York. She could take the children there. She could be where she could drop in on Ellen at the Babylon Arms (preposterous name!). She would watch and aid them in their progress toward success and glory. Ah, she could wrest anything from life. It was, after all, nothing more than a question of energy and persistence.

These thoughts were whirling madly about her brain as she turned the corner into Sycamore Street in time to see a group of children congregated before the path that led into the shaggy domain of the Tollivers. They appeared to be watching something and clung to the gate peering in through the lilacs at the vine-covered house. Unconsciously she increased her pace, and as she approached the gate they fell back, with a look of awe and the sort of animal curiosity which comes into the eyes of children gathered on the scene of a catastrophe. Through their ranks and into the house, she made her way like a fine ship in full sail.

Once inside she learned the news.

It was this—that upstairs in the room once occupied by Ellen there lay on the bed the unconscious form of her father, the invincible Jacob Barr. They told her that the patriarch, while superintending the loading of hay in his mows, had made a misstep and so crashed to the floor twenty feet below. They had brought him to her house on a truss of hay. The doctors, the same doctors whom Gramp Tolliver had baffled, said he might die suddenly or that he might live for years, but he would never walk again.

When she had put the place in order and driven out the confusion which accompanies physicians, she seated herself in a chair opposite the unconscious old man and presently began to weep.

"What good is it now? What difference does it make?" she repeated bitterly over and over again.

Where before there had been but one, there were now two old men to be managed, and Hattie Tolliver, understanding that it was now impossible to follow Ellen, settled herself to waiting. For what? Perhaps for death to claim her own father. It would have been, as she said, a blessing, for the fracture concerned far more than a hip bone; the very spirit of old Jacob Barr was crushed in that fall from the mows. Sinking back upon the pillows of Ellen's bed, he gave up the struggle. A life in which there was no activity was for him no life at all. He became again like a little child, like his own little children whom his daugher Hattie had cared for through all the years of his widowhood. Sometimes he sang songs and there were hours when he talked to himself and to Hattie of things which had happened when she was a very little girl or before she was born. He lived again in the Civil War and in the days preceding it when the fleeing niggers hid in his great mows. Passers-by in Sycamore Street sometimes heard snatches of singing in a voice now cracked, now loud and strong and defiant. . . . *John Brown's Body lies a-moldering in the Grave, But his Soul goes marching on. Glory! Glory! Hallelujah!*

But Gramp Tolliver in his high room walled with books kept spry and alert, triumphant now in the knowledge that he had survived old Jacob Barr, that the stern virtue of the old Scotsman had not prolonged his health and happiness by so much as an hour. He read his old books and scribbled on bits of yellow paper, ageing not at all, remaining always spare, cynical, vindictive.

In these days his daughter-in-law rarely addressed him, and less and less frequently she came to see that his room was in order. There were other cares to occupy her energy. There was a husband, working now, and two growing boys and her own father to care for; in addition to all these she had taken to sewing, secretly, for friends whose fortunes were better. (She was a magnificent needle-woman.) And she had each day to write a long letter to Ellen, though the letters in return came but weekly and sometimes not so often.

They kept her informed of the bare facts of her daughter's life. They told her, in a new, amusing and somewhat cynical fashion of Ellen's adventures among the music teachers of the city . . . of weeks spent wandering through the bleak and drafty corridors of studio buildings, tormented with the sounds made by aspiring young musicians. They described the charlatans, the frauds, which she found on every side, teachers who offered every sort of trick and method by which fame and fortune could be reached by the one and only short cut. There were women called Madame Tessitura and Madame Scarlatti, who had been born Smith or Jones and knew less of music than May Seton, and men who wore velveteen jackets and insisted upon being called "Maestro." There were the usual adventures (alarming to Hattie Tolliver who saw her daughter still as a little girl) with lecherous old men. Indeed, in this connection Ellen wrote with a certain hard mockery that was utterly strange and carried overtones of an unmoral point of view, as if such things were to be treated more as preposterous jokes than as "grave offenses." And in this Mrs. Tolliver fancied she discerned some traces of Lily's influence. To a woman like Lily, such things didn't matter. She took them too lightly, as a part of the day's experience . . . carefree, charming, indolent Lily, so impossible to combat.

And at last, wrote Ellen, she had stumbled upon the proper person . . . an old man, a Frenchman, who bore the name of Sanson. He knew what music could be, and so she had settled with him, working under his guidance. In his youth he had known Liszt, and he had been a friend of Teresa Carreño, until a quarrel with that temperamental beauty ended the friendship. Ellen, he had hinted, might one day become as famous as Carreño (she was like her in a way) but she must work, work, work and not lose her head. It would be a long hard path with Paris at the end! (It was always this thought which filled Mrs. Tolliver with a nameless dread. Paris! Paris! And Lily!)

But what troubled her most was the absence of any comment upon Clarence beyond a simple statement that he was well. By now she must have realized that Ellen had no love for him. From her letters it was clear that she had not found him actually offensive. He was a good enough husband; he did everything for Ellen. It was, indeed, clear that he worshiped her. But on her side there appeared to be only a great void, a colossal emptiness where there should have been the emotion that was the very foundation of her mother's life.

Mrs. Tolliver worried too about the expenses of her daughter's household. In such matters, distance made no difference. It was her habit to remark to her husband, "If only I could be near Ellen I could teach her so much about managing. Clarence must make a great deal of money to have such a flat and pay for her lessons too."

And when she questioned Ellen in her letters, she received the reply that Ellen had spoken to her husband and been told that there was no need to worry. He had, he said, plenty of money . . . eight thousand a year.

It is possible of course that Ellen never loved him for an instant; it is probable that the state of her affections never progressed beyond the stage of the kindly pity which is akin to love. She was not a bad wife. She cared for him admirably. She kept his house in order. She even cooked for him delicacies which she had learned from her mother. He insisted that she have a servant, declaring that he could easily afford it. She gave him all that he asked, even of herself, and yet there was a difference . . . a difference with altered everything. It was that difference which Hattie Tolliver, expert in such things, sensed in the letters of her daughter. It filled her with a vague suspicion that Ellen had sold herself to satisfy a thing no greater than mere ambition.

Of Clarence's sentiments there could have been no doubt. He sang his wife's praises to the men at the Superba Electrical Company, to the men whom he met on those trips into the west when Ellen was left behind alone in the Babylon Arms. He bought her present after present until, at length, the whole aspect of their little apartment was changed. Bit by bit the furniture altered its character. First there was a small grand piano, and then a sofa and presently a chair or two, and at last the brass beds

which he and Bunce had once occupied gave place to twin beds
of pale green ornamented with garlands of salmon pink roses.
And strangely enough as the apartment brightened, the little man
himself appeared slowly to fade. In contrast with his handsome
and energetic wife, he grew more and more pale. It was as if
he were being devoured by some inward malady. Yet there was
nothing wrong. Doctors could discover nothing save the usual
weakness of his heart.

If he desired a more demonstrative affection than that given
him by Ellen, he said nothing of the desire. He never spoke of
love. Indeed, long afterward, when Ellen followed back her
memories of their life together she was unable to recall any mention of the word. If he desired her passionately he sought her
silently and with timidity, as if each caress she gave him were far
beyond that which he had any reason to expect. He was a shy
man and with Ellen it was impossible to speak of such things;
there was a coolness about her, a chastity of the sort which sur-
rounds some women regardless of everything. And always it was
she who dominated, always she who gave, coldly and without passion, as if she felt that in all honor she owed him a debt.

With the passing of the months the breach between Ellen and
Mr. Wyck became complete. The other friends came sometimes
to the Babylon Arms where Clarence, with a sudden expansion of
temperament, entertained them in lordly fashion and beamed with
pride in his wife. But Mr. Wyck no longer came. There had
been no open quarrel, not even a hasty word. Quietly he had
dropped from the habit of seeing Clarence at home. It was a
change so imperceptible that before Clarence understood it, it was
complete.

They met sometimes at lunch in one of the cheap restaurants
frequented by Mr. Wyck, for Clarence, so far as his own needs
and pleasures were concerned, had taken to a program of economy.
And there, over greasy food, they talked of the old days together,
Clarence speaking with sentiment and Mr. Wyck with a curious
wistfulness. He too had grown pale and cadaverous upon the

diet in his Lexington Avenue boarding house. He hated Ellen. He had hated her from the moment she had stepped through the door of the apartment, so cool and arrogant, so sure of herself. But he was too wise to betray his feeling save in subtle gibes at her and references to the jolly old days that were passed. He was lost now in the obscenities of a boarding house, a nobody treated scornfully even by the old aunts in Yonkers who looked upon him still as an anemic little boy with Fauntleroy curls playing among the iron dogs and deers of their front lawn.

And no one, of course, knew that Mr. Wyck, wrapped in his shabby overcoat, sometimes walked the streets after dark in the neighborhood of Riverside Drive, the gale from the North River piercing his bones, his pale eyes upturned toward the pleasant light that beamed from the top floor of the Babylon Arms.

22

One night nearly two years after they were married, Clarence asked, "What do you hear from your cousin?"

And Ellen, who had been playing all the evening, turned and asked, "What cousin?"

"Miss Shane."

"Oh, Lily!" And a shadow settled on her face as if the mention of Lily's name suddenly aroused memories which she had been striving to forget. "Oh, Lily!" she repeated. "I haven't heard from her in weeks. She never writes. You know she is indolent. . . . When I last heard from her she was all right. She wrote from Nice."

Clarence kept silent for a moment. "Nice must be a beautiful place. A man from the office was there last year, our foreign agent. Nice and Monte Carlo. I guess they're quite close together."

"She has a house there. It's called the Villa Blanche."

Again Clarence remained thoughtful for a time. The newspaper had fallen from his hands and lay now, crumpled and forgotten by his side. Presently he blushed and murmured, "D'you think she might lend us the house some time. . . . We might be able to go there. . . . Not now, but when we have more money. I'd like to see Nice."

And the shadow on Ellen's face darkened. "We will . . . some day. When I'm famous and making money too."

"But I don't want to do it that way. I want to take you myself and pay for everything. . . . We might have Lily come and visit us."

Then to fill in the silence Ellen fell to playing again, softly now so that it did not halt the conversation; yet the sound in some way protected her. It was like the frail veil of lace which Lily wore. It shut her in suddenly. Clarence talked no more. He lay back in his stuffed chair, one hand strumming thoughtfully the wooden arm. A look of loneliness, more and more frequent of late, came into his brown eyes.

It was Ellen who turned to him presently, in the midst of the soft music and said, "I have good news for you. I am going to play to-morrow night in public. I am going to be paid for it. Sanson arranged it. I'm going to play at a party. It will mean money for us both."

But Clarence wasn't pleased. On the contrary he frowned and kept a disapproving silence.

"It's silly to feel that way about it," continued Ellen. "Why should I work as I do if not to make money in the end? Why shouldn't a wife help her husband? There's nothing wrong in it."

And then more music and more silence, while she destroyed slowly, bit by bit, his hopes of grandeur, of conquering a world for the sake of the woman he loved. He saw, perhaps, that despite anything he might do she would in the end surpass him.

"You see, we understood this when we married, Clarence. It's nothing new. . . . Is it? . . . Nothing new. Some day I shall be famous." She said this quite seriously, without the faintest trace of a smile. "Some day I shall be great and famous. I mean to be."

By now Clarence was leaning forward holding his head in his hands. His glasses had slipped from his pointed nose and lay forgotten in his lap. Presently he interrupted the music to say, mournfully, "And then I shall be Mr. Tolliver . . . husband of a famous woman."

As though amazed by this sudden resentment, Ellen ceased playing for an instant and regarded him with a curious penetrating look.

"It won't be like that," she said. And there entered her voice an unaccustomed note of warmth. It was the pity again, an old sense of sorrow.

"Besides," she continued, "the day will come when I must go to Paris. . . . You see, I will have to polish off there . . . I can live with Lily. It won't cost anything. You see, we can't forget that. We have to think of it. It's nothing new. . . . I told you that in the beginning."

For a long time there was no sound in the room save that of Ellen's music, soft, beautiful, appealing, as if she used it now as a balm for the wounds caused by all she had been forced to say. Presently her strong beautiful fingers wandered into the Fire Music and the tiny room was filled with a glorious sound of flame and sparks, wild yet subdued, thrilling yet mournful. And then for a time it seemed that, wrapped in the color of the music, they were both released and swept beyond the reach of all these petty troubles. When at last the music ceased, Clarence roused himself slowly and, coming to her side, knelt there and placed his arms about her waist, pressing his head against her. There was in the gesture something pitiful and touching, as if he felt that by holding her thus he might be able to keep her always. The little vein in his throat throbbed with violence. There were times when his adoration became a terrible thing.

It was the first time in all their life together that he had ever done anything so romantic, so beautiful, and Ellen, looking down at him in a kind of amazement, must have understood that there were forces at work quite beyond her comprehension—something which, for the moment, overwhelmed even his shame of love. The act, by its very suddenness, appeared to strike a response in the girl herself, for she leaned toward him and fell to stroking his hair.

"I didn't know," she said softly, "that you could be like this. . . . It frightens me. . . . I didn't know."

His arms slowly held her more and more tightly, in a kind of fierce desperation. "You won't go," he murmured, "you won't leave me. . . . There would be nothing left for me . . . nothing in the world."

"I'll come back to you. . . . It won't be for long. Perhaps, if there is money enough you could go with me."

But all the same, she was troubled by that simple act of affection. Somehow, she had never thought of *his* love in this fashion.

The rest of the evening was raised upon a different plane, new and strange in their existence together. Some barrier, invisible as it was potent, had given way suddenly, out of Clarence's dread of the future it seemed that there was born a new and unaccountable happiness. Ellen, watching him slyly with a look of new tenderness, played for him the simple music which he loved.

But at midnight when, at last, the music came to an end Clarence asked, "Where are you going to play to-morrow?"

"At the house of a Mrs. Callendar . . . I don't know who she is."

"If it's Mrs. Richard Callendar . . . she's rich and fashionable. One of the richest women in New York. . . . Rich and fashionable. . . . " But the rest was lost in a sudden return of a bitterness that seized him of late with a growing frequency. He knew of Mrs. Callendar. Wyck, in his snobbery, had spoken of her. One saw her name in the journals. It may have been

that he had thoughts of his own which no one had ever guessed
. . . not even Ellen.

"It *is* Mrs. Richard Callendar," she said.

23

IN the beginning Mrs. Callendar had regretted the sudden
indisposition of the great pianist she had engaged. It was,
she said, *embétant*. But presently as the hour of the reception drew near, the things which old Sanson had said of his unknown prodigy began to have their effect and, being like most
women of affairs, a gambler as well, she saw in the approach of
the unknown substitute the possibility of an adventure. She was,
in any case, willing to take the word of old Sanson; he was, when
all was said and done, no humbug. He knew a performer when
he saw one. He did not go about his studio in a coat of velveteen
calling upon his pupils to address him as "Maestro." In a satisfactory way, he got down to brass tacks. What he had to offer
must at least be interesting.

The drawing-room of the house on Murray Hill was enormous.
It extended the full length of one side of the house, finishing in
a little alcove where to-night space had been made for the performers, who sat shielded by a lacquered screen reaching almost
to the ceiling. Before it a little place had been cleared and a
small dais, covered with black velvet, erected to serve as a stage.
There was a great piano at one side and then more cleared space
reaching out to where the row of collapsible chairs had been placed
for the guests.

The room itself was painted gray and high up near the ceiling
hung in a row portraits of the Callendars, male and female, who
had existed since the immigrating member, an honest Dutch chem-
ist, founded a fortune in America by buying farms that lay north
of Canal Street. The usual furniture had been pressed back
against the sides of the room or removed entirely, but some of

the pieces remained . . . chairs and sofas of gilt and salmon brocade, American adaptations of the monstrosities of Louis Philippe—the furniture of some preceding Mrs. Callendar. And in gilt cases of glass there ranged the famous Callendar collection of Chinese bric-à-brac . . . bowls and idols of jade, porphyry, and carved sandalwood, row upon row of tear bottles (it was for these that the collection was especially noted) in jade, ivory and porcelain. All these ornaments represented the second period in the fortunes of the Callendar family . . . the days when the clipper ships of Griswold and Callendar carried cargoes around the world from Singapore, Shanghai and Hong-Kong. The fortune was now in its third stage. The clipper ships had vanished and the money they once represented was now safe in the best stocks and bonds it was possible to buy.

The room had never been brought up to date. Indeed it had remained untouched since the Seventies, for Mrs. Callendar spent only a month or two of the year in New York and, being thrifty, had not found it necessary to alter anything. The caretaker, once a year when her mistress returned, sent for a small army of charwomen, dusted, cleaned and scrubbed the old house and engaged a corps of servants. The rest of the time it remained empty but solid, immersed in the quiet dignity which is acquired only by houses of great bankers, a symbol in the midst of less enormous and somber dwellings, of all that is enduring and respectable in a changing effervescent world.

At ten o'clock on this particular evening the lacquer screen concealed behind its shimmering walls the figure of a Russian tenor, a Javanese dancer (really a low caste Hindu woman who had her training in some brothel of Alexandria) and the unknown American girl whom Sanson recommended as a fine artist. They were entertainers, mountebanks, brought together only to divert a crowd of guests, who presently would arrive, jaded and somewhat torpid, from monstrous dinners of twenty courses held in houses from Washington Square as far north as the east Sixties. In the behavior of the three performers there was no great cordiality.

They sat apart, without interest in each other; indeed there were in their manner unmistakable traces of jealousies as old as their very profession.

Sometimes the tiny dancer, with skin like *café au lait* satin, stirred restlessly, setting all her bangles into jangling motion, to address the Russian tenor in bad French. He was an enormous blond man with a chest like a barrel and hands that rested like sausages upon his knees, a man gauche in manner, a little like a bear let loose in a drawing-room . . . a mountain between the little Hindu woman and the American girl who sat a little apart, slim and tall as Artemis, her black hair wound low over a face that was pale with excitement. She knew no French and so, after the first exchange of "Goot eefning!" with her two weird companions, she lapsed into a silence which concentrated all its force upon a crevice in the lacquered screen. Thus she was able to see the whole length of the great drawing-room and witness the spectacle of the arriving guests.

At first there appeared only her employer, a squat, plump woman laced until her figure resembled the hour glass shape of the ladies in Renoir's pictures of bourgeois picnics at St. Cloud. From sources hidden in a veritable upholstery of satin and velvet, so cut as to emphasize all her most voluptuous curves, little ladders and tongues of jet sprang forth and glittered darkly at every motion of her tiny plump feet. The face too was plump and, despite a drooping eyelid (which in her youth might have been fascinating and now only made her appear to be in a constant state of sly observation), it must have been lovely, perhaps even subtle. The tight little mouth had an expression that was pleasant and agreeable. It was as if she said, "Ah, well. Nothing in this world surprises me. It will all come out right in the end."

The sleek black hair she wore pulled back into an uncompromising knot, though in front it was frizzed into a little bang which once might have passed for a weapon of coquetry. Over all this was flung the glittering sheen of jewels, prodigal, indecently

Oriental in their extravagance. Above the fuzzy bang reared a tiara of emeralds and diamonds and beneath, sweeping over the mountainous curve of her bosom so that it entangled itself in the plastrons of diamonds fastened beneath, hung a necklace of emeralds. All these repeated their glitter in the rings on the plump hands emerging from long tight sleeves of black satin, which stretched perilously at each dominating gesture employed to direct the small army of servants. But all the jewels were a little dirty. It was probable that no money had been wasted in cleaning them in more than twenty years.

This, then, was *the* Mrs. Callendar, appearing to-night in *grande tenue* to receive a small and shrewdly picked list of guests at her only entertainment of the season. To Ellen, peering with breathless curiosity through the crack in the screen, this plump middle-aged woman must have appeared a highly bedizened figure of fun; for Ellen, having come freshly from the provinces, could have known nothing of all the glamour and power that lay concealed in the hour glass of velvet, satin, and soiled diamonds.

There was no secretary hired by this thrifty woman to send lists of her guests to the daily papers and see that her picture or paragraphs concerning her appeared once or twice a week. She did not even give twenty course dinners interrupted by false endings of Roman punch, nor circus entertainments like those of some women who filled the pages of the noisier journals with columns of diversion for shop girls. Through the barbaric spectacle of the late nineties and the early nineteen hundreds she made her way quietly and firmly, knowing perhaps that she was above these things, a power beyond power, living most of the year abroad, seeing only those persons who amused her (for she had learned long ago that in order to survive one must be selective). Indeed her name was more likely to appear upon the pages devoted to stocks and bonds than in the columns given over to what was known variously as the *beau monde* and the Four Hundred.

Queerest of all was the fact that behind this stout-willed dowager lay an impossibly romantic past.

In the early Seventies when the steam freighters were making their final inroads upon the business of the clipper ships, the house of Griswold and Callendar, Shippers, Importers and Bankers with offices in Liverpool, New York, Marseilles, Bombay and Shanghai, was already on a decline. Already the capital was being shifted into bonds. In these days there remains of this firm no importing business at all but only a great banking house with offices in Wall and Threadneedle Streets and the Boulevard Haussmann; but in the Seventies it was still a great shipping company whose ships circled the globe and dealt alike with Chinese, Indians, Frenchmen, Greeks, and the men of half a dozen other nations. In consequence of these dealings there arose from time to time many disputes, so that always there was some member of the firm on business in a distant quarter of the world. It was to Richard Callendar, the youngest and most vigorous member and the only Callendar in the firm, that most of this traveling fell; and so, in the course of time, he found himself in Constantinople on the business of settling claims with a crafty fellow, one Dikran Leopopulos, whose bank had offices in Calicut and Alexandria with the main house at the Golden Horn.

The contest between the two was drawn out, resolving itself at length into a battle between Yankee shrewdness and Levantine deceit. Leopopulos, a swarthy fellow with narrow green eyes, opened the engagement by an onslaught of hospitality. He entertained his young visitor in the most lavish and Oriental fashion. There were dinners to which the *chic* foreign world of Constantinople were invited . . . ambassadors, secretaries and their ladies, French, German, English and American, in the banker's palace in Pera; there were *pique-niques* beside the River of Sweet Waters, and moonlight excursions in caïques propelled by dark oarsmen, on the Bosphorus near the Greek banker's summer palace; and excursions in victorias to the ruins of Justinian's fortifications. He sought as a wily means of gaining his end to dazzle the blond, romantic young American, to coddle him by eastern luxury into a false bargain. And to make the entertainment complete, he brought from her seclusion his young daughter, a girl of eighteen, slim, dark, fresh from a French convent, dressed in the very latest modes from Paris, to preside over his entertainments. The girl's mother was dead, having swooned and later passed away of the heat and confusion at the great Exposition in Paris whither she had gone to visit, after many years, her great-aunts. For the wife of Leopopulos had been French, the daughter of an impoverished, moth-eaten Royalist, and in her child, the slim young Thérèse, there was much that was French . . . her wit, her self-possession, her sense of knowing her way about the world. But there was much too that was Levantine.

When at last the revels came to an end, there were bickerings and bargainings in which Yankee shrewdness, in the end, got the better of Levantine deceit. The green-eyed Leopopulos to hide his sorrow gave a farewell dinner aboard the young American's ship (a Griswold and Callendar clipper named *Ebenezer Holt*) and so, he believed, closed the incident. It was not until the following day, when a veritable army of fat Greek aunts and cousins, wailing and lamenting, burst at dawn into his green bedroom, that he learned the full extent of his sorrow. His daughter, the dark-eyed Thérèse, had sailed on the *Ebenezer Holt* as the bride of young Richard Callendar.

Thus Thérèse Callendar came to New York, a stranger out of the oldest of worlds entering into the newest, confused a little by her surroundings and by the primness of her husband's family, so like and yet so unlike the caution of her own Greek aunts and cousins. In those early days at long dinners in rooms hung with plush and ornamented with Canalettos and Cabanels, her sensations must have been very like those of an ancient Alexandrian, civilized, cultivated, and a little decadent among the more vigorous and provincial Romans of Cæsar's day. In that age of innocence she found it, no doubt, difficult going; for there was in New York no warm welcome for a foreign woman, no matter how great her beauty, her cultivation, or her charm; much less for a Greek from such a frontier as Constantinople, the capital of the cruel and abandoned Turk. An alien was a creature to be regarded as a curiosity, to be treated, unless he possessed a great title, politely but with suspicion. She was, to be sure, probably the first Greek who came to live on Manhattan's rocky island; but despite this and all the other barriers, she succeeded in the end, because she was, after all, older than any of them, more civilized, more fortified by those institutions which come only of an old race. In her French blood she was old, but in her Greek blood how much older! She was as old as the carved emerald which she wore always upon her little hand, now so plump with middle age, in a ring which legend had it survived the sack of Constantinople. In tradition she was as old as Justinian and Theodora. The family of Leopopulos was proud—so proud and so old that one no longer discussed its pride and age.

After two years she bore a son, and before the end of that year she became a widow when her ardent young husband, swimming in the surf off Newport, went in his reckless way too far out and never returned. The son she called Richard, after the father, and together with her he inherited the great Callendar fortune, to which was added with the passing of years the gold, the olive orchards, the vineyards, and the palaces of the green-eyed old Banker of Pera. But Thérèse Callendar never married again; she devoted herself to the upbringing of her son and to the husbanding of a great fortune which by shrewdness and will she had long since doubled and tripled. She was, in her soul, a Levantine; thrift and shrewdness were a part of her very flesh and bones. She lived here and there, always on the move, now in Constantinople, now in Paris, now in London, now in Cannes, now in New York, even making at times trips to such outlandish places as Bombay and Sumatra; a woman of sorts, of vast energy and sharp intelligence. And slowly as she passed down the corridor of the years the slim chic figure became an hour glass hung with jet and diamonds. Her eyes were no longer good and she was able to see now only with the aid of lorgnettes through which she stared with a petulant intensity into the faces of all her companions.

But she was rich; she was respected; she was fashionable. Indeed in those days of the Nineties and the early Nineteen Hundreds when European titles had not yet acquired a doubtful character, she achieved an added glamour through the unsought visits of bankrupt Royalist relatives, distant in relationship but much in need of American heiresses. And at least two of them took home as brides the respective daughters of an American nickel plate king and a wizard of Wall Street. They were gaudy days, less pleasant perhaps in the eyes of Thérèse Callendar than the quiet provinciality she had known in the beginning as the bride of Richard Callendar. This capital of the new world she knew, in the depths of her racial instinct, to be an awkward affair, flamboyant, yet timid; vulgar yet aspiring; arrogant but still a little fearful. It was the day of twenty course dinners and banquets at which the cost of feeding each guest was estimated in the daily press. The Greek woman knew that some day this city would come of age.

So Ellen, trembling with excitement in her hiding place behind the screen, must have caught a little of the smoldering magnificence that lay hidden in the plump corseted figure, for presently she forgot entirely the bearlike Russian tenor and the exotic dancer with her outlandish bangles. She had eyes only for Mrs. Callendar and the guests who had begun to arrive.

That wise hostess might have written an entire book on the subject of an amusing entertainment. From the procession of guests it was clear that she considered them a part of the evening's diversion, a kind of preliminary parade about the arena which provided variety and color. She understood that people came when you provided rich food and amusing types, the more preposterous the better.

A Tzigane orchestra, much in fashion, assembled itself presently and played an accompaniment to the grand march of arriving guests. Among the first were the Champion girls and their mother. These represented the old families. The two girls, already past their first youth, wore gowns made by Worth, cut low back and front, which fitted their thin bodies in the Princess style. But these gowns, Thérèse saw instantly, they had ruined; for in a moment of caution the deep V's, front and back, had been built up with modest inserts of lace and tulle, and short sleeves of similar material had been inserted to shield the upper portions of their white arms. They held themselves stiffly. Nothing of them remained exposed save the fact that they were virgins.

Close upon their heels, so close that the mother in her haste appeared to shuffle her daughters into a corner with the air of a hen covering her chicks from a hawk, came that elderly rake, Wickham Chase, and Mrs. Sigourney, the latter dressed tightly in black and diamonds rumored to be paste—thin, piercing and hard, too highly painted, a divorcée. (None but Thérèse Callendar would have dared to ask her.) And then Bishop Smallwood, whom Sabine Cane called "The Apostle to the Genteel," a Bishop with a See in the far West, who managed to divide his time between New York and Bar Harbor and Newport . . . a fat, pompous man with a habit of alluding too easily to "My wa'am friend Mrs. Callendar" and "My wa'am friend Mrs. Champion" and "My wa'am friend Mrs. So-and-so" ad infinitum through the lists of the wealthy and the fashionable. Trapped between the Scylla of Mrs. Champion and her Virgins and Charybdis of the questionable but very smart Mrs. Sigourney, the poor man found himself at once in an untenable position. Seeing this, the small eyes of his hostess glittered with a sinful light.

Next came the Honorable Emma Hawksby, a gaunt Englishwoman of some thirty-eight summers with a face like a horse, projecting teeth, and feet that appeared to better advantage in the hedgerows than in the ball room. To-night they emerged bargelike from beneath a very fancy gown of pink satin ornamented with sequins and yards of mauve tulle. It was in her direction that the anxious Mrs. Champion steered her two virgins. Was she not a cousin of the notorious Duke of Middlebottom?

And then the four Fordyce sisters, arriving unattended in a hollow square formation, large, dark, powerful girls ranging in age from twenty to thirty-one, filled with an inhuman energy and zeal for good works, the very first of those who struggled for the enfranchisement of women.

Then one or two nondescript bachelors, of the handy sort seen everywhere as conveniences, stuffed with food and wine taken at some monstrous dinner in the Thirties; and on their heels Mrs. Mallinson, who belonged in the category of Mrs. Champion and her virgins, but who had escaped years ago into the freedom of the literary world wherein she wrote long novels of society life. She was a hard woman and beginning to sag a little here and there so that she threw up against the ravages of decay bulwarks in the form of a black satin ribbon ornamented with diamonds about her dewlapped throat. She lived outside Paris in a small château, once the property of a royal mistress, and spoke with a French accent. Because she was literary, she was considered, in Mrs. Champion's mind, also Bohemian.

In her hiding place behind the painted screen, the dark eyes of Ellen Tolliver grew brighter and brighter. Behind her the Javanese dancer and the Russian tenor had relapsed into a condition of moribund indifference.

More and more guests filtered into the room, old, young, dowdy, respectable, smart, one or two even a little déclassée. They regarded each other for a time, slipping into little groups, gossiping for a moment, melting away into new and hostile clusters, whispering, laughing, sneering, until the whole room became filled with an animation which even the great dinners of two hours earlier could not suffocate.

With the arrival of Lorna Vale the excitement reached its peak; even the gipsies played more wildly. She was an actress! And in those days it was impossible to imagine an actress and the

Champion virgins in the same room. The Bishop stared at her, somewhat furtively to be sure, and Mrs. Champion, quivering, again executed her swooping gesture of protection toward her two daughters. But Mrs. Sigourney, perhaps seeing in her an ally, pierced the surrounding phalanx of eager young men and found a place by her side. Each benefited by the contrast, for the one was large, an opulent beauty with tawny hair, and the other, thin as a hairpin, black and glittering.

Then, during a brief pause in the music, the wide doors opened again and there entered Sabine Cane and Mrs. Callendar's son Richard.

At their approach there was, even in that nervous, chattering throng, a sudden hush, a brief heightening of interest as if the crowd, like a field of wheat, had been swayed faintly for an instant by the swift eddy of a zephyr. Then all was noisy again. It was a demonstration of interest, polite, restrained, as it should have been at a gathering so fashionable, but a demonstration that could not be entirely disguised.

It was in the women that the excitement found its core . . . women who saw in the dark young man a great match for their daughters, girls who desired him for his fortune and his rakish good looks and found the legend of his wild living a secret and sentimental attraction; widows and spinsters who discerned in him matchmaking material of the first order. Beyond doubt the glittering Mrs. Sigourney and the tawny Lorna Vale held other ideas, not to be expressed in so polite an assemblage. He had been, after all, notoriously attentive to both though they were years older. But there was one element in the situation which raised the interest to the pitch of hysteria; it was his attention to Sabine Cane, a fact of growing importance which many a jet-hung bosom found hard to support.

She was a year or two older than Richard Callendar (every woman present could have told the very hour she made her entrance into society) and she was not, like most of young Callen-

dar's women, an acclaimed beauty. Yet there were other qualities which set her aside from the commonplace round of marriageable girls. She was easily the most smartly dressed in all the
room; there was about her clothes a breathless sort of perfection
that bespoke the taste of an artist. In place of an overwhelming
beauty, she had developed a wit that could be infinitely more dis-
astrous. In this, she resembled Cleopatra, Madame de Staël and
the Montespan. These things made her perilous and caused
many an ambitious mother hours of sleeplessness.

A long nose, a generous mouth frankly painted, green eyes set
a trifle too near each other, a mass of brick red hair and a marvelous figure . . . these things comprised the physical aspect of
Sabine Cane, a combination that was changeable and a trifle bizarre and therefore, as Thérèse Callendar had observed more than
once, enormously *intrigante*. But there was more than this, for
in the green eyes there lay a light of humor and malice and beneath the brick red hair a brain which had a passion for the
affairs of other people. What disconcerted her enemies most
was her air of entering a room; she did not walk in, she made an
entrance. It was as if such women as Mrs. Sigourney and Lorna
Vale did not exist. Lily Langtry or Cléo de Merode were less
effective. To-night she wore a brilliant yellow dress with a wide
full train. It was as if she understood shrewdly her ugliness and
made capital of it.

Sabine knew things about these people who filled the drawing
room—little bits of gossip, scraps of information picked up here
and there in the course of her twenty-six years. She knew, for
example, that Mrs. Champion (mother of the virgins and most
rarefied of aristocrats) had a grandmother known as Ruddy Mary
who in her first assault upon the social ranks had invited people
to a monstrous ball by invitations written in red ink, and so
gained a sobriquet that was now forgotten. She knew that Wickham Chase had a maternal grandfather who had been a Jewish
pawnbroker and laid up the money which he now spent. She
knew that the Honorable Emma Hawksby (niece of the no-

torious Duke of Middlebottom) was without a cent in the world
and found an easy winter in New York by living off those who
liked to speak of the dear Duke's cousin. "Honorable" was not
a great title, but it went far enough in those days to keep the
Honorable Emma in bed and board for the winter. She even
knew that a brother of the Apostle to the Genteel had to be kept,
at some expense to the Apostle, in an out of the way country town
in order that he might not make a drunken spectacle of himself
before the Apostle's many "wa'am friends."

Sabine kept a great many family skeletons in her clever memory and it was impossible to know the moment when she might
bring them forth and rattle them in the most grisly fashion.

It was clear that her companion, shrewder than the well-fed
young men about him, penetrating with those instincts which came
to him from the plump bundle of satin and diamonds who stood
receiving the guests, understood perfectly the atmospheric disturbance. He was young, clever, handsome in a fashion that was
a little sinister, and very rich, so rich that the whispers of gossip
that clustered about him—even the talk of Mrs. Sigourney and
Lorna Vale—made no difference. Mrs. Champion found him
not entirely beneath consideration as a possible match for Margaret or Janey, the redoubtable virgins.

"Look at Boadicea and her daughters," Sabine whispered maliciously in his ear as they came abreast of this virtuous group.

Young Callendar was tall, with dark skin, closely cropped
black hair and a wiry kind of strength that was an heritage of
his green-eyed grandfather, the Banker of Pera. When Sabine
said "Boadicea," he laughed and showed a row of fine teeth set
white against an olive skin. It was this same dark skin which
gave his eyes a look of strangeness. The eyes should have been
brown or black; instead they were a clear gray and had a way
of looking at a person as if they bored quite through him. People
said he was fascinating or wild or vicious, according to their
standards of such things. The women morbidly watched his
greeting of Mrs. Sigourney and Lorna Vale, but they discovered

nothing. All the talk may only have been gossip. He was, after all, only twenty-four . . . . a boy. But, of course, he had French and Greek blood and had lived on the continent. "That," said Mrs. Mallinson, the escaped novelist, with an old world air, "makes a difference."

Behind the screen, the Hindu dancer had begun to droop a little with boredom, like a dark flower turning on its stem. Close by her side the bear-like Russian :nor had fallen asleep, his enormous blond head bent forward against his rumpled shirt front; his enormous hands, bursting the seams of his civilized white kid gloves, hung limp between Herculean thighs clad in black broadcloth that would have benefited by a visit to the cleaners.

Only Ellen remained alert and nervous, peering through her crevice, all interest now in the handsome young man and the bizarre red-haired woman at his side. These, her instinct told her, were characters, individuals, powerful in the same fashion that the plump little woman covered with dirty diamonds was powerful. And deep down in her heart a tiny voice kept saying, "This is the great world. Some day I shall be on the other side of the screen, seated no longer with mountebanks."

Behind the screen she experienced a swift tumult of emotions, confused and ecstatic like the sensations she had known on sight of her first play in a real theater. The scene was glamorous, extravagant. Perhaps for an instant she caught a sense of what was really passing before her eyes; it may have been that she understood the spectacle even more clearly than any of the participants save only Thérèse Callendar . . . that these people were not gathered in the tomb-like room because they were drawn by any bond of affection, but rather because they had been summoned, each of them, to play his little rôle in a comedy of manners which the world called fashionable life. There was the Bishop who played a part quite his own (two bishops would have been too many and so, by giving the evening a clerical aspect, have dulled the edge of its *chic*). Mrs. Sigourney, wicked and painted, played the rôle of Sin, a fascinating and indispensable part, just as Mrs. Champion and her virgins as Virtue, Purity and Chastity, were her foil; and Mrs. Mallinson and Lorna Vale were the Muses of Literature and the Drama. Others stood for Family, and Wealth and what-not, while Mrs. Callendar, hidden behind the drooping lids of her near-sighted green eyes, understood all this and pulled the strings. She made for the piece an admirable showman.

Ellen, watching them, grew excited, and out of this excitement there emerged slowly a new ambition, which had nothing to do with a career in music. It was, rather, a passionate desire to conquer this world as well, so that she might fling her triumph back into the world of the Town; it would serve as an admirable weapon to flaunt in the faces of those who had mocked her poverty. For she had not yet escaped the Town; she had not even learned how difficult it would be ever to escape.

The Russian tenor was a dismal failure. Save for the fact that he was Russian and therefore wildly exotic, he would have been impossible, for he sang in a bleating voice a popular ballad or two by Tosti and a dreary bit of folk music, still half-caught in the mists of slumber. In the back of the room, seated against the wall so that the figures of the other guests rose in silhouette between them and the lights of the low stage, Richard Callendar and the ugly Sabine sat like naughty children, jeering. They were bored by such spectacles; they were interested only in the individuals which comprised it. They saw that the others were a little restless.

And then there was a brief hush broken presently by the music of the Tzigane orchestra augmented by drums and clarinets, rising slowly at first and then breaking into a crescendo of Arab music, filled with insinuating and sensual rhythms, accentuated by the beating of a tom-tom, and from behind the lacquered screen there arose a faint tinkling sound like the music of a million tiny bells heard from a great distance. Then as the music rose to a climax the sound grew suddenly more and more clear and from behind the screen sprang the Javanese dancer, gyrating, now bending low, now rising with a motion of a tawny lily swept by a breeze. It was a beautiful body, soft yet muscular, wild yet restrained. She wore the costume of a Burmese dancer, all gold with a towering hat like a pagoda made all of gold. Her breasts were covered with gold and her thighs, and on her hands she wore gauntlets of gold that ran out into long tapering pinnacles; but the rest of her was naked. The skin of *café au lait* satin glistened, voluptuous and extravagant. There were tiny gold bells on her wrists and ankles.

For an instant a faint gasp, barely audible, swept the little group seated on collapsible chairs. From her hiding place in the shadows Sabine Cane nudged her companion and whispered again, "Look at Boadicea!"

Before her eyes, between her and the dancer, Mrs. Champion had raised her fan; her daughters had done likewise. Between her and "his wa'am friend" Mrs. Mallinson, the Bishop stirred uneasily. Some leaned forward; others feigned indifference. One or two of the men assumed expressions of boredom. For none of them, save in brothels in Paris, had ever seen a woman dancing without tights, utterly naked.

Withdrawn a little from the others Thérèse Callendar sat staring at the dancer through her lorgnettes. She was immovable but interested, as if the barbaric music and the sight of the Hindu woman's naked body roused in her a train of dim racial memories. And slowly in another part of the room Sabine Cane became aware that Thérèse Callendar's son no longer had any interest in her. He no longer heard the malicious sallies she uttered in a whisper. He had risen now and was standing so that he might have a clearer view of the little dais bathed in light where the golden dancer swayed and whirled to the wild music of the Tziganes. Slowly his body stiffened and into the weird gray eyes there came a look of fierce concentration. The dark muscular hands, clasping the chair, so near to Sabine that she could have touched them, grew taut and white. It was not mere sensuality that was roused by the sight; Sabine, with her hard intelligence, must have known that it was something more profound, something that savored of a passionate and barbaric excitement, as if the man was stirred in the depths of his spirit. She must have understood then for the first time that he was of a race so different, so alien that there was a part of him forever beyond comprehension.

Sabine said nothing. Fascinated, she watched him quietly until, as the music died suddenly, the dancer stood motionless as a statue of bronze and gold. There was a ripple of embarrassed applause and she disappeared, then another hush and the nervous murmur of many voices. On her little throne Thérèse, like a plump Buddha, nodded her approval and beat her plump hands together. "C'est une vraie artiste," she murmured, leaning toward Mrs. Sigourney, in whose eyes there glittered the light of jealousy at being outdone in spectacularity by a hired entertainer.

In her corner Sabine said, "Beautiful!" To which young Callendar made no reply. He fingered his mustache and presently, smiling slowly, he murmured, "Mama shouldn't have done it. She has shocked some of them. This isn't Paris. Not yet!"

They were different from the others—Thérèse and her son.

While he was still speaking the gypsies deserted the stage, leaving it bare now save for the great piano. Again a brief hush and there emerged from behind the painted screen with a curious effect of abruptness and lack of grace a tall girl, very tall and very straight, with smooth black hair done in the style of Cléo de Merode and cheeks that were flushed. She wore a plain gown of black very tight and girdled with rhinestones that, shimmering, threw off shattered fragments of light as she walked. Her strong white arms were bared to the shoulder. There was pride in her walk, and assurance, yet these things hid a terror so overpowering that only those who sat quite near saw that her lip was bleeding where she had bitten it.

On her little throne Thérèse Callendar in cold blood waited. She wondered, doubtless, whether Sanson had failed her, and slowly she began to perceive that he had not. Somehow as she emerged from behind the screen, the American girl captured the imagination of her audience; it was as if she dominated them by some unreal power. They stirred and looked more closely. It was not altogether a matter of beauty, for the dancer who had preceded her was by all the rules far more beautiful. It was something beyond mere physical beauty. It emanated from her whole body, running outward, engulfing all the little audience. They became aware of her.

"Hm!" murmured Mrs. Callendar. "Here is something new. Something magnificent. A born actress . . . crude still, but with magnetism!" And she raised her lorgnettes and peered very hard with her short sighted little eyes.

To Richard Callendar, Sabine murmured, "Interesting! Who is she?"

"She's very handsome. . . . A discovery of Mama's."

And then, seating herself the girl began after a shower of liquid notes, to play, softly and suggestively, a Chopin valse, one that was filled with melody and simple rhythm. After the hot passion of the dancer she filled the great room with the effect of a soft wind infinitely cool and lovely, serene in its delicacy. She appeared presently to forget her fright and gave a performance that was beautiful not alone in sound but in manner as well. It may have been that old Sanson taught her that a great performance meant more than merely making beautiful sounds. All her face and body played their part in the poise, the grace of every movement, the sweep and the gesture. But it is more probable that she was born knowing these things, for they are a matter more of instinct than of training and lie thus beyond the realm of mere instruction.

There could be no doubt of the impression she made, yet in all the audience there was none, unless it was old Thérèse Callendar, who suspected that she had never before played in the presence of

anything but a small town audience. There was in her performance the fire of wild Highland ancestors, the placidity of English
lanes, the courage of men who had crossed mountains into a wilderness, perhaps even the Slavic passion of a dim ancestress brought
from Russia to live among the dour Scots of Edinburgh, the hard,
bright intelligence of Gramp, and the primitive energy of Hattie
Tolliver. There was all the stifled emotion pent so long in a
heart dedicated to secrecy, and the triumph of wild dreams; and
there was too a vast amount of passion for that little company who
believed in her, whom she dared not betray by failure . . . for
Lily whose very gown she wore, and the withered Miss Ogilvie;
for Gramp, and young Fergus who worshiped her with his eyes,
for her gentle father and the fierce old woman in Shane's Castle;
but most of all for that indomitable and emotional woman whom
she must repay one day by forcing all the world to envy her.

When she had finished she was forced to return because
overtones of all this wild emotion had filtered vaguely into
the very heart of the restless, distracted audience on stiff collapsible chairs. They applauded; it was as if she had suddenly
claimed them.

Then she played savagely the Revolutionary Prelude and disappeared behind the lacquered screen. There was a hush and
then more talk and then a sudden excitement which began at the
screen and ran in little ripples through all the stiff gathering.
From the alcove there emerged the bass rumbling of the Russian,
stirred suddenly into somnolent activity, and again a wild tinkling
of little bells and a torrent of French in the shrill voice of the
Javanese dancer. The screen parted and the dancer, half naked,
covered only by the heavy gold ornaments and a wrapper of scarlet silk, emerged chattering French and gesticulating. She addressed Mrs. Callendar who stirred herself into a sudden dull
glitter of movement. The son left the ugly Sabine and joined
his mother, calm but with a fierce, bright look in his eyes. The
American girl . . . the unknown pianist had fainted!

24

WHEN at length Ellen became conscious of her surroundings, it was with the faint odor of stables in
her nostrils and in her ears the jingling of harness
and the steady, brisk clop! clop! made by the hoofs of spirited
horses upon wet asphalt. The cabriolet, flitting through the
streaks of light made by street lamps on the wet pavement, was
passing through an open space where the light shone on the bare
branches of trees and banks of wet and dirty snow. Otherwise
everything was silent.

When she stirred presently and moved into an upright posture,
she saw by her side a mass of sable, the sudden glint of a brilliant
yellow dress, captured and fixed by a stray beam of light and then
the face and bright lips of the bizarre woman with red hair, who
stirred and murmured,

"It's all right. I'm Miss Cane. On the other side is Mr.
Callendar . . . Mrs. Callendar's son."

The dark man removed his top hat and bowed. "We're taking you home," he said, "to the Babylon Arms. . . . That's right,
isn't it?"

There was a faint trace of accent in his voice . . . vaguely
familiar, confused somehow with a memory of mimosa and the
figure of Lily standing beneath the glowing Venice in the drawing room of Shane's Castle. The same sort of accent. . . .

"That's right, isn't it?" continued the voice of the dark young
man. "The Babylon Arms?"

Then for the first time, Ellen spoke, slowly and with a certain
shyness. "Yes. I live there. . . . But how did you know?"

The man laughed. "Two reasons," he said. "First. Sanson
told my mother. Second. My mother owns the Babylon Arms."

Again a wandering ray of light flitted across the window of
the cabriolet illuminating for an instant the brilliant lips of Miss
Cane. The lips were smiling, as if conscious that they were
shielded by the darkness, but it was a mocking smile and the mem-

ory of it haunted Ellen long afterward. It was as if the painted lips were really speaking and said, "The Babylon Arms is a preposterous pretentious place." And for the first time, perhaps, Ellen doubted the magnificence of that vast pile.

Her next speech was dictated by the careful precepts of Hattie Tolliver. "I'm sorry," she said. "I shouldn't have fainted. . . . It ruined everything."

There was a stifled laugh from Sabine Cane. "Nonsense! It gave us a chance to get into the air."

Then silence once more and the echoing clop! clop! clop! clop! regular as the beams of light which flashed past the open door of Thérèse Callendar's cabriolet.

Long after midnight the carriage came to a halt before the gigantic Syrian lions of cast iron that ornamented the entrance to the Babylon Arms. It was young Callendar who descended first, lending his arm with a grave and alien grace to Ellen who, having recovered entirely, emerged with a sure and vigorous step. The third occupant, instead of remaining behind as she might well have been expected to do, followed them, driven by an overpowering desire to miss nothing. So with Ellen between them, Callendar in a top hat, and Sabine Cane, muffled in sables and holding her full yellow train high above the wet pavements, descended upon the astonished negro who ran the elevator.

Here Ellen bade them good night. "I'm all right now. . . . It was good of you to have come."

But they insisted upon accompanying her. There were protests, into which there entered a sudden note of desperation as if the girl were striving to conceal something which lay hidden at the top of the flamboyant apartment.

"But you might faint again," protested Sabine firmly. "I shan't be satisfied until I see you safe in your flat."

"Besides," observed young Callendar, smiling, "some day the Babylon Arms will be mine. I should like to see what it looks like, abovestairs."

So they pressed her until at last she yielded and in their company was borne aloft in the swaying elevator. As it jolted to a halt, she bade them good night once more, saying, "The elevator only runs this far and I live two flights above. I'll go the rest of the way alone."

But they went with her through the red painted corridors under the light of the flickering gas up the flights of stairs to a door which she opened with her own key. There at last the farewells were made, for she did not invite them to enter.

"My mother will call in the morning," said Callendar, "to see that you are not really ill. . . . Oh yes! You couldn't prevent her! You don't know her as well as I do!"

"Good night."

"Good night."

And as the door closed they caught a sudden glimpse of a man, standing timidly in the dim light of an inner room, listening with an air of curiosity to their talk. He was a small man and rather thin, and stood dressed in a shirt and trousers. His hair was rumpled; obviously he had been "sitting up." Behind him there was a table covered with papers and accounts. All this the shrewd eye of Sabine captured in one swift instant.

As they descended under the guidance of the negro, Callendar said, "The man . . . who was he?"

"Some one . . . perhaps her lover. Musicians have lovers. . . ."

Her companion turned sharply. "No . . ." he said, "not a lover. A woman with such spirit wouldn't have that sort of lover."

Sabine laughed softly and with a hint of wickedness in her voice. "You don't know women . . . how queer they can be. Besides . . ." And she indicated with a nod of her red head the listening negro. "One must be careful." But she regarded Callendar with a new interest and during the long ride back through the park she remained silent save to comment now and then upon the bits of gossip which he discussed. Knowing him so well, perhaps she understood that a new source of disturbance had crossed his path. There was between them a remarkable sense of intimacy, as if each expected the other to understand him perfectly.

By the time they reached the solid house on Murray Hill the party was already on the wane and the guests had begun, in a motley stream, to leave. Mrs. Champion and her daughters disappeared among the first after Mrs. Callendar had the audacity to bring forward the artists and beg them to join the guests. The Russian tenor stood awkwardly alone and in a corner and the tiny dancer, in a turban and gown of crimson and gold brocade, sat surrounded by young men. She had learned the business of entertaining during those early days in Alexandria.

25

The prediction of young Callendar came true, for in the morning, while Ellen sat in a purple wrapper practising her scales, the bell rang suddenly and into the room came Mrs. Callendar, dressed coquettishly in a very tight black suit, a hat much too large for her short, plump figure, and a voluminous stole of sable. The climb up the two flights of stairs above the elevator had been very nearly too much for her and she greeted Ellen with much panting and blowing.

"Good morning, my dear," she said. "I hope you're none the worse for last night's experience."

Ellen smiled respectfully and bade her guest seat herself in the padded arm chair that was the property of Clarence. "I'm all right again. I can't imagine what could have made me faint. I'm sorry. It must have spoiled the party."

At this Mrs. Callendar, settling herself in the chair, chuckled, "Not at all. Not at all. They'll talk of it for days. You could not have done better. It was dramatic . . . dramatic."

"I'm all right. You needn't have come. It is good of you."

"Perhaps you lace too tightly," suggested Mrs. Callendar, returning to the subject of Ellen's collapse.

"I don't lace at all," said Ellen. "I can't play if I'm all boxed in."

Mrs. Callendar threw back her stole and nodded her head sagely. "You're much wiser, my dear. Much wiser. When I was a girl I was famous for my waist. Sixteen inches it was . . . only sixteen inches." And she brought together her plump fingers in a gesture which implied that once she might have encircled her waist with her two hands. "But I fainted . . . I used to faint daily. I don't lace tightly any more, but it makes no difference. It's just stayed that way. You see, my corsets are quite loose." And she thrust a finger into the space between her ample bosom and her corset to prove her statement. "I know my figure is bad in these days. Too many curves and too little height. But I'm past forty and it doesn't matter so much."

Secretly Ellen must have compared the figure of her guest with that of her own vigorous mother. Mrs. Tolliver was ten years the older, yet her appearance was that of a woman much younger than Mrs. Callendar. It was in this difference that the Levantine blood of the latter betrayed her. She was a friendly woman, certainly, and one who was quite sure of herself, fortified clearly by the conviction that the king can do no wrong.

"You shouldn't have climbed the stairs just to see if I was all right."

"But you see," said Mrs. Callendar, "I'm interested in you. Sanson tells me you have a great future. He doesn't tell me such things if he doesn't believe them. . . . But don't let that turn your head. Nothing comes without work . . . least of all, anything to do with the arts."

For a moment Ellen did not reply. At last she said, thoughtfully, "I know that."

"You are bitter," observed Mrs. Callendar, "and perhaps unhappy," she added with a shrewd glance of her near sighted eyes. "Well, that's a good thing. It shows character, and no artist ever existed without character. Character is the thing that counts." Here, having regained her breath, she rose and placing the lorgnettes against her slanting eyes, she wandered to the window. "It's a fine view you have from here," and after a moment's consideration, "Not so fine as it appears at first. Too many locomotives and signboards. You see," she added, turning toward the girl, "I came here this morning for other reasons too. I own the Babylon Arms."

"So your son told me."

"But I've never seen it before. I'm only in New York for a month or two at a time. I own a great deal of property here and there. I don't have to look at it. I have a good agent . . . a young Jew, trustworthy . . . a fellow who knows values up and down. I pay him well and he knows that if he played me a trick, I'd throw him out at once. Oh, I can trust him. Besides, I'm a Levantine myself and in every Levantine there is a Jew hidden away. We understand each other . . . Minsky and I. It's a fine building but the elevator ought to run all the way up. Then I could charge you more rent. I suppose there's no room for it. The architect made these upper floors too fancy. No eye for comfort and common sense."

And having uttered this torrent of opinions, she returned to the plush chair and said, "But tell me about yourself. I have a terrible curiosity about people. You're American, aren't you?"

"Yes," replied Ellen. There was about this preposterous visitor a quality that was irresistible. It was impossible to know whether you liked or disliked her, because she gave you no time to consider. Even if you decided against her, it availed nothing; she swept over you with the persuasion of a mountain torrent . . . a powerful woman and one whose friendliness was disarming. For a moment or two, the absurd thought that she might have been drinking lingered in Ellen's mind.

"Well," observed Mrs. Callendar, "some day this raw country is going to produce a superb art. Maybe you're one of the first artists. Who can say?" Fumbling in the reticule of black jet she brought out at last a tiny cigarette case, made of onyx with the name Thérèse in small diamonds, a bizarre box which in the possession of a woman less powerful and less foreign would have been vulgar. "I suppose you smoke?"

"No," said Ellen, "I never have."

"Well, you will." And she thrust the case back into the reticule. "You don't mind if I do?"

"Certainly not." Ellen brought out the small table consecrated to the smoking apparatus of her husband. It was a violation of Clarence's principles. On this subject he had spoken to Ellen many times, saying always, "Women who smoke are all of one kind."

"Wouldn't you have a cup of tea or a bit of cake?" asked Ellen. "I owe you something for the climb up the stairs."

"Thank you, no. Not at this hour of the day, and besides there is my figure to consider. It is real suffering to possess at the same time a tendency toward fat and an appetite for rich food."

She paused for a moment to breathe in the smoke of the tiny scented cigarette. All this time her eyes, aided by the lorgnettes, had been roving the room, as if somewhere within its walls she might find other clues to Ellen's history. To Ellen this action must have been disconcerting, especially since the drooping lid which half concealed one eye of the visitor made it impossible ever to know in what direction or in what object she was interested.

"But tell me about yourself," she continued. "You like Sanson?"

"He is a good teacher."

"No monkey business about him . . . no fanfaronade and nonsense. I've known him a great many years. I see him in Paris more often than here. He's not so busy over there."

Ellen sat on the edge of her chair, like a school girl in the presence of an elderly aunt. In the age and self-possession of her guest there was some quality which caused her to feel an awful sense of youth and inexperience. "I'm going to Paris to study in a year or two," she said modestly. It was almost as if Mrs. Callendar had the power of making her enact a rôle.

"Of course. So you must. Nobody here would pay to hear an American musician. And you must take a foreign name. That's important. Some day it won't be. But it is now. We're still afraid to trust ourselves. People spend money for names as well as music. You must have a good foreign name, the fancier the better so long as it doesn't sound like a music hall. Have you any friends over there?"

"I have a cousin." Her manner was better now, a little more contained and far less shy, for the amazing friendliness of Mrs. Callendar had begun to accomplish the inevitable effect. This dowager was perhaps the first woman in all the city who had been friendly toward her, the first woman who had not been a little on her guard, a little uncertain . . . the way Bunce's wife was uncertain and hostile. And there was something in the manner of Mrs. Callendar which must have reminded Ellen of her mother . . . a certain recklessness, a quality that was quite beyond barriers of any sort.

"Is the cousin male or female?" asked Mrs. Callendar, "because in Paris it makes a difference."

"Female," replied Ellen.

"Indeed! Perhaps I know her?"

"Her name is Shane," said Ellen. "Lily Shane."

For a time Mrs. Callendar regarded the blue smoke of her cigarette in silence, thoughtfully. "Shane," she murmured, "Shane? I don't think I know any one named Shane? I know most of the Americans in Paris. Has she lived there long?"

"Many years."

"Shane? Shane?" Mrs. Callendar continued to murmur with an air of searching the recesses of her excessively active brain; and then, all at once, she grew alert. "Shane! Shane! Of course. Reddish hair. Tall. Beautiful. Madame Shane. I've never met her, but I've seen her somewhere. She's been pointed out to me . . . maybe at the races, maybe at the Opéra. Madame Shane . . . to be sure. A beauty! A widow, isn't she?"

There was in Ellen's reply no haste: indeed she waited for a long time as if turning the simple inquiry over and over in her mind. Lily a widow! Lily who had never been married! She did not, as her mother might have done, spring impulsively to a blundering answer. Perhaps out of her memory there emerged old thoughts, old gossip, bits of instinct and emotion which presently fashioned itself into a comprehensible pattern—such things as her own pride of race, the tribal sense that was so strong in her family, the memory of gossip about a child, indeed all those fragments of mystery which surrounded the existence of her cousin. When she replied it was calmly in a manner that protected Lily. "Yes," she said, "a widow. That's the one," as if nothing had occurred that was in the least surprising.

"A beautiful woman," continued Mrs. Callendar crushing out the ember of her cigarette upon the tray dedicated to the ashes of Clarence. "And now," she added, "coming to the point, I wanted to know whether you would come sometimes and play for me in the evenings. . . . Not a performance, you understand, but simply to play once in a while for me and perhaps my son and Miss Cane and one or two friends. . . . Miss Cane—you may remember her—came home with you last night . . . a clever woman. I'd pay you well . . . understand that. I'd like to have you once or twice a week. I don't go out frequently. I love music but I dislike musicians. You'll understand that when you come to see more of them."

For Ellen it was, of course, the opening of a new world in which she might become independent, a world such as she had imagined the city to be. It was as if, overnight, the whole course of her life had been changed. There were chances now, subtle, hidden gambits for which she had an instinct.

"Yes," she replied quietly. "I think I could arrange it to come."

"And very likely," said Mrs. Callendar, "I could get other engagements for you." She had risen now and was wrapping the sable stole about her short fat neck. "I'll let you know when I'll want you to come. I'll write you a note that will be a sort of contract between us. I believe in contracts. Never trust the human race. . . . And now good-by, Miss Tolliver. I'm glad you're all right again. You may have fainted out of fright. There were people there last night . . . stupid people . . . who would have frightened Rubinstein himself."

So Ellen thanked her, bade her good-by and walked with her to the top of the stairs. Half way down, Mrs. Callendar turned. "I suppose," she said with a rising inflection, "that you live here alone."

"No," said Ellen; but that was all she said, and Mrs. Callendar, smiling to herself, disappeared amused, no doubt, by the memory of the story which Sabine Cane had told her when she had returned across the park from the Babylon Arms.

Once the door was closed, Ellen flung herself into a chair and sat staring out of the window into the gray clouds that swept across the sky high above the North River. It must have occurred to her then that Mrs. Callendar had departed with an amazing amount of information . . . knowledge which concerned herself and her family, her future, her plans, even the details of the very flat in which she lived. Her guest had, after a fashion, absorbed her and her life much as a sponge absorbs water. By now Mrs. Callendar could doubtless have drawn a detailed and accurate picture of the flat and written a history of its occupant. Indeed she had very nearly tripped Ellen into one unfortunate truthfulness. That was a fascinating thought . . . Lily and her strange foreign life. Lily a widow? What were her morals? How did she live in Paris? Surely no one in the Town could have had the faintest idea. But *Madame* Shane! Still Mrs. Callendar might have been mistaken. It would have been, under the circumstances, a natural error. It was as though Lily was destined in some unreal fashion to play a part in Ellen's own life. Always she was there, or at least some hint of her. Even Clarence talked of her in a way he did not use when speaking of other women. Yet no one knew anything of Lily.

Smiling dimly she rose, and before returning to her music she took the brass ash tray containing the remains of Mrs. Callendar's scented cigarette and cleaned it thoroughly, taking care to bury the offending morsels well out of sight where Clarence could never find them. Certainly she performed this act through no fear of him. Rather it was with an air of secrecy as if already she and her visitor had entered into a conspiracy. It may have been only a touch of that curious understanding which flashes sometimes between persons of great character.

26

THE life of Mr. Wyck was no longer of interest to any one; yet there were times, usually after a stronger dose than usual of his wife's power and independence, when Clarence sought the company of Wyck with the air of a man in need of refreshment and rest. For she had brought into the lives of both men a sense of strain which, during the days of their amiable companionship on the top floor of the Babylon Arms, had been utterly lacking. To Clarence, this new condition of affairs remained a mystery; but Wyck, with an intuition that was feminine, must sometimes have come close to the real reason.

He knew, beyond all doubt, that Ellen, for all her indifference, was his enemy—an enemy who never once considered her foe, an enemy who in her towering self-sufficiency had not troubled to include him in her reckoning. There were times, during the lunches the two men had together in a tiny restaurant in Liberty Street, when he came very close to speaking the truth, so close that Clarence, moved by a shadowy and pathetic loyalty, turned the talk of his companion into other channels. People said that a wife made a difference with one's friends, that marriage ended old friendships and began new ones. There were, to be sure, old ones that had come very near to the end of the path, but in their place there were no new ones. It was wonderful how Ellen appeared to exist without friends.

"She is busy, I suppose," he confided in admiration to Wyck over the greasy table, "and she is more independent than most women but still I don't see how she stands it. She might have had Bunce's wife for a friend."

Wyck said, "Oh, no! *She's* not good enough for her." And then as if he had spoken too bitterly, he added, "I can understand that. Bunce's wife is a vulgar woman." He had never forgiven the contractor's daughter the theft of Bunce. He hated her so strongly that in order to disparage her, it was necessary by comparison to reflect praise upon another enemy.

There were at times long silences when neither man spoke at all, for even their talk of shop came to an end after it had been turned over and over a hundred times. What thoughts occurred in those tragic silences neither one could have revealed to the other because they were in the realm of those things which friends, or even those who cling to the rags of friendship, cannot afford to tell each other.

Clarence with his nose-glasses and neat white collar drank his thin coffee and thought, "Wyck is a dull fellow. How could I ever have liked him? Funny how men grow apart."

And across the table Wyck, finishing his apple sauce, thought, "Ah, if only there was some way to save him. That woman is destroying him slowly, bit by bit. He should never have married her. If only I could get him back where he would be happy again."

There were in these thoughts the vestiges of truth. At one time they were more filled with truth than at another, for no thing is true persistently and unutterably. Yet in their truth Clarence was the happier of the two because he had discovered in his marriage a freedom of a new and different sort; through Ellen he was strong enough to yield nothing to the shabby little man who sat opposite him. In some way he had caught a sense of her independence, a knowledge that she was not as other women, or even as most men. She belonged to the ruthless and the elect. As for Wyck, he had only his sense of loss, for which there was no reward, and a pang which he was resolved one day to heal by some revenge, as yet vague and unplanned. And in his heart he believed that friendship between men was a bond far finer, far more pure than any relation between a man and woman.

"See!" he thought, over his apple sauce, "what it is doing to Clarence. It is destroying him. His love for her is consuming him."

And when they had finished eating and had paid the yellow-haired cashier who sat enthroned behind the till, it was their habit to saunter into the streets and lose themselves in the noon crowds of lower Broadway. Sometimes they wandered as far as the Battery to sit on a bench and watch the fine ships going proudly across a bay of brilliant blue out to the open sea. But there was not much pleasure in their promenade. It ended always in the same fashion with Clarence looking at his watch to observe, "It's time we started back."

And so they would return, back the same way over the same streets and over the same doorstep. There were times when the sight of the blue sea and the great ships sliding silently through the green water filled the heart of Mr. Wyck with a wild turbulence which was beyond his understanding. Those were times when he hated both his friend and the woman who held him prisoner.

But no one was really interested in Mr. Wyck. In the evening when he returned to the gas-lit bed room in Lexington Avenue there was nothing for him to do. He read sometimes, but not frequently, and on warm nights he sat on the doorstep watching the passers-by and exchanging a word now and then with the grim woman who was his landlady. There were long hours in which there was nothing to do but to think, and not even the gray cat, watching the shadow of her tail against the decaying brownstone of the doorstep, could have guessed the dark trend of those secret thoughts.

His life, his happiness had been ruined by a stranger who scorned even to think of him.

Other changes came in the life of Clarence.

Once he had been a great one for organizations. He had been vice president of the Mutual Benefit Association of the Superba Electrical Company and a member of no less than three lodges. In the days before his marriage the duties concerned with all these organizations had required much of his time, but when Ellen arrived he came to stay more and more at home, and little by little these gaieties too lost their place in his life. It seemed that he was content to remain in the flat reading the newspaper, working over his accounts and now and then merely listening to his wife's music with a strange expression of bewilderment as if it were impossible for him ever to understand her; and that little vein in his throat, which Lily had observed with such interest, throbbed and throbbed with a desire which sometimes must have terrified him.

Sitting there in the long evenings, silhouetted as she played, against the brilliant blue of a sky that stretched out interminably beyond the windows of the Babylon Arms, she had an air of lofty magnificence, an aloofness that was unconquerable. There were times when she seemed a very symbol of all that was unattainable; and always she was related to the wild dreams that became gradually less and less turbulent.

When she told him of these new engagements to play for Mrs. Callendar, he frowned and said, "But what of me? What am I to do?"

"It means more money for us . . . and we need money. You see, Mrs. Callendar pays me well. My music will cost me nothing. Perhaps I shall be able to put something aside. Besides there is the experience which must not be overlooked."

These things were true, and of late the mention of the money she might earn seemed not so unpleasant to Clarence as it had once been. He was, it appeared, more troubled by the fear of her escaping him, for he said, "I don't think it's wise to go too much with these people. They're not our sort. . . . I've heard stories of how they live. They're society people."

At which Ellen mocked him, laughing, to say, "But I have nothing to do with them. I work for them. I entertain them . . . that's all."

"And Wyck says that young Callendar has a reputation for being a bad one."

Ellen laughed again, scornfully. "How does he know anything about young Callendar? Wyck and his boarding house. It's because he hates me. I know what he's like . . . a mean, nasty little man who hates me."

"He has friends. . . . His family was rich once in New York."

What Clarence said was true. Wyck did know because, although he had long since ceased to have any existence for such people as the Callendars, there were channels by way of housemaids and distant relatives through which news of their world penetrated at last, somewhat distorted and magnified, to the spinster aunts in Yonkers, and so at length to Mr. Wyck himself. For the old ladies had known young Callendar's father as a boy and they still lived in the world of those early days when, ensconced on lower Fifth Avenue behind plush curtains ornamented with ball fringe, they had received the Sunday procession of fashionables. The vulgar, new city of this early twentieth century, for all its noise and show, did not exist for them any more than they, for all their thin blooded pride, existed for the Callendars. It was after all an affair merely of dollars and cents. The Callendars had increased their fortune; the Wycks had lost theirs.

"I shall go to the Callendars' and play for them because it is necessary," said Ellen. "I am not a fool. I can take care of myself."

To this abrupt statement, Clarence found no answer. He yielded quietly and, presently, on the nights when Ellen played in the great house on Murray Hill, he found himself going back once more to his three lodges and the Mutual Benefit Association

of the Superba Electrical Company. There were members of the
latter organization who thought it queer that their vice president
attended the annual ball, held that year in a Brooklyn Hotel, as
he had always done, alone, without his wife. It happened that
she played that night in the solid house on Murray Hill.

And what then of Ellen herself? She was not, surely, unconscious of all that was happening so slowly, so imperceptibly about
her. It is true that she was one of those who are born to success, one for whom the past does not exist and the present has
reality only in so far as it provides a step into the future. Indeed, during those years in the city, even the Town itself became
a very distant and shadowy memory. She was concerned, desperately, with what lay before her, confused perhaps by a sense
of imminent disaster so vague that it could have for her no real
meaning or significance.

But of course she never spoke of these things to her husband,
perhaps because she was conscious that he might not understand
them. At times the old pity for him, the same pity which had
seized her so unaccountably upon the night of their flight, overwhelmed her, and at such moments it was her habit to be tender
with him in a fashion that sent him into extravagant flights of
happiness. But these moments became, after a while, conscious
things on the part of Ellen so that presently she used them
cheaply to quiet his unhappiness as one might use a gaudy stick of
candy to quiet an unhappy child. Such little things made him
happy.

Sometimes in the night she would lie in one of the green beds
ornamented with garlands of salmon pink roses, listening to the
sounds of the city that lay far beneath them . . . the distant rumble which rose and mingled somehow with the glow of light that
filled all the dome of the sky, a rumble pierced sharply by the
sudden shrill cry of a city child playing late in the streets.
or the faint clop! clop! of hoofs upon asphalt blurred now and

again by the ghostly boom of a great ship's whistle rising from the fog-veiled river . . . marvelous, splendorous sounds of a great world close at hand. There lay in these sounds a wonderful sense of the crowd—in which she herself was not a part. Lying there, her fingers would clutch the bedclothes tightly and presently she would become conscious that in her listening she was not alone, that beside her, separated by the little chasm which divided the two green beds, Clarence too lay awake . . . listening. She must have known in those hours an unreal consciousness of something that was waiting . . . a Thing destined not to become clear until long afterward . . . a Thing which waited silently and with a terrible patience. It was an experience that was not rare; it happened many nights, so that presently she came to be happy in the weeks when Clarence, traveling through the night hundreds of miles from her, was not there at all.

Sometimes her hand would steal out and in the darkness be touched and clasped by another hand that trembled and clung to hers in a sort of terror.

27

ELLEN'S awareness of Richard Callendar came over her slowly, a sensation neither desired nor anticipated, but one which stole upon her in some obscure fashion through the corridors of her own music. It would have been impossible to fix the moment at which this awareness took form; certainly it was not during that first damp drive through the park, when, wedged between his slim body and that of the yellow-clad Sabine, she had her first view of him. On that occasion she had remarked him merely as a young man perhaps of thirty (in this she was wrong by five years) who possessed a beauty of a kind new to her, a beauty of which there were traces to be found among certain of the workers in the Mills that hugged the dying hedges of Shane's Castle. It was, in short, a kind of mystical, unearthly beauty born of an old, old race that was sensual and filled with an intense capacity for suffering . . . a kind of beauty never to be found among her own Scotch and English friends and relatives. It had its determining quality in the extraordinary blackness of his hair, the dark olive of his skin and the unreality of gray eyes so queerly placed in so much darkness.

Sabine Cane, so completely civilized, so disillusioned, understood this beauty with the mind of one capable of an amazing detachment and power of analysis, for she had an extraordinary power of pulling herself up short in the midst of her emotions and saying, "This is indeed interesting. Here am I giving way to a good wholesome passion. Well! Well! . . ." and then, "It's all very good so long as I don't allow myself to be hurt by it." For Sabine had the sort of intelligence which is the equipment of every potential sensualist.

This awareness on the part of Ellen forced its way through a torrent of impressions and emotions into a consciousness never too well organized. At the "parties" of Mrs. Callendar, there were, as the amusing woman predicted, never more than three or four people. There was always herself and usually her son. Sometimes Sabine Cane, whose relationship to the older woman was that of one who shares a complete understanding, was present, and now and then an elderly beau or two, of the sort which appears at concerts and the opera where they sit in the rear of boxes obscured somewhat by bedizened dowagers.

These entertainments, referred to variously by Thérèse Callendar as musicales, parties and soirées, were held in the vast drawing room where Ellen appeared on that first evening. While she played, the others, flanked by brocade curtains of immense dimensions, rows of Callendar family portraits and cases filled with bronze Buddhas and jade tear bottles, sat about respectful, listening, prepared to speak only in hushed voices, for it was true that all of them were wholly devoted to music . . . all perhaps, save Sabine who, it might be said, was present as much because she found Thérèse Callendar amusing and had a profound curiosity regarding the shy, handsome girl who came to entertain them.

Ellen had a capacity for "feeling her audience." She had not played many times before she knew exactly the degree and quality of appreciation in each of those who listened. She came to know that Sabine neither understood music nor cared very greatly for it, and that Mrs. Callendar preferred the compositions which were a little wild and barbaric. In the dark young Richard Callendar there was a quality altogether different from any of the others. It was a kind of appreciation which she had experienced only twice before. Lily listened in that fashion and her own brother Fergus. It was as if they abandoned themselves completely to the sound, as if they became in all their senses quite immersed. For a long time after the music ceased it was difficult for them to return wholly to the world of reality. She herself knew the intoxication; it was an emotion quite beyond the realm of drunkenness; it might be perhaps comparable to the effect of certain drugs. Richard Callendar listened in that fashion, and understanding this she came at length to play for him alone, moved only by an instinct of profound gratitude.

Even Sabine Cane, with all her sharp intelligence, failed to understand what was happening before her green eyes. She knew, vaguely, that there were times when the girl outdid herself, when the sounds she made possessed a beauty unusual in degree and quality, but her penetration seldom progressed beyond this point, because, by virtue of that strange and mystical bond, the other two were raised into a world quite beyond her. If there was a difference it lay in this . . . that to Sabine one would have said that nothing could ever happen, because she guarded herself so carefully.

In the beginning, Ellen had come in only to play in the evenings at nine o'clock when the others had finished dinner and were sitting in the walnut-paneled library over cigarettes, coffee and liqueurs. She came, as a mountebank, to entertain. It was her habit to arrive quietly, to greet Mrs. Callendar and then sit modestly a little apart from the others until the moment came for her to play. They were kind to her, and sometimes quite cordial—even Sabine who, out of an awkwardness born of a nature really shy, talked with her in the most confused and disjointed fashion, sometimes, under the stress of temptation, striving even to pry into the details of her life. Perhaps Sabine, in the recesses of her clear intelligence, speculated regarding the origins, the background, the very surroundings of Ellen. Her own life had been one ordered and held in check by a rigid tradition . . . a nurse, a day school kept by an affected and clever old harridan in impoverished circumstances, a year abroad and at last a coming-out ball. The independence she possessed lay altogether in her own thoughts, a thing hid away deeply. It moved like a mountain torrent confined placidly within the walls of a canal. It manifested itself only in a sharpness of tongue, a restless and malicious desire for gossip. She encouraged her imagination to rebuild the lives of her friends according to some pattern more exciting than that of the straight-laced world by which she was submerged. It was this, perhaps, which drew her to old Thérèse Callendar and her son. In them she found a freedom, a sophistication that elsewhere was lacking. Richard Callendar was not unwilling to discuss such things as mistresses. Thérèse did not treat her as if she were a spotless virgin to be protected against the realities of the world. They provided release to an intelligence bound in upon all sides by the corseted bejetted traditions of the day. They treated her with respect, as an individual. They possessed candor.

And so in the beginning her curiosity had seemed to Ellen, not understanding all this, an impudent thing, to be snubbed quietly in the proud way she had. She understood, well enough, that Sabine possessed the advantage . . . at least in the world of Mrs. Callendar's drawing-room. Sabine was at home there. She had lived always in such drawing-rooms. And yet there came a night when Sabine turned with her strange abruptness and said apropos of nothing, "I envy you."

At which Ellen smiled and asked, "Why?"

"Because," continued the abrupt Sabine, "you will always have the advantage over us (she was quite frank in admitting that they belonged to different worlds). It is always so with those who make their way by their wits."

Once Ellen might have pondered such a speech, wondering whether she should consider herself insulted by it. But in the experience of many talks with Sabine, she came to understand that there lay at the bottom of the observation no more than a complete honesty. Indeed, the remark was so honest that in the very moment it was made, Ellen saw not only its honesty but its truth. She *was* making her way by her wits. Sabine had nothing to make . . . nothing to expect save a marriage which would occur in due time according to the plan that controlled all Sabine's life. And the artist in Ellen leapt at once to assume the rôle. She would make her way by her wits, from now on, consciously. That placed her. It provided her with a certain definiteness of personality.

"People like that are always more sure of themselves," Sabine continued. "I've noticed it. Take Mrs. Sigourney. She's done it. She's outraged some people but she's got what she wanted. . . . She was nobody and now she's chic. It's her wits, always her wits. . . . She never does the wrong thing . . . never puts herself in a place where she can be hurt."

At the end of the speech, Sabine's voice dropped suddenly. There was even a little echo of something . . . perhaps a faint sigh, as if it came somewhere from deep within her. She *had* been hurt then, perhaps a long time ago. Perhaps her flawless clothes, her sharp and witty tongue, her air of entering a room, were all no more than an armor she had raised about herself. She was not, like Ellen, isolated, independent, free . . . belonging to nothing, to no one, save only herself. Her friendship with Richard Callendar may only have been a bit of bravado, to flaunt in the face of the others who desired him.

Ellen saw it, clearly now. In the Town she would have been like Sabine. There, in a community all her own, they could have hurt her. Here in this world there was no one who could do her any injury. Alone, isolated, she was stronger than she had been in the very midst of all those who had known her since the beginning.

"I wish," continued Sabine, "that you would tell me about yourself some time. . . . Tell me and Richard. He's interested in such things."

"But I must play now," said Ellen.

On the same night when the hour came for Ellen to be sent home in Mrs. Callendar's cabriolet, the plump woman said, "The next time. . . . Let's see, it's Thursday, isn't it? . . . You must come for dinner. . . . I'll send Wilkes at twenty to eight."

28

THAT there was any such thing as kindliness involved in all these complicated, new relationships had never occurred to Ellen, perhaps because she had never for a moment expected it. It was only with the invitation to dinner, in itself a tacit recognition of her individuality as something more than a mere music box, that the real state of affairs first became clear to her. It was as if she had progressed a step in the world, as if she had achieved a little already of the vast things she had set out to accomplish. She tried, in her direct, unsubtle way of speaking, to convey something of the idea to Clarence. She wanted him, as always, desperately to understand her actions. She wanted him, perhaps dishonestly, to believe that she could not help acting as she did, that it was not from choice but from a desire to brighten both their lives that she left him now and then to venture forth into regions which it was impossible for him to penetrate. And in her own fashion, as she had done so often with her mother, she told him the truth selectively, so that although she did not lie she managed to achieve an effect that was not the truth.

The great thing which she neglected to admit was this . . . that she had come now to the point where it was no longer possible to take him with her. Even his fantastic dreams could not make him more than he was, and that was not enough. He had come to the end of his tether. She had barely begun. Imagine him in Mrs. Callendar's drawing-room! Fancy the abrupt Sabine Cane talking to him as she talked to Ellen! He, she knew, would suffer more than any one.

She said to him, "I'm sorry, but on Thursday I shall be out for dinner. . . . I've got to dine with Mrs. Callendar. . . . It's business, dear. . . . I must do these things."

And at the speech, Clarence assumed that hurt and crestfallen look which touched her sense of pity. It was the one thing which could alter her determination; indeed there were times when she must have suspected that he used it consciously, as his only weapon. It moved her even now, so that she went so far as to kiss him and say, "It's just one night."

"But it's a beginning." He saw it perhaps, clearly enough, more clearly than she ever imagined. "I wish you wouldn't."

And then she explained to him again the things which it was necessary for her to do in order to win what she must have. She talked long and eloquently, for she was earnest and she pitied him. It was clear that her dishonesty arose not so much out of any evil calculation as out of a desire to have everything, to go her way and still leave Clarence unharmed and happy. It was a thing impossible, of course, yet it never seemed so to her. There was in her so much of her indomitable mother that she was never able to believe in the impossible.

So she talked eloquently and at length she even arranged it for him that he should dine on Thursday night with Mr. and Mrs. Bunce. Thus, by a single act, she accomplished another thing. She dined with the Bunces without having to dine with them.

She knew too that they would be happier with Clarence there alone. It would be like the old days, without strain, an evening when the three of them,—Clarence and Harry Bunce and his rosy wife,—could dine, as one might say, in peace. There would be no strain, no sense of an intruder in their midst. For she was a stranger, always; they were never quite at ease with her.

Thus Clarence found the evening arranged, and he was content in his way, for he liked the Bunces.

Afterward Ellen's clearest memory of the evening was the voice of Sabine drifting from the drawing-room as she entered the hall, saying, "The trouble with Boston people is that they are all descended from middle class immigrants and they've been proud of it ever since."

This speech became fixed somehow in her brain as a symbol of Sabine's queer worldliness, of a strangely cynical honesty that would color her whole point of view up to the very end. If Sabine thought it idiotic to take pride in being middle class, if she thought it absurd not to strive after distinction, she would say it, whether or not people thought her a snob. The world to her was thus and so; it moved according to an ancient pattern. All the orations in the world upon the subject of democracy could not alter the rule of things. Besides, it was a good enough rule. Why pretend it wasn't? Sabine, of course, could afford to take such a position. In a worldly sense, she had nothing to strive for. She had been born to those things.

Ellen, removing the squirrel coat Clarence had given her, turned these considerations over in her mind as she entered the room. She was watching them all to-night as she had watched them once before through the crack in the lacquered screen, cautiously, with an air of an enemy laying siege to their fortress.

There was, beneath the gaze of the Callendar ancestors, only Mrs. Callendar in a dress of jet and sequins, Sabine in a brilliant green gown and Richard Callendar, handsome and dark in his black and white clothes. Richard rose and came forward to meet her.

"Mama," he said, smiling, "has just been talking of you. She believes that one day you will be a great personality."

"We are dining alone, the four of us," said Mrs. Callendar abruptly. It was clear that she meant to keep Ellen forever in ignorance of what she had said.

The dining room was done in the grand manner of the Second Empire, a room copied at the behest of young Callendar's grandfather from a house built by the Duc de Morny for one of his mistresses. It was grandiose, with columns of white and gilt, centering upon a massive table and a group of chairs with backs which ended a foot or two sooner than they should have ended. On the four panels of the walls there hung pictures of Venice in the dry, hard manner of Canaletto . . . Venice at Dawn, Venice at Sunset, Venice at Carnival Time and Venice in Mourning for the Pope. On the huge table stood a silver épergne filled to overflowing with the most opulent of fruits . . . mangoes, persimmons, red bananas, Homberg grapes and pomegranates. It was as if Thérèse Callendar had built this monument of fruit to recapture something of her own Oriental background—the rest of the room was so bad, so filled with the shadows of Cockney demi-mondaines and snuffbox adventures out of the Second Empire. At the four corners of the vast épergne stood four huge candelabra of silver.

Despite the air of depression given out by the monstrous room, it possessed a somber magnificence. To Ellen, the only magnificence approaching it lay in the drawing-room of that gloomy house known as Shane's Castle, set in the midst of the smoking furnaces. Aunt Julia's house was like it, filled with pictures and furniture and carpets which, like these, had been brought out of Europe.

There were wines for dinner, not one or two, but an array of port, madeira, sauterne, sherry and, at the place where Mrs. Callendar seated herself in a chair raised more than the others so that she might dominate the massive table, a pint of champagne for

herself in a tiny silver bucket filled with ice. It was a schoolgirl's dream of magnificence . . . something out of the pages of
a super-romantic novelette. In the beginning, the spectacle, proceeding through course after course, dazzled Ellen and made her
shy. It was superb food, for in the veins of Thérèse there blended
the blood of Frenchman and Greek. It was food that had a
taste . . . not the boiled stuff of Anglo-Saxons.

After dinner, when they had all gone into the dark library, the
moment came at last when Ellen's tongue was loosed. It may
have been the wine she drank or it may have been the cigarette
which, in her new freedom, she smoked over the coffee (for in a
single evening she had broken two of Clarence's rules) ; but it is
more likely that it was the picture hanging over the mantelpiece,
which changed everything.

She looked at it carefully and then said, "Is that by Turner?
My aunt has one by him."

And a moment later, under the subtle urgence of Sabine, she
was telling them everything. She described, for example, the
Town, its Mills, its desolation, the misery of the workers. She
painted for them a picture of her own family, of the Red Scot
who lay now, helpless and childish, in her own big bed. She told
them of her other grandfather, cold and aloof, who had run
away in his youth and lived in the Paris of the Second Empire,
and now existed in a room walled in by books. She recreated before their eyes the gloomy color of Shane's Castle, only to be interrupted in the midst by Thérèse Callendar, who turned to
Sabine and observed, "She is a cousin, you know, of the Madame
Shane we saw once at Madame de Cyon's in Paris. . . . You remember Madame de Cyon, the Russian woman, whose husband was
French minister to Bulgaria. . . . She lived in the Avenue du
Bois. A Bonapartist. Madame Shane was the beauty with red
hair. . . . Miss Tolliver's Aunt Julia is her mother."

And then she permitted Ellen to continue, and the girl meanwhile, even as she talked, understood that Mrs. Callendar had not

forgotten Lily. She had even fixed the place and time of their meeting. It was clear that she had been thinking of Lily, as every one did.

She told the story simply enough, but with an earnestness that was moving. To her the canvas which she painted was not remarkable, but to the listeners it appeared to hold, perhaps because it was so new to them, the fascination of a world which was utterly strange and a little exotic. They listened, moved by the simplicity of her utterance, and Richard Callendar asked her questions about the mills and furnaces, about the foreign population. The recital was a success and out of it she learned something new, —that there was nothing of such power as simplicity, nothing of such interest as individuality. She understood all that from the way in which they listened. It was the first time in all her life when she had thrown caution to the winds. She was, for an hour, her complete self.

But there was one part of the story which she did not tell. It was that part which concerned her elopement and all that had followed it. She said simply, "And so I came to New York to study, and luckily fell into the hands of Sanson. . . ."

Richard Callendar stood up suddenly and poked the fire. His mother said, "You could not have done better," and Sabine observed, "Here in New York we forget that the rest of the country exists. . . . I've never been out of New York except to go to Europe or to some summer place."

To-night, instead of being a performer, one who played in public, she was the guest, the center of the evening.

She played for them the Moonlight Sonata and while she played, she became conscious again of the curious, breathless way in which Richard Callendar listened. It seemed, for a time, that he existed only in a single spirit which somehow enveloped her and the music of Beethoven. All the evening he had been silent and watchful, as silent and as watchful as herself, save in the moment when she was carried away by her own story. When she had finished playing she was conscious of another fact, perhaps even more interesting. It was that Sabine had noticed a difference and was regarding the handsome Callendar with a look so intent that Ellen, turning sharply, caught her unaware.

This new world was a world of shadows, of hints, of insinuations, a world of curious restraints and disguises. Out of these, in the very instant she turned from the piano, she understood that the relation between Sabine and young Callendar was more than a casual friendship. Sabine was in love with him, passionately, perhaps without even knowing it, for it must have required a terrible force to lead a woman so circumspect into such a betrayal.

That night, for a second time, Ellen left the house in company with Sabine and Richard Callendar. It came about that, as they were preparing to leave, young Callendar proposed to accompany them and without further discussion entered the carriage. In the past it had been the custom to send Ellen home in the cabriolet while Callendar followed in the brougham with Sabine. Sometimes these two walked to Sabine's house. She lived in Park Avenue, a half dozen blocks away, in a tall narrow house, exceedingly stiff and formal in appearance . . . a house which one could not but say suited her admirably.

On the way, they talked music for a time and when the cabriolet approached Sabine's corner, she said simply, "I am tired. You can drop me at home."

So she bade them good night without further ado and disappeared into the narrow house. It was a strange thing for her to have done. Ellen and Callendar must have expected her to accompany them all the way to the Babylon Arms and to return alone with him; that would have been the order of things. But she was more subtle than they imagined. If she understood, as Ellen was certain she had, that there was some new thing come into the relations that existed among them all, she was clever. She did not attempt to change or even interrupt this new current; wise in the depths of her shrewd mind she saw that to be an obstacle was

not the same as to be a goal. So she left Richard Callendar with
the stranger who had become her rival. It may have caused her
sleeplessness and torment; she may have felt a keen jealousy, but
it was impossible to know. It may also have been that, knowing
the continental ideas of Callendar, she was not concerned over her
ultimate victory. By the rule of the very tradition which had
shut her in, Callender could not *marry* this stranger.

29

AS Callendar reëntered the cabriolet, Ellen settled back
into her corner to wait. She watched, as always, but
this time she was conscious that there was another who
was watching. It seemed for the first time that there had risen
up in her path a person, perhaps even an enemy, who played
the same waiting game. Callendar sat in his corner, his dark face
visible now and then as a streak of light from the lamps entered the door, and in that uncertain and shifting illumination,
Ellen studied him closely for the first time.

It was a strangely pleasing face; the very dark pallor, so
evenly distributed, so perfectly shaded caught her attention as a
kind of beauty new to her. There was no ruddiness here, no
boisterous energy. Rather it was a silent, subtle kind of beauty.
The power behind it was not so much a crude energy as a strength
that was placid yet possessed of the quality of steel. It was a
strength that revealed itself in the firm, clean line of the jaw and
in the square, almost hard modeling of the intelligent head. If
there was a hint of passion it lay in the red lips that were so full
and sensual beneath the fine black mustache. He wore the collar
of his coat turned up a little, with his hat pulled well over his eyes
so that the whole gave an impression of rakishness and adventure.
Yet her instinct told her that here was something to be feared,
something subtle and rather neat, of a sort strange to her.

They must have ridden several blocks in silence when he said to her, in a voice that was warm and carried faint traces of an accent, "I say, you are a remarkable person. I'd never dreamed how much it took to bring you where you are."

When she answered, Ellen felt a new and absurd inclination to become a helpless, almost arch, young girl. "It's nothing," she said. "I'd never thought about it."

"It was an entertaining story you gave us. . . . You see people like me and Sabine seldom get any idea of what the real world is like." He paused for a moment and then continued as if to make clear what he meant—"I mean a world in which people have to fight for things. We just have them. We forget about the others. And we're in the minority of about . . . shall we say . . . one to a thousand. I've always had what I wanted. . . . I suppose I'll always have it."

This was strange talk, in a queer philosophic vein, to which Ellen answered again, "I don't know . . . I've never thought about the difference. I know what I want and some day . . . I suppose I'll have it."

"You *are* an extraordinary musician . . . you know," he continued. "I wonder if you know how extraordinary."

Ellen did know; she was sure of it. But she saw fit not to answer because she was a little puzzled. In a world bounded by Clarence and Herman Biggs, she had not met a man of this sort. He was younger than Clarence and not much older than Herman but that made no difference. It was something that had nothing to do with age. Rather it was a matter of experience. She knew she was an excellent musician; she must have believed it or she could not have gone her own way with such unswerving directness, but she chose to answer modestly. In the dim light of the cab, it was impossible to know whether or not she actually smirked.

"Perhaps I am. How is one to know? . . . About one's self, I mean."

"My mother and I know about such things," he replied, and then for a time the cabriolet fell into silence. They turned from the avenue into the park, and presently out of his corner he spoke again.

"You're sure you told us everything to-night? You didn't leave out of the story anything that might interest us?"

There was in this an impertinence which Ellen sensed and considered for a time. He was looking out of the window at the bare trees of the park with a splendid air of indifference, which Ellen felt was not indifference at all. Far back in her consciousness an odd feeling of triumph came into existence, a queer, inexplicable feeling that she was the dominant one, that somehow she had caught him now off his guard, as if she found he was not so clever as he thought. She became aware of a genuine sense of conflict, vague and undefined, . . . a sort of conflict between her own intelligence and one that was quite as powerful. She watched the clear-cut ivory profile for a time and then said, "No, I left out nothing that could possibly interest anybody but me."

(That much for his curiosity about the little man he saw for an instant through the open door at the Babylon Arms!)

Callendar turned to her. "I sound impertinent, but I only ask because it seems to me that you are even more interesting than the story you tell."

Again this was bold and even personal, as though he sought to assume possession of that part of her which should belong to no one . . . the part which was *herself,* at which he had no right to pry. The temptation to become feminine seized her once more.

"I suppose," she said, "that that is a compliment. I thank you for it. Of course, I don't know how true it is."

"It *is* true," he replied abruptly. "You are admirable . . . and courageous. Spirit is a fine thing . . . the greatest in the world."

There was one thing for which she was thankful. He did not treat her as if she were a silly girl, as a man might, for example, have treated May Seton. In years he was not much older than herself yet in reality she understood that he was centuries older. Of that, she was certain. What she did not understand was that his approach to life, down to the veriest detail, was one which, by the nature of things, was not only alien but incomprehensible. He had patience, a quality which in her was so utterly lacking as to be inconceivable; he could wait. It was this which puzzled her . . . this and the sense of conflict, so complicated, that was always a little way off, just out of reach and not to be under-stood.

From a great distance, she watched him and even herself, confused, puzzled, but profundly interested. That much she had gained from the blood that flowed in old Gramp Tolliver's veins. She was always watching, waiting, learning.

The rest of their conversation was less interesting. It possessed, to be sure, a strange quality of leisure; there were long silences not in the least awkward and uncomfortable. On the contrary, despite that sense of conflict and watching, there was a certain calmness about them, as of the silences which fall between old friends immersed in a perfect understanding. It was perhaps the same friendliness which she neglected always to take into consideration, in which she would never quite believe.

At the Babylon Arms they passed between the Syrian Lions of cast iron and at the elevator he left her. There was no prying this time, no evidence of curiosity. As he bade her good night, he suggested that one day they might lunch together. Then the swaying elevator bore her upward to Clarence and out of sight of Callendar.

The sense of conflict disturbed her, even after Clarence came in from the Bunces', murmuring apologies for having forgotten her and stayed so late. He apologized too for having, in the enthusiasm of a pinochle game, invited the Bunces to dinner four weeks later when he had returned from his western trip.

30

Mrs. CALLENDAR stayed two months longer than usual in New York. She was kept by the only things which could have kept her away from the sunshine of her adored Cannes; that is to say, difficulties over stocks and bonds, adjustments of the Callendar fortune. She saw to it that there were no slips and no losses. Indeed, by missing the season at Cannes she turned a profit of several hundred thousand dollars which might have been lost in the hands of one in whose veins there flowed less Levantine blood.

Richard, of course, remained with her, though he exhibited a curious indifference toward the affairs which made upon his mother claims so passionate. When she reproached him, as she frequently did, he turned to her sometimes in the dark library of the house on Murray Hill and said, "My God! I'm too rich now. What should I do with any more money? Why should I worry?"

It was an attitude in which there was nothing of softness, nothing of degeneracy; it was not even the case of a son pampered by riches. His mother must have known that, better than any one, because she had encountered in him a will not unlike her own . . . a will troubled in his case by a strange restlessness born perhaps of the bizarre mixture of blood. If he was possessed of any passions they were for women, and for music, which had an effect that was amazing; it was the one thing which held the power of quieting him. There were times when he would sit motionless in the presence of music as if enchanted by it. Its effect upon him was primitive and barbaric like the hypnotism which a tom-tom exerts upon a savage.

There came a night when, as they sat alone over their coffee, estranged and a little silent after her reproaches, she turned to him and without warning said, "What about this *jeune prodige* . . . Miss Tolliver. I hear you've been lunching with her."

At this direct sally, a smile appeared slowly on the dark face of the son. It began gently at first on the sensual red lips, and then spread itself until the effect was utterly disarming. He had a way of smiling thus, after a fashion that was disconcerting because its implications were so profound, so subtle, and so filled with disillusionment. It was a smile in which the gray eyes, lighting suddenly, played a tantalizing rôle—a smile which seemed to envelop its subject and, clinging there for a time, to destroy all power of deceit by its very friendliness. It said, gently and warmly, "Come now, let's be honest and generous with each other." The red lips curved ever so gently beneath the dark mustache. It was the smile of a man born knowing much that others seldom ever learn.

He smiled at her and said, "Ah! Who could have told you that? . . . Who but Sabine . . . who knows everything?"

The very tone of his voice appeared to caress and yet mock his mother. (Sabine . . . indeed all women.) Before such an assault even Thérèse Callendar had no resistance. Shifting her plump body so that the heavy bangles on her wrists jangled and clattered, she waited a moment before answering. Then a faint blush, which appeared to arise from a real sense of guilt, spread slowly up to the edges of her bright small eyes.

"It *was* Sabine who told me," she said. "You can't blame her for that."

"No . . . she always knows everything." He laughed abruptly. "Sometimes I think she must be in communication with the birds . . . or the mice."

"You know what I think . . . I think that it's time you married. It's a responsibility . . . the money. . . . There ought to be heirs. We can't give all that money to charity or some drafty museum." While she knocked off the ashes from her cigarette, he watched her silently with the same caressing, mocking smile. "You're past twenty-five, you know. . . . I want my grandchildren to be the children of young parents. I believe in it."

Then suddenly, he pierced straight into the thing which she

had avoided mentioning. "I shan't marry Sabine," he said. "I'll find some one. I haven't found her yet."

"Sabine is excellent. She is well brought up. . . . She is rich. She is one of the few American women we know who is *mondaine*. I want you to marry an American. We need new blood. She knows her way about. She dresses superbly. . . . She will make an excellent hostess. She will be at home everywhere."

"But I am not in love with her," he said smiling.

For an instant a glint of hard anger appeared in her eyes. "You are old enough . . . or at least wise enough not to be romantic."

"It is not a question of romance, Mama. . . . It is more a question of necessity. I should prefer to be faithful to my wife."

At this speech, she clucked her tongue, and crushed out the end of her cigarette. "*Ça ne marche pas*," she observed coldly. "You can't expect me to believe such nonsense."

Thérèse was by no means innocent. She had lived in the world, always. She knew what things went on about her and, being Levantine and French, she expected even less than most women of experience. She understood that there were such things as mistresses and that most men of her world were not unacquainted with them; so she could not for a moment have supposed that her son, smiling at her in his knowing fashion, possessed a purity that was virginal. Indeed, it might be said that she knew more of his adventures than he ever supposed. Once she had scandalized Mrs. Champion by saying, "My son has an intrigue with the wife of one of my best friends in Paris. It puts me in a most uncomfortable position."

Nevertheless she had said this in a tone that implied satisfaction; the mistress of her son was, at least, a lady and not a woman of the streets. There was only one thing (she was accustomed to say) that she regarded as unforgivable; it was that he should make a fool of himself or waste great sums of money on any woman. And this, she must have known, was extremely unlikely.

After their disagreement they sat for a time in the sort of strained silence that envelops a conflict between two people of extraordinary will. It was Thérèse who, with a sudden embarrassed cough, interrupted the stillness.

"This girl . . ." she said. "I hope you're not entangling yourself with her."

Again he smiled and replied, "No, I haven't entangled myself."

"Because, it is dangerous with a girl of that sort. . . . She's an American, you know, and not the sort one finds among musicians in Paris. . . . *Autres choses*. . . . She's well brought up . . . *bourgeoisie,* I should say, of the provinces."

This time Richard laughed. "Not so *bourgeoise* as you might think."

She leaned forward a little. "That's just it!" she said. "She's not easy to win. . . . She's not the ordinary sort. She's a woman of character . . . of will." Then she moved back, folding the chubby hands, glittering with rings, on the brief expanse of her black satin lap. "No, you'd best keep clear of her. . . . Whatever happens is without my approval."

"She is interesting," the son replied. "I've never seen a woman quite like her."

This, it appeared, was the cause for new alarm. After regarding him for a time curiously, she murmured, "You can't marry her, of course. She's too inexperienced. . . . Sometimes, she's *gauche*. But that's not the chief thing. . . . If you married her, I don't think I should object . . . not very greatly. . . . It's new blood . . . healthy blood. But I advise you against thinking of such a thing. Wherever she goes, trouble will follow. She's born, like most people with a touch of genius, under a curse." He would have interrupted her here, but she checked him with a gesture of her fat hand. "She is certain to affect the lives of every one about her . . . because, well, because the threads of our lives are hopelessly tangled. Oh, don't think I'm talking nonsense or saying this to discourage you. . . . I know it. . . . I'm sure of it. . . . Marry her if you will, but don't expect happiness to come of it. She would doubtless bear you a son . . . a fine strong son because she is a fine cold animal. But don't expect any satisfaction from her. She knows too well exactly where she is bound."

During this long speech the son stood smoking silently with a shadow of the mocking smile on his lips. When she had finished he did not answer her but sat, with a thoughtful air, looking out into the garden which Thérèse this year had not bothered to have planted.

After a time she spoke again to say, "Surely you don't fancy you could ever control her. . . . She's a wild young filly. . . . No man will ever control her . . . not for long."

"I've never thought of marrying her," he replied quietly. "Why, she has a lover already."

At this Mrs. Callendar's countenance assumed an expression of passionate interest. "But she is not that sort . . . not a *demi-mondaine*. She is an honest woman . . . a cold woman. One can see that."

He smiled, this time even more softly and mockingly and into the gray eyes there came a gleam of ironical humor. "It was Sabine who said she had a lover," he said. "You remember, Miss Tolliver told us nothing of what has happened to her since she came here. . . . Besides, cold women are the most successful. They do not lose their heads."

31

IF Ellen had ever had any use for such a creature as a confidante, she would have told her no doubt that life, at this moment, was an exasperating puzzle. Between the manners of Herman Biggs and Clarence and the manners of such a man as Richard Callendar, there lay a vast gulf, a sort of blank page in the book of her experience, an hiatus that left her uneasy and disturbed.

Clarence and Herman Biggs, she understood, represented to a great degree the husband and lover of her own country. They were the ones who came seeking, the ones who idolized the object of their affections. They were, if not fascinating, affectionate and docile. They were perhaps, even convenient, so long as they did not get under foot. There was in them a certain childlike innocence, complicated alone by a Quixotic code of chivalry and honor which allowed them to be despoiled. Either they overlooked or were innocent of the ways of the world and so clung to the sentimental image of women as pure, devoted creatures who were always good and generous. There were, of course, such things as "bad women" but these did not concern them; such women were of a class apart, without any real relation to good women, a third sex one might have said, with its own uses. The women of their world had changed abruptly, swiftly, in a generation or two, from helpmates on a rude frontier adventure into creatures of luxury; and men like Herman and Clarence had not kept pace. These were the men whom Ellen had always known. There had never been any one like Richard Callendar.

In the absence of Clarence among the factories of the middle west Ellen lunched, not once, but several times with Callendar. Out of the money she had earned by her playing she was able now to dress herself in a fashion which, if not smart, was at least simple and charming. With the approach of the warm days, they lunched at Sherry's (for he made no effort to conceal his attentions) in an open window which gave out upon the Avenue and the stream of carriages, disordered now by increasing inroads of noisy automobiles. She must have understood, out of the depths of her mother's teachings, that what she did was an improper and even a dangerous thing. It was, at least, a misstep, taken through lack of experience . . . a step which later on she might not have risked.

There was Callendar himself to be considered. It was clear that, despite all her coolness, he had an effect upon her. There were times when she would blush as if suddenly overcome by a sense of his presence, for he was charming to her—gentle, understanding, full of a fire which leapt up in sudden gusts to join the flame of her own triumph and zest in living. In the window overlooking Fifth Avenue there were moments when she must have forgotten everything save the future, hours when they talked of Europe, when he described to her with something very close to passion the brilliance of Paris or the smoky glow of London. Both were naïve, Ellen in the fashion of the inexperienced and Callendar, so dark, so charming, so utterly new, in the fashion of a man whose directness of action had nothing to do with the question of conventions. It was impossible for either to have understood the emotion that drew them together, for it was a romantic thing to which both were then insensible, the one because life had taught her not to expect such a thing as romance, the other because he had never believed in its existence.

One bright afternoon in May they walked all the way from Sherry's through the park to the Babylon Arms. It was a soft day when the park appeared veritably to reflect its greenness upon the air itself, a day when the willows were softened by a haze of new leaves, and the rare clusters of cherry trees appeared in faint blurs of delicate pink. Along the edges of the lake, freed now of its burden of ice and not yet burdened anew with the old newspapers of sweltering August, the nursemaids divided the iron benches with vagabonds and old ladies who had come there simply to rest, to sit relaxed, silent, as if they were sustained somehow without effort by the very softness of the air. The quality of this pervading gentleness appeared to have its effect upon the two; for a time they were enveloped by a languor which drugged the intelligence and warmed the senses. They walked lazily, side by side, Ellen in a tight gray suit and a large picture hat, Callendar looking at her now and then out of his gray eyes and poking the fresh green grass with his malacca stick. At times they stopped and laughed, for Callendar was in a charming mood when he became a *blagueur,* irresistible and caressing. Under the influence of the day even the hardness of Ellen, which could be at times almost pitiful, appeared to melt away. She laughed at him. She even watched him slyly from the corner of her eyes, but not in the old hostile fashion. It was more the way one would watch a charming little boy, fearful lest his knowledge of the admiration might give him an advantage.

It could not have been the weather alone which so changed her. There were other things, among them beyond all doubt Callendar himself and the friendship which he had given her, the same friendship which his mother and even Sabine in her brusque, shy way had offered. They were friends in a way no one, save Lily, had ever been before. It is possible that there came to her on this soft warm day a knowledge of her kinship with these people, of a bond which if undefinable was none the less certain and secure. They had nothing to gain from her and they were not concerned with subduing her; they did not seek to change her in any way at all. They were like her old Aunt Julia and the mysterious Lily, who had warned her not to let people make her fit a pattern, not to let them drag her down to the level of their own mediocrity; she understood now what Lily meant. These were people who, by some quality of honesty that was almost a physical thing, had attained an aristocracy of their own, a state which had its foundations in that very honesty. There was, too, a distinction about them of a sort beyond such individuals as the genteel, decayed Mr. Wyck, May Seton and her giggles, Mr. Bunce who was so robust and kind, and (this thought must have occurred to her) even Clarence whose kindly humbleness barred him forever. They were not muddled; they stood outlined, for all their strangeness, with a sharp clarity.

It was an understanding that had come to her over a long time dimly as through a mist. To-day she knew it. She began to understand why there were some people whom she admired and some for whom she could have in her heart contempt or at best an emptiness that bordered upon pity.

So she walked very happily with the fascinating, dark young man, content perhaps that she might go on thus forever, that she might always have him and Sabine and Thérèse quite as they were, without any change. And in the depths of her heart it would have given her a sharp, leaping pleasure to have encountered suddenly on one of those asphalt paths May Seton and others of her townspeople. It would have pleased her to have had them witness her triumph. For she had not yet escaped the Town.

Into the midst of this a new knowledge came, sharp and unforeseen.

Under the shadow of Daniel Webster in the bronze attitude of a pouter pigeon, Callendar halted sharply and turned toward her with a swift directness, looking at her so closely that for an instant she blushed.

"Might I come in with you this afternoon?" he asked. "Will you be alone?"

Faced by the disarming gaze of the gray eyes, she forgot for a moment her game of watching. She answered, "Why, yes. I'll be alone." And then, as if she could not control herself, she looked away and started walking once more.

He did not speak again until they had reached the outer barrier of the park when he said,

"I'd like to have you play for me . . . alone. I've never heard you save in a crowd. I fancy you would play best for an audience of one."

They turned presently between the Syrian Lions of the Babylon Arms and, after being borne silently aloft in the swaying elevator, they climbed the two flights of stairs to the door of the tiny apartment which Ellen opened with her key. The room was in darkness until she lifted the shades which (on the advice of that passionate housekeeper, her mother) were drawn to protect the cheap, bright carpet from the sharp rays of the spring sun, and then the light revealed a shabby little room stuffed with the things which Clarence had bought her. There were chairs and sofas and pillows, pictures, ornaments and little tables. In one corner the grand piano stood somewhat apart in a little bay cleared of furniture. Richard, leaning on his stick and viewing the confusion gravely, must have thought her lover a poor sort, who could offer her only a great profusion of things in the poorest of taste. Yet he did not smile, perhaps because he was not greatly interested in the room. In the midst of all the stuff, Ellen, taking off her picture hat and blushing still with a hazy sense of confusion, possessed an air of aloofness, of being detached from all the shabby things. She rose above them as once before she had risen above the furniture in the Setons' dismal parlor.

The gaiety that had flourished in the bright park became dampened now by a queer sense of strain, an awkwardness which made itself apparent in the silence of both. They were no longer in the bright open park: the walls which shut them in had changed everything, sharpened in some indefinable way the power of their senses. For an instant they stood regarding each other shyly, and presently Ellen said, "Do sit down there. . . . And I'll play for you. What do you want to hear?"

Richard told her that the choice must be hers, and then he seated himself in Clarence's leather arm chair and lighted a cigarette with the matches from Clarence's smoking table in the Mission style. Without speaking again she began to play. It was as if she had said, "I will talk to you in this fashion," and after the first few chords had fallen the sense of strain and conflict disappeared, swallowed up again, this time in the man's attitude of passionate listening.

She played for him, first of all, some Schumann which was so like the shadowy, soft consciousness of this new feeling born with such abruptness there in the park; and then she played some of his beloved Chopin and turned at last into the Sonata Appassionata. She played as she played only for Fergus who listened in the same fashion, slumped down in his chair, his eyes half closed, his curling, golden hair all rumpled, with the air of one intoxicated by sound. It must have occurred to her, for the first time, that there was between her brother and this stranger a certain likeness, a capacity for wild abandonment that was terrifying. To-day all the things which for so long a time had been shut up within the walls of her bitter secrecy poured forth and overflowed into the music; and with this there was united a new fire, a sudden warmth that was strange to her. She knew a strange desire to share all that she possessed, a curious, aching desire close to the border of tears. It was so, perhaps, because love would always be to her like this . . . a wild and passionate heightening of the senses which found its manifestation in an unearthly unity of spirit. For a time she carried Richard with her into the ecstasy she was able to invoke.

And when at length the last chords drifted slowly away, they permitted the silence to remain unbroken for a long time while he sat, still slumped in his chair, his eyes half closed, watching her with the air of one on whom a spell has been cast.

He sat there in Clarence's chair in Clarence's place, magnificent like herself in all that desert of commonplace things. There was a sense of unreality about the whole scene. She must have known, deep within that hard intelligence of hers, that what she saw was at best an illusion since between them both there lay differences, circumstances, facts that were not to be overcome.

He went presently, after they had exchanged a few stupid phrases drawn by sheer force from the depths of an emotion which neither was willing to betray save by their silence. They did not even speak of another meeting; nothing happened; upon the surface their parting was strangely empty and bare. And when the door had closed behind him, Richard halted for a moment in the dark hallway and leaned against the wall. Perhaps he remembered what his mother, so old in her wisdom and so shrewd, had told him. *She's not the ordinary sort. . . . You'd best keep clear of her.*

The mocking look had gone out of his eyes. Something had happened to him, an experience that was altogether new in a life by no means limited in such matters . . . a thing which opened the fancy to a new magnificence, a new rapture, a new intoxication. It was a vision which he may have doubted because he had never believed in its existence. But between him and this wild adventure there stood a barrier against which he could make no progress. It was an invisible wall of a sort he had never encountered in any woman, not even in the terrible serenity of Sabine. Hard it was, and clear like crystal, protecting something which he might see but never touch. *She's not the ordinary sort. . . . You'd best keep clear of her.*

On the opposite side of the door Ellen flung herself down on the ugly divan and wept, silently and horribly, as she had wept once before in the dark solitude of her own virginal room, while the autumn rain drenched the garden outside. And again she could not have told why she wept. It was a passionate sensuous weeping which exhausted itself presently and left her weary and quiet until long after the lights had begun to twinkle through the smoke along the river.

Yet nothing had happened—nothing at all of which she could say, "It is this or that."

32

MEANWHILE from the Town there came to Ellen in the weekly letters of her mother bits of news which sometimes interested her but more often did not. There was the news of May Seton's marriage to Herman Biggs, an evening wedding in the Methodist church with a supper afterwards at which Skinflint Seton, in a gesture of triumph and vindication, had flung loose the purse strings and gone so far as to provide an orchestra which played behind a screen of smilax and carnations.

"Herman," wrote Hattie Tolliver, "looked a gawk, with his freckles, and May was too fat for her dress. It was cut princess fashion and trimmed with duchess lace. She carried a shower bouquet of white roses and sweet peas. Herman's trousers bagged at the knees. At least this is what Cousin Eva Barr, who went to the wedding, told me. I wasn't invited. They say that the Setons have been living on cold hash ever since.

"They went to French Lick Springs on their honeymoon and now Herman is back at the factory learning the corset business."

Miss Ogilvie had not been well lately and Aunt Julia was becoming more and more eccentric. She had shut up all but one great room at Shane's Castle and would see no one but the Doctor and Hattie Tolliver. "I go to see her three times a week. She needs some one to take hold of that great house. There's no one else, so I do it. Miss Ogilvie comes in to sit with Pa while I'm gone. She's given up some of her pupils. She says she finds she can't do as much as she once could.

"Your father is doing well at the bank and I've managed to lay aside quite a sum after the debts were paid. We'll need it to send Fergus to school. I've sold the rings that Aunt Julia gave me and we're now on the prosperous side of things once more. If your father had only listened to me, we'd have been rich to-day, but he always said he knew best, and he trusted people too much. Before long we'll have enough to come East. I want to be with my children."

Then there were inquiries after her health and Clarence's welfare and endless cautions and advice concerning the management of the flat, for distance made little difference to Hattie Tolliver when it concerned the interests of some one she loved. It was as if she ran Ellen's household as well. In one letter she was even bold enough to ask whether there was any hope of her becoming a grandmother.

Each of these letters, though it bore a great similarity to all the others, was in a sense an epic. They recorded in sentences vigorously written and crowded with a host of details, the daily history of a community. They were fiercely personal and colored by the prejudices of Hattie Tolliver. In her enemies there was nothing good and in those she loved best nothing bad. Her world was one of a savage intensity, painted like Skinflint Seton's entirely in blacks and whites.

She inquired frequently whether Clarence would be coming West, insisting that he must stop and see them in the Town and tell them all the news. And the credulous woman was put off with the story that Clarence had given up traveling and would not be in the West again for a long time. It was a lie that Ellen invented to protect him, since he was too timid ever to risk meeting any one who might recognize him as spiritual ravisher of Mrs. Herman Biggs (née May Seton).

And at length there came a letter containing the news that Grandpa Barr had died.

"He passed away," wrote Mrs. Tolliver, "quietly. I was in the room and he was just lying there looking at the ceiling and singing an old song that he used to sing when Ma was still alive and I was a little girl. They used to sing it as a duet. 'I will find my rest in the eagle's nest,' it was called, and they sang it in the long summer evenings when all the chores were done and they sat out under the trees. I can remember it well. He was humming this when suddenly he tried to sit up, and said, 'Why, Ma. . . . There you are, come to meet me. . . . I'm coming to you. . . . In just a minute, as soon as I get the little red cow in from the field by the cairn.' And then he lay back and died without another word. (It was indeed a long way from Grandpa Barr, dead now, with his memories of the frontier, to Thérèse Callendar and her carved emerald saved from the sack of Constantinople.)

"It was a good thing because he wanted to die for so long. It was hard on a man like that who had always been so active. He was like a little child. For a long time he hadn't said anything sensible. I did everything for him and I don't regret it. It was hard sometimes with so much else to worry me and take up my time.

"Aunt Julia is getting worse and worse. She can't leave her bed now and can only eat things without sugar. I make her cakes every week and custards, the kind she likes. I can't even have a holiday, because she grows restless and worse when I'm away."

And then there was a significant paragraph, brightened by a certain spice of resentment. "Gramp remains just the same . . . not a day older and just as strong as ever. It looks to me as if he'd live forever. *I don't see what I've done to bear such a cross!*"

The letters from Ellen grew steadily fewer and more unsatisfactory. With her old instinct, she wrote only of those things which were of no importance, bits of news concerning the health of Clarence and herself, comments on the heat, even stories which she had read in the newspapers. Of her unhappiness she said nothing, though it was at the moment the one thing which dominated all her existence.

After the stifled farewell on the afternoon in May Callendar appeared to vanish. Clarence returned and they gave their party for the Bunces—a party to which Mr. Wyck, somewhat uppish and deeply wretched, brought a spinister heiress from Brooklyn. They played pinochle and drank beer which the radiant Clarence brought in from a delicatessen store. Ellen, it must be said, behaved beautifully and played for them to dance until the tenant from the floor below, a retired actress with yellow hair and a white poodle, made a profane protest to the janitor. She was kind to Clarence and even affectionate, as if in some way the tenderness brought her peace.

Only once was there an unpleasantness and this occurred when Mr. Wyck, finding her alone in a corner looked at her out of his green eyes and observed, "I understand you're growing famous. I hear that you play a great deal in public . . . at fashionable parties."

For an instant, Ellen looked at him sharply and then, believing perhaps that he knew nothing, replied, "Not often . . . now and then. . . . It is profitable."

He did not address her again but sat meditating in a sour fashion, absorbed apparently in the color of the beer he held in his long soft hands, and presently, with the air of emerging from a fog of thought, he observed, "It's too bad Clarence can't enjoy the parties too."

"He would hate them," said Ellen abruptly.

This observation Wyck turned over in his mind and when he spoke again, it was with an air of confidence, of making a concession.

"No," he said, "I understand that. He wouldn't feel at home. He'd be the most miserable person there."

But the look in his eye, the soft insinuation of his voice said, without saying it, "No, you and I are different. We were made for the fashionable world."

Ellen laughed, but there was in the laugh a little sudden choke of bitterness. She came to her husband's defense. "I don't think he'd like it, but it wouldn't be on that account."

It was the most friendly conversation they had ever had, and although he did not address her again during the remainder of the evening, she was aware at odd moments that he was watching her. The sight disturbed her, perhaps because she understood vaguely that the anemic little man possessed an amazing sense of intuition. She understood too that, under the air of condescension which he observed toward the other guests, there was at work all the old hostility, heightened now by a new knowledge that had come to him from some mysterious source. It was as if she were in combat with a woman, sharp-witted and feline, over the possession of a man whom she had no desire to own. Absurdity enveloped the idea of any one fighting for possession of Clarence. He was so easy to possess.

Not even when she went to the Callendars' to play did she have a glimpse of Richard. The group had dwindled now as one by one the friends of Mrs. Callendar betook themselves into the country. There remained during the hot months only the good-natured hostess and occasionally Sabine who was staying in town until Mrs. Callendar sailed. They made excuses for Richard; they told her when she noted his absence that he was at Newport, or in Philadelphia, or vaguely that he was in the country; they kept up a little game in which Mrs. Callendar and Sabine told lies and Ellen accepted them, and both sides knew that the other had no belief in the deceit. Beyond the shrewd probing which the plump Greek woman practised on the evenings when Ellen came to dine with her alone there was no sign on either side. Yet a grayness enveloped them all, altering in its descent the whole tone of their days.

Sabine gave least evidence of the change, but with her it was impossible from her behavior ever to discover the faintest knowledge of her heart, impossible to know anything that lay behind the shield of her terrible self-possession. She had betrayed herself only once, for an instant. Beyond that one could only judge that she was waiting . . . waiting . . . waiting . . . with an overpowering patience, as if she knew the rules of the world in which she lived would give her the prize in the end. There was magnificence in the sight of her, sitting there in the evenings, marvelously dressed, not beautiful but fantastically attractive, listening quietly to the music made by a woman whom she had every reason to hate.

They all talked of the same things, in the same fashion, refusing to admit that anything had happened to change the pleasant, even way of their existence; and each knew that the other knew exactly what she knew. There were times, after dinner in the dark library, when there would be long silences broken only by the faint click of a tiny coffee cup against a saucer. Each of them watched the others, and in those long evenings the two who were so old, so wise in experience, came to respect the newcomer who played the game quite as well as themselves.

A night or two before Thérèse Callendar sailed, Ellen came to dine with her alone. Throughout the long dinner, which the Greek woman had served in the library at a small table, they kept up the game. It was not until the cigarettes and coffee were brought in that Thérèse as the servant closed the door behind him, said abruptly, "I want to talk to you about my son."

It came so suddenly, after so much waiting, that Ellen said nothing. She blushed and the tears came into her eyes. She kept silent.

"I think I know what has happened," said Mrs. Callendar. She did not speak now in her old cynical fashion, slipping quickly from one thing to another. All the evening she had been grave and now, mingled with the gravity, there was a curious warmth, a sympathy which reached out and touched Ellen. She understood, it seemed, that the matter had arrived at the point where it was necessary to go beneath the thin surface of their pretense, when she must delve under all those polished little speeches that made life move along an easy path and deal, directly, with a thing that was stronger than any of them.

"We all know," she continued softly. "We played the game very nicely, but now something must be done about it. Sabine knows it too. She's known all along and it hurts her perhaps more than any of us because she understands that in my son there are things which are beyond her control. . . ." She coughed. "For that, my dear, you are much better equipped. I hope you respect Sabine for an extraordinary woman . . . civilized. I think you might put her to torture and never succeed in making her cry out."

Ellen, sitting now with her head bowed as if she had been accused, said, "I know. . . . I know that."

"I know my own son . . ." repeated Mrs. Callendar gravely. "I know him well. We are very different in some ways . . . but I know him." Here she paused for a moment and stirred her coffee with the tiny silver spoon. "I've seen him when he fancied he was in love with a woman." She raised one plump hand and the soiled diamonds glittered darkly. "Oh, this has not been the first time. It has happened before. But this time there is a difference." She coughed and added, "This time instead of pursuing the object, he has run away from her. . . . That makes it serious."

Ellen, mute and frightened by the frankness of the older woman, sat awkwardly, like a little girl, regarding her. Surely she had never heard any one talk in quite this fashion . . . so honestly and yet so calmly. In a moment like this she had expected anger, even denunciation; she had prepared herself for it.

"I don't know what is to be done about it . . ." continued Mrs. Callendar, "because I don't know everything. . . . In a case like this, one must know everything in order to make sense. You have done something to him. I don't blame you. . . . It is simply one of those things which happens. . . . I fancy if you had not met each other as you did, you would have met in some other fashion. . . ." Her green eyes narrowed and her lips contracted so that all her plumpness appeared to shrivel and vanish. She seemed suddenly to become vastly old and wizened. "Yes, I am sure you would have met. Nothing could have kept you apart." And then, plump and kindly once more, she said, "I don't know what it is you have done to him. I don't fancy he knows himself, but he's miserable. . . . You see, the trouble is that he is really romantic . . . just as I am romantic . . . and he's always pretended he was an experienced, cynical *homme du monde*. . . . In that one thing he is dishonest."

She reached over and in an unexpected gesture touched the hand of the girl so that Ellen, taken unaware by this movement of sympathy, began to cry softly.

"I *am* romantic," said Mrs. Callendar softly, "though you might not believe it. Listen!" She leaned forward. "Listen! I'll tell you a story about myself and you'll see. You'll understand then perhaps that I have sympathy enough to be of use in this matter . . . because in a time of this sort, it's sympathy that's needed more than anything else."

And then she settled back and between puffs on her cigarette related bit by bit, from the very beginning, the romantic story of her elopement with Richard Callendar's father. She told the story with an Oriental sense of color, and slowly before the eyes of the girl she recreated the color of Constantinople in her youth, all the magic of the summer palace and the Bosphorus by moonlight, all the desolation of the Greek aunts, all the crafty manner of the rich old Dikran Leopopulos, and above all the somber glow of the love she had known for the blond and handsome young American. Under the spell of her own tale she began to speak half in French, half in English, but Ellen, listening, became so caught up in the magic of the story that she understood it all, even those things which Thérèse Callendar related in an alien tongue. The tale set fire to a vein of warmth in the girl which until now had gone undiscovered, save only at times when, lost in her music, it had emerged translated into a beauty of sound. For the moment even the plump Greek woman herself appeared no longer to be old and ugly and covered with diamonds in need of cleaning. In the fervor of her story, she attained for a passing instant the quality of youth and of a fleeting beauty out of the Levant.

And when she had finished, she leaned back and said, with a wicked chuckle, "*Voyez.* I am ugly now and fat. But I was not then." Then she sighed quickly and looked down at her rings. "You see the thing is that he died . . . he was drowned before we had been married two years."

Again Ellen kept silent. There was nothing for her to say that would not have been trivial and idiotic. She waited and presently Thérèse said, "You see, I can understand. . . . I wanted you to know that. . . . One would have said that he and I were separated by a thousand things. None of them made the least difference."

It was Ellen who in the end interrupted the strange, breathless silence which enveloped them at the conclusion of Thérèse's story. She murmured, "It was nothing that I meant to do. . . . It happened. . . . I don't know how. . . . It happened without either of us saying anything. It was," (she groped for the words and collapsed into banality), "It was like a flash of lightning."

"It would be," said Thérèse, "with him. I don't believe he understands what it is."

"And I haven't seen him since."

"He has never spoken a word of it. . . . Always he tells me." Something of the girl's awkwardness had vanished now, and between them there was a sense of a sympathy that had not before existed. It was the manner now of two women who were confidants.

"There is nothing I can do," said Ellen, "nothing. It is hopeless."

"You were a brave girl to go on coming here."

A flash of Ellen's old spirit returned as she said, "What could I do? Running away helped nothing. . . . It's hard because I have had no one to speak to . . . no one I could talk it over with. . . . You see, I am really alone. . . . It never mattered before. . . . I mean . . . the loneliness."

They faced each other, two women, each possessed of intelligence and honesty, striving to discover some way out of the tangle in which they were caught. Being wise, they knew perhaps the uselessness of violence. They waited, each knowing well enough that there was much more concerned than simple romance. Thérèse knew, no doubt, that the young woman who, stripped now of her fierce secrecy, sat opposite her, frightened and tearful, was not simply an adventuress seeking to gain a husband and a vast fortune. She knew, too, how much these things would have meant to the girl, and she understood well enough that Ellen, face to face with an unaccustomed tangle, lacked the experience which could have helped her.

On Ellen's side, she must have been conscious of facing a mystery. The plump woman, covered with dirty diamonds, was her friend, yet, despite her kindliness, she was remote, separated from her by differences of blood, of tradition, of a million things. She was as remote, as beyond comprehension in the subtlety of her wise, old mind as her dark son, even in the moments when he was most disarming. Her own people Ellen might battle and overthrow, but these were different. She could not even fathom the woman's friendliness.

"I am not a cheap adventuress," she repeated. "Don't believe that."

"My dear girl, I am not such a fool. . . . I was not born yesterday. . . . I have dealt with women of that sort."

"You see," said Ellen, folding and refolding her handkerchief like a little girl, "I am quite alone. . . . I looked on him as a friend . . . as I might look on my own brother. . . . I never thought of such a thing."

At this Mrs. Callendar made a clucking noise and bowed her head for a time in thought. At last she said, "Ah, but that is where the trouble lay! That is where you were wrong! . . . Such a thing is not possible with him. . . . There is acquaintance and the next step is the other thing. He is not, after all, like your American men."

Ellen looked up now and ceased to plait the handkerchief. "I can see that . . ." she said. "I've learned a great deal. I've thought of nothing else for weeks. . . . It frightens me because I can't stop thinking of it when I want to . . . not even at night. There's never been anything like it before." She looked directly at Mrs. Callendar. "Could I talk to you . . . ? Could I tell you the truth?"

"My dear, it is the only way we shall arrive anywhere."

"I've got to tell some one . . . I've thought and thought about the whole thing. I don't know what it is he wants of me. He has never said anything. . . . We have never even mentioned it." She smiled faintly. "Perhaps I am a fool and silly. We've never mentioned it in any way. . . ."

Mrs. Callendar interrupted her. "Ah, but that's it. That's what makes it serious. . . ."

"Perhaps I'm talking of something that doesn't exist."

"Oh, it exists all right." Thérèse knocked the ash from her

cigarette. "You would know it if you had seen him." She
turned sharply to Ellen. "Why do you think he is avoiding you?
It's not because he regards you as a virgin not to be defiled. It's
himself he's thinking of too."

"But there is nothing to be done. . . . Nothing can be done."

"Do you love him?"

Ellen smiled again. "How should I know that? I've not been
in love a hundred times. I had never met anything like this. I
had my whole life planned, perfectly, to the very end. I don't
know what's to happen now."

Before she answered Mrs. Callendar sighed. "If there is
enough of love, anything is possible." She raised her plump hand.
"Oh, I'm not being a romantic fool. I only mean that if there
is enough of passion . . . If you believe that it is the greatest
thing of all, worth all else in the world, then take what life can
give you. Let nothing stop you. It will come to an end soon
enough and you will be unhappy, but you must understand
that in the beginning. If you are to have remorse, have it before
you act and be done with it. . . . That is the only rule for intelligent people, and they are after all the only ones who dare
know such a rule."

For a time Ellen sat quietly regarding the floor, lost in consideration of all her companion had said. It was a bewildering
speech and colossally unmoral. She must have thought, then or
later, of the vast distance which separated the girl who sat in
Mrs. Callendar's drawing-room from the girl who sat on Hattie
Tolliver's knee the night that Jimmy Seton rang the bell and
brought Clarence into her life; yet she had only gone a little way.
Turning the speech of Mrs. Callendar over and over in her mind,
she became aware that it savored curiously of Lily. It was a consciousness always present, an awareness of Lily's charm, her
beauty, her curious soft independence, the beauty, the talk, the
scandal that centered about her. . . . If Hattie Tolliver could
have known it, the influence of wicked Lily was stronger at that

moment than it had ever been. Out of all the talk, the experience, the sorrow, Lily was emerging slowly from the well of mystery that engulfed her.

"It is impossible," said Ellen slowly, "because I could not marry him." She hesitated for a moment and then added in a whisper, "I have a husband already. . . . I've never told any one."

She began to weep once more, gently and wearily, while Mrs. Callendar, poised and remote in black satin and diamonds, regarded her with an expression of astonishment.

At last the older woman said, "You should have told me this. It changes everything. Sabine told me that you had a lover . . . that she had seen him at your flat."

"That was my husband."

"You never spoke of him, so we had nothing else to believe." She smiled suddenly and touched Ellen's hand once more. "I was right then. I did not believe it possible."

Ellen looked at her silently, in amazement. "But you had me to your house, as a friend. How could you have done that when you thought me a woman of that sort?"

Across the gulf that separated them, Mrs. Callendar laughed and said, "But that would have made no difference. I learned long ago not to be concerned with the morals of my friends. You are what you are and I like you, my dear, whether you had one lover or fifty, except that if you had had fifty I should have known you to be a woman of no taste." She paused and lighted another cigarette out of the box she had sent her from Constantinople. "I had no idea," she continued thoughtfully, "how wide the difference was. . . . Besides, you are a musician . . . an artist. One does not require of an artist the morals of the *bourgeoisie*. One expects such things. It is so because it is so, and there's an end to it." She puffed for a time, slowly, lost in thought, and then added in a kind of postscript. "My poor girl! What a lot you have not learned! You will not be free until you do what you see fit . . . regardless of any one."

And now Ellen found herself once more where she had begun. In all their talk they had arrived after all nowhere, because they had been talking all the while of two different things. Mrs. Callendar, conscious perhaps of the hopelessness of the muddle, rose and began to walk slowly up and down the room, an absurd and untragic figure, plump and much laced but energetic and clever. After a time she came and stood by Ellen's chair.

"I take it then," she said, "that you do not love your husband."

"I don't know," Ellen replied dully, "I don't know. It is nothing like this new thing . . . nothing at all. I am sorry for him. Perhaps that is it."

"It is a match then that your parents made?"

"No. . . . It is not that. . . . It's quite different. . . ." She hesitated for a moment and then said in a low voice, "I ran away with him. . . . I eloped. It was not because I loved him. It was because I had to escape. I wanted to be a musician. . . . I wanted to be great. Lately I have thought sometimes I was only a fool . . . that I have only confused and ruined everything."

This Mrs. Callendar pondered for a time, returning to her chair and lighting another cigarette before she spoke. "And why do you pity him?" she asked presently.

"It is because he is so good and so humble. I am afraid of hurting him. He has been good to me and generous. It is almost worse than if I had loved him. . . . Don't you see?"

"You would not divorce him?" asked Mrs. Callendar.

"No," Ellen cried suddenly. "No, I could not do that. . . . I couldn't. . . ."

"And you would not run away from him?"

"It is the same thing in the end. . . . It would hurt him. It might kill him. . . . He's such a good man . . . so kind, so helpless. He wants me to love him always. . . . He's done everything he could for me . . . everything and more than he is able to do. You see. I told you there was nothing to be done."

"No," said Mrs. Callendar slowly, "I'm afraid there is nothing to be done. . . ." Again she rose from her chair and walked over to the window. "You had best think it over." She turned and faced Ellen. "I will talk to Richard. I will not sail to-morrow. I will stay. It must be settled somehow, for the sake of all of us. . . . I have not forgotten Sabine. She must be considered."

33

It was long after midnight when Ellen, entering the cabriolet at last, was driven off by the impatient Wilkes to the Babylon Arms. When she arrived, she found Clarence in the lower hall pacing up and down with a pitiful air of anxiety.

"I should have telephoned," she said, "but I forgot. I did not know how late it was. You see we talked for a long time afterward."

And then she kissed him gently, swept again by the old sense of pity. During all the drive home, in the long moments when she had been alone in the dark cabriolet, she had struggled, bitterly, with the puzzle that confronted her, knowing always in the back of her mind that whatever happened she could never run away with Richard Callendar. She might fall ill, she might die, she might go mad, but there were some things which she could not do. Deep down in her heart there was a force that was quite beyond her, a power that was an instinct, as much a physical thing as her very arms and hands. It was the part of her that was Hattie Tolliver.

There had been the other way out, but when she kissed Clarence she knew that it too was impossible. When she saw him waiting, his eyes wild with anxiety, his whole face suddenly lighted up with joy and adoration at sight of her, she knew too that she could never divorce him. His very weakness destroyed her, for she knew that if she had asked him he would have freed her. There was nothing that he would deny her . . . nothing that he was able to give; and what she wanted from him, he would never be able to give because he was, after all, only a poor thing.

But the hardest part of the ordeal lay before her. It was the meeting with Callendar when, for the first time, they would both be forced to recognize the truth and deny it, forever. She understood this well enough; she was in a way even eager to have it occur at once so that she might put the memory of it behind her, so that she might stamp out the incident forever and go on her triumphant way. It came at last when Callendar, in a brief note, asked if he might call upon her. The letter, in a headlong handwriting so unlike the mocking cynicism which he cultivated, gave no hint of what was in his mind. It asked merely that she set a time and place.

She bade him come to the apartment in the Babylon Arms and he came, strangely sobered and quiet, with a chastened look in his gray eyes. At sight of him he appeared to her, as it seemed long afterward, for the first time in any semblance of reality; he existed with a new clarity, a new distinctness of outline. It was as if she had never seen him rightly before, as if until now he had been to her some one whom she accepted vaguely without questioning. Only one quality carried over completely into the new Callendar; it was the old sense of conflict, of will against will, of a pleasurable, almost perverse sensation of struggle. The new Callendar was an older man in a fashion she could not altogether define, save that the impression was related to the effect which his mother had upon her, of weakening and diminishing all reliance in herself.

The first thing she said to him was, "I am frightened."

He took off his hat and laid it quietly on the divan by the side of his stick and then he turned and looking at her with his strange gray eyes, replied, "I too am frightened."

Among the cheap furniture that crowded the room the old sense of his superiority returned to her, mingled this time with a new consciousness that he was utterly alien, stranger than she had ever imagined until now. She sat down quietly while he drew a chair to her side.

"I've talked to my mother," he said. "Or rather she talked to me. She's told me everything."

Under the gaze of the gray eyes, Ellen turned aside, discomfited, wretched. "I wasn't honest," she murmured. "I'm sorry, but I hadn't meant to be dishonest. I never thought it would make the least difference to any one."

"It has made a difference though . . . a great difference. It's changed everything." He reached over with a tenderness that suddenly weakened her and took one of her hands in his. She knew his hands; she knew them as she had known Clarence's on the night in the Setons' parlor when she had judged him nice enough but a bit of a prig. Callendar's hands were slender, dark and strong, beautifully shaped in a way that made her fear them. When they approached her, she became weak; she felt that she was losing herself. She could not have explained the feeling save by a sense she had of their power. He was talking again, softly in the low voice with the thin trace of an accent, like Lily's.

"I was foolish," he was saying. "I should have known that the thing which made me afraid of you was the thing that would have kept you from taking a lover. I'd never encountered anything quite like it before." He smiled and touched his mustache gently. "I was a fool. I should have known better. I thought perhaps you would love me some time . . . not without a struggle. No, I never expected that. I thought we might understand each other. . . ." For an instant the incredible happened. Callendar was blushing. It was a thing which she had not seen happen before. "I thought that one day we should come together. . . . I thought you were an artist, living as artists I have known do live. I was idiotic. I should have known better. You'll forgive me that . . . won't you?"

For a moment she did not answer. The sound of his soft voice, the touch of the dark hands, had taken possession of her. Dimly she knew that she should have been insulted, yet she had no feeling at all, no sense of indignation; there was only a curious faintness that made her afraid. Somehow she understood that all this in reality had nothing to do with insults, with conventions, even with laws. It was something which might never again come her way and yet something which was to be feared, because it might destroy her forever. At last she said, "Why should I forgive you? It would make no difference now. . . ."

"It would make a difference. . . . It would make a difference," he said quickly. "I want you to marry me. . . . We can arrange everything. It makes no difference how." And then after a sharp silence, he added in a low voice, "There is a magnificence about you, . . . a bravery . . ." And the rest of the sentence trailed away so that she did not hear it.

Out of a great depth as if by a great physical effort she returned into the daylight. She found her lips moving. She found herself saying over and over again, "I must remember. . . . I must remember. . . . I must not ruin everything." He had never even asked whether she loved him. He had accepted it as a fact. He had asked her nothing. He had come simply to take her.

Then she withdrew her hand slowly and sat staring at it with an air of looking at some object unfamiliar to her. "I can't marry you," she said slowly. "I can't. . . . I can't. . . . There is nothing to be done. . . . There is nothing to be done." And she began to cry silently, so that the tears fell down upon her hands.

The speech appeared to astonish him, for he made no effort to regain her hand but sat staring at her as at a stranger. When at last he spoke it was in a voice that was low and caressing, but the tenderness had slipped away and in its place there was a hardness, as of steel; it was like a sudden glimpse of claws emerging from a soft and furry paw.

"Is it because you won't give him up," he asked, "as you told my mother?"

"It is because I cannot give him up. . . . I cannot treat him that way. . . . I cannot . . . cannot."

The steel in the voice emerged a little more sharply. There was an edge to it now, sarcastic, cutting. "Is it because he is so fine . . . so handsome . . . so magnificent . . . so dazzling?"

He repeated thus all the things that Clarence was not, and so he gave her the last bit of strength that she required, for the sound of his voice, the sharp edge of the sarcasm, filled her with a sudden anger and a wild desire to protect Clarence as something which was her own. She found herself fighting for a man who was none of these things against a man who to her was all of them. It struck somehow at her sense of gallantry . . . that Callendar who had everything should sneer at poor Clarence who had nothing.

She said, "It has nothing to do with that. . . . There are some things that one cannot do. . . . This I will not do." She dried her eyes and sat more erectly. "There is no use. . . . There was no use in your coming here. . . . My mind was made up . . . long before you came."

At this he turned angry. "You are like all your women. . . . Love to you is nothing. . . . It is something to be controlled. You don't know what love is. . . . You would exploit it. . . . You are like all your women."

So he talked thus for a time in a childish vein strange and new while she sat impassive, conscious all the while of the power he could exert over her, a power that had to do with the beauty of his hands, with the strange quality of his eyes, with the sound of his voice, with the soft catlike way in which he moved; yet she remained in some mysterious way safe from that power. It was, perhaps, her intelligence which saved her, for as she watched him she gained slowly a curious intuition of what he might do to her if she yielded. The old sense of conflict was fanned into a new life, more intense than it had ever been. He sought to overpower her will. She knew all at once that this was the very essence of his confused, unreasonable emotion.

And as she listened to him her woman's instinct for the dramatic came to her aid. She saw herself sitting there calm and a little cold, slowly but surely winning in the battle. She listened to his abuse. It did not enrage her. It did not even make her weep. It seemed rather to increase her coldness, her very strength. She felt him beating against the wall of her serenity and a kind of fierce triumph flowed through her body. For a time she possessed truly a great magnificence. At a little distance, she stood outside herself and watched the spectacle. She saw him standing by her, white with anger.

"You have lied to me. . . ." he was saying. "You have never cared at all. . . ." And again the reproach. "You are like all your women . . . cold . . . magnificent . . . not worthy of love." He came nearer to her. "I will love you. . . . I will teach you what love can be. . . . What does he know of love . . . ? Nothing. . . . I will give you a happiness such as you never dreamed of. . . . I . . . I am a lover. . . . I know these things."

And then he went down suddenly upon his knees, the steel gone swiftly from his voice; the warmth and tenderness flowing back. "You will not refuse me." He leaned forward and pressed his head against her. "You cannot. . . . I will give you everything . . . all the things which he cannot give you. . . ." And again he took her hands and this time kissed them passionately in a fashion that frightened her and filled her with the old weakness.

The spectacle of his humility, of this sudden collapse of what to her was his dignity, his will, his strength, astonished and embarrassed her. In her coldness it seemed to her incredible that any woman, least of all herself, should possess such power over any man. It was all unreal, beyond belief, and yet it fed her pride and gave her strength with which, one might have said, to destroy her own happiness, to resist the force of circumstances, even of nature, as she had defied it once before in marrying Clarence.

At last he rested his head against her knee and she bent over him, touching his dark hair with gentle fingers.

"Don't," she said. "Don't. . . . Please don't. . . . It is no good. I know better than you. . . . I should always be thinking of him. . . . I should never be happy, so neither of us could be happy. There are some things which I cannot do . . . and this is one. It is impossible."

They said nothing more. Richard remained kneeling with his head against her knees and slowly the old peace which she had not known in months took possession of her, heightened now by a new knowledge of her completeness and power. It was a kind of satisfaction which was new to her, an emotion which was heady and intoxicating. She was uplifted, free now of Callendar, free of Clarence, free of everything in all the world . . . alone, liberated, triumphant. She had defeated them all. And when he turned toward her for the last time there was a look in her eyes which said, "Is is no use. You need have no hope. It can never be."

On leaving, he kissed her hand, gently this time as if the passion had gone out of him. All he said was, "I shall do then what they expect of me. Some day you may wish for what you have thrown away. . . . I don't imagine a thing like this happens every day."

He was polite but, like herself, he was unbroken. He appeared to have regained possession of himself, to have become cold and calm and even a trifle indifferent. That was all he said and when he had gone the sight of his back, so slim, so strong, so inscrutable, filled her with a sudden weakness, for she knew that she had closed the door not alone upon Callendar but upon his mother, upon Sabine, upon the big house on Murray Hill, upon all that she had built up with such terrible patience.

He did what was expected of him. In a fortnight there appeared in the newspapers an announcement of the engagement of Richard Callendar to Sabine Cane. It described the great fortune of the prospective bridegroom and enlarged upon the social position of the happy couple. On the same day there was a paragraph

apprising the world of the fact that Thérèse Callendar had sailed
as usual to spend the remainder of the year abroad. But there
was nothing said of the girl whom the world had seen lunching
with Richard Callendar in Sherry's.   She was talked of, to be sure,
in the circles in which Mrs. Champion and the Virgins, Mrs.
Mallinson and the Apostle to the Genteel, were shining lights.
They agreed that it must have been the clever Thérèse who disposed of the girl (perhaps paid her well) and made the match she
desired; and they predicted with some satisfaction an unhappy life
for Sabine.   But Sabine in the end had won her game of patience,
though she never knew the reason.

34

IT was in the weeks which followed the final meeting that
Ellen came really to suffer. Together there in the shabby
little room she had been sustained by the very struggle between them, by all the excitement that warmed and strengthened
her. Now that he was gone forever, he kept returning to her in
a fashion more terrifying than he had ever been in the flesh.
Even at night when she lay in the apple green bed, so near and
yet remote from Clarence, trying always to conceal from him the
faintest suspicion, she could not free her memory from the sound
of his voice and the persuasion of his hands. The memory of him
haunted her, so that she grew pale and thin and Clarence, filled as
always with nervous anxiety, urged her to go away into the country. In moments of depression she even reproached herself with
being a fool for having thrown away what Callendar could have
given her . . . his wealth, which she needed, the place which he
could have given her in the world. Indeed when life seemed
altogether hopeless, she went so far as to contemplate a return to
the Town, a thing she had sworn never to do save in triumph.
Clarence, understanding dimly that she was unhappy, sought to
help her with a kindness that hurt her more deeply than any

cruelty could have done. There were nights when he lay awake
listening until the gray light appeared over the river and the
sound of her regular breathing told him that at last she was asleep.
Beneath the strain he too became pale and thin. His nose grew
more pointed and his little round shoulders more and more stooped.
In the mornings when Ellen, busy over his breakfast, caught rare
glimpses of him, as he patiently did his exercises on the floor of
the bath room, she was smitten with the old sense of pity at
the thinness of his poor body. It hurt her in a fierce way because
it was so different from the catlike suppleness of the man who was
gone now forever. It was the valiant quality in Clarence, the
struggle to be worthy of her, to make her always love him that
made her helpless. Until now she had never clearly understood
the power he had over her. It was the terrible power which the
weak have over the strong.

It proved a hot, breathless summer when the asphalt turned
spongy and the carriage wheels left great ruts and ridges. Even on
the top floor of the Babylon Arms there was no coolness save on the
rare nights when the wind, blowing up the river from the free
and open sea, penetrated the high windows. It became more and
more difficult too when Clarence came to her one evening and
said, "I'm sorry dear, but we must economize. I find that we
have been living beyond our income."

He said it so meekly, so apologetically and he looked so weary
that she kissed him and replied, "I have money saved . . . money
that I earned this winter. We can use that if we're in a tight
place."

But he refused it. He assured her that there was no such deep
necessity. He would not, he said, take anything she earned. He
must support them always. And when she told him that this was
absurd, he straightened himself and grew indignant.

"I couldn't do that," he said. "If you'll give me time, we'll
be rich one day. . . . I'm getting ahead. It's not easy. There's
so much competition. Don't think I'm a failure." He took her

hand and pressed it savagely. "You won't think that . . . will you? . . . Just be patient and give me time. I'll be rich some day."

Time! Time! She knew then what she had always known—that time would make no difference with Clarence. There was no way out. Whatever was to be done, she must do it herself. The old passion swept her. She would not sink. She would not yield to circumstance. She would die rather than fail!

35

WHEN Fergus came in early September to make his home in the little flat atop the Babylon Arms, the strain, the weariness, the very heat itself appeared for a time to dissipate. He was, of course, a novelty. Into an existence which had become flat and stale through the long routine of petty things, into a monotony which even the energy of Ellen was unable to dissipate, the brother carried a sense of excitement. At seventeen he bore a resemblance to his father, but only in a physical sense, for there was more dash, more vitality in him than there had ever been in Charles Tolliver. Tall, with wide shoulders and blue eyes that looked out from beneath sensuous drooping lids, he possessed the same blond charm which in Charles Tolliver's youth had made the vigorous Hattie Barr his slave. In the son there was even the same echo of that quality which the world, in its stupidity, called weakness and which was not weakness at all. The boy as yet was too young to understand what it was; the father, long past middle age, knew that it was a precious gift, a quality which protected him against the pettiness of the same stupid world. It was a disarming tolerance and geniality that made him friend alike to every one, beggar or prince, who passed his way. Father or son would have been at home in any part of the world; they would have found friends among the Lapps as easily as among the farmers of their own county; the Moros would have received them as honored comrades. It was a quality that transcended limitations of family, of nationality, of race; it was a simple friendliness. And in their way they loved life as passionately as Ellen and Hattie Tolliver; the difference lay in the fact that their joy was a warm, glowing, steady emotion less spectacular and vivid.

It was Clarence who suffered the first onslaught of the brother's charm, for Fergus arrived to find his brother-in-law lying in one of the green beds, alone in the flat. Carrying bundles of luggage carefully prepared by the hand of Hattie, he burst into the room and came suddenly upon Clarence, asleep beneath the blankets, his mouth open a little way, his face a shade near to the green of the painted beds. Asleep and off his guard, Clarence was not a spirited picture. Fergus could not have remembered him distinctly, for he had seen him but twice and then long ago in the days when he was courting May Seton. More than three years had passed and Fergus, standing now at the foot of the bed, big and placid and blond, regarded his brother-in-law with the air of a stranger. Clarence slept quietly; his narrow nose appeared more pinched than it had been; the brown tousled hair had thinned until at the back of his head there appeared a tiny island that was entirely bald. The nervous, knotty hands lay outside the cover, pale and covered with pallid skin that was transparent and showed beneath it a network of tiny blue veins.

If Ellen had come in that moment, her brother, in his naïve honesty, might have turned to her and asked, "What have you done to him?" But she did not come and, as he turned to leave the room, Clarence stirred and opened his eyes. Out of the depths of his sleep he emerged painfully, leaning for an instant on one elbow and staring silently in reply to the cheery "Hello" of Fergus.

"It's me—Fergus," said the boy. "I just came in."

Again Clarence stared for a time and then murmured slowly. "Oh! yes. It's you! . . . I didn't recognize you at first. . . . I was having a dream . . . a bad dream. Won't you sit down?"

It was a stiff greeting, somewhat awkward, not because the boy was unwelcome but because Clarence, who would have welcomed the devil himself for the sake of his wife, was ill at ease. It may have been the dream that disturbed him.

Fergus pulled up a chair beside the bed, and asked if his brother-in-law were ill.

"It's nothing," was the answer. "It's just a bilious attack. I have them every now and then. . . . I'll be over it in a day or two."

Then he lay back once more, wearily, and asked Fergus about his trip and about his mother and father and the people in the Town—all save the Setons. They made polite conversation to each other and Clarence, beneath the spell of the boy's friendliness, melted a little so that the stiffness presently slipped away. But after a time the conversation for want of interest died back into silence and Fergus went to the window to feast his young eyes on the panorama of the river and the great city into which he had escaped. The boy was happy with an animal sort of joy which showed itself in the very lines of his tall body, in the brightness of his blue eyes. He too was free now, a rover, attached to nothing.

"It's a great place," he said presently, and turning from the window, added, "I think I'll get settled. . . . Where do I hang out?"

He had picked up his hat before Clarence said, "Wait. . . . There's something I want to talk to you about. . . . Just a minute." And then humbly after a pause: "It won't be long."

So the boy seated himself again and waited while Clarence sat up in bed, looking thin and worried in his mauve pajamas, and, after coughing nervously, said, "It's about Ellen. . . . You know her better than I do. . . . I've lived with her for three years but she's more like you. . . . She's not like me, at all."

Fergus stirred nervously and blushed a little, perhaps in doubt of what Clarence was to say.

"It's about Ellen," Clarence repeated, looking down at the quilt. "I don't think she's happy and I don't know what to do about it."

The boy laughed. "Oh, she's always like that. . . . It doesn't mean anything. She used to be cross with us at home most of the time." He knew Ellen well enough. She was a cross, bad-tempered girl whom you could control if you understood the method.

"I don't mean that. . . . I've known her when she's like that. . . . This is different." He halted for a moment and fell to tracing the design on the quilt with his thin finger. He was thinking, thinking, trying to explain. "No, it's not like that," he said presently. "It's worse than that. She never complains. . . . She never says anything. Only it doesn't go away. . . . It hangs . . . like a cloud. I'm not meaning to complain about her. . . . It's my fault if it's any one's. . . . But she's sad now . . . in spite of anything I can do." And then he added painfully, "She's unhappy."

Fergus waited. He sat with the air of a man desiring to escape, as if he would in some way repel these confidences and force Clarence into silence. He hated confidences, sorrow, trouble, of any sort. But Clarence was not to be silenced. He even grew a little excited.

"You see, the trouble goes back farther than that. . . . I can't explain it. . . . I don't know how. . . . Only she's never belonged to me at all. She's always escaping me. . . . And I try and try."

"It's her music," repeated Fergus. "She's crazy about it. . . . She always has been." Sitting there he seemed the symbol of a youth which could have no belief in disaster. He would never be hurt as Clarence was being hurt.

Clarence, ignoring the interruption, continued. "I married her and she's my wife. . . . She's a good wife and she does everything for me. . . . She never refuses me anything. . . ." He coughed and, looking down, added, "Not even herself."

The color in Fergus' cheeks flamed out now. He too became ill at ease.

"Don't think," said Clarence, "that I mean to complain. It's all my fault. A man ought to be able to make his wife happy. . . . I've tried hard. I've tried to make money. I'm good to her . . . but . . ." He trailed into silence for a time and when he returned it was easy to say, "But somehow she escapes me always. . . . There's something in her that doesn't belong to me. I don't know what it is because I've never been able to discover it. . . . And you can't talk to her about such things. . . . I've tried. Once I got almost to the point and she said, 'Don't worry, Clarence. You mustn't take things so seriously. . . . I'm all right. Don't think about me.' But I can't help thinking, because when she's unhappy I am too, because I love her so much. I'd do anything for her."

He lay back and fell to regarding the ceiling. Fergus, in silence, watched him now with a look of intense curiosity. Perhaps he guessed what it was Ellen had done to him. Perhaps he realized that, without knowing it, he had himself come to look upon Clarence in the same fashion that his sister regarded him . . . as a nice, kind, good man whom one tolerated. He was older and paler and more insignificant than he had been in the days when he courted May Seton. What the man needed perhaps was some one—a wife—who would lean upon him, who would think him a wonderful creature. And instead of that he had Ellen. Clarence rose on one elbow and said slowly, "But don't tell her. . . . Don't say I spoke of it."

It was the end of their talk. They never mentioned the thing again, but in some way the conversation appeared to bring Clarence a kind of dumb relief.

Of course, there were things that Fergus could not have known. He could not have known—Fergus, who took life so lightly—that the little man's only experience with love had been Ellen. He could not have known that Clarence was the victim of a sensual nature placed by some ironic trick of fate in the body of a prig.

He could not have known that the man was the victim of that little vein, so amusing to Lily, which with the march of the years beat less and less passionately. He could not have known that Clarence had discovered love in the body of Ellen and was now love's victim—that he was being destroyed because he had never known, even now, what love might be.

Of this secret Fergus said nothing to Ellen, perhaps because Clarence had asked him to keep silence and perhaps because he came to understand in the succeeding days that in her present mood, it would serve only to increase the strain. It was not until years afterward that he broke his silence and wrote her that he had known from the first day how matters stood. In his good-natured way, he sought rather to drive away the mood entirely. During the remainder of the week, while Clarence lay in bed, the brother and sister made excursions together into various parts of the city and Ellen, for a little time, grew again eager and filled with the old restless energy. They understood each other, this pair, in a miraculous fashion, though they were in many ways so different. They looked upon the world in the same way, as a great pie from which plums are to be wrested. They knew the same delights of being free and alone, the strange joy of being a part of a vast spectacle from which they were, at the same time, curiously aloof. For neither of them did the past exist. They lived wholly in the future. If there was a difference it lay in this—that Fergus looked upon the future as a land filled with a host of careless delights; to Ellen the future was a country in which lay the rewards of fame, of wealth, of vindication. She would force those who had mocked to bend their knees. As for these, Fergus never even thought of them. The world to him was a friendly place.

He began presently to attend his classes. Clarence recovered and returned to the offices of the Superba Electrical Company, and Ellen, pondering secret plans for the expedition to Paris and Lily, returned to her endless practising. In the evenings she played magnificently, for she had now a superb audience in the person of

Fergus who, sprawling on the divan with his eyes closed, listened to her in a sensual abandonment. There were times when it must have seemed to her that Callender had returned and listened. The old likeness, so elusive, so indefinable, came to live again in the long evenings. She could not say what it was, save that they both possessed a wildness not to be hindered by ambition or restraint or even laws. They were both among those who were born free.

But as the month of October advanced, a depression appeared slowly to envelope her. To Fergus the change became apparent and to Clarence it was acute. She betrayed herself by no single thought or action; it was far less simple and direct. Outwardly she went through the old motions of living. Sometimes in the autumn evenings when the husband and the brother sat listening to her music, Clarence would turn his pale eyes toward Fergus with a look which said, "You see what I mean? What am I to do?" The grayness trapped them all, even the genial, careless boy.

In the hours when she was alone, she did things which might have betrayed her, had they been known. Instead of spending the long hours at her piano she walked for miles, sometimes along the river, sometimes in the park. And she developed a new interest in newspapers, an interest which centered itself upon the columns setting forth the doings in the world of the rich and fashionable. From these she learned that Thérèse Callendar and her son had returned from abroad, bringing with them Sabine and a trousseau which cost fabulous sums. She discovered that the wedding party was not to be in Sabine's narrow house (it was too small) but in the solid brownstone house of the Callendars. The wedding, said the columns, was to be not in the flamboyant new St. Jude's on the Avenue but in St. Bart's two blocks away, a small church of dark brown stone, rather shabby but really distinguished. Knowledge of this sort she had picked up in the course of her brief adventure into the world. She understood the difference between St. Jude's which was the richest church and St. Bart's which was the most fashionable. These things were put away in the little pigeonholes of her observing brain (so like the pigeonholes in Gramp Tolliver's walnut desk).

She learned all this and never once did she betray any sign of her knowledge or her interest. Clarence would have known nothing of the wedding save that Mr. Wyck, over one of their greasy lunches far down town, mentioned it to him with the sly suggestion that his wife might be interested and would no doubt be invited. Wyck appeared to know most of the details, for in the secrecy of his bleak room he read the society columns, and there was always the backstairs gossip which came to him through the two aunts in Yonkers. Over the apple-sauce, and under the eye of the peroxide blonde cashier, he insinuated other things, suggestions that Ellen might even be more interested than her husband imagined, but Clarence either was too stupid to understand these hints or in his loyalty saw fit to ignore them.

But when he returned to the flat he did say to Ellen, "I see your friend Mrs. Callendar's son is being married. I suppose you'll be invited to the wedding."

Ellen glanced at him sharply and then returned to her work. "No," she said calmly. "I don't think I'll be invited. Why should I be?"

"I didn't know," he replied awkwardly. "I thought they were friends of yours."

"No. I worked for them. . . . A thing like that means nothing."

After that he was silent and for a time wore an air of disappointment. She knew, beyond all doubt, that it would have pleased him to know that his wife ·had been invited to a fashionable wedding. The old ambitions, less vigorous now, stirred more and more rarely. To-night, for a moment they had been kindled, but it was the last time they ever raised their dangerous heads. Clarence read his newspaper and did not speak again of the event.

On the afternoon of the wedding the temptation was not to be overcome. For a long time she fought it and at last, putting on a large hat and a veil she descended from the Babylon Arms and made her way by tram car to the neighborhood of St. Bart's. Before the church there was a great crowd (a fact for which she was doubtless thankful) which pressed close against the awnings and peered at the carriages that were beginning already to arrive. There was, she felt, something at once comic and pitiful in the spectacle of men and women crowding and pushing into the gutters for a glimpse of the fashionable people who descended and swept across the red carpet into the church. Among the arrivals there were dowagers who strained through the doors of tiny cabriolets, cow-eyed young girls, elderly bachelors dressed with the stiffness of starch, whole armies of relatives and friends, moving forward with a concentrated air of indifference to the stares, jostled fairly by men with cameras who climbed about on the steps and even as high as the façade of the church in order to capture brief glimpses of such people as the Apostle to the Genteel, Mrs. Champion and her Virgins, the questionable Mrs. Sigourney (who was always news), and the dewlapped Mrs. Mallinson.

With the arrival of the bridegroom's mother the jam became terrifying. Women fought with one another to catch a glimpse of a fat little woman clad in purple satin with a bird's nest on which a few violets had been carelessly planted, perched high on her head. Ellen, taller than most of the crowd, was able to see without being seen. She caught a swift glimpse of Thérèse as she emerged from the door of the cabriolet, only to see her swallowed up at once in the press of the onlookers. She appeared calm and had the air of a woman well satisfied. After all, she had succeeded in uniting two great fortunes. The bride was all that she should have been. The future was assured.

Of Richard Callendar himself, Ellen caught only a swift glimpse—a flash, no more, of a dark handsome face paler than she had ever seen it. A moment later the bride arrived, but of

Sabine nothing was visible; her face was covered by a long veil of lace. The mob of democratic citizens rocked and quarreled and pushed; dowdy women from the suburbs elbowed their way through stenographers and errand girls; clerks and fat old men trod on the toes of angry females; and Sabine was swallowed up.

Ellen leaned against the stone of the church as if she had become suddenly faint. Here the sounds of the music came to her, distant and triumphant, now swelling, now diminishing, until at length it died away altogether to make silence for the ceremony.

It was not until the bridal party, still jostled by the crowd, came out of the church and descended the steps that she saw them fully. Standing now on a jutting piece of stone she saw Callendar and Sabine move toward the waiting carriage. They smiled as if that were what the world expected of them and once Ellen fancied that the bridegroom looked toward her. Of this she was not certain and she was sure that he could not have recognized her through the veil, but she slipped from her eminence and dropped to the sidewalk where she vanished in the pressing mob. Nevertheless she was suddenly happy and strong, for in the one swift glimpse of the .two faces she had divined her victory. The face of Callendar, for all its fixed smile, was pale and a little drawn, and in the eyes of the bride there was a bright fixed look of unhappiness. Sabine, so intelligent, so grotesquely clever, must have known what Ellen .knew—that although she had married Callendar she was not the one who possessed him. In the end she might perhaps lose her game of patience because, after all, it was not a simple game; there were in it elements beyond the control even of so shrewd a pair as herself and Thérèse Callendar.

All the way back to the Babylon Arms, Ellen hurried with an hysterical air of triumph. It may have been that she knew a profound feminine satisfaction in the sense of vanity gratified. She hurried too because Clarence would be waiting for her, tired and pathetic and hungry. It would please him to find her so happy.

so excited. In this strange confusion of moods she passed between the lions of the Babylon Arms and made her way up to the tiny flat. She was neither happy nor unhappy; it was emotion beyond either thing, entangled somehow with the old sense of triumph.

The dark hallway with the red walls was the same; the red carpeted stairway, its splendor gone now and the cordage showing through, was unchanged, as it had always been. It was only when she ascended the very last step that she discovered anything unusual. The door of the apartment stood open a little way so that she was able to look through the room into the distant stretches that lay beyond the river. For an instant she halted, looking about her. The key was in the lock. On the smoking table there lay the remnants of the cigar which Clarence always smoked on his way home from the office. His coat and waistcoat, which he was accustomed to hang neatly in the closet, lay on the divan. They had been thrown down carelessly. The red sunset above the river illuminated the shabby room in a fiery glow.

Standing quite still in the center of the floor she waited, listening for some familiar sound; and presently when there was no interruption of the stillness, she called "Clarence! Clarence!" in a voice that sounded queer and strange to her. The excitement had gone from her now, drained away by a curious sense of foreboding. In that narrow life where every day each small act followed exactly the same plan, the sight of a coat flung down carelessly terrified her.

She called again presently and, receiving no answer, she opened the door of their bedroom. It was empty. The room in which Fergus slept was likewise undisturbed. In the kitchen there was no one. Then slowly she made her way to the door of the bathroom. It stood open a little way as if inviting her, maliciously; yet it was not open wide enough for her to see what lay beyond. Gently she pushed it back until it struck some object that blocked its motion. Again she pushed, this time more firmly, and the obstacle gave way, moving a little to one side so that a foot became visible. It was then in a single, unreal moment, that she

divined what had happened. She pushed harder and the door
flew back. Behind it on the rug where he had done his exercises
so patiently lay Clarence, face down, motionless. He had fallen
forward and from beneath him there flowed a thin, dark stream.
It had touched the white of his shirt and discolored it.

There was no doubt that he was dead. There was no doubt
as to how he had died. The pistol, which had always been in the
drawer of the bedroom table, lay beside him on the white floor.
In the gathering darkness she knelt down at his side and began
to weep, wildly, hysterically, like a savage. The darkness and the
silence engulfed her.

It was thus that Fergus found her when he came in at last.

A doctor came and after him a policeman, but there was nothing
to be done. The man was dead, and, as they observed to Fergus,
you could see how he came to die. There would have to be
the nasty business of an inquest. The news filtered through the
apartment and the elevator man and the defunct actress with
the white poodle in her arms came and stood at the doorway,
whispering together and offering sympathy. It was Fergus who,
with all the efficiency of Hattie Tolliver herself, "took hold" and
managed things.

As for Ellen, she shut herself away, with a knowledge that
roused in her a new agony infinitely more profound and terrible
than the first brief outburst. In the darkness of her room she
lay, alone now, on one of the apple green beds, silent and quite
beyond so paltry a manifestation as tears. In one hand she
held a note, crumpled and damp, which had been read again and
again.

It was brief although the dead man, in his agitation, had written some things over and over again. It was simple, humble, inarticulate, more real, more vivid than he had ever been in all
his mild existence. It was as if all the mysterious substance that
was his soul had been poured out in that last moment upon the
crumpled bit of paper. He had written it in a great speed; it

seemed that, under the stress of fate, he had suddenly gone mad, flamed for an instant into a pitiful kind of heroism and then gone out forever. He had been almost poetic.

"Forgive me, beloved, for what I am doing. It was all that remained. It is better . . . everything is better now, and you will be free again as you once were.

"I must tell you what you will soon learn. No one can keep it from you. I am a thief. I have stolen money and now there is no way to escape. If I ran away, it would be the same as what I am doing. . . . It would be the end. I would never dare ask to see you again. I would never tell you where I had gone. What I am doing is the only way out."

(Here he had, in his agitation, written the same sentence twice as if he begged her not to hate him because he had been the cause of so much trouble. He had almost said, "Forgive me for being a bother to you.")

Then it continued, "It was wrong from the beginning. I should never have asked you to run away with me, because I was not good enough. I tried to be and failed. I was a poor thing. So now, after I am gone again, there will be nothing to hold you . . . not even from the man you really loved . . . if it is not too late. You see, I know the truth! I know the truth! I discovered it in time. Forgive me, dearest. I love you always."

Slowly during the long hours of the interminable night, the whole tragedy assumed a clarity of form. While she lay on the green bed, in a silence penetrated only by the faint nocturnal sounds that rose from the distant street, the little pieces fitted together . . . bits of the past and the present, sudden stabbing memories and poignant flashes of intuition, odd scraps of old emotions vanished now forever . . . the little pieces fitted together until, like a picture puzzle, they assumed a swift and startling completeness. She saw the answer in a quick bright flash; it was that she had destroyed him; she it was who had driven him into the abyss. The bitterness lay in the fact that all the while she had tried to save him, to make him happy.

If he had stolen money it could have been for one purpose alone —to give her more than he had been able to give her, to make her believe that he was far greater than he could ever have been. She understood that he had fought for her sake to create an illusion of grandeur, to raise before her eyes the figure of a man, successful and clever, who was not Clarence at all but a creature who existed only in the troubled flights of his ambition. And it was this very figure which, toppling from its pedestal, had destroyed him. She had known all along that there was no such creature. She could have told him. . . .

His humbleness pained her. Even in the end he had chosen to destroy himself in a corner where it would make the least trouble.

There was, too, the vague confused affair of Callendar. The note said so little; it left the fear so incomplete. *There will be nothing to hold you, not even from the man whom you really loved.* He must have known that he had not freed her, even by his death, for he knew that in almost the same hour Callendar had himself ceased to be free. All that was gone now, lost forever, and a little time before it had been so near, quite within her grasp. In trying to have everything she had lost all save her soul and the fire which burned there. . . . *If it is not too late. . . .*

But the thing which hurt her most was the memory of two words which he had used. They were, strangely enough, words of endearment, of affection, even perhaps of something so strong as passion. He had dared in his note to say "dearest" and "beloved." He was gone now; he would not have to face her, knowing that because his love had fallen upon barren ground he was ridiculous. In life these were two words which he had never dared to use. They burned now like scars that would never heal.

She could not talk to him now; she could no longer still his uneasiness with empty words and a kiss which cost her nothing. He lay near her, just beyond her door, upon the shabby divan, but she could not reach him. To the dead there was nothing she could say, nothing which she could explain. In death he had come to possess her, for it was she who was humbled now.

She did not hide herself away. When morning came she appeared, calm and cold, to aid a strangely subdued Fergus in all the bitter tasks of caring for the dead. She arranged the telegrams and even chose the wording for the one that went to his sister in Ogdensburg. In all of them she said merely that Clarence had died suddenly. The truth she withheld. (There was always his weak heart to lend credence to such a tale.) In the newspapers there appeared only a brief line or two recording the fact of one more suicide in a great city and this, of course, was never read in the Town or by the people who had known Clarence as a boy. So in the end, his mother was the only one who knew the truth and even of the truth there was a portion which she never learned; it was that her son was a thief.

Out of all the tragic confusion only one thing remained to puzzle her; it was how Clarence had come to know of Richard Callendar. The answer, never entirely clear, came to her from a source she had never considered, from a man whom she treated, when she bothered to think of him at all, as beneath her contempt.

In the midst of that first gray morning the door opened and Mr. Wyck came in, shabby and downcast, to pay his condolences. He returned to the flat where he had known the only happiness which had ever come his way, but he returned, clearly, under circumstances he had never foreseen in the most gloomy and portentous of his bitter imaginings. At the sight of Ellen, cold and capable, in the midst of her grief (for she did grieve in a fashion she would not have done for a man whom she had loved), his green eyes turned toward the tips of his boots and he murmured, "Ah, this is terrible . . . terrible," in the professional manner of an undertaker.

In his heart, he may have thought, "It was you who ruined him, you, who came here into this very flat, a nobody, to use him

for what he was worth . . . to turn me out into the streets."
But he kept silent, perhaps because she had always terrified him,
filling him with a sense of one standing upon the rim of a volcano.
He was afraid of scenes, Mr. Wyck, and so his hate found its
way into the open through devious, hidden channels. He had
not the courage, it seemed, even to look at her now.

They stood for a time in silence by the divan, symbols of that
queer, distorted figure of which the dead Clarence formed the third
angle—a figure all awry, perverted out of all drawing—Clarence,
so white and still, gone now beyond the reach of either of them.

Mr. Wyck muttered oily and incoherent consolations. . . . "It
is a bitter blow. . . . One must be brave. . . . He was a good
man. . . ." All the old banalities which somehow took on
a bitter, ironical ring. And presently he snuffled and wiped his
eyes, as much in pity for himself who had lost the one thing
for which he had gambled, as for the man who lay quiet and
still upon the divan.

Ellen, watching him, was filled with a slow, burning anger.
She wanted suddenly to crush him as she had once wanted to
crush poor May Seton, because he was sentimental, and silly
and without strength. And suddenly it occurred to her to say
abruptly, "It was not a case of suicide. It was not Clarence
who killed himself. . . . It was others who killed him."

She had spoken in a sudden moment of humility, acknowledging
her own guilt, and the speech, so abrupt, so unexpected, produced
upon Mr. Wyck the strangest effect. He looked at her sharply,
for the first time, and then averted his eyes; but in the brief glance
she discovered the answer to the mystery. It was Mr. Wyck
who had betrayed her secret. It was Mr. Wyck who had told the
story of Callendar, distended no doubt, and perverted by his
malice. She knew it by the look of terror in the shifty eyes.
He had used this secret as his last stake. . . . And he had lost,
forever, beyond all hope.

Almost at once he turned away from the morbid fascination
of the divan, bade her good-by and hurried out of the door;

and Ellen, watching his narrow back with the weak, sloping shoulders, knew that she would never see him again. She was sure now that it was this poor, furtive creature, with his strange, perverted love, who had given the dead man his final push over the abyss into eternity. For even the theft would not have driven Clarence from her; it could have been only the knowledge that she was lost to him forever.

So it was a man whom she had scorned, a creature whom she ignored and who hated her, who in his poor fumbling way had set her free.

36

SHE went to his own town for the funeral and there met for the first time his mother, a grim, tragic sort of woman with sharp, searching eyes and straight black hair pulled into a tight knot at the back of her neck. It was this woman with whom she shared the secret; none of the others knew, not even his sister (the one he had said played the piano), a mild, weary woman rather like Clarence, who was the mother of five children and went about throughout the visit weak and red-eyed with weeping. The neighbors flocked into the house, mostly middle-aged women and spinsters, black and crow-like, moving about in melancholy clusters with the air of vultures. They came and went, speaking always in whispers, saying the same things, wearing the same mournful countenances, talking always of their own losses and calamities, speculating always upon the deaths of certain well-established invalids in tne community. Always they reached in time the same refrain. It was this—"If he'd been an old man it would have been different, but he was so young and so clever. He was such a brilliant fellow and doing so well in the city. He'd have been a big man some day. We were all proud of him here in Ogdensburg."

And Ellen, handsome and pale in her mourning, sat by quietly, listening while they surveyed her with a distant air of disapproval.

She kept silent. Perhaps to these crow-like women, Clarence had been a brilliant and powerful figure.

In the Babylon Arms there was little to be done. Ellen paid a visit for the first time to the offices of the Superba Electrical Company and there learned that Clarence had stolen money which he collected and failed to deliver. The amount was something over fifteen hundred dollars. When she heard it she murmured, "It was so little too! Why, I could have paid it if he had told me. To have killed himself for so little!"

But she knew, of course, that if he had confessed he would have destroyed that splendid creature which he fancied he had created in her eyes. He had preferred himself to be destroyed. In death it would not matter that she discovered the fraud: he would not have to face her.

She paid the money, out of her savings and out of the amount brought by the sale of the furniture. She sold even the piano he had bought her as a wedding gift. And when she had finished there remained but little more than a hundred dollars.

On the very day the furniture was being taken from the flat she told Fergus the whole truth concerning her plans. They sat together amid the wreckage, brother and sister, both understanding for perhaps the first time that they were faced by the new problem of Hattie Tolliver. Both knew that she had set her mind upon coming to them, and having tasted freedom, neither was willing now to turn back.

"There is Ma," said Ellen. "I don't know what's to be done about her. She'll be coming here to live before long and I won't be here. She's worked all these years to come where she can be near us and now I've got to go away. I'm going to Paris. . . . It's the only thing left."

Fergus looked at her. "But you don't know French," he said, "and you haven't any money."

"I can't turn back now. If I went back to Ma, it would be the end of me. I know that. I couldn't. . . . I couldn't ever

begin again. I've enough money to take me there. . . . I'll manage after that. . . . Besides, there is Lily. . . . She promised to
help me when the time came. . . . The time has come. . . . I
can't turn back."

Fergus listened in silence, moved perhaps by the new dignity
that had come to her, a dignity touched with bitterness. She
was ·beautiful too in a new fashion, more placid, more serene.

"You must be good to Ma," she continued. "She'll hate my
running away, but I've got to go. She's a wonderful woman.
She's the one who has sacrificed everything. She's always done
it . . . for all of us. I couldn't go if I didn't know that you're
the one she loves best of all. You're the one she worships. She
loved you enough to let you go. I had to run away. You know
it, Fergus, as well as I. You must be good to her. If anything
happened to you, it would kill her. You mustn't disappoint her.
One day we must all make her proud of us. I mean to do it, and
then when I'm rich, when I'm successful, I can reward her."
She paused for a moment and then added. "You see, she loves
you best because you're so like Pa. You're the way he used to be
when she fell in love with him."

The boy's face took on an unaccustomed gravity. He rose and
looked out of the window over the beloved and magical city.
"I'll do my best," he said presently. "I'll do my best. . . .
She's a wonderful woman." (Yet neither of them would turn
back now.)

In the room there was no sound for a long time save the tick-
ing of the clock, wrapped now in paper to be carted away. At
last he turned and said, "But you're going to Lily. . . . Ma will
hate that."

"I know she will. . . . She's always been afraid of Lily. She
needn't worry though. I can take care of myself. I imagine
nothing very serious can ever happen to me again."

It was Lily again, always Lily who was concerned in the
whole course of Ellen's destiny. Yet Ellen never knew how great
a part she had played for she never knew, of course, that if

chance had not thrown her glamorous cousin into the path of Clarence on a wintry night years before, he might have been alive and happy now, the husband of a stupid woman who would have thought him as wonderful as the figure he had given his life to create. He had looked for an instant at the sun and been blinded.

So perhaps, in the end, Skinflint Seton had been right. *Women like that can ruin men . . . just by talking to them.*

37

THE world of Lily had its center in a house which stood in that part of Paris beyond the Trocadero in the direction of Auteuil and the Bois. Here she had lived for years, since the moment when she had found it agreeably necessary to live abroad. For her purposes the house possessed every advantage; it resembled, after a curious fashion, those convents of the eighteenth century to which ladies of fashion retired at the moments when they desired solitude and rest and yet wished not to be cut off entirely from the gaiety of the world. As the Baron had once observed, Lily herself belonged to the eighteenth century; there was about her always so much of luxury and indolence, so much of charm and unmorality.

The house stood in the Rue Raynouard a short distance from the place where it rushes down a slope to join a half dozen other streets in a whirlpool known as the Place Passy surrounded by magasins, cafés, and tobacconists' shops. It was, in all truth, an eighteenth century house, built in the beginning as a château in the open country on the outskirts of Paris between the city and the Grand Trianon of Versailles. Here in the open fields the Marquise de Sevillac, an ugly, clever and eccentric woman, held a court of her own, a court indeed which in some respects outshone the splendor of Versailles. In her house were to be found the poets, the wits and the philosophers of the day. She corresponded with Voltaire, and the Encyclopedists came frequently to work in the rooms which overlooked the little park and the sheep pastures beyond. Indeed the Sage of Ferney on his triumphant return to Paris had planned a visit to the Marquise and was only prevented by the fatal illness which overtook so swiftly his skinny old body.

The Marquise had been the last of her family. There is a Marquis de Sevillac living to-day but the title is Bonapartist and has nothing to do with the ancient splendor of the true family. As an old woman, the Marquise clung to her house even with the approach of the revolution. During that cataclysm, which she faced in a bold and cynical fashion, she was allowed to survive because the people remembered her as the friend of the radicals and the philosophers ·who plagued their stupid King. She allied herself with the Girondists and took Madame Roland perilously to her bosom, and when the débâcle came at length her bony old body would have been dragged off to the guillotine along with the others save that she was so old and that Danton and Terezia Tallien intervened. So she died at last in her bed and the château became the property of the Directory.

Since her death it has known many occupants. For a time it served as a museum; it housed the American ambassador Benjamin Franklin, who gave his name to a street nearby; it passed through a period of neglect and emptiness and at last fell into the possession of a wealthy manufacturer of soap and chocolate. It was during his day and the day of his son that the château came to be pressed upon by other houses and by apartments in the florid German style, until there was left at length only the house itself and the little park designed by Le Nôtre which still remained the largest private garden in all the city of Paris.

The house turns to the world a deceptive face, for on the side facing the Rue Raynouard it is but one story high with a commonplace door and a single row of shuttered windows. It is this side which in the days of the Marquise faced the stables and dovecote; so the house now turns its back upon the world and preserves for its friends the glory of its three story façade of Caen stone. The façade, broken by rows of tall windows, looks upon a high terrace lined with crumbling urns carved in the classic Greek manner and a garden with a reticulation of paths laid out by Le Nôtre to center upon the pastry-cake pavilion erected to the God of Love. Inside the high wall which shuts out the noise and dust of the Rue de Passy there are great plane trees with trunks mottled like the backs of salamanders, and laburnums that cluster close about the Temple of Eros.

One could live forever within the boundaries of the ancient house and garden, surrounded by luxury and beauty, receiving one's friends, seldom going into the world. It was an admirable house in which to live discreetly, almost secretly, and it was an admirable house for one of so indolent a nature as Lily's. For Lily had succeeded the chocolate manufacturer, and the château of the Marquise de Sevillac with its ghosts of Voltaire and the Encyclopedists, the wanton Terezia Tallien and the clever Madame Roland, was tenanted now by a rich American out of a country which in the days of the Marquise had been no more than a howling wilderness—a woman the world knew as a widow, beautiful, charming, discreet and indolent, living under the guardianship of the most respectable and stuffy of Bonapartists, the ancient Madame Gigon.

On a dripping morning of December, of the sort which makes Paris a wretched city in midwinter, a carriage drew up before the door of this house and out of it stepped Ellen Tolliver, pale from traveling but unusually handsome in the black of her widowhood. There was with her a small thin young woman, trimly dressed rather in the practical style of a professional traveler, with red hair and pretty bright eyes which had a way of observing the slightest things which occurred in her vicinity. The stranger (after haggling with the driver over the fare) paid him

and then, changing her mind, bade him wait for her. She pulled
the bell with a swift, energetic jerk.

"It is a modest house," she observed to Ellen in short, ironic
syllables colored by an accent that was indefinable. "A modest
house for a rich American. Usually they are more flamboyant."

Impatiently she pulled the bell a second time and presently the
commonplace door was opened by a Breton maid in a white
cap who bade them enter. Inside, away from the dripping cobblestones of the Rue Raynouard, it was clear that the stranger
succumbed to the magic of the house. For an instant, she
remained silent, staring in astonishment at the long sweep of
stairs and the array of glittering crystal. Then she made a
grunting noise and addressed the maid in French.

"Madame Shane. . . . Is she in?"

"No," replied the girl. "She is at Nice. . . . She has been
gone since two weeks."

The stranger translated the speech and for a moment there
was a silence in which the face of Ellen, pale and handsome in
her mourning, was shadowed by a sudden look of terror. It
vanished quickly and she said to her companion, "Ask for Madame
Gigon."

Madame Gigon was in. She never went out any more. At
the moment she was in the drawing room. Should she ask if
Madame Gigon would see them?

"This," observed the bright ferret, to the maid, "is Madame
Shane's cousin. She has come to pay her a visit."

The stairway before them led downwards in the most unexpected fashion. Between panels of satinwood adorned with
plaques of gilt and rock crystal and filled with candles, it swept
down for the depth of two stories, past a gallery which led away
on both sides, into a dim vista of polished floor at the end of
which there was a high window with small panes of glass that
gave out upon a garden. At the sight, a faint touch of color
appeared on the cheeks of Ellen and her eyes grew bright with

interest. It was all far grander than she had ever imagined, more magnificent than she had hoped. In such a house she might stay quietly, interfering with no one. It was possible to remain hidden in its depths for weeks at a time.

"Shall I stay?" asked her companion.

"I can manage. . . . It's my affair. There's no use troubling you any further. It was good of you to have bothered."

"But what about speaking French?"

"Madame Gigon speaks English. She once had a school for English and American girls. . . . My great-aunt went to it."

Up the long stairs, remotely, the maid was returning now.

"Bien," she said. "Madame Gigon will see you."

"Au revoir," murmured the stranger. "If you want me, I shall be at the Ritz until the end of the month. . . . Miss Rebecca Schönberg. . . . You have my card. . . ."

And with that she vanished through the rain into the waiting cab.

At the foot of the long stairs Ellen found herself suddenly in the great drawing-room. Beyond, through the tall window draped in blue brocade, she had a vista of dripping trees and a wet garden dominated by a white pavilion that resembled a pastry. The room was long and rectangular, for all the world like the drawing room at Shane's Castle, save that it was not, even on this wet winter day, a gloomy room. There was in it far too much color. Even the satinwood paneling appeared warm and soft. At the far end before a neat fire of cannel coal she discerned among the shadows the figures of a tiny old woman and a small boy, sturdy, handsome and red haired. He sat at the feet of the crone, reading aloud to her in English and nearby lay two fat and elderly dogs, an Aberdeen and a West Highland. It was not until she had come quite close to them that they realized she had entered the room. The boy stood up and the old woman turned toward her with a curious dazed look in her eyes.

It was the old woman who spoke first. She peered, apparently without seeing her, in the general direction of Ellen and asked, "Are you Mees Tolliver?"

The boy regarded her, frankly, with a pleasant friendliness.

"Yes," replied Ellen, "I am Madame Shane's cousin."

In an instant, as she watched the child and faced the sharp old woman, she grasped the identity of the boy. It came to her quickly, as a revelation out of all the mystery of the past. Of course she knew all about Madame Gigon; it was the boy for whom she was not prepared. About him there could no longer be any doubt. He was Lily's child and the old story was true. It gave her a quick, inexplicable feeling of relief, as if after so many years she stood in the open, knowing at last the truth. It did not produce any shock, perhaps because she had been for so long prepared for the knowledge. So she had said without hesitation *Madame* Shane, just as a little while before in order to take no chance in protecting Lily, she had said *Madame* Shane to Miss Rebecca Schönberg.

The old woman coughed and said slowly, "I don't speak English very well any more. I'm so old. . . . I almost forget. . . . Est-ce que vous parlez français?" And then, "Asseyez vous."

Ellen simply stared at her, and in the emergency the boy, polite and eager, said in a piping voice, "She wants to know if you speak French. . . . She wants you to sit down." His English was colored by an accent which struck Ellen with a remote sense of unreality. Lily's child! Her own cousin! Speaking English as if it were a foreign tongue!

"I don't," said Ellen. "Will you tell her that I know no French?"

It was the old woman who answered in labored English. "Oh, I understand. . . . I know what you say. . . . I can no longer *speak* English. . . . Asseyez vous. . . . Sit down."

It was only then that Ellen understood the peering look in the eyes of the old woman. She had been sitting down, all the while. The old woman, who peered at her so earnestly, was blind.

"Did Madame Shane know you were coming?" asked Madame Gigon.

"No, I had no time. . . . I left America in haste." She held back the truth. She did not say that she had come, deliberately and without warning, because she could take no chances on being refused. Sitting there, with only a few francs in the world, she felt secure. She was in Paris now in a house that was big and beautiful. The rest could be managed.

"She did not tell me. . . . She would have been here," continued Madame Gigon. Then, as if her brain were fatigued by the strain of speaking English, the old woman addressed a torrent of French to the little boy. When she had finished he advanced to Ellen, shyly, and held out his hand.

"She says," he repeated in the same piping voice, "that I must welcome you as master of the house. She says you are my cousin." He smiled gravely. "I never had a cousin before. And," he continued, "she says that if Maman had known she would have been here."

He stood regarding her with a look of fascination as though so strange and exotic a thing as a cousin was too thrilling to be passed over lightly. Touched by the simplicity of the child, Ellen drew him near to her and, addressing both him and Madame Gigon, said, "You are good to believe that I am Madame Shane's cousin. How could you know?"

Madame Gigon smiled shrewdly. She was withered and had a little black mustache. Again the boy translated her speech. "She says," he repeated, "that you have . . . une voix honnête." He hesitated. . . . "An honest voice . . . and that she knows the voice because she taught my mother in school and before her my grandmère. She says it is like my grandmère's voice."

As he spoke the old woman smiled again and wagged her head with extraordinary vigor. "Je connais la voix. . . . Je la connais bien."

Then she addressed the boy again and he translated her speech. "She says she is blind and will you come near so that she may touch your face?"

Ellen drew her chair closer so that it disturbed the fatter of the two dogs and allowed Madam Gigon to pass her thin hands in a fluttering gesture over her handsome throat and the fine arch of her nose.

"Ah," said the old woman triumphantly. "Le nez . . . the nose. . . . C'est le nez de vôtre tante . . . le même nez . . . précisement. C'est un nez fier . . . distingué."

"It is a proud nose," echoed the interpreter gravely. . . . "A high distinguished nose. . . . A nose like your aunt's."

And the old woman, wagging her head, fell suddenly into a silent train of old memories.

"My name is Jean," said the boy shyly. "I am ten years old. Would you like to see my book? It is in English. I can read English just as well as French." And he brought her Tom Brown's School Days and showed her the picture of the boys climbing the tree to rob the rook's nest. Ellen, leaning over his shoulder, was softened and showed a warm enthusiasm over the other illustrations. She even listened while he told the long story of Tom Brown.

Presently Madame Gigon joined their talk and for a long time they held a conversation, translated always by the boy, that was animated and illumined by a warm friendliness. It was this which presently filled Ellen with a passionate desire to weep. She took off her hat and sat on the floor with Jean and the dogs, while Madame Gigon and the boy asked questions about America and old Julia Shane whom Jean called "grandmère" and whom he had never seen. And presently the Breton maid appeared with tea (for Madame Gigon, though she was French, had learned the custom of tea among the English) and over Ellen there swept slowly a strange feeling that, at last, after having been away a long time, she had come home. It was here that she belonged, here that she would be happy, in this great, beautiful house that was so friendly.

Jean was allowed one gâteau and the fat dogs devoured two apiece.

"She says," translated Jean, "that Maman told her you would come some day . . . just as you have come. She says she is not surprised . . . your great-aunt, my grandmère, would have done the same."

After tea, she was led away by the Breton maid up the stairs and along a gallery into which opened an endless procession of doors, until she came, at length, to the end, where a door was opened which revealed a square room dominated by a great bed hung with a canopy of brocade. The tall windows gave out upon the park which, lying now in the fog that succeeded the rain of an hour or two before, appeared blue and mysterious. In the heart of the mist the white pavilion showed vaguely, and beyond it, above the top of the garden wall, yellow globules of light from the lamps in the Rue de Passy cast the trunks of the old plane trees into sharp black shadows.

When the maid had left, she sat down before the bright small fire and without moving regarded the room closely, point by point, detail by detail. It was large and warm and beautiful, but the quality which moved her most profoundly was its elegance . . . the same quality that was so evident in the great drawing-room belowstairs. She had never dreamed that there could be such warm, old beauty. There was nothing here of the barren, gas-lit pomp of Mrs. Callendar's dining room out of the Second Empire, and nothing of the vast Callendar drawing-room lined with grim Dutch ancestors and gilt cabinets of tear bottles and Buddhas. This room . . . this lovely house . . . had been there always. It had been like this in the days of the ugly Marquise de Sevillac. The chaise longue on which she sat, the gilt chair that stood before the writing desk, the very mirror, with its dim rectangular panes of glass, had the effect of softening her. Indeed, for a time, these things made her dimly uneasy; far back in her consciousness there rose a grotesque fear that if she once succumbed to the splendor of that great bed, she might never rise from it again, that it might weaken her by its very luxury. She regarded it almost with suspicion, touched by an actual fear of all that was too beautiful and too splendid. She might become, like Lily, indolent and idle and charming. And slowly the realization swept over her that she was changed. She became aware that she was a woman now; she no longer wanted to be like Lily. She was strong, as she had never been before, strong as Lily would never be. Luxury, idleness, charm were not the things she desired. It must be something stronger than that, more heady, more challenging.

Dimly she understood the appeal of the room and of the dark misty garden with its white pavilion. It was insidious and peaceful, like an enchanted palace that swam mirage-like in the blue fog. And again she was overcome by a sense of returning home after having been away for a long time. The white squares of Paris, seen through the rain-spattered cab-windows on the way from the Gare du Nord, had moved her deeply; they had given her a wild sense of freedom, of escape. But this was different, more languorous, more intimate. It was the thing for which she had been born, the thing which, all her life, she had struggled to attain. It lay on the opposite side of the earth from the black Mills and the plain houses of the Town.

And then, pathetically and slowly, there came over her the wish that, as once she had planned, Clarence might have known this old splendor . . . the splendor he had talked of seeing, "some day when they were rich enough." There was that white villa at Nice. . . .

She had understood, well enough, while she sat on the deck of the *City of Paris,* damp and chilled by the fog, that Clarence was not gone forever, simply because he was dead. She understood (indeed she thought of it constantly, even in the hours when she had listened in fascination to the talk of Rebecca Schönberg) that since his death he was more real to her than he had ever been in life. While he had lived there had never been time to consider him. There was only time, now, when he was gone. The very affection she had for him in life was nothing to the affection she now experienced, and in this new emotion there was no pity, because pity had been effaced by self-reproach. The one desire which obsessed her was a desire to see him, to explain, to justify herself . . . Ellen, who had never bothered to justify her faintest whim. The power of the weak over the strong was still stirring. It had not altogether died.

Mingled with these very thoughts was the knowledge that somewhere in this strange city that was so familiar, Callendar and Sabine were living. They must be there quite near her; she was sure of it. They were moving about, dining, going to the theater and the opera, all the while in ignorance of what had happened to her, knowing nothing of her presence. For them, her reason told her, she was forgotten; yet something stronger than reason, a belief which beyond all doubt had its roots in the memory of Callendar's face upon his wedding day, told her that she was not forgotten. She had been there, with them, all the while, . . . perhaps, she thought triumphantly, even upon their wedding night. It was a thought utterly free from any desire to hurt Sabine; indeed, toward Sabine she had no feeling at all. Callendar was the one who roused her malice; she wanted to torment him, to be herself the one who dominated. The thought would have appeased her vanity save for the fact that she could never capture the whole truth; it was impossible because, in the months that had separated them, she had returned again to the old feeling that she did not know Callendar at all, that there was a part of him beyond her understanding, which escaped her always. She was afraid of him.

She dressed to the accompaniment of water dripping from the high roof on to the white terrace of the garden and, under the stimulus of physical activity, she came presently to forget both Clarence and Richard Callendar. Her thoughts turned to Miss Schönberg, that small, good-natured, ferrety creature who was so kind to her. The encounter had occurred, by chance, on the *City of Paris* when the stranger, watching Ellen as she paced in her tireless way round and round the deck through the fog and the blowing rain, finally offered her a book to read. Ellen did not, as a rule, read anything, but she accepted the book, gratefully enough, more as a symbol of the stranger's friendliness than for its own qualities. She could not, now, even remember what it was, nor anything about it save that it was bound in green and was written by a man called de Morgan. She was, at that time, engaged in thinking of her own story, which was indeed quite as good as anything concocted by a novelist. For the sense of rôle, the awareness of herself as a dramatic figure "living by her wits," had grown upon her steadily, until in her mind there had been born a suspicion that such a rôle possessed a value. She was not, after all, commonplace. Already, though she was but twenty-four, tremendous things had happened to her . . . things which were romantic and even tragic, but things in which she found satisfaction. She had wished, as far back as she could remember, to have a life that was eventful. She wanted not to die until she had known her share of life, and in life she did not seek, like Lily, simple happiness and contentment. She desired experience, and so she resembled greatly old man Tolliver.

It may have been a sense of all this which attracted the stranger, for Miss Schönberg despite all her fine clothes and her habit of wandering from one spot to another, lived vicariously. She searched breathlessly for excitement. At thirty she was a confirmed and passionless virgin who lived on the fringes of life, perpetually stimulated by her sense of the spectacle. She had no real home nor any real nationality, unless one might identify as a nation that army of restless wanderers which moved from hotel to hotel across the face of Europe. Her best friends, or at least those who knew her most intimately, were the proprietors of such establishments as the Hotel Negresco and the Beau Rivage, the Royal Splendide, Claridge's, the Cavendish, the Adlon, the Ritz and sometimes, for the sake of atmosphere, such a place as the France et Choiseul. She was an orphan and rich. In Vienna she had an aunt; in Trieste a handful of cousins; in New York an uncle who traded in diamonds. She was a Jewess and an emancipated woman, regarded with suspicion by the orthodox members of her tribe. And her emancipation had the fierce quality which envelops Jewish virgins who have determined at all costs to be free. It was a sort of aggressive freedom. She had never succumbed to or even understood love and it was extremely unlikely that her bright, shiny mind would ever be weakened by an emotion so sentimental.

All this Ellen had learned from her, either by intuition or by her own confession, for Miss Schönberg was much given to conversation, especially of the self-revelatory variety. From Ellen, in turn, she had learned what the girl chose to tell her, fragments of the truth strung together in such a fashion that the whole seemed an honest but rather dull and erratic tale. Yet she knew more of Ellen than the young widow ever guessed, for if Ellen had been as dull and uninteresting as the story she told, Miss Schönberg would never have bothered to address her a second time.

And now Ellen, as she dressed to dine alone with the blind old woman belowstairs, wondered why Rebecca Schönberg had been at all interested in her. She had, it was true, faith in her own star; she knew that she would one day be famous. That any one beside herself could have any intimation of this appeared on the surface preposterous.

When she descended, she found that Jean had gone to bed and before the fire there was only Madame Gigon with Criquette and Michou, the dogs, who had not stirred from their places but lay fat and lazy, basking in the warmth of the blaze. With the eager interpreter gone, Madame Gigon, under the stress of necessity, cudgeled her old brain into speaking a very passable sort of English. At dinner, she told Ellen that Lily was stopping in the white villa at Nice. (It was not in Nice proper but Cimiez, high up on the hill beside the ruined Roman arena with a magnificent view overlooking Villefranche and the Bay of Angels. It lay just above the statue of Queen Victoria carven with a very realistic reticule and an umbrella.) She had telegraphed Lily to come home and greet her cousin properly.

After dinner they went, followed by the dogs, back again into the drawing-room to the luxurious chairs by the fire, and after a time Ellen rose and played at the request of the old woman some Brahms, an air from La Belle Hélène and finally a waltz or two of Chopin. It was a beautiful piano, for Lily respected music, and the sound of its low, mellow beauty led Ellen into playing more and more passionately. When at last her hands dropped into her lap and she sat listening to the distant sound of the boat whistles along the Seine, Madame Gigon began to talk.

She had seen George Sand once a long time ago when, as a bride, her husband, M. Gigon (who had been a curator at the Musée Cluny and had been dead now for more than half a century) had taken her one night to dine at Magny's where he might show her the celebrities of the town. She had seen George Sand, she repeated, come in with no less persons than Flaubert, yellow and bent, and the exquisite Théophile Gautier, to dine in a private room before the répétition generale of her play Le Batard, at the Odéon. The writer was an old woman then, come up from her farm, and bedizened with cheap jewelry, but every one noticed her. She had vitality. She was a sensation. . . .

And she could remember too the funeral of Jules de Goncourt and how they stood in the rain quite near to this same Flaubert. . . .

But Ellen had never heard of George Sand and knew, beyond his music, very little of Chopin, so it merely confused her to hear Madame Gigon call a man "she." Lest she betray her ignorance she kept silent, and sometimes she did not listen at all, because this ancient talk did not interest her, though it seemed to be the very core of all the life that remained in the blind old woman.

Madame Gigon talked far into the night, with the air of one who had long been shut in solitude, and as she talked her English became more and more clear. She spoke almost as easily as she had spoken in the days, half a century earlier, when she had taken Lily's mother and the other girls of the school on *pique-niques* in the woods along the Seine at Sèvres. And after a time as the dull glow of her memories took fire, she fell to talking of old Julia Shane herself. But she talked of a Julia Shane who was still a young girl and not the sick old woman who, lying ill in her house among the black mills, was the last link in the chain that held Hattie Tolliver from her children.

And as Madame Gigon talked on and on to the accompaniment of the distant sounds from the misty river, there swept over Ellen a consciousness, new but unmistakable, of a delicate unity running through all of life. It was bound together, somehow, in an intricate web composed of such things as love and memories, hopes and sorrows and sentiment, but it was a web without pattern, without design, a senseless, crazy and beautiful thing. She saw then that she could never exist apart, in isolation, from all these others; there were filaments which bound her even to so remote and insubstantial a creature as this blind old woman. It was the web which made her uneasy. She must be free of it, somewhere, sometime. . . .

Criquette began to wheeze and Madame Gigon prodding him with her toe said, "Heigh-ho! . . . We must go to bed. . . . Even the dogs have begun to snore."

38

AT the end of the week Lily returned from the south, wrapped in furs and shivering in the damp of Paris. She was a warm, sensuous creature who loved the sun and traveled north or south according to the variations in temperature. Even on the Riviera she was not content and, on the occasion of a mistral, she had been known to pack her bag and embark into Italy for Capri or Taormina where the sun was brighter and the flowers more fragrant.

She arrived early in the morning in company with the Baron, Madame Gigon's nephew, and together they came upon Ellen, not yet fallen into the luxurious habits of the French, having breakfast alone in the dining room with Jean, who sat across the table from her plying her all the while with questions about his grandmère and about America and the Town where his mother was born. She was describing it to him. . . .

"It is not a nice Town. . . . It is full of big Mills and furnaces and the soot blackens everything. . . . There's nothing pretty in the Town . . . nothing in the whole place half as pretty as your garden. . . . Your grandmother had a garden once that was as pretty as this one but it's all dead now. The smoke killed it. . . ."

Here Jean interrupted her to say, "I know! . . . I know! . . . Maman has a friend . . . a Monsieur Schneidermann who owns Mills like that. Once when we were up north, we stopped at a town called Saarbrücken and saw the furnaces. . . . It was a long time ago when I was only seven . . . but I remember. . . ." He became silent and thoughtful for a time and then, looking at her wistfully, he added, "I'd like to go to that Town . . . I'd like to see my grandmère. . . . But Maman says I can't go . . . at least until I'm grown up . . . I suppose grandmère will be dead by then. . . . She's an old, old woman. . . ."

"But she's not so old as Madame Gigon. . . . Think of it,

Madame Gigon taught your grandmother in school when she was a young girl. . . ."

She wanted by some means to escape from the ·subject of the Town. She could not, of course, tell the boy why he could never visit the Town; she could not tell him there were scores of old women who had been waiting for years just to know for certain that he existed at all. She could tell him about the smoke and filth, but she could not explain to him the nasty character of those women.

"I'm going to England to school in the autumn," the boy said. "Maman has arranged everything. . . . I'll like that better than going to school here. . . . Perhaps grandmère might come to visit us some time."

"She might . . ." replied Ellen, "but she's very ill. . . . My mother is taking care of her now. You see, my mother lives in the Town. She's your mother's cousin . . . her real first cousin. That's how it comes that I'm your cousin."

"And your mother? What is she like?" asked the boy.

For an instant Ellen observed him thoughtfully. "She's not a bit like your mother . . . and yet she's like her too in some ways."

She did not finish the description, for at that moment, through the long vista of the rooms, she saw moving toward her Lily and a man who carried a handbag and across his arm a steamer rug. As they came in, Jean sprang from his chair and ran toward them, clasping his mother about the waist and kissing her as she leaned toward him.

"Maman has come back! Maman has come back!" he cried over and over again, and then, "I have a new cousin! I have a new cousin!"

The man laughed and Lily, smiling, bade the boy be quiet, turning at the same time to Ellen, whom she embraced, to say, "So you've come at last! I hope you're going to stay a long time."

It was the same Lily, a shade older, a shade less slender, but still warm, lovable, disarming. As they embraced, the faint scent of mimosa drifted toward Ellen and the odor raised a swift, clear picture of the drawing-room at Shane's Castle with all the family assembled on Christmas day . . . the last Christmas day they ever came together there. Old Jacob Barr was dead now. Ellen and Lily were in Paris, Fergus in New York. The drawing room was shut up and abovestairs in her vast bedroom Julia Shane herself, cared for by the capable Hattie, lay dying. In a few more years there would be none of the family left in the Town. They would be scattered over the world. It remained only for grandmère to die.

All this passed through Ellen's mind as she spoke, "Yes, I shall stay a long time . . . if you will have me." She turned away. "I had to come," she said. "There was nothing left to do. . . . But I'm sorry I brought you back from the south."

"And this," said Lily, "is Monsieur Carrière . . . César. He is the nephew of Madame Gigon and a great friend of Jean and me."

The stranger bowed and murmured, "Enchanté," adding in English, "You are the musician . . . Madame Shane expects you one day to be great."

He was a swarthy man, rather handsome with sharply cut features and fierce mustachios, a Colonel of the Cuirassiers who had most of his time free. He smiled pleasantly, yet underneath the smile there was a hint of hostility, a mere spark which, however, struck a response in the breast of Ellen. It was on her side, perhaps, a resentment of his arrogance, of the very assurance with which he conducted himself. It was as if he welcomed her to his own house. And it may have been that for reasons of his own he resented her presence. She too, was arrogant and assured, even though she said pleasantly enough, "If you will have me." Underneath all that false humility, there ran a vein of domination, a strength which one less good-natured and indolent than Lily could discern at once. Still Lily had told him, long ago, that he would not like her cousin. . . .

They were a handsome pair, Lily and the Baron, the one so blonde and voluptuous, the other so dark, so brusque, so like a bit of fine steel. There was about him a sense of something familiar, which tormented the dim recesses of Ellen's memory.

"Well! Well!" he said, throwing down the coats and bags. "Let's have some breakfast." And with the same proprietary air he moved across and rang for the maid and ordered chocolate and rolls for himself and Lily.

When they had gone at last into the drawing-room and Madame Gigon, groping her way down the long stairs, and followed by the two fat dogs, had come in, Ellen understood what it was she had recognized at once in the swarthy Monsieur Carrière. It was nothing that had to do with his appearance; it was far more subtle and complicated than that. It was his manner, the very intonation of his voice when he spoke either to Ellen or Lily herself. He approached them, for all his smooth politeness, as if they were, in the final analysis, creatures inferior to himself, creatures who should be delighted to grant his every whim. With Lily, so good-natured, so generous, he may have been right; with her cousin it was as Mrs. Callendar used to say, "autres choses." The girl bristled with subdued anger. As they sat there, the three of them, smoking before the bright fire, she knew they were destined to hate each other.

Yet it was this very quality, so hauntingly familiar, that reminded her of Richard Callendar. He had not asked her if she loved him; he had taken it simply for granted that she should do as he wished. The memory, in spite of everything, made her miserable. She heard his voice again, more gentle and soft than the voice of the Baron, and saw his hands, fascinating and persuasive.

He was somewhere in this same damp white city on his wedding journey with Sabine.

Presently the Baron observed with a brusque, important air that he must be off; Madame Gigon summoned Jean to the school-

room for his lesson, and the two cousins were left alone. Before
the others they had carried on a sort of made-up conversation,
suitable for the ears of strangers, and neither had spoken honestly nor fully. As Madame Gigon, guided by Jean and followed
by the waddling dogs, disappeared round the corner of the stairs,
Lily took off her hat and observed, "Well, now I suppose we
can have a long . . . long talk. Come up to my room where
we'll be alone."

The family, again after so long a time, asserted itself.

It was a large room, closely resembling the one in which
Madame Gigon had placed Ellen, save that it was even more
luxurious and smelled faintly of scents and powders. There was
a canopied bed and on the wall hung reproductions of four draw-
ings by Watteau. It was not until Lily had removed her corsets and, clad in a peignoir of lace, had flung herself down on the
bed that the sense of strain disappeared utterly.

"Sit there on the chaise longue," she said to Ellen, "and let's
have a good talk. There's so much to say."

Ellen, stiff and severe in her mourning, sat down by the side
of her glowing cousin and Lily, lying back among the pillows,
appeared by contrast more lovely, more opulent than she had
seemed an hour earlier. To her cousin, so changed since they
had last met, so much more indifferent to such matters, there was
an air of immorality and sensuousness in the room. Beside Lily
she felt as lean, as spirited as a young greyhound.

"You know about Jean," Lily observed casually. "You understand then why I did not insist on your coming to live with me.
I was foolish perhaps . . . but when the moment came there
was always something which wouldn't let me betray the secret. . . ." She lighted a cigarette and lay back once more
among the pillows. "I suppose it *was* a secret," she added, complacently.

"People talked, but no one knew anything."

"No one knows anything here. . . . No one save Madame
Gigon. They know less here because they haven't so much time

to think of other people's affairs." Slowly a smile crept over her face, from the rosy mouth up to the violet eyes. "Ah, wouldn't they like to know in the Town?" But her voice was bitter.

Ellen smiled again. "It makes no difference. They say what they want to believe anyway. . . . They said that I ran away with Clarence because I was going to have a baby . . . and I've never had it yet. It's been a long while coming."

"I wanted you to come . . . always, but I was too lazy ever to come to the point. You can stay as long as you like and do as you please. This is a big house. . . . You need never see the rest of us if you don't care to." She spoke with the carelessness of one who was fabulously rich; there was a certain medieval splendor in her generosity. Ellen smiled again.

"Why do you smile?" her cousin asked.

"I was thinking that all this money comes out of the Town . . . the same dirty old Town."

"There's satisfaction in that . . . to think that people like Judge Weissmann are paying us rent."

It was extraordinary how clearly the Town rose up before them. The thousands of miles which lay between made no difference. They belonged to the Town still, by a thousand ties. They were, each in her own way, American. All the years that Lily had lived in Paris could not alter the fact. She was extravagant as Americans are extravagant, content to live abroad forever as Americans are content to do. Yet all her wealth came out of America, out of the very factories in the dirty Town which they both despised. It was perhaps the Scotch blood in them that made them content wherever they saw fit to settle. In a strange country they would not, as the English do, strive to bring their native land with them; they would simply create a new world of their own. Their people have done it everywhere . . . in St. Petersburg, in Constantinople, in Paris, in the Argentine and on the frontiers of Africa.

"And your husband," began Lily. "Tell me about him. . . ."

I met him once, you know, coming out on the train to the West. He was going then to see a girl called . . ." She frowned slightly. "I've forgotten her name. . . ."

"Seton," murmured Ellen. "May Seton." Lily was rousing memories now, which seemed far away and yet were faintly painful.

"Seton! That was it! . . . I'd never heard of them and it seemed to hurt him. I wrote you when I heard of his death. The letter must have passed you."

"I never got it . . . perhaps it'll be forwarded."

"Had he been ill long?" She must have wondered at the look in Ellen's eyes. It was not a look of sorrow or desolation; rather it was a look of numb pain.

"He hadn't been ill at all." The girl frowned suddenly and looked out of the window. "All the same," she continued, "you might have said he had been ill for a long time." Then she rose and stood before the small panes looking out into the wet garden. "I've got to tell some one," she said with an air of desperation. "You see . . ." And her voice became barely audible. "You see . . . He killed himself."

The veil was torn away now. Between them there remained no barrier. Each had made her confession, Lily concerning the child, Ellen concerning her husband, and in the torrent of emotion which engulfed them Lily sat up and drew her cousin down to the bed beside her. They both wept and each (with as little real cause) pitied herself.

Ellen told her story, punctuated by sobs, from the beginning. She confessed that she had never had any love for Clarence. She spoke of many things which, at the time of the tragedy, were not clear to her and which she had come to understand later during the hours of solitude on windswept decks. In the emotion of the moment she understood the whole affair even more clearly. She told Lily that she had tried, valiantly, to make Clarence happy. She had done her best to preserve his happiness and her own at the same time. There had come a time when this was no longer possible.

"Perhaps," she said, when her sobbing had quieted a little, "it is not possible for two people to be completely happy together." If she had spoken all that was in her mind, she would have added, "When one of them is ambitious and a genius." But this would have been preposterous because there was then no proof of such a thing. Another chapter of the tale she chose not to reveal. In all her torrent of sobbing and talk she never mentioned the name of Callendar.

When they had become more quiet, Lily kissed her and said, "You have been too unhappy. You must stay now with me . . . forever, if you like. You must study and become a great musician. I am rich. I can help you. . . . If you won't take the money, you can borrow it from me and pay me back when you are successful and famous. . . ."

Lily rose languidly and brought a bottle of cologne and they both bathed their eyes. All the strangeness was gone now. Their tears, in the way of women, had brought them close to each other. The sun had come out and the little park was filled by its slanting rays. Belowstairs one of the tall windows opened and they heard on the gravel of the terrace the slow steps of blind Madame Gigon who, wrapped in an antiquated coat of fur and followed by the dogs, was moving up and down in the unaccustomed warmth. There was something in the sound which, as they listened, filled the room with the atmosphere of a conspiracy. For an instant the current of kinship ran swift and high, as high indeed as it had run in the old days when all the clan assembled for the annual feast at Shane's Castle.

"She is growing feeble," observed Lily. "Think of it. She's eighty-five."

Life was short. Only a little time before Madame Gigon had been a young widow come to the school of Mademoiselle Violet de Faux to teach, among others, an awkward young American called Julia Shane.

When Ellen had gone to her own room, she sat for a time before the fire, thinking, and slowly the face which she saw reflected in the dim old mirror began, though it was quite alone in the room, to smile back at her. It had not been difficult. It was all done now. The future was certain. She had gotten what was necessary, without asking for it; in some inexplicable fashion, quite without any planning, it had happened. She had not even been forced to say that all she had in the world were the seven francs that lay in the sunlight on the Louis Quinze console.

39

In this one fleeting instant life had been briefly a perfect and exquisite thing. In the great house, surrounded by beauty, by warmth and friendliness, the past and, even for a time, the future did not exist. It was a moment which could not have endured; with such a person as Ellen a moment of that sort might have been called a miracle to have happened at all. As the months passed the very comfort which surrounded her degenerated into a sort of dulness. After a time, Lily returned to her beloved south and there remained in the house only Ellen, Madame Gigon and Jean. The endless talk of Lily's guardian, which in the beginning had seemed vaguely diverting, became in the end merely the garrulity of a childish old woman. But there were worse things to bear.

She soon discovered that Lily, in her indifference, had virtually given over the house to Madame Gigon, and the old woman, poverty-stricken until Lily appeared on her horizon in need of a companion and watchdog, now used it to make up for all the years she had spent alone in a single room in a Versailles pension. Her friends were coming and going constantly, at the most inconvenient times, an endless procession of dowdy widows and spinsters. It was their habit to fortify themselves in the great drawing-room at just the moment chosen by Ellen for her practising. This they

did with an air of the utmost assurance, as if their great age in
some fashion gave them precedence over all else in this world.
Thus they would sit for hours talking volubly in a tongue which
so far as Ellen was concerned might have been Greek or Rou-
manian. But gradually as she came to understand a word here
and there, the mystery surrounding their impassioned conversation was dissipated, and out of the fog there emerged the prosaic
fact that their excitement had no foundation. They became as
wild over the price of cheese or the health of Criquette as if
they had been engaged in a battle to preserve *la glorie de la patrie*.
Yet they were all rich; the very fingers which they shook so
violently in the excess of their excitement glittered with diamonds
and emeralds. And presently, as her knowledge of French increased, Ellen came to the dismal realization that the bulk of their
talk was concerned with gossip. Gathered in a cluster about the
blind old woman, they tore reputations as they might have torn
cheese cloth. The words "maîtresse" and "intrigue" leapt from
the conference a score of times within a single afternoon. Heads
wagged and crêpe flowed, (for all of them were so old that they
were perpetually in mourning for a husband or a brother or sister; indeed, they went beyond this and mourned darkly the demise
of the most remote cousins). Madame de Cyon, the youngest
of the lot and the one whom Mrs. Callendar had mentioned so
long ago, had a way of narrowing her green eyes and saying,
"Tiens! Tiens!" over some choice morsel, with an air of sniff-
ing a bad smell. There were times when Ellen felt that if she
said "Tiens! Tiens!" another time she would strangle her.
Madame de Cyon was Russian but no better than the rest. They
were all, Ellen came to understand, like the women of the Town;
they visited Madame Gigon because she was blind and did not go
out, and the remainder of their time, it seemed, was spent in
collecting morsels for the delectation of the old woman.

There was but one thing which diverted the stream of their
gossip and this was the mention of the sacred name of Bonaparte.

She gathered, after a time, that there was a Prince Bonaparte
in whom the existence of all of them had found its core. She
learned to her astonishment that they ignored the very existence
of the Republic. A tottering old man, the son of a plumber's
daughter and a dubious prince who was a homicide (all this she
gathered from their talk) was, to them, a shining figure invested
with all the glory of the Corsican's golden bees.

At length, when she could bear it no longer, Ellen had a piano
brought in and placed in one of the great empty chambers in
the gallery above the drawing-room, and there she played for
hours in defiance of "le Prince" and his court of old women belowstairs. There were times when the music (especially the
compositions of some of the hateful new composers) became so
violent that it threatened to drown the gossip of Madame Gigon's
cronies. At such moments the blind old woman would raise her
sightless eyes toward the ceiling and observe to the others, "That
is Madame Shane's cousin. She is a violent woman (une femme
sauvage). . . . She suffers from an excess of élan."

At which Madame de Cyon would wag her head and observe,
"Tiens! Tiens! Perhaps if she had a lover it would help! A
young widow like that. . . ."

During the long months two things sustained her. One was,
of course, the old passion for her music. The other was Jean.
As they came to know each other, a warm and touching affection
developed between them, for the boy, despite the good manners
and the quiet grave charm born of his long association with older
people, had in him a spark which the presence of his cousin
fanned into a flame. The life he led was, to be sure, of a queer
sort . . . a life spent almost entirely within the walls of the
beautiful old house with little company save old Madame Gigon,
her fat dogs and the fussy music master who came twice a week
to give him lessons. It was a somber, quiet life which changed
only during the delirious summer months when, in company with

his mother and old Madame Gigon, he went to stay in the
country at Germigny l'Evec in the lodge of the park owned by
Madame's nephew, the Baron. There he could ride a pony,
sometimes alone and sometimes following his mother and the
Baron on their long rides at early morning through the damp
forest on the opposite bank of the Marne. And there were the
farmer's boys for playmates.

But in winter everything was changed. Until his cousin came
from America he played alone day after day in the little park
dominated by the white pavilion. The fascination of having a
cousin . . . a real new cousin . . . seemed likely to endure forever. Indeed the power of the novelty was so great that at
times he slyly deserted old Madame Gigon and made his way
secretly up the long stairs and along the gallery to sit on the floor
outside Ellen's door and listen, breathless, to the flood of music
that welled up to fill all the house.

When Ellen took him walking in the Bois she did not, like
his mother, walk in an indolent regal fashion; she moved rapidly,
quite the way a person ought to walk, and she talked of the people
they passed and sometimes even halted beside the pond and threw
stones far out into the water.

The boy was, at that time, her only companion for, shut in by
her ignorance of French and an incurable dislike for the stringy
American students who sometimes sought her acquaintance, she
had no opportunity for making friends. Yet she was content
to be lonely, for she had always been so, save in two brief moments . . . once when she had been overcome by the presence of
Callendar and again when Lily had wept and embraced her.
Jean worshiped her without claiming any part of her. He was,
in this, like his mother, for Lily, in the wisdom and indolence of
her nature, allowed Ellen to go her own way. It may have been
that in this grain of wisdom lay the secret of her charm and her
power even ove. the old women who came to gather about
Madame Gigon's chair and gossip. They succumbed to her like
all the others, like the Baron. . . .

There were times when the presence of César troubled Ellen. During all those months the first hatred she had for him failed to abate; she came to tolerate him, perhaps because she saw that it was necessary just as once it had been necessary to tolerate Mr. Wyck and the Bunces. She must have known that he worked against her. Yet in a strange, abstract fashion, she was able to understand the fascination of his hard and wiry masculinity. It was, of course, a thing which she herself could not have suffered for an instant, but she understood that to Lily it was a necessity. Beyond this point, however, her shrewd mind was unable to penetrate; it was impossible to fix the relationship of the pair. Lily never spoke of him, save in the most casual fashion. Indeed, Ellen, who could not bring herself to pry into such matters, never knew whether the Baron had been at Nice with her cousin or whether he had met her at the railway station. Madame Gigon spoke of him as her devoted nephew. She praised his virtues, and his constant presence at the house she interpreted as an interest in herself. At times Ellen could have cried out, "Rot! It's not your nephew who's supporting you and making you comfortable. It's Lily. And it's not you that he comes to see. It's Lily."

But she said nothing. The strangest thing of all was that she did not much care what their relationship might be. Once it might have disturbed her; now she looked upon it as a matter of no concern, a thing which had nothing to do with her. Yet there were moments in the evenings when, sitting with them in the long drawing-room, she felt vague, faint envy of her cousin. They came in the long silences when she would suddenly discover that Lily, so happy, so radiant, so lovely, in the long gowns of black velvet which she wore in the evening, was watching the Baron as he sat smoking his pipe, his feet stretched out before him toward the fire. The dogs adored him. He was the one person for whom they would desert Madame Gigon.

It was then that Ellen became conscious of her loneliness as a distant, almost physical pain. She learned to kill the pain.

Usually she rose, lighted a cigarette, and sitting at the piano, fell to playing wild and boisterous music out of the music halls.

Miss Rebecca Schönberg did not abandon her. She came once or twice to the house, where her bright shiny eyes penetrated every corner. She inspected, absorbed Madame Gigon and, having exhausted the possibilities of the old woman, put her forever out of her mind. She would, no doubt, have found marvelous material in Lily and the Baron but, as chance had it, they were never present. She took Ellen with her to the theater and twice to the opera, once to hear the inevitable Louise and once to hear Götterdämmerung, with all the guttural power of its German diction ironed out into smooth, elegant French. They called it Le Crêpuscule des Dieux, a whimsy which caused Ellen endless mirth. And at the end of two months, the restless Jewess having placed Ellen with an excellent teacher of French, left the Ritz and set out to visit an aunt who was married to a rich Gentile merchant in Riga.

But before she left she said to Ellen, "When I return we will arrange some entertainments. You must know the right people. That is vastly important. You must be modern, because during the next ten years to be modern will be to be chic."

It occurred to Ellen that Miss Schönberg, with remarkable speed, had undertaken the position of guide and messenger toward the heights of success. She was like a trainer who had taken in charge a new animal to teach it a whole set of tricks. She did not protest, because Rebecca Schönberg did not annoy her; on the contrary she was vastly amusing. In her restless energy there was a quality akin to the vitality of Ellen herself. They went everywhere; they saw everything; they absorbed the people about them, and returned late at night as fresh as they had started.

"Vitality," observed Rebecca, as they lunched at the Ritz on the day she left for Riga, "is nine-tenths of success. With one grain of genius and nine of vitality, any one can succeed."

As she made this observation, she regarded Ellen with an in-

tense and speculative scrutiny. The girl was looking about her
with a naïve interest in the people who sat near them. Her
whole manner was one of a vast wonder, as if she thought, "I,
Ellen Tolliver, lunching at the Ritz in Paris. It is not possible
that I am awake!" Miss Schönberg must have seen that she was
still a bit crude, still not quite free of the multitude, but she had
an unmistakable air, a certain distinction born in her which had
to do with the superb poise of the head, the slight arch of the nose
and the line of the throat. It had been sharpened and polished
mysteriously during the few months in Paris. The clothes were
right for her style . . . simple almost to severity, fitting the tall,
strong, energetic body to perfection. They came from dress-
makers, Miss Schönberg reflected, who knew their business.
Madame Shane must have had taste to have guided the girl so
well. A touch here and there and she would be perfect. What
she lacked was a sense of the bizarre which the public expected
from artists. There was plenty of time to accomplish that. . . .

"As I was saying," continued Miss Schönberg, over her *coupe
marron,* "vitality is everything. I once saw Mary Garden at a
rehearsal on a stage cluttered by the jumbled scenery of Pelléas
and Melisande. There were scores of people on the stage . . .
carpenters, musicians, a director, journalists . . . all alive and
moving about, but one didn't see them. One saw only Mary
moving back and forth, in and out among them. No one
else existed. It was a case of vitality. She is ninety-nine per
cent. vitality . . . nothing else. She hypnotizes the public.
Why, she has even adapted the French language to suit her own
ideas."

The men and women who sat at the adjoining tables must
have found them an interesting pair; they were both so neat,
so trim, so *raffiné.* It was not without reason that more than
one person, in the years that followed, spoke of Ellen as resembling a fine greyhound. The one, it was plain, was a Jewess and
very likely, if one could judge from the bright shrewd eyes, a
clever one. The other might have been anything . . . Russian,

French, American, Hungarian; it was impossible to say. And she was young and handsome.

"You must exercise," continued Miss Schönberg, "so as not to lose your figure or your vitality."

So after Miss Schönberg had gone, Ellen took up riding, a thing she had not done since the days when, as a wild young girl, she had ridden her grandfather's horses over fences and ditches without a saddle. And in the Bois, as in the Ritz, people came to notice her, that she rode magnificently and was dressed by the best of habit makers. Presently, Lily's friend Paul Schneidermann, who sometimes called at the house in the Rue Raynouard to see young Jean, took to riding with her. He was a languid young man, devoted to the arts, who led a sybaritic life, but he came presently to rise at dawn in order to ride by her side through the dewy park.

In those days, she did not forget her mother; on the contrary she wrote to her more frequently than she had ever done, and her letters were real letters, filled with the details of her progress. She wrote that Sanson had placed her with the proper teachers, that she had been to see the great Philippe and that everything had been arranged for her to work under him. She described Rebecca Schönberg.

Sometimes in the letters that came from the Town, Ellen discerned a note of subdued and passionate jealousy which had, somehow, taken the place of her mother's old distrust of Lily. She understood all that well enough; Hattie Tolliver hated Lily for giving her daughter all those things which she had herself desired so earnestly to give. But there was in Hattie's letters no sense of remoteness, not the faintest note of her having yielded the possession of her daughter. She treated Ellen still as a little girl. She saw her still as she had seen her on that last afternoon, a stiff, proud, awkward girl carrying her skates as she stepped through the door of the Tolliver house into the bright sunlight on her way to Walker's Pond.

40

It was the death of old Julia Shane which set in motion the next event of importance to the Tollivers. Things happened like that in their family. For a time all would go forward, much as a wave moving in a great smooth swell approaches a reef, until presently some event interrupted and the courses of their lives had all to be redirected. The old woman was, perhaps, the center, the one who at that moment held all the skeins in her withered bony fingers. She chose at last to die, and so brought Lily back to the Town and freed her niece, the faithful Hattie.

Together they cared for old Julia; together they sat by the side of her bed and slowly, under the circumstances, being so close to death, there grew up between them a new and unaccustomed affection. It was Lily herself who, a day or two before her mother died, told Hattie that the old story about her having had a child was true. The existence of Jean shocked Mrs. Tolliver less than might have been expected, less even than she herself had expected it to do, perhaps because always deep in her heart she was certain that Lily had had a child born out of wedlock. It was old gossip, which she had endeavored always to crush, yet it was gossip which she knew had its foundations in truth. She knew it, always, just as she knew the days when it was certain to rain or to be windy. She could not have explained the feeling, save that she had always distrusted Lily's charm. One could not be like Lily and still be a good woman. . . .

For the sake of morality, she made known with an acute frankness her disapproval of such conduct, and when this had been done in conscientious fashion she came to the subject nearest to her heart, the question which interested her more profoundly at that moment than anything in the world.

It happened a day or two after the funeral when the old Julia, dressed for the last time in her mauve taffeta, was borne through the Flats past Mills made silent by the long awaited strike, up to the bleak hill where they buried her by the side of her brother-in-law, Jacob Barr, the pioneer.

The two cousins, Lily and Hattie, sat together in the gloomy drawing-room before a fire of cannel coal, surrounded by pictures which stood in piles against the wall and rosewood furniture wrapped in ghostly cheesecloth. Shane's Castle, they both knew sadly, would no longer be a source of talk and excitement for the Town. Harvey Seton need no longer view it distantly with all the cold horror of a Calvinist. Its history was ended; there would never be within its walls another gathering of the clan.

The gentle melancholy which filled the old house had, it seemed, an effect upon the two women. Lily, clad in a loose gown of black velvet, sat watching her cousin with a curious look of speculation. She was as lovely as she had always been, so lovely, so gentle, so amiable that the Spartan Hattie in heart could not believe that she had changed her scandalous way of living. The older woman was, as usual, busy; it was as if her tireless fingers could cease only in sleep or in death. She sat now mending a bit of old lace which they had found while ransacking the vast attics of Shane's Castle.

"I will mend it and send it to Ellen," she said. "It is fine lace, better than anything she will be able to get in Paris."

Lily smiled, perhaps because Hattie thought so little of Paris and the laces it might offer, perhaps because it seemed to her that lace was so wildly inappropriate to Ellen. What was lace to a creature so proud and fierce, so ruthless? For she had discovered what the others had not known and what Hattie, even in the moments when her daughter hurt her most savagely, would never believe—that Ellen *was* ruthless.

"I am trusting you," she murmured over the lace, "to look out for Ellen. She is young and even if she is a widow she knows little of the world."

Lily smiled again. She thought, "As if it were possible for any man to seduce Ellen unless she chose to be seduced. She was born knowing the world!"

"Do you think she knows her way about with you away from her?"

Lily leaned forward and touched her cousin's strong, skilful fingers. "Don't fret over Ellen," she said. "Why, Ellen is safer in Paris than I am. Nothing can ever happen to Ellen. . . ." She bent her head and the warm color came into her cheeks. "I mean nothing of the sort that could happen to me. Why, Ellen's complete. . . . You don't understand how independent she is. She could go into the middle of Africa and land on her feet. She has no need of friends or guardians. Why, she's never even homesick."

Hattie's fingers paused in their work. "Never?" she asked in a low voice. "Never?"

And Lily, understanding that she had hurt the proud woman, hastened to add, "Oh, not that she doesn't want to see you all. She speaks of you constantly. . . . She wants some day to have you near her always. . . . You see, now she has to work. . . . I don't think you understand how ambitious she is."

Slowly, as Lily spoke, the cloud passed a little from Mrs. Tolliver. When her cousin had finished, she raised her head and said in a low voice, "Oh, I know all that. I've been thinking about it all lately . . . thinking a great deal. Only I never understood why it was she never came home before she went to you."

"There were reasons," said Lily. "Good reasons. . . . One was that she hadn't the money and wouldn't ask you for it. She doesn't know that I discovered that . . . but I did . . . I know just how much money she had. When she came to me, there were only seven francs left. . . . D'you know how much that is? It's a little more than a dollar. That's all she had left. A girl who would take such a risk is not likely to fail. You'll see her famous some day, Hattie. You can be sure of that. You'll be proud of her."

The fingers were busy again with the lace, and Lily knew suddenly that she had hurt Mrs. Tolliver again, this time in quite a different fashion. She had touched the old pride that had to do with money . . . that curious, hard vein of pride so incomprehensible to Lily who had never thought of money, save only as something that was always at hand to make the wheels of life run smoothly.

"To think," murmured Mrs. Tolliver, "that there wasn't enough money to bring her home to me." A tear slipping down the worn cheeks dropped into the web of old lace and Lily hastened to speak.

"It wasn't only that," she said. "Money would have made little difference. She couldn't have come back. . . . She didn't dare to come. You see, she was discouraged. . . . How can I say it? She told me the whole story. She said that if she had turned back then she would have been lost forever. She would have turned into a pitiful old maid like Eva Barr. She could never have married any one in the Town. There was no one with enough spirit. The ones with spirit . . . enough spirit for her, all leave the Town." Then after a silence: "You see the death of her husband was so tragic. . . . It hurt her."

For a second Mrs. Tolliver raised her head and faced the beautiful cousin. "She never loved him. . . . I know that."

Lily, a little frightened, kept silent for a time. She had come close to betraying the awful secret. "No," she said, presently. "I suppose she didn't love him. He was a creature without spirit . . . a nice man, but no mate for an eagle."

"You knew him?" asked Hattie. "Where? You never told me that."

"I met him on the train . . . the last time I came here. I think," she added with a faint smile, "that he was a little *épris* of me . . . a little taken by me. I know the signs. . . . But he was terribly frightened . . . timid like a rabbit."

And then Mrs. Tolliver came round again to the old observation. "I always said he wasn't good enough for her. I couldn't see why she had anything to do with him."

"Ah," said Lily. "You don't know your own daughter yet . . . Hattie. He helped her to escape."

But she knew that Hattie would never believe such a thing.

It was a strange circumstance that Lily—the Lily whom Hattie had always feared and distrusted—became in those days the one to whom the vigorous woman turned for comfort and companionship. Somehow the indolent Lily, so filled with understanding and knowledge of the world, served as a bond between the mother and the daughter in far off Paris. She succeeded in softening all the wounds made by Ellen in the abrupt notes which came with an efficient regularity, for Lily possessed a great power in such matters; it was a power which had more to do with the sound of her warm, low voice than with any logic in the arguments she used. Her arguments were neither logical nor profound; usually they were only observations as to the shyness of Ellen in all the range of affection, and the fierce ambition that tormented her.

"You will understand some day," she said, "that all she is doing is more for you than for herself. It is because she wants you to be proud of her."

"I don't care about that . . ." Hattie would say over and over again. "Not very much. But I don't want her to escape me forever. I couldn't bear that. She's different from Fergus. He is warm and shows his love. But there are times when I'm afraid I'll lose Ellen forever."

And Lily, in the depths of her placid mysterious soul, knew that here again it was a matter of possession . . . the same possession which the Baron must always have over herself, the possession which Ellen, without willing it, had exercised over poor Clarence. Hattie would not abandon her claim to her children. She could not say to Hattie, without hurting her, that her daughter was a creature whom none had possessed or ever would possess even quietly, secretly, as Lily knew that she possessed the Baron, despite all his boisterous show of domination.

41

ON a gray winter morning early in the year 1912, the Tolliver family stood on the platform of the Town station, a dirty affair covered with soot and shameful in a community so prosperous. There was no new station because none could be built so long as Shane's Castle stood upon the only site worthy of so grandiose a building as the Town had planned. The old woman was dead but her daughter Lily refused to sell, and Hattie Tolliver, standing now on the platform with the air of a field marshal surrounded by his troops, took satisfaction in this knowledge. Her family was on the retreat now before the onslaught of the Mills and she herself stood in command of the tiny rear guard.

"They'd give a lot for that land," she remarked to her husband. "I hope Lily will keep it. She doesn't need the money."

It was her parting shot at the Town. She stood now, free of it forever, surrounded by her husband, her son Robert and the everlasting Gramp. There was money in her pocket, money which Aunt Julia had left her, and so there were no perils ahead for a little time at least. And in her heart there were no qualms over leaving the place in which she had been born and lived a life filled with petty cares and worries. She regarded it, on the contrary, as a malignant desert from which two of her children had fled as soon as they were able, a pest-hole filled with factories and furnaces which had ruined her husband and forced her into poverty. She left nothing behind her for which she had the faintest affection; for the dog was dead long since of old age. Out of a family whose founder had settled the wilderness on this spot, only one remained . . . the hard and pious Eva Barr. They were all gone, the uncles, the brothers, the cousins, the sisters . . . all of them . . . dead now or gone out into the world.

Of this world, her ideas were still somewhat vague, for she never had been outside the borders of the state: it was perhaps a great, roaring place full of adventure, or again it might be very much like the county. It really made very little difference; she was free now, with money in her pocket, setting out at last in pursuit of her children.

A little way off, wrapped in a shawl and the coonskin coat, Gramp Tolliver sat peering indifferently through the fog that had settled over the Flats. In the depths of his heart, he respected his enemy. She stood there in command of the party, beside her son and her husband, so self-assured, so utterly fearless of the future. She might have been, he thought, a prophetess, a leader in an Old Testament migration. . . .

Only a week earlier there had been a skirmish between them over the matter of his possessions. Hattie had been for leaving them behind altogether with much of the family stuff; she had been for brushing aside carelessly all his shelves of books, his beloved rocking chair and the ponderous, antiquated desk. He would, she told him, be able to find all the books he wanted in the libraries of so great a city as New York. (As if, indeed, books out of libraries were the same as his own in which he had written along the borders such remarks as "excellent," "penetrating," or "tosh," and "rubbish"!)

Gramp had learned long ago the great power which lay in simple inertia; by taking no course of action, one became the possession of other people. He knew that they could not cast him aside like a piece of old furniture. He was a relative, a father; and one could not abandon a father. So he waited, and when Hattie threatened not to send his books and chair and desk along with him, he had refused to go at all and threatened her wickedly with the awful scandal of staying behind and entering the poorhouse. He knew the keeper well, he said (lying) and there at least they would let him keep his books.

In the end he had won. The desk, the rocking chair, and ten cases of books had been shipped ahead. With those things he would be content. He would be able again to raise his sanctum somewhere among the buildings of New York.

"The train is late," observed Hattie with irritation. "Why is it that it is never on time?"

She spoke with the air of an experienced traveler,—Hattie who had never been outside the state. She begrudged every moment that she stayed in the Town as a moment which kept her out of the future.

Bidding her not to worry and observing that eventually the train would come as all trains did, her husband turned away and began to walk silently up and down the worn bricks of the platform—the same bricks, he remembered, that he had trod on the night he set out upon his futile pursuit of his daughter.

It was one of those moments which occur sometimes between lover and mistress, between husband and wife, between those who have loved each other for years—a moment when it is impossible for the one to tell the other what is in his heart because it is quite beyond understanding. He could not say to her that he was sad because he was leaving so much that he had loved; she, his own wife who loathed it all so deeply, would think him a little mad. He could not say that he was sad because he would never again see the pleasant farms of the county, never again talk with his cronies of the Grand Circuit and quarrel about Pop Geers and how he had driven his latest race. Never again would he have those long arguments over horses in hotel bars and parlors during racing week, never again see the sap running from the trees in maple sugar time, never again talk with old Bayliss and Judge Wilkins about their Guernseys and Shorthorns. He was leaving a world which, despite all the disappointments it had brought him, he loved. There were friends in this world which it pained him to believe that he would never meet again.

He was lonely in a way he had never known until now.

For a moment, at the far end of the platform, the gentle man halted and fell to regarding his wife and his father with a strange and distant expression, as if they were strangers to him. The one was so restless, the other so indifferent. The one had love only for her children, the other had love for nobody and nothing. No, they could not understand. It was easy for them. . . .

Far off a whistle sounded and he saw his wife hasten for the fifth time to put all the luggage in order and pry old Gramp loose from his throne of indifference upon the baggage truck. At the sight he turned and as he moved, walking slowly toward them over the worn bricks, it occurred to him that it was Ellen whom they were all pursuing and that he was being dragged along with all the others.

He knew then what he had known before—that they would never recapture her. She was gone forever.

From his eminence on the baggage truck old Gramp had been meditating the selfishness of Julia Shane. She had left Hattie a fat sum of money, enough to escape, but she had kept it until she died, allowing Hattie to live for years on the very edge of poverty. Poor Hattie! She never saw the reason; she never understood that the old woman had kept her poor so that she might have her by her side as illness and old age claimed her. It was poverty that gave Julia Shane possession over her niece, and she had guarded the possession until the day her will was read, long after she had grown cold in her grave on the bleak hill above the Town. She was beyond help from Hattie now, and so, when she could keep her niece no longer, she had set her free.

The train screeched over the crossing, through the mills and into the station and Hattie, all agitation and worry now, jarred the old man loose from his meditation and steered him in the direction of their car.

Five minutes passed and the great locomotive with a series of demoniacal snorts pulled the train out of the station into the unknown. It carried an old man, a middle-aged woman, her mild husband and a boy. It was the last time that any of them ever saw the Town that bore the name of Hattie's grandfather.

42

THE house in Paris to which Sabine and Richard Callendar returned after their honeymoon stood in the
Avenue du Bois-de-Boulogne. It belonged, properly
speaking, to Thérèse herself, an enormous florid house of white
stone built in the baroque German style which came to dominate
the new parts of Paris in the early part of the twentieth century.
In all honesty it could be said that Thérèse was not responsible
either for its architecture or its decoration; the house came to
her in partial payment for the loans she had made a year or two
before the mysterious collapse of the international banking firm,
Wolff and Simon. It had been the property of Wolff, and
Thérèse, examining it one day shortly after the transfer to her
possession, decided that it would suit her admirably as a *pied-à-
terre* in Paris. Instead of turning it into cash she kept it and
used it, unchanged, during her visits.

Wolff, in the heyday of his prosperity (long before he shot
himself after fleeing half-way across Europe from such tender
creditors as Thérèse) had fancied himself as a collector of art.
The house remained as a monument to his bad judgment in this
matter; in a German fashion he had absorbed quantities of sentimental pictures and rococo bronzes that hung or stood on marble
pedestals between enormous second-rate tapestries. All pieces
of any value had vanished long ago when Wolff, in a frantic
effort to save the collapse of his firm, had summoned a dealer
who stripped the place of its Degas, its Rodins, and even the
Seurat and the Rousseau which a mistress had led Wolff into
buying against his will because she thought it chic to "buy mod-
erns." All that remained were remnants, grandiose, vulgar and
sentimental, among which Thérèse Callendar moved and lived
with as great an indifference as she displayed toward the
solid house on Murray Hill. The vast mass of marble and
tapestry satisfied, it seemed, an Oriental longing for pomp and
splendor. All that was Greek in her and much that was

French exulted in this phantasmagoria of marble, red plush and mirrors.

The house depressed Sabine from the very moment she crossed the threshold and beheld with a shudder the expanse of tesselated floor, the red plush stair rail and the drawing-room beyond with its modern gilt furniture set upon an authentic Savonnerie beneath sentimental German pictures of the Dresden school. Unlike her mother-in-law she had an Anglo-Saxon feeling that a home should be a place in which one was surrounded by warm and beautiful things. To Thérèse Callendar a house was a house. She owned houses in London, New York, Paris and Constantinople. A house was simply four walls within which one found rich food and soft beds during the brief weeks between journeys from one capital to another; and so the houses she possessed, like the one in the Avenue du Bois and the one on Murray Hill, came to have the indifferent air of great caravanseries. The only rooms which might have attained the dignity of the word "home" were those occupied by the concierges and the caretakers.

It was in this house, after the turbulence of her honeymoon, that Sabine found the time to analyze, with all her passion for such things, the exact character of her position. The process began during the first week when her husband, a little gruff over her dislike for the place, left her a great deal in solitude. She found that he expected her, during the day, to amuse herself; at night he was devoted enough, but the days clearly were to be his to be spent among his friends of the Jockey Club and else-where. The afternoons she passed languidly in a sitting room which adjourned their bed-chamber and had once served as a boudoir for the same mistress who led Wolff into buying a Seurat.

Sabine understood perfectly the character of the room; indeed, she found amusement in reconstructing from the evidence furnished by the atrocious house, the character and history of the suicide banker; and, though she never knew it, she came miraculously close to the truth.

The former boudoir had a marble floor on which were spread a tiger skin from India and a white bearskin from Siberia. There were mirrors on every side; the lady who had once occupied the room could not have turned her head without encountering a dozen reflections of her pink voluptuous body. (Wolff, being a German and a Jew, was certain to choose that sort of mistress.) The walls were covered with black satin on which had been painted a Parisian decorator's version of Tokyo in cherry blossom time. The chaise longue, fashioned like an Egyptian couch with carved lions' heads at both ends, stood almost hidden beneath great piles of cushions of fanciful design and color . . . mauve, yellow, green, crimson and black, all decorated with a profusion of tassels and gold lace. Lying upon it Sabine gazed at her innumerable reflections and thought that being a lady was much more satisfactory than being a demimondaine; only to laugh aloud the very next moment at the picture of her mother-in-law in respectable black satin and jet moving complacently about amid such vulgar and guilty splendor.

But all her thoughts were not amusing ones. For a bride, they were remarkably cynical and disillusioned. She was troubled by the change which had come over Callendar since their marriage . . . a change of which she had become aware almost at the moment she turned away from the altar of St. Bart's. Being the wife of Richard Callendar, she understood, was not the same as being his friend. This new relationship had altered everything. As a friend she might have found him satisfactory until the day of her death; as a husband . . . she did not know. She was puzzled. It seemed to her that in gaining a husband, she had lost a friend.

She understood, quite coldly and without conceit, that she was much more clever than most women of her age. She was not silly; she had few illusions. Nor was she, perhaps, romantic; though of this she could not be so certain.

It puzzled her that in becoming the wife of Richard Callendar, she had forfeited so quickly the old understanding, the habit they had of exchanging jests and of mocking people in the manner of naughty school children. She had tried from the first to revive the old intimacy, but when he failed to respond to her sallies and regarded her with a queer look of disapproval, she had grown depressed. It was as if the new intimacy, so intensely physical with a man like Callendar, had killed the old; as if by becoming his wife she had attained a position immeasurably remote from that of his friend.

Would he, she wondered, treat a mistress in this fashion, as if she were an institution? And an institution over which he had complete authority?

It was not that she thought him in love with her. Reflecting now with some bitterness, she knew why he had married her. From his point of view, the time had come for him to marry; she was suitable, and he must have known that a woman so clear-headed would cause him no difficulties, no scenes, no unpleasant-nesses. His mother had desired it because she liked Sabine and because it increased the already vast fortune for which she cared so tenderly. Lately, when they dined out together, she had come to understand even more—that he had perhaps chosen her because she made the best of herself, because she was a woman of spirit who, on entering a room, made an impression. There was in Callendar a strange sort of vanity which demanded satisfac-tion, a vanity which was, perhaps, another and a masculine man-ifestation of his mother's passionate sense of property. It would have been impossible for him to have married a woman, no matter how pretty she might have been, who was simply commonplace, sweet and insipid. He demanded in his wife an element of the spectacular. He had devoted himself to the tawny Lorna Vale, to the black and glittering Mrs. Sigourney, and to that strange, uncivilized musician from the middle west. About them all, there had been a spectacular quality, an undercurrent of fierce vitality, of outward distinction from the mob which appeared to have fascinated him.

She did not flatter herself that he had married her through desire; yet from the moment of their marriage he had been passionate after a fashion which shocked her. It was confusing to find that a man who was so polite and indifferent, so free from the little tendernesses which, to be honest, she had never expected, could at times display a passion so fierce and unexpected. It was as if in some way, love, passion, desire—she could not in his case define it precisely—were isolated, a thing apart.

There were reasons enough why she had married him. He was a great match; women would have desired him even if he had not been rich. And, she reflected with astonishing coldness, to have won him in the face of so much competition was a triumph worth paying for with much unhappiness. It was a victory over women who hated her and had sought with all the bag of their nasty feminine tricks to outwit her. She had married him too because she had come very nearly to the conclusion that she could never fall passionately in love with any man and that, therefore, it was far better to choose an interesting husband than a dull one. It was impossible, she felt, for love to survive such a passion as hers for dissection and analysis; love could not stand being pinned down and pulled apart. She did not then expect great love, and for the rest of it, Callendar had fascinated her as no other man had ever done, because he had always eluded her, just as he was eluding her now that he was her husband. In a sense, he offered her material vigorous enough to last a lifetime.

More than once in the midst of such reflections there returned to her the memory of the night when the raw young creature, whom she now thought of as "that musician," had fainted. She remembered how, on this occasion, she had regarded Callendar minutely as he stood, his hands clenching the back of a chair, watching the naked Burmese dancer swaying to the insidious rhythm of tom-tom and flageolet. She remembered how the dancer and the barbaric music had shocked her a little as being wildly out of place in the big stuffy drawing-room. It was music which to her meant very little save that it was mildly exciting. Upon Callendar and his mother it had produced the most astonishing effect. Could it be that in this lay the clue alike to his fascination and to her failure to fathom that obscure thing which people called his soul? Though he had been her husband, even her lover, for a long time, she knew him no better than she had known him on the night of his mother's absurd soirée.

And lying in that preposterous boudoir that had once belonged to the mistress of Wolff, she found herself admitting that slowly and certainly he was gaining complete possession of her imagination. It troubled her because she valued above all else in the world her own aloofness; so long as she did not lose her sense of being a spectator, no one could hurt her, not even her own husband. It troubled her too because she could not be certain whether this new interest had any relation to love or whether it had its roots in a sort of perverse attraction, fundamentally intellectual in quality . . . an attraction which carried an element of the sensual hitherto entirely foreign to her nature. Day after day she found herself smiling over the thought that this sensual attraction should have been a little shocking and was not. In one sense he had overwhelmed her. He was a cruel, a passionate lover. If she had been less intelligent, more innocent, more sentimental, he might have wounded her very soul; but the curse which made romantic love impossible also saved her. Never, for more than a passing moment, had he been able to dissipate her awful awareness.

He had come to her, after all, from Lorna Vale, from Mrs. Sigourney, perhaps even from that American girl (though of this

she could not be certain) and, doubtless, from many other women.
So much experience, she understood, made him dangerous to any
woman possessed of curiosity.

During those first weeks in Paris, it amazed Sabine to find that
her husband knew so few of his own countrymen; he told her
that most Americans who chose to live in Paris were either silly
or depraved and so revealed for the first time the fact that he did
not consider himself American. He became sulky when she asked
him to dine with a school friend of hers whose husband chose to
live in Paris.

"I know her husband," he answered in contempt. "He is an
ass who tries to live like the French. He's not a Frenchman.
His money comes out of a New England shoe factory."

But he went all the same, perhaps because she managed to convey to him without saying it, that he was neglecting her. During
the day she spent a great deal of time with friends and acquaintances, mostly women who had married foreigners of one sort or
another. In their company she went from shop to shop buying
an endless number of clothes. The same taste which caused her
to shudder at the monstrous house in the Avenue du Bois led her
to love clothes passionately. She knew too that beautiful
clothes satisfied the strain of vanity in her husband which demanded a wife who was dressed with taste and distinction. She
had begun already to plan how she might attract and keep him.

One evening, while they were dressing for the Opera, he said
to her as she came out of the boudoir and faced him, "It is true
what Jacques said at the club to-day. It takes the Parisian to
make the clothes and the American to wear them. The Americans are the best dressed women in the world."

And he looked at her in such a way that she grew warm suddenly in the knowledge that her figure was superb, that her
shoulders were marvelously white and beautiful, and that her
clothes were perfect. Until lately she had dressed, like most
American women, for the sake of other women; now she under-

stood that, without knowing it, she had been dressing of late to please a man, because she had found one who understood the beauty and importance of clothes. There was, despite all her other doubts, great satisfaction in that.

She discovered too that his friends were not among the Americans and the English but among the French and the Russians. She found herself, night after night, at dinners watching him as he stood, straight, dark and handsome, his queer gray eyes wrinkled a little with laughter, talking to some friend who was a foreigner, and at such moments she was aware of his great difference from her own people. He was, in some obscure fashion, linked with that preposterous boudoir and its florid decorations. Perhaps, secretly, he really liked the awful house as much as his mother liked it.

She saw too, with the green eyes which took in everything, that the women about her were intensely conscious of him, and she knew then that she had been at the same time lucky and tragically unlucky. It would be so easy for him . . . a man of so much intelligence and a beauty like that of a fine animal.

Toward the end of the first winter, a day or two after she had made certain that she was to have a baby, she interrupted her shopping long enough to have lunch at the Ritz. She had a table, alone, in one corner of the big room and, having no one to talk with her, she fell to observing the types at the other tables and reflecting upon the vulgarity and self-conscious glitter which marked the patrons of such hotels the world over. So she was startled when she found that the personality of some one who entered the room at that moment had the power of distracting her.

Two women came in together and stood for a time surveying the room. The one (it was she who was disturbing) was tall, slender and handsome, dressed smartly in a black suit with a black fur. The other, plainly a Jewess (who understood perfectly the manipulation of head-waiters) was small, with a ferrety, good-natured face and an energetic, chattering manner. They took a table at a little distance so that Sabine was able to watch them.

In the beginning, as she realized that there was some reason for her having noticed the pair, she became aware of a sense of familiarity in the taller woman. Then, as she watched them, the reason became quite clear. It was the American girl . . . the musician, in Paris and in the Ritz of all places, and no longer dowdy but handsomely dressed!

By long established precedent, Sabine made no move toward approaching the newcomer. It was her habit to avoid involving herself with too many people; such a course made life far too tiresome and complicated. She had known the girl well enough, but there was no point now in renewing the acquaintance; indeed, it seemed idiotic even to consider the idea. Vaguely, she reflected, it was a good idea to leave what was well enough alone.

But the old, insatiable curiosity had been aroused; she found herself puzzled as to the presence of Ellen . . . (Tolliver, that was her name) . . . in Paris. She had been poor. She had been, she told Sabine during those stark conversations in the house on Murray Hill, hindered by a hundred obstacles. Yet here she was, in Paris, dressed handsomely in clothes which the appraising eye of Sabine told her had come from one of the best establishments, probably Worth or Chanel. Sabine was curious too regarding the whereabouts of the husband . . . the husband whom she had once mistaken very stupidly for the girl's lover. And slowly, in the midst of the noisy room filled with a fantastic assortment of people, there rose in her memory a picture of that vulgar apartment the Babylon Arms, and a glimpse as they opened the door of the tiny top floor flat, of a mild little man in shirt sleeves. What had become of him?

She remembered too the confidences which she had exchanged with her mother-in-law in the days when the young musician seemed so near to upsetting their carefully laid plans. Mrs.

Callendar had mentioned the mild little man, saying, "I'm certain the girl doesn't care a fig for him. She's tied to him by pity. That's all. But we can be thankful for him. He stands between her and Richard."

Where was the little man to whom she was tied by pity?

Any one noticing Sabine as she made ready to leave the dining room might easily have taken her for an adventuress. She drew her veil over her face and holding her fur almost up to her eyes, she hastened out, taking care on the way that her back was toward the tall girl and the busy little Jewess. In the battle between an overwhelming curiosity and a vague instinct of fear, it was fear which, unaccountably, won the victory.

As her motor, very small and very expensive, sped away along the Rue de Rivoli and across the white spaces of the Place de la Concorde into the Avenue des Champs Elysées, Sabine succumbed to an inexplicable sense of depression. It occurred to her that she did not really know whether the girl had ever been the mistress of her husband. She could not even be certain that Callendar had ever asked Ellen Tolliver to be his wife. Thérèse Callendar had the word of the girl that there had been nothing; yet with Callendar, it was impossible to know. If he had asked her to marry him, it must have been but a step toward seducing her from her husband, the mild little man. It did not occur to Sabine that with two women a man might be two quite different persons.

The motor sped smoothly along the asphalt past the Elysée Palace, around the Arc de Triomphe and on toward the huge house in the Avenue du Bois.

It might be, she thought, that Callendar himself knew the girl was in Paris. It might even be that he had arranged it for her to be there.

And again Sabine reflected that in her good fortune there was a tragic element of bad luck.

Callendar came in late for tea. She heard the footman speaking to him as he came through the vast hall across the tesselated floor. She waited for him, sitting behind the silver tea things in the small sitting room at the back of the house, and as he entered she was seized again by the disturbing fear of losing herself. He kissed her, casually, and said, "Well, have you had a busy day?"

"Nothing. . . . I went shopping with Madeleine and lunched alone at the Ritz."

She might easily have added, "And whom do you think I saw there?" But she did not. On the contrary, she said, "It's a funny show . . . the Ritz . . . And you? . . . What have you done?"

She did not hear his answer, because her attention was swallowed up by a sharp sense of his presence . . . a vivid image of the dark face and the fine, muscular hand as he raised his silk kerchief in a familiar gesture to stroke his mustaches. In the back of her mind a small voice told her that it was perilous and awful to have such emotions.

She poured his tea but he did not drink it.

"I'll have a glass of port," was his reply. And then, "I had luck to-day. I won eleven thousand francs at baccarat . . . playing with Henri and Posselt, the Russian."

"Good," was her reply, and again it was not what she might have said. This gambling worried her. It was not that he would bring them to poverty by it; that was almost impossible. But there was in her mind a feeling of disgust at the picture of men spending five hours of daylight in gambling. She tried to reproach herself by the thought that the idea was American and provincial. But she understood why his mother sometimes reproached him for not thinking more of his business. (Always he retorted that she liked business and he did not.)

There was silence and presently Sabine said, "I wonder, Dick, if we can't do something about this house . . . either take one of our own or clear out some of this rubbish."

"It's very comfortable. . . . There's every luxury."

She laughed. "Too much luxury . . . I feel at times like a kept woman. Wolff had it for his mistress . . . I'm sure he did."

Callendar smiled. "That's true," he replied. "Some of it is very bad, but can't we stick it out until spring? We'll go to the country then or to England for a time."

She had spoken of the matter before and the answer had always been the same. She now revived the discussion without hoping for any solution; she wanted to know whether he really liked it, whether he was really linked in some way to the extravagance of that awful boudoir. Watching him as she spoke, she believed that he did.

For a time they smoked in silence and then Sabine, crushing out the ash of her cigarette, observed with a magnificent air of indifference, "I wonder what has become of that American girl . . . the musician. You remember, 'Miss Tolliver' was her name."

She saw that he looked at her sharply and then, disarmed by her indifference, that his face assumed an expression which matched her own.

"I don't know. I suppose she's still in New York. She was very talented."

"She planned to come to Paris some day. If she does, it would be a nice thing to do to look her up."

Her husband smiled before he answered her, a quiet amused smile such as he used to display when he caught his mother in some intricate feminine plot.

"I don't see why we should. She probably wouldn't like it. After all, it wouldn't be the same, would it?"

From this she could make nothing. All that he had said might mean anything at all. It seemed to her that the more she talked, the more confusing, the less clear everything became.

"I simply happened to think of her. She's a remarkable girl. She's had a struggle from the beginning."

"A damned fine lot," was his comment. "You'll hear from her some day."

She must have understood that all her slyness was of no use, that methods such as this brought her nowhere, for she fell silent after this until Dick rose and said, "Shall we go up? My nerves are on edge from playing all afternoon. I think I'll sleep a bit."

Then while she watched him, as from a great distance, it occurred to her that all this was scarcely the behavior of a bridegroom on his honeymoon; it was, on the contrary, as if already they had been married for years.

As she rose to go with him, a sudden decision crossed her mind. Without thinking why she was employing it, she used the one stake which she had at hand.

"Dick," she said abruptly, "I am going to have a baby."

He turned, and into his face came an expression of pleasure the like of which she had not seen there before. He smiled and, moving toward her, took her gently into his arms.

"That's fine," he said softly. "That's wonderful." And she felt him kiss her gently after a fashion that was new and disarming. It was neither a casual kiss, nor a passionate one; those two moods she knew very well. This was something new. She felt almost that she were an animal, a pet for whom he had a great affection and a strong desire to protect.

"Your mother will be pleased," she said, frightened again by the old dread of losing herself. (She was ashamed too that he should feel her tremble so.)

"She will be delighted. She wants an heir. She thinks I'm not much good at taking care of all her money." And he kissed her again in the same tender fashion.

"But it might be a girl."

He laughed a little. "No, I'm lucky . . . Think of my eleven thousand francs!"

But she saw that he wanted a boy, desperately, that he was not in the least interested in a girl. It was very foreign of him . . .

that desire for some one to carry on the name, to inherit all the fortune.

After they had gone up the stairs with the rail of red plush, he came into the sitting room again to kiss her gently and to ask if she were feeling well, and when he had gone Sabine, as she lay in the darkness among the gaudy pillows of the chaise longue, understood clearly and bitterly for the first time the change which their marriage had brought about. He was being gentle and loving not because she was a woman or because he loved her, but because she had become now by the course of nature an institution, a wife, a prospective mother. He was being tender not toward her but toward an idea. He placed her a little apart, so that the old sense of companionship was no longer possible. She was a symbol now . . . the wife and mother who was the rock and foundation, the one who produced sons to carry on name and property, but not by any chance the one who was loved because she was a woman.

43

OF all the events, the emotions and the tragedy that occurred during the turbulent years spent in the Babylon Arms, nothing had hurt Ellen so much as the fashion in which Mrs. Callendar, after such a show of friendship and interest, vanished quickly and completely from her life. Even the affair with the son and the death of Clarence had had in them elements which her feminine mind found not unpleasing; there was a certain romance in the idea that it was herself whom Callendar really desired and not Sabine at all; there was even more romance, though perhaps a trifle bitter, in the idea that a man had taken his own life because he loved her too much to spoil her existence. In her headlong fashion, she was conscious that these elements contributed to her own personality; they made her an important figure with enhancing shades of romance and tragedy. That the facts were known to so few persons as to be almost secret, only increased their fascination. Sometimes, as she walked along the boulevards or rode in the Bois beside Schneidermann, paying little heed to the accompaniment of his pretty speeches and comment upon people, pictures or music, she found herself filled with a triumph at her secret knowledge. She thought, "People who see me and talk with me little know all that has happened. They do not know that they are talking with a powerful person. They do not know the mystery and tragedy."

She began even to think that she had consciously planned each step of her progress, and she came after a time to forget that all that had happened to her had been born either of headlong impulse or through some senseless operation of circumstance.

Nevertheless there were times when she grew troubled by a sensation of insecurity. Mrs. Callendar had deserted her without a word. Rebecca might easily do the same. It was only Lily in whom she placed any real trust; with Lily there were ties of family and of blood.

She was troubled too because she knew that there was still need of the Jewess. For all the arrogance that came more and more to assert itself in her nature, for all the confidence and the secret triumph with which she looked out upon the strangers who passed by her on the boulevards and in the Bois, she understood that she was not yet ready to stand alone. She needed the guidance of persons like the gentle Schneidermann and the busy Rebecca. They knew the world; they knew the tricks by which one advanced to fame; they knew the people who were the right ones to know. She could not try her own wings because they were not yet strong enough.

Yet she must have the aid of such as Schneidermann and Rebecca without once acknowledging it. The old, twisted pride forbade her to lean upon any of them. It was a hard business.

And she would pull in her horse so that the languid Schneidermann might come abreast of her and talk without having to shout at her back. She would smile indifferently at him and say,

"It is a beautiful morning. . . . Look at the dew shining beneath the hedge. And the spider webs like nets of shining silver."

Sometimes Schneidermann rode silently by her side, stealing glances at the color in her cheeks and the blue black of her hair as she rode so straight and so proud and yet so careless of her horse, reining him in at will or galloping him madly through the long tunnels under the dripping linden trees. He was a tall thin man with an arched nose and a blond drooping mustache, rather pale and mild, who never disputed with her the choice of bridle paths or the hour they were to return. She understood that he was interested in her; he had helped her with her accent, though in this they had made little progress, for she had a stubborn, careless way of sticking to her own version of the tongue just as she had never lost completely her way of saying "dawg" for dog and "watter" for water, and persisted in the burr which came to her doubly through a Scottish heritage and a middle-western childhood. She suspected sometimes that he might even be falling in love with her and this made her knit up her brows and scowl at him furtively. She did not want him, even with all his money. She had had one husband who was mild and gentle and a bit stupid. Schneidermann was, to be sure, more intelligent than Clarence, and he knew far more of the world; it amused her to talk with him of music and art and politics, but a relationship more intimate was to her inconceivable. Aside from this worldly knowledge he was like Clarence; he possessed the same humbleness, the same physical paleness. .It annoyed her to believe that she attracted only men who must be dominated.

Yet there was Callendar. Unconsciously she came to compare the humbleness of Schneidermann and Clarence with the cat-like virility of Callendar. It was as if she were putting aside all other men in the knowledge that some day, at some time if she waited long enough, she would come to possess him. Yet when she thought of him, as she frequently did after she had gone up to the luxurious room looking out upon the white pavilion, she grew angry at the memory of that last visit to the Babylon Arms.

He had watched her, cat-like, until, driven by some obscure desire, he could no longer play the game of waiting.

She came slowly, as she grew to know and understand the world, to see that he had looked upon her always as a naïve and helpless creature, awkward and a little ridiculous. It gave her a sort of restless and unhappy satisfaction that she had shown herself the more powerful.

It was not strange that she did not encounter the Callendars in Paris. The world in which they moved was more remote from hers than the Babylon Arms had been from the house on Murray Hill. True, the crêpe-hung Madame de Cyon was an acquaintance of Thérèse, but Ellen took good care that this fat, bedizened gossip should never learn of her acquaintance with the Callendars, and so it did not occur to "Tiens! Tiens!" ever to mention them. Of their life Ellen sometimes read a paragraph or two in the Daily Mail or the Herald; they were off to New York or England or had just returned to their house in the Avenue du Bois. She knew nothing of the feverish, cosmopolitan society which surrounded them, nothing of the seedy, impoverished Royalists who were the poor relations of Thérèse and lived in fine, damp, decaying houses in the remote provinces, clinging to the splendor of the past because so little else remained; she knew nothing of the rich American women who had married titles.

At the lovely old house in the Rue Raynouard there were always the friends of Lily and Madame Gigon, dowdy, bourgeois and dull, among whom Lily moved with the calm of perfect security, as the one American who had ever penetrated with any success the inmost circle about the doddering Prince Bonaparte. The presence of so vigorous and arrogant a creature as Ellen they resented bitterly and sometimes openly, so that Ellen in the end was thrown for companionship, a thing of which she stood very little in need, upon Rebecca Schönberg, Schneidermann and all their hodge-podge of musicians, artists, writers and patrons of art.

Rebecca, as the months turned into years, had come to devote more and more of her time to the house in the Rue Raynouard. When she returned from Danzig, or Rome, or Vienna or wherever it happened to be, she came day after day to Numéro Dix where it was her habit to sit quietly in the big empty music room and listen with extraordinary attention while Ellen played hour upon hour. She watched Ellen's progress with an interest of such intensity that Ellen at times grew ill-tempered and wished heartily that the sandy haired creature would disappear forever. She would, doubtless, have committed some act to sever their relationship forever save that always in the back of her mind was the certainty that the Jewess was valuable to her.

It was really the sense of Rebecca's domination which at once annoyed and confused her; otherwise she liked her well enough. It was Rebecca who suggested the number of hours which she should practise; it was Rebecca who bullied her into going out in the world; it was Rebecca who insisted on helping her choose her clothes; it was Rebecca who even brought to the Rue Raynouard people who sent Madame Gigon into the most distant part of the house where she would be safe from the noise of their violent, modern music. It was Rebecca who at times set the house by the ears and threatened to bring about an open quarrel between Ellen and the Baron.

For a long time the enmity between these two had grown less and less concealed. Lily must have sensed conflict and in her quiet, indolent way have chosen to pretend that no strain existed. There was irony in the fact that a woman who sought only quiet and leave to do as she pleased should have found herself suddenly the battleground between two natures so violent. In dealing either with insolence or domination Lily had no difficulty; always she had gone quietly her own way achieving in the end by some unviolent coup her own desire. When she chose, even the dark, bumptious César obeyed her as a pet dog might have obeyed. She was even able to cope with Ellen (though she seldom interfered) in the very midst of the girl's most stubborn moods. Yet when César and her cousin came into conflict, she grew helpless; it was

like living perpetually on the edge of a volcano. She knew, perhaps by instinct, what it was that caused the trouble . . . that
each of them sought to rule the household.

So the peace had gone presently from the lovely old house. On
one side were ranged César and his aunt, the blind old Madame
Gigon, reënforced by the cohorts of crêpe-laden old women who
came to her salons and impressed upon her the sense of her injury.
On the other were ranged Ellen and her ally, the shrewd Rebecca.
Between the opposing armies stood Lily who wished only peace
and luxury and indolence.

One night early in May, before Lily's household had moved to
Germigny, Rebecca failed to appear for a concert they had planned
to attend. There had been good reason; an aunt of Rebecca's,
very rich, had arrived without warning from Vienna. Yet Ellen
was unreasonable and believed that Rebecca had failed her deliberately. She had gone out for a time to walk sullenly along the
Seine and when she returned, she went silently to her room and
locked the door. The disappointment, the softness of the evening,
the look of the lights floating in the river . . . all these things
created an overwhelming and terrible nostalgia.

Once inside the room she flung herself down on the canopied
bed, her blue black hair all tossed and disheveled, and, weeping,
reproached herself bitterly. She was, she believed, a horrible
creature. She had treated her mother cruelly; she had forgotten
the existence of her brother—of Fergus, with his humorous blue
eyes and magical sympathy and his uncanny way of understanding
what it was that terrified her, what it was that made her unhappy,
what it was that drove her on and on without rest or peace. She
saw too her father, a mild man who loved her without making
any claim, without once speaking of love. On all these she had
turned her back in a heartless fashion.

And Clarence . . . poor Clarence . . . was always with her in
these terrible moments of solitude. She knew him then as she
had never known him in life; she saw him with a terrible clarity,

moving about meekly with the awful look of pleading in his near-sighted eyes. He had not been like that in the beginning; he had changed while he lived with her, changed, as it were, beneath her very eyes. And she saw him too as he lay for the last time on the divan of the little flat in the Babylon Arms, peaceful at last and untormented by a woman who always eluded him, a woman whom he loved so much that he made way with himself that he might hinder her no longer. And *him* she could never repay; it was impossible even to explain or to beg for forgiveness, though he would have said, no doubt, that there was nothing to forgive.

Then growing a little more quiet, she asked herself in one of her rare moments of reflection what power had driven her to act as she had done. To this there was no answer; it was quite beyond her. She knew, as indeed she had always known, that she must go her way, solitary and ruthless, to fulfil a rather shadowy ambition, a confused desire for vindication, a hunger for the sight of the world at her feet.

It would do no good now to turn back, because such a course could only create disaster. Sitting up among the pillows of the canopied bed she fell to staring hopelessly into the darkness. For a long time she sat thus, pale and disheveled, her long black hair streaming over the crimson peignoir. She had discovered an awful thing. She, Ellen Tolliver, who had wanted only to be free, was entangled and caught beyond all escape. She could not turn back. She could only go forward along the path which she herself had chosen, and it was a lonely path, a path so enveloped in solitude that she fell to weeping again over the desolate waste of its loneliness.

There was a moon which painted all the garden outside with a pale green light; the pastry-cake pavilion of Le Nôtre had turned to silver and the leaves of the old plane trees, rustling together now in the soft spring air, cast black shadows across the white terrace. Lured by the faint stream of silver that spilled in through the darkness at the tall window, Ellen rose presently and, sitting on the chaise longue, looked out over the garden. To-night the familiar, distant sound of the boat whistles along the Seine seemed very close. The hoofs of a horse passing along the cobblestones of the Rue de Passy struck up a slow tattoo that leapt the garden wall and came up to the very window. It was a foreign horse, passing along a foreign street and the garden had become remote and melancholy with a new sort of beauty. It was as if she suffered from an enchantment, as if all that had happened since the day she had gone off to skate alone on Walke's Pond had been an hallucination, detached from all reality. She might wake and find herself once more in the shabby comfortable sitting room of the house on Sycamore Street. Still it could not be a dream; because if she returned to that shabby room, she would find it occupied by strangers she had never seen. Her mother would no longer be there, darning in the firelight, nor her father sleeping on the great divan, nor Fergus, nor Robert. They were all gone now . . . gone, strange to say, in pursuit of herself. Perhaps one day they would come as far as this lovely garden. Ma would like it only because her children were there, but Fergus would know its meaning, how much of old beauty that was beyond expression lay in the silver pavilion, in the mottled trunks of the old trees and in the black filigree of shadows across the white terrace. If only Fergus could be there she would not be lonely. . . .

And for the first time in all her life, she became sharply aware of the passing of time. She heard it rushing past her and knew that slowly, like a tide rising upon a beach of shingle, the years were stealing upon her, the years and a desperate haunting loneliness which it seemed impossible ever to escape.

Sitting there in the moonlight, the whole of the past rose up in a queer, muddled procession. There had been in the progression of events neither rule nor reason. Fate, one might call it, but fate was a silly name. It meant nothing; it could not explain

how Clarence had turned toward her and so changed all the course
of her existence; it did not explain Mr. Wyck and his muddled
part in the suicide of Clarence; it did not solve that sudden,
passionate interval with Richard Callendar. It was all senseless
and muddled.

People might judge her as hard and cold and calculating but
that, she thought, would be unjust. She had been forced to make
her own way, to clear her path by the best means at hand. She
had tried always to do it without harm to others. She was not,
like Sabine Cane, born with all that one needed in this world.
If she had been born, having those things, she might have been
more happy, less lonely, less aloof. Sabine, she reflected bitterly,
had everything . . . wealth and friends and happiness. Even
her husband had been delivered into her hands, a man who, if
chance had been less cruel, might not have been hers. She envied
Sabine.

So she fell to thinking of Callendar. What might have happened if she had hurt Clarence deliberately and gone away with
her lover? Callendar would have married her. She would have
been rich. She would have been free. There would have been no
more of this struggle.

But she could not be certain. For the first time, thinking of
him now out of the detachment of her loneliness, she doubted him.
He might not have married her, after all. Why should he have
done it? And if he had married her he might not have been
stronger than this other thing which kept driving her on, this
terrible ambition that was like a disease with which one was born.

What would love have been with a man like Callendar? She
trembled a little at the memory of him, grown softer now with the
passing of time and more sentimental. With Clarence love had
been a poor timid growth, choked and inarticulate, a thing that
somehow he made shameful. Callendar was not like that. Love
with him must be a great glowing passion that would overwhelm
all else, even her own terrible awareness.

She sighed and bound up her hair. All that had passed long ago and was done. She might die now without ever knowing anything more wonderful than the stifled, timid embraces of Clarence.

Idly, out of nowhere, into her brain there strayed presently a memory of old Julia Shane. It had happened when Ellen was a little girl and she could not think why she had remembered it, yet unaccountably it was there in her head, very clear, like an old photograph found by chance after many years. She saw old Julia sitting in the big drawing-room of Shane's Castle on a Christmas day talking with Grandpa Barr. She was thin and hawklike and leaned forward now and then on her ebony stick to give the coals in the grate an angry poke. She had been quarreling with the vigorous old man and presently she said sharply, poking the fire for emphasis, "Fate! Pooh! Robert! Fate is no great tide that sweeps everything before it. It is a river that goes this way and that, and the smart fellow is the one who jumps when it turns in his direction!"

Aunt Julia has been right. Fate was like that and, Ellen reflected, she had jumped when she saw it coming her way, but by ill luck she had jumped sometimes full into the midst of the stream and been swept along by it.

Lost in this sudden memory she was interrupted sharply by a murmur of voices arising from the garden. Without stirring she listened and, presently, recognizing that one was Lily's and the other that of the Baron, she made no attempt to move out of hearing. Once, a long time ago when she had first come to Paris, she would have moved away or have let them know by some sign that she was nearby, watching and listening; but that time had long gone by. She listened now either because she was shameless or because in the mood of the moment it did not matter what things she learned. And in some way the sight of the two dark figures, moving so close to each other up and down the white terrace, dissipated the terrible loneliness.

The pair below her knew, no doubt, that Madame Gigon was

long since snoring among the gimcracks of her bedroom, and they believed that she herself was out, at the theater with Rebecca. In the French manner, the servants did not matter; it is probable that of all the people in the house they knew most of Lily and her life.

The Baron's voice, deep and rich, drifted up to the open window. "Jean, you say, will be back from school in June?"

He wore his uniform, and the perfection of its lines emphasized all the trim, masculine hardness of his slight figure. Beside him in her black gown, with the stole of sable thrown round her for warmth, Lily was soft and lovely. His voice it seemed, caressed her.

"He is growing big now . . . fourteen. Think of it. . . ." He laughed softly. "*You* with a big boy of fourteen! It is impossible . . . *incroyable!*"

Lily said something which was not audible and then, "Yes. We must be more careful. He will begin to see things."

"In England boys are not so sharp . . . at least not about affairs between men and women."

In silence they walked for a time, once up and once down the terrace. The leaves of the plane trees rustled and a boat far below in the Seine whistled faintly. Once more they passed beneath the window.

"June is more than a month away," said the Baron. "We could go to Nice for three long weeks."

Lily, it seemed, was unwilling, for he argued with her, saying in a voice that would have melted steel, "Think of it. . . . We have not been alone for months. Think of it . . . the mornings . . . waking together . . . looking out over the bay. . . . Alone . . . alone." He paused suddenly and seizing her in his arms kissed her. For a long time they stood thus. Ellen could see them quite plainly, standing in the shadow of one of the white urns, Lily with her head against his shoulder while he kissed her again and again.

Then slowly, with the air of waking from a dream, Lily raised her head and passing her hand against her eyes, murmured, "I should not like Ellen to know."

At this he laughed and a new note, one of hard anger, entered his voice. "She knows already if she is not a fool."

At the intonation Lily withdrew and leaned against one of the white urns. "She doesn't. I'm sure of it. She has said nothing."

Again he laughed, scornfully. "She's no fool. She knows it would be more unpleasant for her than for you. She needs a home and money . . . just now. She'll not open her eyes so long as it might harm her plans."

Sitting there in the darkness, Ellen succumbed to a slow anger that rose to her head like a fever. She had believed that he spoke against her; now she was sure of it. She hated him vaguely, because he dared even to say such a thing to her cousin. He was so sure of himself, the amorous beast.

She was hurt too, as if some one had struck her, because what César had said was so near to the truth.

But Lily turned away from him. "I won't have you say such things," she said. "It is ridiculous and unjust."

He did not use words in defense of himself, perhaps because words were to him such weak and awkward weapons. Instead, he simply took Lily once more in his arms, and beneath his kisses, Ellen saw that all resistance, all anger melted from her. It was like a bit of wax touched suddenly by a flame. . . . An amazing sight which seemed to illumine sharply the whole of Lily's strange life.

After a moment, he placed his arm about her waist and they moved away down the steps into the shadow of the plane trees. Once they halted for a time while he kissed her again and then, resuming their way in the same state of enchantment, they disappeared through the filigree of black shadows into the white pavilion, silvered by the moon.

And in the room above the terrace, Ellen slipped from the chaise longue to the floor where she lay flung out, weeping passionately. The loneliness returned now more terribly than ever before.

44

IN the morning, after coffee and brandy, Ellen rose at dawn to ride in the Bois. She went purposely without Schneidermann, leaving him to a vain pursuit, in order that she might be alone; and when she returned she found that Lily was already awake and had come down from her room to breakfast on the terrace. The May sunlight poured into the garden and beat against the stone of the façade, enveloping her with its reflected warmth, as she sat at the iron table before a bowl of hot chocolate, a dish of rolls and two piles of letters. One heap had been opened and the contents lay scattered over the table and on the flagging beneath. As Ellen, tall and slim in her riding habit and hard hat, stepped through the tall window Lily put down a letter and said, "I brought your mail out here. It isn't interesting this morning . . . mostly bills."

Ellen throwing down her crop and hat, ran her fingers through her dark hair and seated herself on the opposite side of the table, while Lily sent for more chocolate and hot rolls.

"You look tired," observed Lily. "Were you out late?"

"No. Rebecca couldn't go with me, and I was tired so I didn't go at all. But I slept badly."

Lily turned the page of the note she was reading. "You work too hard," she said. "Try taking a rest. Come down to the country with me in June."

"No, I can't do that . . . I'm going to play in London. Rebecca and Schneidermann have arranged it. It will be my début."

She announced the news abruptly, without any show of emotion.

Lily put down the letter and leaned toward her. "You didn't tell me it would be so soon."

"I only knew it for certain last night. I'm superstitious about speaking of things until they're certain. I'm to play in Wigmore Street on the third."

Her cousin was all interest now. She drew her chair a little nearer and carelessly pushed her letters off the edge of the table.

"Have you chosen a gown? We'll send for the motor and choose one this morning. That's important, you know . . . especially in England where they recognize good clothes but never wear them."

"I can't go this morning. . . . I'm going to Philippe."

"To-morrow then," said Lily. "I shall go over to London for the concert and bring Jean back with me. . . . Perhaps César can go too."

"Not him!" Ellen interrupted sullenly. "He'd spoil everything."

For a moment the two cousins regarded each other in silence. In Ellen's face there was a look of bitterness that appeared more and more frequently of late, a sort of devil-may-care expression that puzzled Lily and disturbed her. They had never recognized the breach before . . . not, at least, openly.

"Why shan't César come?" she put forward gently.

"He hates me! I know that!"

Lily endeavored to pour oil on the waters. "It's not true. You're rude to each other . . . both of you. Why is it? There's no reason. He doesn't really dislike you?"

For a time, Ellen came very close to being unpleasant; she was tempted to reveal all she had seen and heard from the window above the moonlit garden. The memory of César's words rang in her ears, a taunt in which there was too much of truth. But she could not say that she hated César because he never allowed her any peace of mind. She could not say that she never saw him without thinking of Callendar.

"It's nothing . . . nonsense, I daresay, on both sides." The power of Lily's eager friendliness overwhelmed her. "I'm sorry," she added, "that I'm disagreeable sometimes. . . . I've been worried lately. I know the quarrel is my fault too." She tore open one of her letters and then, looking very pale, she added, "Bring him, if he would like to come. . . . It won't matter."

And Lily never knew what it was that softened her so abruptly. She did not know, of course, that Ellen was thinking of Callendar.

hoping desperately that he could be there to listen to her music as he had listened so many times, with all the passionate abandon which meant so much to her. She needed Fergus too, for she was frightened now that the chance, awaited so long, was at hand. With César present she would at least be reminded of Callendar. It would be the next best thing to having him or Fergus in a cold audience of strangers.

On the top of the little pile of letters was one from her mother from which she read portions aloud to her cousin.

"We are settled now in seven rooms in East Seventieth Street. There is room for Fergus and Robert and Papa and I, and a room for Gramp and his books, which he would not leave behind. And an extra room which I have let to a young man who works with an electrical company. He has nice manners and seems to be of a very good family. He talks a great deal about them. It seems that his family was rich once, a long time ago. He was very unhappy in a boarding house, but he likes it here. . . ."

Lily, who had been listening closely to the news, looked up as Ellen suddenly stopped reading and allowed the letter to slip to the ground. She saw that her cousin reached down hastily and recovered it, as if she wished to conceal her agitation.

"Not bad news?" asked Lily.

"No. I was just surprised for a moment by something in the letter. I think . . . I think I know the young man she writes of. Still I can't understand what chance brought him and Ma together. . . . It's an idiotic world. . . . There's no sense in it." She lighted a cigarette, and after a thoughtful silence added, "Ma is a remarkable woman. Think of her, tearing a whole family up by its roots and transplanting it without a thought."

Then she continued reading. The family, she learned, were all very comfortable in their new home. Fergus might be going abroad in a year or two . . . some sort of writing work, with a newspaper. Hattie had recaptured him only to lose him again at once. Robert was the same, the plodder of the family, silent, unbrilliant, a sort of rock and foundation as old Jacob Barr had been before him. They were hoping to see Ellen soon now. She must come home, now that they were settled in New York. And in the end there was the usual refrain. *I am looking forward to the day when I can make a home for all my children.*

When she had finished reading, they both sat for a time in silence and at last Lily said simply, "She'll never give up, will she?"

In the same pile there was a note from Rebecca sent by hand from the Regina where she was stopping. It read:

"I'm sorry about last night but it couldn't be helped. How was I to know that Aunt Lina was arriving from Vienna and hadn't been in Paris for twenty-five years? She had to be looked after and will take a great deal of my time, I suppose, as she plans to stay a month if I cannot get her off before that. She is important because she is very rich and has no children. Uncle Otto owns a sapphire mine in Cambodia. And I am her god-daughter. (Her real name is Rebecca, but in the family they call her Lina because there are so many Rebeccas.) Besides, some day she may be of use to us in Vienna, especially when the time comes for you to play there. She is rich and has myriads of rich friends who all spend money on the arts.

"I won't let her interfere with the plans for London. I've talked to Schneidermann and in case I can't get away at once, he will go over and arrange things in plenty of time. He knows the ropes. Don't let Lily help to choose your gown without my being there. She has beautiful taste but it's too quiet for an artist. The public, especially in England and America, expects something spectacular from a musician. I'll try to run out for a moment to-day if I can get rid of Aunt Lina. Perhaps I can make her believe she is tired from the journey and stay in bed all day. Here's to the triumph in London!

REBECCA."

The note troubled her, so that when Lily rose, and murmuring something, went into the house to dress, Ellen took no notice of her but got up and walked, in her slim black riding habit with the skirt pinned high (she did not ride astride, because she thought it ugly) down the steps into the garden.

If Rebecca failed her now, either through Aunt Lina or otherwise, she felt that she would not have courage to go on. She would kill herself because there would be nothing left. She fancied the humiliation of playing before row upon row of empty seats. If fate played her such a dirty trick, she would put herself out of fate's way. She was sick to death of being buffeted about, this way and that, achieving neither success nor happiness.

Angrily she beat her skirt with her riding crop. If Schneidermann went to London, it would only put her hopelessly in his debt. She might have to marry him out of gratitude, and she wanted no more weak husbands to clutter up her life.

And then this business of Wyck turning up suddenly as a lodger in her mother's house! It could be no one else; her mother's description fitted him too perfectly . . . *a man whose family had been rich once, who worked with an electrical company, who talked a great deal of past splendors.* He had reappeared, armed with her secret. She could fancy her mother caring for him, making him comfortable, giving him all the attentions he yearned for and never received in a world which kicked him about. She could trust Fergus, but Mr. Wyck was nasty, feminine. Still he had not betrayed his acquaintance either with her or poor Clarence. If he had done that, her mother would have spoken of it in her letter. . . . A friend of one of Hattie's children would be like a child of her own. It may have been that he felt as guilty as she herself felt; if that were true, he would not be likely to betray her. She thought of his shifting green eyes, his mincing manner and his habit of talking perpetually of the past. He was a worm . . . something one might find on lifting a stone!

Twice she had made the round of the garden, indifferent now

in the midst of her own worries to the nearness of the guilty pavilion, when she saw Augustine, the maid, coming toward her with a card. For some reason, she was overcome by a sudden feeling that this bit of paper which the red-faced Breton girl held in her hand was of immense importance. She found herself hurrying forward to meet her. She found herself reading the name and then, looking up, she saw in one of the tall windows that opened on the terrace, the figure of Sabine Cane . . . Sabine Callendar . . . standing in the brilliant sunlight, dressed all in gray, superbly, with a gray veil that fell over her shoulders . . . the same Sabine, poised, indifferent, striking. Nothing had changed save that she looked old, surprisingly so considering the perfection of her make-up.

The call must indeed be important, since Sabine had followed Augustine straight into the garden.

They sat in the long drawing-room where they might look out over the sun-drenched garden with its blue flame of irises lighting up the expanses of gray stone.

"What a lovely house!" remarked Sabine as she drew off her gloves. "I suppose it is your cousin's."

The speech was stiff, constrained by the vague shadow of hostility that had enveloped them, almost at once—an intangible thing, which it is probable both women felt but failed to understand, because each fancied herself too intelligent to be the victim of jealousy.

"Yes. It belongs to Madame Shane."

Sabine laughed. "It's the sort of house I would like. You see we live, when we're in Paris, in a sort of World's Fair exhibit in the Avenue du Bois."

It surprised Ellen to find that a single, small word such as "we" could cause her any feeling. She found too that the presence of Sabine had turned back the years; she was watching her now, as she might watch an enemy, as she had watched her in the days when she had gone, a young and awkward girl, to the big house on Murray Hill. She had not "watched" people in quite this fashion for a long time now.

She felt herself quite a match for the wordly woman who sat, carefully, with the brilliant light at her back; she could no longer be taken at a disadvantage.

"It is strange," said Ellen, "that we have not met before."

Sabine's scarlet lips curved in a bright hard smile. "I saw you once, in the distance, at the Ritz. It was nearly four years ago. You went out before I was able to speak to you." She coughed, nervously. "So I lost trace of you. I was sorry, because I was interested to know how you had come to Paris so soon."

"I just came. There was nothing strange about it."

"But I thought there were so many difficulties."

"They happened to disappear very quickly . . . through a series of chances."

The old Sabine, the one Ellen had known so well, the Sabine who was always prying into the affairs of other people, showed itself now, yet there was a difference, impossible to define save that now her interest seemed to be more personal, more intense, not so cold and abstract.

"You see," she continued, "Mrs. Callendar found your address through Madame de Cyon."

(So Mrs. Callendar had known all along that she was in Paris.)

"I have not seen her," said Ellen, "since I left New York."

For a moment, the shadow of a mocking, bitter smile crossed Sabine's face.

"She is just the same. . . . Just as vigorous, just as determined."

"I should like to see her again. . . . Perhaps she will be interested to know that I make my début in London in June."

At this, even the indifferent mask of Sabine betrayed a flicker of surprise. "So you're still working at your music."

Ellen laughed. "Of course. What did you think?"

"But it has taken a long time."

"Naturally. It meant work. I was taking no chances."

So they talked, rather stupidly, fencing with each other, making no progress. It was clear that Sabine had not called at such an hour simply through politeness, nor was it likely that she called because she sought to renew an old acquaintance. Both women were too intelligent to have misunderstood each other. As for Ellen, she found herself excited by the consciousness of a shadowy struggle; there was a devilish satisfaction in finding herself with an advantage over so experienced a woman as Sabine. The visitor wanted something; beneath all her indifference, she was clearly excited and nervous. Once Ellen caught her pulling a button from her gray gloves.

It occurred to her suddenly to be bold and strike at what might be the root of the matter.

"How is Mr. Callendar?" she asked, amused at the thought of speaking thus of him.

"He is well," Sabine replied with a terrible quietness, and then, after a little pause. "Do you see him frequently?"

For an instant Ellen was very near to losing her temper, a thing she might easily have done now that she found herself a match for Sabine. But she did not; instead she waited and said, "What do you mean? How could I have seen him? I have not seen him since I came to Paris."

The answer was so honest, so obviously true, that even Sabine was discountenanced. She looked at the floor and murmured, "I didn't know. I thought perhaps you had."

"Why didn't you ask him?" suggested Ellen.

"It would have done no good. Besides he would have thought me jealous." There was something pitiful in the terrible control exercised by the woman. Even Ellen forgot suddenly the strange sense of enmity. She kept silent and it was Sabine who spoke.

"Besides." she said. "You never spoke of him or of Mrs.

Callendar to Madame de Cyon. That made me think you might have seen him."

"It would only have made complications," replied Ellen. "If you knew Madame de Cyon, you would understand." Her voice suddenly grew cold. "Did you think," she asked, "that he had brought me to Paris? Did you think I was carrying on an affair . . . secretly?"

The more they talked, the clearer grew the likeness of the one to the other. They were in both the same restraint, the same watchfulness, the same determination that the world should not hurt her.

When Ellen looked at her visitor again she saw that she had been weeping, silently; she was putting a handkerchief, stealthily, to her eyes, ashamed clearly that she should have so revealed her unhappiness.

"I have been wretched all day," she said. "You see little Thérèse and I . . . that's my little daughter, she's three years old . . . found a starving kitten yesterday. It had fleas and we washed it with carbolic soap. It's sick. I'm afraid we've hurt it and it may die. Little Thérèse is very fond of it."

Then, quite silently, the tears began to stream down her face. It was the only sign she gave. She did not sob. Her hands did not tremble. She simply wept.

It was a terrible sight, because Ellen understood plainly that the kitten had nothing to do with the tears.

Presently, after she had had a glass of port, Sabine took Ellen's hand and murmured, "You must forgive me. I was spiteful and rude . . . and unjust too. But you see there were so many things. You knew my husband a little, so you can guess perhaps something of the story."

Then pressing her hand to her head, she was silent for a time. "You see I have had a child . . . a daughter . . . and I can never have another. Mrs. Callendar and Richard want a son . . . I know that. . . . The old woman wants some one to care for all her money. You see, he's no good at it. They've never said anything, but I know she wants me to divorce him so that he can marry again. I can feel all their will working against me. . . . It's horrible. It's sinister. It's always concealed by smiles and smooth words. I can't do that. . . . I can't. . . . Not yet . . . perhaps some day." The tears began to flow again, for even Sabine could not keep from pitying herself. "And I know there are other women. . . . I think I am a little mad to behave in this fashion . . . to come to you, like this." She coughed nervously. "You were always so strong and so independent. So was I . . . once."

She rose and dried her eyes and powdered her nose. "Now," she said, "I look presentable again." Then she took Ellen's hand and murmured: "You'll forgive me, won't you? I've been a fool. . . . And you'll say nothing?"

Ellen moved with her toward the long stairs that led up to the door opening upon the street. Together they climbed them, quite close to each other in the friendliest fashion, and from the doorway Ellen watched her, composed once more, chic and worldly, step into her tiny motor and drive away.

As she turned from the door and descended the stairs, it occurred to her suddenly that save for chance she might have been the unhappy woman entering the motor. It was amazing what Callendar had done to Sabine. Last night she had been envying her, and to-day Sabine had come to her almost, one might say, seeking help. . . . Sabine who had been so cold and impregnable and aloof.

And in a strange way, in spite even of Sabine's insults, she had given her sympathy. It was as if they had, tacitly, become allies in the battle against him.

45

AUNT LINA did not interrupt the plans, for she spent only two weeks in Paris and left declaring that it had changed for the worse during the twenty-five years that had passed since her last visit. The new houses looked just like the houses in Vienna; her friends had died or gone away; in fact she could see no reason at all for ever having left Vienna. So Rebecca went over to London to make the arrangements and Schneidermann did what he could in Paris.

Between them, they set in motion a caravan of gossip and small talk which found its way through devious channels into Berlin, Munich, London, Rome and New York. Sometimes news of this new pianist (who was so remarkable) was carried by word of mouth; sometimes it was relayed by letter to the members of Rebecca's tribe scattered across the face of Europe. After a conference in the Rue Raynouard, attended by Lily, Schneidermann, Rebecca, Ellen and César (who took part resentfully until it occurred to him that if Ellen could be made famous he might be free of her forever), a name was chosen. "Ellen Tolliver" was commonplace and carried no implications that were not solid, respectable and bourgeois. The name which emerged after three hours of frantic argument was "Lilli Barr," a name compounded out of Lily's name and the name of old Jacob Barr . . . a name that might be anything, a name that had a slight turn toward the Hungarian, a name that was abundant of implications. A musician called Lilli Barr could have no past that was not glamorous and romantic; and between them, Rebecca and Schneidermann proceeded to invent just such a past by creating out of nothing the most amazing tales.

In all the hubbub and preparations Sabine was forgotten, but the memory of Callendar remained. Ellen, now Lilli Barr, prayed that he might reappear for just one night.

The success of the concert in Wigmore Street is now a part of musical history. In London Rebecca drafted the services of an immense family connection; fully one half the seats were taken by Bettelheims, Rakonitzes, Czelovars, Schönbergs and Abramsons; there were even one or two Rothschilds present in a box. Schneidermann recruited another group, less numerous but more cynical and hostile, from the musical world. Pictures of Lilli Barr (who photographed splendidly) appeared in the illustrated papers, and the critics, instead of sending their second or third assistants to the concert, appeared in person.

It was all admirably managed. The shrewd brain of Rebecca forgot nothing. In those busy days the friendly little Jewess with the red hair and ferrety eyes stood forth for the first time in all the glory of her rôle as impresaria; and when the concert was over and the notices read, it was clear that she had been right in the instinct that had led her to speak to the pale, disagreeable girl in black who had paced the deck of the *City of Paris* five years before. Rebecca had loved music always; she had wished earnestly all her life to be an artist of one sort or another; she had spent years in rushing madly from one capital to another in search of diversion or occupation, and now she was settled. She had found her place as "the exploitress," as Schneidermann expressed it, of Lilli Barr, the new star upon the horizon of music.

But there was one thing of which Rebecca knew nothing and which Ellen chose to keep a secret because it could have been of interest to none save herself. After she had played the first group on her program and returned to the platform in response to the applause, she caught a glimpse among the shadows in the back of the hall of a dark, familiar face. It astonished her that she should have noticed it at all, and once she had seen it, the rest of the audience failed to trouble her; it no longer had any existence. From that moment there had been a strange lift apparent in her music, a wild sort of ecstasy which carried every one with it. She played for one person. Among the shadows at the back of the hall Callendar sat, listening, his dark sleek head bent forward a little. He was alone.

It was Rebecca who saw to it, in the months which followed, that Ellen was seen at the proper places, dressed with just a touch of fantasy so that she might attract notice and yet not be taken for a demi-mondaine; it was Rebecca who saw to it that Ellen's fierce dark beauty (so confident now in her triumph so arrogant) was set down for posterity by the most fashionable portrait painter in England, a man with a romantic reputation whom the gullible public would in time connect with Lilli Barr in some hazy intrigue which had never existed. It was Rebecca who saw to it that Ellen was photographed beside this composer and that one, and that the photographs, skilfully made with an eye to public attention, fell into proper hands and traveled to America where they looked forth from the pages of the Sunday supplements into the startled, proud faces of Charles and Hattie Tolliver and Fergus and Robert. They even found their way, after the rest of the family had exhausted the possibilities of the papers, into the cell of Gramp Tolliver who chuckled with wicked satisfaction over the spectacle of the ruthless granddaughter who had, after all, escaped.

And they found their way back to the Town where Mrs. Herman Biggs (née Seton and now the mother of three children) clipped them and showed them to the neighbors and to her brother Jimmy, a spindly, nervous youth of nineteen, who in his childhood had been honored more than once by cuffs from the hands of Lilli Barr which the newspapers said (via Miss Schönberg) were insured for one hundred thousand dollars.

In her boarding house, Cousin Eva Barr, last of the family, dominated the greasy meals for more than a week by the stories of the childhood of Lilli Barr. Under the spell of the reflected glamour, she forgot even the charities she administered so grimly, and spent most of her day at meetings and walking along streets where she would be likely to encounter people who would ask about her cousin. For in all the excitement, it seemed that in some way she herself had at last escaped the tradition that made a vigorous, unmarried woman into a grim, forbidding dread-nought.

Miss Ogilvie too shared the triumph though in a different fash-ion. It was she, after all, who had discovered Lilli Barr; but it was not this which warmed her fluttering heart so much as the old secret of the missing five hours, which even now she shared with no one. It was Miss Ogilvie—poor, timid, Miss Ogilvie—trapped like Cousin Eva Barr in the tradition of an earlier genera-tion, who had helped this Lilli Barr to escape. And in her thoughts (she being a sentimental creature and knowing nothing of the truth) the little parlor took on a new glow of romance and glamour. At times, when her secret seemed almost too difficult to keep, she fancied that some day, after she herself was dead, they might place on the front of her house a little tablet with an in-scription which read, "It was from this house on the Fifth of January, 1903, that Lilli Barr (then Ellen Tolliver) eloped . . . etc. etc."

So, in the first years of her fame, Ellen remained a little dazed by her success. She moved, terrified always on the eve of a con-cert, going between concerts her hard-working, secretive way, so that there grew up about her, in addition to all Rebecca's marvel-ous lies, a legend of mystery. Few people knew her or anything at all of her real life. There were only the gaudy stories of Rebecca's fabrication which people believed and yet did not believe because there were so many of them and they were all so conflict-ing. In place of the old coldness and restraint, which melted only when Ellen's fingers touched the keyboard of a Bechstein or a Steinway, Rebecca managed to create such a sense of splendor and unmorality that presently the newspapers, as old Sanson had done long ago, came to speak of her as a second Teresa Car-reño.

She caught too from Rebecca something of the latter's contagious sense of showmanship and came to understand presently that if one wished to be sensationally successful it was necessary not only to be a fine musician but something of a charlatan as well. She learned not simply to walk out upon the platform; she made an entrance. In Paris, where Rebecca managed to buy up most of the press, she had a great following. Women came to the concerts for no other reason than to see her clothes and to study the youthful perfection of her figure.

Success and triumph flared up in her path in whatever direction she turned, yet there were times when the old doubts, the old self-reproach, assailed her bitterly.

One night, as she left the Salle Gaveau after a concert, and stood waiting with Rebecca for Schneidermann's motor to come up, the sight of an *affiche* bearing the name LILLI BARR in great letters filled her with a kind of terror. Silently she gazed at it, fascinated by the name and the program in small letters beneath it . . . Bach, Schumann, Moussorgsky, Chopin, Debussy . . . all the great names dwarfed beneath the gigantic LILLI BARR. She knew that on the sidewalk, almost within arm's length of her, there stood students, hungry and a little threadbare, who waited by the door to catch a glimpse of her as she left the hall. She knew that this Lilli Barr, whose name was set forth in letters so gigantic, had every reason to be content. Lilli Barr . . . Lilli Barr. . . . She stared at the name with a curious sensation of strangeness, of detachment. Lilli Barr was herself now, and Ellen Tolliver was dead, swallowed up by a fantastic creature whom Rebecca and Schneidermann between them had created. To the world Ellen Tolliver had no existence; she had never lived at all, and she had now to play a rôle—to put on a false face —that the world might not discover it had been deceived. She was still playing the mountebank, the charlatan, as she had done in the drawing-room on Murray Hill behind a painted screen with a Russian tenor and a Javanese dancer. For a moment she hated Lilli Barr with a passionate hatred. She had lost possession forever of Ellen Tolliver. In the midst of her pride there had always been the grain of humility, fiercely hidden from the world, which made her in spite of everything an artist.

The voice of Rebecca, shrewd and sleek with her success as an "exploitress," sounded in her ear.

"Here's the motor. . . . We'll be late and the others will have arrived without you." (Always hustling . . . Rebecca . . . always pushing from one thing to another.)

César, for all his hopes, had not yet lost her. At that very moment the house in the Rue Raynouard was filled with people whom Schneidermann and Rebecca hàd called in . . . actresses, writers, rich bankers with a fancy for art, musicians, perhaps even a demi-mondaine or two . . . all the rag, tag and bobtail gathered from a dozen cities of Europe. What was she doing among them? She? Ellen Tolliver? Had she lost possession of herself?—that precious self she had guarded always with such secrecy?

It was not Ellen Tolliver who was going to this noisy party. It was Lilli Barr, a creature who had been made out of nothing. Ellen Tolliver would have gone to her room and wept a little over her loneliness.

The voice of Rebecca again . . .

"Ravel is coming to-night. He wants to speak with you about the new suite he has done. . . . It is important. Be nice to him."

It was all a long way from Walker's Pond.

For two years she lived, thus, almost in public, sustained always by the glorious vitality descended to her from Hattie Tolliver and guided by Rebecca who allowed her to miss no opportunity. She was tireless. She appeared everywhere. Yet there was a remoteness about her which none penetrated, save perhaps Callendar whose dark face appeared now and then in the back of some concert hall, now in Paris, now in London, now in Rome, wherever his path chanced to cross that of Lilli Barr. Sometimes as she came upon the stage she caught a fleeting glimpse of him, watching her as he had watched on that first awful evening in

Wigmore Street, when so much had hung in the balance. He was always alone.

During the second summer she set out with Rebecca to visit Vienna and exploit Aunt Lina and her friends, and to play in Salzburg; but they never arrived, for on the day they left Paris the Archduke Ferdinand was shot in Serajevo.

On the same day Fergus sailed for London.

46

IT was Fergus who first called Gramp The Everlasting. The name was not original; he found it in one of the seed catalogues which his father brought into the apartment; for Charles Tolliver, shut up all day in a government office and all night in a city flat, led vicariously a life which in happier times had been a reality. The living room was cluttered with the catalogues of gardening houses and journals which dealt with agriculture, stock breeding and horses. The outward life of the gentle man was scarcely more than an illusion; a man with Charles Tolliver's face and dressed in Charles Tolliver's clothes lived at an address in the east Seventies of New York City; the same man worked at the Customs House, eating his lunch modestly in one of the little restaurants where Clarence and Mr. Wyck had once taken their gloomy meals. But the real Charles Tolliver was not to be found in any of these places. He lived perpetually among the farms of a county in the Midlands, or in the hotel bars and parlors of the Town, talking endlessly of the Grand Circuit races. And sometimes he was to be found seated with a fishing rod on the banks of a clear stream a thousand miles from the greasy current of the North River. When he was not in such places, he could be found among the catalogues which displayed gay colored pictures of gigantic beets and ears of sweet corn, or in the pages of journals which had splendid pictures of prize cows and great herds of cattle grazing knee deep in alfalfa. Sometimes he found pictures of his old friend Judge Wilkins' prize shorthorns and on such occasions he grew sentimental and talked of the county as an old man talks of the love affairs of his youth. One would have thought that the triumph of each new blue ribbon won by Judge Wilkins' prize bull, Herkimer Sextant, was a personal triumph of Charles Tolliver. The city had for him no reality; it was a dreary episode, a nightmare from which he would in time awake as he awaked reluctantly from the pleasant dreams he had when, carefully tucked in on the divan by Hattie's capable hand, he escaped for a little while from the ugliness of the hard, unreal city. Since he had come from the Town, the habit of sleep had grown upon him: it was a drug . . . hashish or opium.

It was in one of his garden catalogues that Fergus found the name. Seizing the booklet in hilarious triumph, he bore it to his mother and, holding it open, he showed her a large picture in color of a gigantic raspberry advertised as bearing throughout the season. Underneath in bold letters there stood forth in an amazing coincidence the name—TOLLIVER'S EVERLASTING. The name stuck and from then on the family referred to Gramp with humorous disrespect by that name. At length the old man himself overheard it and was delighted. He resolved then to see his hundredth birthday. In the solitude of his room, he felt amazingly brittle and young. Time rushed past him; tremendous things happened to the family, but he remained passive, unchanged because he had no emotions left to exhaust him.

The war that trapped Ellen and Rebecca Schönberg somewhere in the neighborhood of Trieste dawned upon the Tollivers in the most conventional fashion. At first they talked of it as impossible and absurd, and for the first time in years Gramp emerged from his seclusion to discuss with Robert (for whom he had an intense dislike) the Siege of Paris, which he had lived through in his youth. Indeed his interest attained such a magnitude that he very nearly revealed a secret hope that one day he might be taken, a

millstone about his daughter-in-law's neck, back to the city where
he had spent what she would have called "a profligate youth."
But he took care not to mention the wish for fear that Hattie, in
revenge for so many defeats over so many years, would do all in
her power to thwart it. At ninety he wanted to see Paris again.
He developed a passion for the military maps which appeared in
the newspapers and used up all the pins in the house tracing the
advance of the Germans toward the Marne.

As for Hattie, she gave small heed to his eccentricities, for she
was occupied with other things. Her son, her best-beloved, was
in England; she could not trust him. He might join in the war.
She knew him well enough to know that he would not stop to
weigh the chances of death; such a spectacle would fascinate him.
And she knew that her daughter, in the company of an unearthly
creature called Rebecca Schönberg (whom she had come to regard
darkly as a sort of procuress), was lost somewhere in Austria.
Until now, these foreign nations had meant little to her save that
they were in the part of the world from which came the hordes
of aliens who jostled her in the street. But now all was changed;
a great war was no longer a distant affair to be treated with indifference. Her children were involved. She fancied Fergus already ill and wounded. She saw Ellen taken for a spy and im-
mured in the sort of a dungeon one saw in the lurid pictures of
the Sunday papers.

The news that came at last into the midst of her frantic anxiety
brought her no peace. The two letters arrived by the same mail.
The one from Fergus contained the information that he had gone
to France, that vaguely he was trying to find a place where he
might see the war. He was all right, he wrote. She must remember his excellent luck. It was all terrible, tragic, incredible
. . . the sights he had already seen, the things he had already heard.
Yet it was magnificent too; somehow between the lines of a letter
which he had meant to be reassuring and a little cold, she caught
a sense of his reckless enthusiasm. She understood that he saw
the war as a great spectacle. She remembered him as a little boy,

wild with excitement at the glitter and pomp of a circus parade, intoxicated by the splendor, captured by the romance.

And she knew that she could not stop him. She knew that all the ink in the world and all the words she might write with it would not hold him back. It was all so clear in his letter. The image returned to her again and again . . . a little boy, running recklessly, wildly toward the gaudy parade. . . . Only this time the parade was tragic and wound its length half way across the face of Europe. And because it was so gigantic, it was all the more powerful, all the more glamorous. What could she do against it?

Sometimes she cursed Gramp, The Everlasting, for the wandering spirit he had passed on to her children, and sometimes she reproached her own people for their strength and energy. If her children had been poor weak things she would never have lost them; she could have guarded them always. Sometimes when her worry and despair became overwhelming, she had a terrible premonition that in the end she would be left, alone, with that terrible sardonic old man, her father-in-law.

But Ellen was coming home! Ellen was coming home! She wrote from a place called Genoa to say that she was sailing in two days with Rebecca Schönberg, whom Hattie pictured as sallow, dark and sinister. Ellen had escaped from Austria, out of the midst of the war! She had been arrested with the dangerously international Miss Schönberg, but in the end, due to Miss Schönberg's Aunt Lina and Uncle Otto, everything had been set right and they were allowed to go by boat from Pola into Italy. It was a wretched experience. The police, the soldiers . . . every one was stupid and a little insane. Ellen would, she wrote, be thankful to get away from such a madhouse as Europe had become. *Damn them!* she wrote, *for starting a war just when I had planned a tour of Austria and Germany!*

There was hardness in that one line, of a new and amazing kind.

The entry into New York was made, due to Rebecca's shrewdness, the proper sort of event. Two women straight (as the newspaper men managed to make it seem) from the front line! Two women who had been detained as spies! Two women who were good for at least two columns of space, paid for at so much a line, not to speak of the large photograph showing them on the deck of the *Giuseppe Verdi* with a great black Swiss shepherd dog that belonged to Lilli Barr! Two women with (almost) the dust of the trenches on their shoulders! The papers were full of Lilli Barr, and Miss Rebecca Schönberg, her manager. Every one got something out of it. Lilli Barr got a vast amount of attention. Rebecca Schönberg found herself in the newspapers and rose correspondingly in the eyes of all the relatives and acquaintances, (there were Bettelheims and Czelovars and Schönbergs in New York as well as in London and Paris and Vienna) to whom she had been known until now as Raoul Schönberg's eccentric niece. The newspaper men earned extra money on space and the public had a first hand account of the war. It was all arranged magnificently. Lilli Barr got in under the line before the hundreds of other musicians who likewise damned the war and turned their faces toward a new world that had suddenly acquired an enormous importance.

Hattie Tolliver, dressed in shabby black, and weeping with joy, was on the pier, and with her, Robert, stolid and a little cynical of the grand manner with which his arrogant sister descended the gangplank. Seven trunks were gone through by customs men. Hattie Tolliver discovered that Miss Schönberg, instead of being a dark, sinister species of procuress, was red-haired, good-natured and immensely excited and triumphant. Robert, to his disgust, was told that he was quite a man, and Hattie was told that she was not a day older, that she must have a new hat . . . a half-dozen new hats . . . at once. And, at length, under the eyes of bedazzled fellow-passengers, the entire party, with immense gusto got under way.

It was all different from the damp December day when a lonely
young widow, secretly terrified, waved farewell to Fergus as the
doddering old *City of Paris* slipped away from the pier. It was
not Ellen Tolliver who was returning. She had been left behind
somewhere in Europe. It was Lilli Barr.

The seven trunks did not go to the apartment in the Seventies;
they were sent instead to the Ritz, to the rooms arranged by Raoul
Schönberg, the diamond merchant, in accordance with instructions
from his niece. Miss Schönberg went with the trunks and the
wolf-like dog, but Ellen, with her hand clasped in both her
mother's, smiling in triumph beneath the gaze of her mother's tear-
stained eyes, went straight to the apartment. All the way Robert
sat opposite them, stolidly. He was the bourgeois member of the
family. For him there were no transports of joy and sorrow, no
wild soarings of delight, no gay irresponsibility, no intense passions, no violent depressions, no fierce desire to set off wandering
about the earth. And so it happened that he, the most dependable,
the most unselfish, was the one whom all the others took for
granted. For him there would never be any celebration to mark
the prodigal's return. Darkly he knew all this, and was in his
quiet way, content. Somehow he had escaped the heritage of
The Everlasting. Secretly he thought there was a great deal of
bunk about Miss Schönberg and his sister Ellen; he suspected that
their adventures had not been, in fact, so exciting as Miss Schönberg, with a magnificent embroidery of detail, made them seem.

Still, he knew nothing about their profession. Such nonsense
might be necessary. Thank God, it was not necessary in the bond
business to behave like a three ring circus!

It was long after midnight when Ellen at last joined her manager at the Ritz. Dressed in the smart clothes in which she left
the ship, she remained at the apartment surrounded by her family,
talking, laughing, even weeping a bit when the rich, violent emotion of her mother engulfed them all save Robert and The Everlasting in a sort of sentimental orgy. Gramp joined them too, for

in a city apartment it was no longer possible to keep him shut away as they had done in the days when he occupied a room above the kitchen.

There was but one thing to sadden the reunion; it was the absence of Fergus. Ellen learned for the first time, when she asked for him, that he had gone to Europe. It was rotten luck, because in the depths of her heart he was the one she had wanted to see above all the others. He would have appreciated the grandiose triumph of her return; he would have laughed at it but he would have understood the importance of the spectacle. He would have known how well it was done. She needed his little touch of mocking humor, his complete sympathy. . . . And now he was gone. There was even a chance that she might never see him again.

The others had no interest in the spectacle. Her mother, it was clear, was proud that she was famous; but she really cared nothing at all for Lilli Barr. It was Ellen Tolliver who absorbed them all. They wanted to recapture Ellen Tolliver, pin her down and keep her with them forever. And that, of course, could not be done, because there was so little of Ellen and so much of Lilli.

Once, as they talked frantically, she caught a sudden twinkle in the eye of The Everlasting as he sat, silent and mocking, a little beyond the border of the family group. It was a brief twinkle, which vanished as quickly as it had come, but it told her that he, like Fergus, understood. He knew that she had carried the war into the enemy's country and had won. They hadn't, after all, pulled her down and clipped her wings.

And then, during a brief silence, in the flood of talk there sounded through the room the familiar echo of his demoniacal chuckle. He was thinking, perhaps, of the winter night when he threw a fit and so allowed Ellen to escape.

The occasion was so great that Gramp was allowed to have his dinner with the rest of the family, a privilege which had not been granted in more than fifteen years; for on that first night Hattie would have welcomed the devil himself and placed him on her right hand. Sitting there with his dim spectacles tilted on the end of his high thin nose, he watched them all without taking any part in the celebration. He listened while Ellen described Lily's house in the Rue Raynouard, and he understood, what the others failed to understand, that of course the Baron was Lily's lover. He saw quickly enough that Ellen had closed her eyes to all that took place in the lovely old house. And he knew what the others did not . . . that Ellen had not really returned to them at all, that she had learned the wisdom of going her own way and allowing others to do the same. She had, in short, discovered freedom; she had found her way about in a strange world and had learned the tricks which gave her the upper hand. He was proud of her to have been so smart, to have learned so quickly.

This was no longer the stormy, unhappy Ellen who had run away with a drummer. This was Lilli Barr, a woman of the world, hard, successful, with smooth edges. She glittered a bit. She was too slippery ever to recapture. She sat there, in her chic, expensive clothes, self-possessed, remote, smiling, and a little restless, as if she were impatient to be gone already back into the nervous, superficial clatter of the life which had swallowed her.

The others would discover all this in time, later on. The Everlasting knew it at once.

At one o'clock, Robert summoned a taxi and drove with her to the Ritz. It was a strange, silent ride in which the brother and sister scarcely addressed each other. They were tired, and they were separated in age by nearly ten years. (Robert had been but ten when Ellen eloped.) The one was an artist, caught up for the moment in the delirium of success. The other sold bonds and was working at it with a desperate, plodding persistence. They might, indeed, have been strangers.

Ellen, watching in silence the silhouette of her brother's snub nose and unruly red hair against the window of the taxicab, began to understand, with a perception almost as sharp as the old man's, what it was that had happened. It made her sad and a little fear-

ful lest she should discover that Rebecca had already gone to bed
and she would find herself alone in the gaudy hotel. She was
afraid, more and more of late, to be left alone.

Still, she reflected, there would be Hansi . . . for company
. . . Hansi, a big, black, wolfish dog who devoted himself to her
with a fanatic affection.

And the thought of Hansi turned her memories in the direction
of Paris, which lay safe for the time being from the Germans;
for Hansi reminded her always of Callendar and the day, just before they left for Vienna, when a fat little old man brought the
dog with a note to the house in the Rue Raynouard. . . . A note
which read . . ."I send you Hansi because he is like you. He
will look well by your side and be devoted to you. He may remind you sometimes of me, even in the midst of wild applause.
It would be easy now to forget one who has known since the beginning that you were a great artist.

C"

That was all . . . just a line or two, but enough to remind
her of what she had forgotten—the awful sense of his patience,
which seemed always to say with a shrug that all life was merely a
matter of waiting.

The solid voice of Robert roused her.

"Here we are," he said, and stepping from the cab, she was
washed for an instant by the brilliant white glare of electricity
and then vanished through the whirling doors into the Ritz.

In all the hubbub of those busy, noisy days there were intervals
when, for a moment, she found time for reflection . . . odd moments between tea and dinner, or in the hours after midnight when
the roar of the city and the small revealing sounds of the great
hotel had abated a little; or moments when Rebecca, buoyant,
triumphant and full of business interviewed in the sitting room
the men who came from musical papers suggesting a sort of polite
blackmail. Rebecca handled them all beautifully because she had
in her the blood of a hundred generations who had lived by barter.

So Ellen escaped them, save when it was necessary for her to be interviewed. Rebecca arranged the concerts that were to be given. She was busy, she was happy, she was content in her possession of Lilli Barr.

It occurred to Ellen after a time that she had not seen Mr. Wyck. In all the confusion there had been no mention of her mother's lodger. He had not been about. So when her mother came to lunch the next day in her sitting room at the Ritz, she asked, after the usual warm kisses had been exchanged, concerning the mysterious lodger.

"He went away the week before you arrived," said Hattie. "I could never understand why. He had seemed to be so satisfied."

Ellen endeavored to conceal her sense of pleasure at his disappearance. "Perhaps," she suggested, "he was leaving town."

Hattie frowned. "No. It wasn't that," she replied. "He said that he must have a room nearer his work. . . . It seemed a silly reason."

Ellen called Hansi to her side and the big black dog threw himself down with his head against her knee, his green eyes fastened on her face with a look of adoration. She stroked the fine black head and murmured, "You never told me his name."

"His name was Wyck," said Hattie. "We grew to be very fond of him. He was no trouble at all, though he did sometimes talk too much concerning his family. Still, I can see that he had nothing else to talk about. He didn't seem to have any friends but us. Fergus was the only one who didn't like him."

Ellen looked up suddenly. She had forgotten Fergus. She had forgotten that Wyck had seen him on the morning when Clarence lay dead on the divan in the Babylon Arms. Perhaps they did not remember each other. Certainly it was clear that Hattie knew nothing. Fergus must have known and, distrusting the nasty little man, have kept his secret. It was a strange world.

There was champagne that day for lunch because Rebecca had asked her uncle Raoul and his daughter, a handsome dark Jewess. Together they sat about a table laden with food which was rich and bizarre to Hattie Tolliver. The sunlight streamed in at the windows and the waiters bobbed in and out of the room serving her daughter. The champagne she refused to drink and when the diamond merchant filled Ellen's glass, she frowned and said, "I wish you wouldn't drink, Ellen. You never know what it leads to."

And when Mr. Schönberg, after telling one or two risqué stories, held a match to Ellen's cigarette, Hattie frowned again and the old look of suspicion came into her eyes. It was Lily Shane who had taught her daughter to behave like a fast woman. She knew that.

It was only when the first excitement of Ellen's return had worn away that Hattie began to feel the dull ache of an unhappiness which she could neither understand nor define. With all the vast optimism of her nature she had fancied the return of Ellen as something quite different from the reality. A hundred times during the long years while her daughter was away, she lived through the experience in her imagination; she saw Ellen taking her place once more in the midst of the family, quarreling cheerfully with Robert, helping her mother about the house, going and coming as the mood struck her. She fancied that Ellen would be, as in the old days, sullen and sometimes unhappy but always dependent just the same, always a rather sulky little girl who would play the piano by the hour while her mother saw to it that there was no work, no annoyance to disturb her.

And now it was quite different. She scarcely saw Ellen save when she went to the Ritz to eat a hurried lunch of fancy, rich foods under the bright eyes of the cheerful Miss Schönberg. The old piano stood in the apartment, silent save when Hattie herself picked out her old tunes in a desperate attack of nostalgia. Ellen had played for her a half dozen times but always on the great piano in her sitting room at the Ritz; it was not the same as in the sentimental, happy days when Hattie, as ruler of her household, sat darning with her family all about her. There was no time for anything. And Ellen herself . . . she had become slippery somehow, happier than in the old days, but also more remote, more independent, more "complete" as Lily had said. She had no need of any one.

There were days too when Hattie felt the absence of Mr. Wyck. Of all those who had at one time or another depended upon her . . . old Julia, Fergus, Ellen, Wyck and all the others . . . none remained save her husband. And somehow she had come to lose him too. Here in the city, living in his farm papers and in his memories, he had escaped her in a way she failed to understand. He slept more and more so that there were times when she was worried lest he might really be ill. Robert and The Everlasting were aloof and independent; they were no help whatever. But Mr. Wyck had come to her, wanting desperately all the little attentions which she gave so lavishly. And now he was gone, almost secretly and without gratitude. It hurt her because she could not understand why he had run away.

At times it seemed that with on one to lean upon her, the very foundations of her existence had melted away; there were moments when, for the first time in all her troubled and vigorous life, she feared that the world into which she had come might at last defeat her.

47

SCARCELY a week after the landing of Ellen and Rebecca, Thérèse Callendar landed in New York, almost willingly and with a sense of relief. In the solid house on Murray Hill, the usual army of charwomen arrived and put the place in order against her coming, but on her arrival she closed most of the rooms and chose to live between her bed-room and the library. She was, oddly enough, confused and a little weary. She had been, all her life, a match and more for the shrewdest of men; she had outwitted bankers and brokers and even swindlers, and now she stood confronted by a catastrophe which she was unable to dominate. A third or more of a vast fortune stood in danger . . . that part of it which she had been unable to save when the maelstrom broke over Europe. Much of it, fortunately, was transferred into safety. Through bits of information and advice picked up here and there in the course of her wanderings, she had divined that one day there was certain to be a war, and accordingly she had taken money out of Germany and placed it in England, disposed of Russian bonds and reinvested the money in America, shifted credits from Vienna to Paris. Yet there still remained a great sum which, for the time being, was lost in the confusion . . . part of the fortune she had tended with the care of a gardener for his most prized orchid.

In the midst of the turmoil she had stayed for days in the office of her lawyer in Paris, wiring now to London, now to Trieste, now in New York—sitting with him, a shrewd, bearded man, in conference with bankers, brokers and men who simply juggled money into more money. And in the end even she, Thérèse Callendar, had been no match for the war. She wakened one morning to find the Germans at the gates of Paris and the Government fled to Bordeaux. She was alone; Richard and Sabine and little Thérèse were in England. So alone she had paced the tesselated floors of the monstrous house in the Avenue du Bois, until all had been done which could be done. And at last, glad to leave the Europe which Ellen had called a madhouse, she turned back for the first time in her life with pleasure and relief to the quiet of the brownstone house on Murray Hill.

She had come to New York, as may be said of great people, incognita. Only her banker and her lawyer knew she was in town—a strange state of affairs for a woman who had lived always in public, going from one capital to another, seeing scores of people day by day.

It was not the money alone which troubled her. There was

the matter of Sabine for which there seemed to be no solution. As she sat alone in the dark library three days after her arrival, she turned the matter over in her mind.

She thought of the interview which took place with Richard a day or two before the Archduke was shot in Serajevo . . . an interview which occurred after lunch in the house in the Avenue du Bois before he took the Boulogne express to join Sabine in Hertfordshire. Over her coffee, she saw him again . . . a dark handsome son of whom a mother might have been proud if he had cared more for the things which were the foundation of her life. There was bitter disappointment in all that . . . his neglect of business and his indifference to money. Here he was, a man of thirty-five, who did nothing but amuse himself. He gambled a bit, he bought a picture now and then, he had a passion for music, he fenced and swam and rode beautifully. Yet there seemed to be no core to his existence, no foundation, unless the satisfaction of his own desire for pleasure might be called the dominant thread of his character. It was satisfaction—no more than that: it was never satiation. If he had been weak or dissipated or a waster, there would have been more to be said against him; but he was none of these things. In this, fortunately, he took after her own people. He had not, like young Americans who had money, gone to pieces. He took good care of himself. He had no habit which had become a vice. He had all the curious strength that comes of an old race.

Sitting over her coffee, she saw him again as he stood with the old mocking smile on his too red lips while she argued across the spaces of Wolff's house in the Avenue du Bois. He stood, rocking a bit on his toes, with the easy grace which came of a supple strength, looking down at her out of the mocking gray eyes.

"But there is no one whom I want to marry," he had said, "even if Sabine would divorce me."

At which she had grown angry and retorted, "Women interest you. It would be easy enough. . . ."

"It would be a nasty, unpleasant business. She is not a bad

wife. I might do much worse. I am sorry that she can't have more children, but that is none of my doing. I do not want to hurt her. I might not have another wife as satisfactory."

To which Thérèse had replied, "She is unhappy. I know she is. She can't stand indifference forever, even if she is a cold woman. Besides she's in love with you. She can't go on always living with you and yet not living with you. She'd be happier free . . . to marry some one else."

Then he had mocked her out of the depths of his own security. "Do you think love is such a simple thing that it can be turned on and off like water from a tap?" (She knew that love with him was just that . . . something which could be turned on and off, like water from a tap.)

"Besides, it was *you* who wanted me to marry her. I had other ideas."

"You mean Ellen Tolliver?" she asked. And then, "You would not have married her if you could have escaped it . . . if you could have got her in any other way."

But she saw that the look of mockery had faded a little at the sound of the girl's name. (She was of course no longer a girl but a successful woman of thirty or more.)

"I don't know . . ." he had said, "I don't know what I should have done. Only I fancy that if I had married her there would have been a great many little heirs running about."

She had delivered herself into his hands. As a woman of affairs she knew that one could not argue sensibly about what might have happened; and for what had happened she herself was responsible. In that he had been right.

"Would you marry her to-day?"

"How can I answer that? Probably she wouldn't have me. Why should she? We're both different now. . . . It's been years. . . . She's rich now . . . successful . . . famous. It isn't the same."

"People don't change as much as that . . . especially if they have not seen each other. They are likely to keep a memory of that sort always fresh. It's likely to grow strong instead of weak."

"I've seen her since . . . several times . . . at her concerts."

She saw, with her small piercing eyes, that she had uncovered a weak place in his armor . . . a single chance on which to pin all her hopes.

"Have you talked to her?"

"No."

She knew too that he was, in a sense, invincible. Sabine, so far as the world was concerned, made an excellent wife. She was worldly, distinguished, clever. So far as he was himself concerned, she gave him no trouble. She did not make scenes and she did not indulge in passionate outbreaks of jealousy. She did not even speak of the love which he sought outside his marriage . . . the intrigues that were always taking place and now made him invincible in the face of her argument. She effaced herself, and as she had done once before, waited. But on that occasion she had waited for marriage, and had won. Now she was waiting for love, which was quite a different matter.

"If it's an heir you want, I have one already." He smiled. "He must be nearly twelve by now. Of course, he is the grandson of a janitor and the son of a music hall singer. . . . Still, he is an heir. We might legitimatize him."

By this stroke he had won, for he had made her angry . . . the thing he had been seeking to do all the while.

"I hear from him twice a year . . . when my lawyer sends his mother money."

"You'd do well to forget his existence."

And then they had talked for a time without arriving anywhere. As usual it was Richard who had won. He had gone back to Sabine as if nothing at all had occurred.

Thérèse drank the last of her coffee and then laid her dumpy figure down on the divan in the dark library. She was tired for the first time in her life, as if she had not the strength to go on fighting. She might have but a few years longer to live and she must hurry and settle this matter. There must be an heir to whom she might pass on the fortune . . . not a sickly girl like little Thérèse but a man who could manage a responsibility so enormous.

Though her body was weary, her mind was alert. There still remained a chance. In the gathering darkness, she knew that the chance depended upon two things . . . the hope that Ellen Tolliver still loved Richard as she had so clearly loved him on the night years earlier when the girl had talked to her in this very room; and the hope that Lilli Barr was as honest, as respectable, as bourgeois as Ellen Tolliver had been.

She got up and in the darkness made her way to the bell. When the butler appeared and switched on the lights, she said, "Please get me a box for the concert of Lilli Barr. . . . It's a week from to-morrow." And, as he was leaving, she added, "I shall give a dinner that night. See to it that the rest of the house is got ready."

This was the first step.

48

ON the very same night in her weathered house sheltered by lilacs and syringas in the Town Miss Ogilvie, trembling and fluttering like a canary set free and preening itself in the sun, packed her trunk for the trip to the East. Any one looking on might have believed her, save for the wrinkled rosy cheeks and the slight spare figure, a young girl on the eve of her first party. After all, it was an event . . . the first trip she had made to the East since the Seventies when she had sailed as a girl for Munich. And she was going East to hear Ellen Tolliver play . . . Ellen who had been a chit of a girl when she had last seen her, Ellen who was now Lilli Barr, whose name and picture appeared everywhere in the papers, Ellen who had hidden on the night she fled the Town in the nest-like parlor of this very house.

Miss Ogilvie, packing her best taffeta with its corals and cameos to wear at the concert, indulged in an orgy of memories . . . memories that went back to the years before Ellen was born, to the days in Munich when for a delirious week, until the heavy hand of her father intervened, she had fancied she would become a great musician and play in public.

Pausing beside the old tin-bound trunk, she thought, "No, I never could have done it. I was too much a coward. But Ellen has . . . Ellen has. . . . And to think that I advised her to do it, that I told her to go ahead."

In the long span of a gentle life in which there had been no heights and no valleys, this occasion eclipsed all else . . . even the day she had herself sailed on the black *paquebot* for Europe.

"It happens like that . . . in the most unexpected places, in villages, in towns. . . . Why, even in a dirty mill town like this."

It all came back to her now, all the conversation between herself and Ellen on that last day when, weeping, she said to the girl, "I no longer count for anything. You are beyond me. Who am I to instruct you?"

And she remembered too with a sudden warmth the old bond between them, the hatred of this awful, sooty Town . . . a desert from which Ellen had boldly escaped, which Miss Ogilvie had accepted, hiding always in her heart her loathing of the place.

"And to think that she remembered me . . . a poor, insignificant old woman like me! To think that she even paid my way!"

For Miss Ogilvie could not have come otherwise. As the years passed she had grown poorer and poorer in her house behind the trees.

Her conscience pricked the old lady. "I wonder," she thought, sitting on the edge of her chair before the old trunk. "I wonder if I should confess to Hattie Tolliver that it was I who helped them to escape. It would be more honest, since I am going to stay with her."

And then she grew worried for fear Ellen might be ashamed of her in her old-fashioned taffeta with coral and cameo pins. Ellen had been living in Paris with Lily Shane; she would know all about the latest thing in clothes. And to convince herself that the dress was not too bad, she put it on and pinning fast the coral and cameos, stood before her glass, frizzing her hair and pulling the dress this way and that.

In the midst of these preparations, she was interrupted by the distant jangle of the bell and the sound caused her to blush and start as if she, an old dried-up woman, had been caught by an intruder coquetting before her mirror.

She knew who was at the door. It was Eva Barr and May Biggs come to send messages to Ellen, for they too shared a little her excitement. They would talk, the three of them, about Ellen as they remembered her until long after midnight; for all three hoped that Ellen might be induced to play in the Town, especially since there was such a fine new auditorium. They too had claims upon her, claims of friendship and blood and old associations.

49

ON the night of the concert Ellen wore a gown of crimson velvet, according to a plan of Rebecca who determined that the occasion should be a sensational one not to be forgotten. The house was filled and when Lilli Barr came through the door at the back of the stage there was a quick hush, a sudden breathlessness, caused not so much by her beauty (for she was never really beautiful in the sense that Lily was beautiful) but by the whole perfection of the picture. The crimson dress fitted her tightly and was sleeveless and cut low to show the perfection of her strong, handsome shoulders. Her black hair, so black that in the brilliant light which showered upon her from overhead (a device of Rebecca's) it appeared blue as the traditional raven's wing. She wore it pulled back tightly from her smooth forehead and done in a small knot at the nape of the neck. In her ears she wore old Portuguese rings of paste and silver. She was superb, glittering, slender, strong, and possessed of the old brilliant power to distract thought and concentrate attention.

In that instant the battle was half won. There were those in the audience who felt that the mere sight of her was enough.

In her box on the first tier, Mrs. Callendar sat up with a start, raised her lorgnettes and said "Tiens! Quel chic!"

Beside her Mrs. Mallinson (the lady novelist) murmured, "Superb creature!" and the Honorable Emma Hawksby (back again to live off the Americans on the strength of being a niece to the disreputable Duke of Middlebottom) thought again that the big feet of Englishwomen were a serious hindrance and that perhaps her countrywomen went in too much for walking. The elderly rake, Wickham Chase, sighed bitterly at the tragedy of old age and the loss of vigor. Bishop Smallwood (whom Sabine had dubbed the Apostle to the Genteel) thought, "She looks like my wa'am friend, Mrs. Sigourney," but, considering the impression, thought better of it and said nothing, since Mrs. Sigourney had long since overplayed her game and become utterly déclassée. And the third, a nondescript bachelor, strove to peer between Mrs. Mallinson's supporting dog-collar and the bony back of the Honorable Emma Hawksby. If he had any thoughts at all, they were not very interesting; for thirty years he had been sitting in the back of boxes at plays, concerts and the opera, peering between plump backs and skinny ones.

Below them the audience stretched away row upon row, in dim lines marshaled into neat columns like an advancing army seen through a mist.

Mrs. Callendar thought, "Ah! She is magnificent. The transformation scarcely seems possible. . . . Still, the girl had it in her always." And a little voice kept saying to her, "You will win. She is an admirable pawn. You will succeed. You will get what you want if you work hard enough and are clever about it."

Down among the dim rows spread out below them sat Hattie Tolliver, in a new gown chosen by Ellen. Large and vigorous she sat, looking a little like a powerful and eccentric duchess, by the side of Miss Ogilvie in her mauve taffeta with the corals and cameos, her thin hair done elaborately in a fashion she had not worn since she was a girl. They sat there, the eagle and the linnet, trembling with excitement, the tears very close to the surface of the emotional Hattie.

Presently, as Ellen took her place at the piano and struck a few crashing chords, Hattie could bear it no longer. She leaned toward the stranger at her side, a woman with short hair and an umbrella, and said in triumph, "That's my daughter who's playing."

The stranger stared at her for an instant and murmured, "Is it indeed?" And the music began.

Hattie really wanted to tell them all—the row upon row of strangers, obscured now by the darkness.

Charles Tolliver at his end of the row closed his eyes and slipped presently into the borderland between sleep and consciousness, a country where there is no reality and all is covered by a rosy mist. Through this the music came to him distantly. He fancied he was back once more in the shabby living room with Ellen playing sullenly at the upright piano. And for a little time he was happy.

Robert, who had no ear for music, felt uncomfortable and disapproved of his sister's low-cut gown. Robert was a prig; he took after his grandfather Barr, "the citizen."

The Everlasting was not to be seen. He had been left at home, because it was impossible to say how he would behave on such an occasion. One dared not take the risk.

In the mind of Hattie, sitting there in the shadows of the great hall, there could be no question of failure. Was it not her Ellen, her little girl whom she had once held upon her knee, who now sat, as it were, upon a throne before a world which listened breathlessly? All those people who filled the seats about her and above her might have risen and left, but to Hattie the evening would have been a great success, a triumph in which the judgment of the world had been wrong. They did not leave; instead they sat, leaning forward a bit or slipped down in their seats with closed eyes, bedazzled as much by the perfection and grace of this new musician as by the music itself.

Rebecca, standing in the darkness at the back of the great hall, understood all that. She knew that in part the triumph was her own, for had she not tricked them, hypnotized them? They would not be able to forget. She, like Hattie, felt with every fiber of her body, the very sensations of all those people who listened—people from great houses of the rich who had heard of Lilli Barr from friends in Europe, people from the suburbs who would rush away in frantic haste for the last train home, people—young people—like the one who sat next to Hattie, in shabby clothes and worn shoes, who were fighting now desperately, as Ellen had once fought, to reach that same platform, that same brilliant shower of light. They listened, enchanted by the sound, caught by the spell of one woman's genius and another's brilliant trickery. Possessed they were, for the moment.

And presently the tears began to stream down Hattie's face. They dropped to the hands worn and red, concealed now by the expensive gloves which cramped her uncomfortably.

The applause rose and fell in great waves, sweeping over her with the roaring of a great surf heard far away, and through it the voice of Miss Ogilvie, saying gently, "Who would have believed it?"

And then at length, when the sound of the last number had died away, an overwhelming surf which would not die even when the woman in crimson appeared again and again under the brilliant shower of light; until at last Lilli Barr seated herself before the great satiny piano and the crowd, which had pushed forward to the stage, grew quiet and stood listening, waiting, silent and expectant . . . the people from great houses, the people from the suburbs, the young people with worn shoes and shabby clothes. And into the air there rang a shower of spangled notes, gay and sparkling, embracing a rhythm older than any of them. For Lilli Barr—(or was it Ellen Tolliver)—was playing now The Beautiful Blue Danube. It was not the old simple waltz that Hattie had picked out upon the organ in her father's parlor, but an extravagant, brilliant arrangement which beneath the strong, white fingers became fantastical and beautiful beyond description.

Hattie Tolliver wept because she understood. It was as if Ellen—the proud, silent Ellen—had been suddenly stripped of all the old inarticulate pride, as if suddenly she had grown eloquent and all the barriers, like the walls of Jericho, had tumbled down. Hattie Tolliver understood. Her daughter was speaking to her now across all the gulf of years, across the hundred walls which stood between them. This was her reward. She understood and wept at the sudden revelation of the mysterious thread that ran through all life. All this triumph, this beauty, all this splendor had its beginning long ago on the harmonium in the parlor of old Jacob Barr's farm.

When the lights went up and Hattie, drying her eyes and suffering her hand to be patted by Miss Ogilvie, was able to look about her, she saw with a feeling of horror among the figures crowded in a group before the stage a coonskin coat and a sharp old face that was familiar. It was The Everlasting. He had come, after all, alone, aloof, as he had always lived. He stood with his bony old head tilted back a little, peering through his steel rimmed spectacles at the brilliant figure of his granddaughter.

For an instant Hattie thought, triumphantly, "Now he can see that my child is great. That she is famous. He will see," she thought, "what a good mother I have been."

But her sense of triumph was dimmed a little because she

knew that Ellen belonged also to him . . . all that part which she had never been able to understand. It was Gramp's triumph as well as Hattie's. To her horror she heard him shouting, "Bravo! Bravo!" in a thin, cracked voice, as if he were a young man again listening while Liszt played to an audience of foreigners.

In the box, looking down on the crowd below, Thérèse Callendar waited to the end. She sent Mrs. Mallinson, the Honorable Emma Hawksby, the Apostle to the Genteel, Wickham Chase and the nondescript bachelor away in her motor, bidding the driver return for her. She sat peering down through her lorgnettes, plump and secure in her sables and dirty diamonds, a little bedazzled like all the others but still enough in control of her senses to be interested in the figures below. Among them she too noticed the extraordinary figure of a skinny old man in a coonskin coat, who stood a little apart from the others with a triumphant smile on his sharp, wrinkled face.

At the moment she was in an optimistic mood because there had occurred in the course of the concert an incident which, with all the rich superstition of her nature, she interpreted as a good omen. Between the two parts of the program when dozens of bouquets (mostly purchased by Rebecca) were rushed forward to the platform, she saw that Lilli Barr leaned down and chose a great bunch of yellow roses. It was the bouquet which Thérèse had sent. It was an omen. If there had been any wavering in the mind of Thérèse it vanished at once. Ellen could not consciously have chosen it. She was sure now that she would succeed.

Behind the stage whither she turned her steps when the last of the applause had died away and the lights were turned out, she found Ellen standing surrounded by a noisy throng. Among them she recognized only Sanson, who had grown feeble and white since last she saw him. And there was an extraordinary, powerful woman, handsome in a large way, who wore her white gloves awkwardly; and beside her a little old spinster in an absurd gown of mauve taffeta adorned with cameos and coral pins. These two stood beside the musician, the one proud and smiling, the other a little frightened, as a bird might be.

It was all exciting. Thérèse waited on the edge of the throng until all had gone save the big handsome woman and the little spinster in mauve. Then she stepped forward and saw that Ellen recognized her.

"Ah," said Ellen, coldly. "Mrs. Callendar! Were you here too?"

Thérèse did not say that the concert was magnificent. She knew better than to add one more to the heap of garish compliments. She said, "It was the first time I have been where I could hear you. I knew you would do it some day. . . . You remember, I told you so."

There was a look in Ellen's eye which said, "Ah! You forgot me for years. Now that I am successful everything is different." Then drawing her black cloak about her crimson dress, she laid a hand on the arm of the big, handsome woman.

"This is my mother . . . Mrs. Callendar," she said. "And this is Miss Ogilvie, my first music teacher."

Mrs. Tolliver eyed Thérèse with suspicion, and Miss Ogilvie simpered and bowed.

"I came back to ask you to come home to supper with me," said Mrs. Callendar to Ellen. "We could have a sandwich and a glass of sherry and talk for a time. I've opened the house."

For a moment the air was filled with a sense of conflict. The suspicion of Hattie, as she saw her daughter slipping from her, rose into hostility. In the end she lost, for Ellen said, "Yes, I'll come for a little time." And then turning to her mother, she added, "You and Miss Ogilvie go to the Ritz. I'll come there later. Rebecca has ordered supper."

But it was not Thérèse Callendar who won. It was some one

who was not there at all . . . a dark man of whose very existence
Hattie Tolliver had never heard.

50

MEANWHILE in the front of the concert hall a little
man whom none of them had seen slipped away before the lights came up, into the protecting darkness
of the street. He had come in late to sit far back in the shadow
beneath the balcony. Rebecca had noticed him, for he sat almost
beside her and behaved in a queer fashion; but never having seen
him before, she gave the matter no further thought. In the midst
of the concert he had suddenly begun to weep, snuffling and drying his eyes with a furtive shame. He was a small man with a
sallow face and shifting eyes which looked at you in a trembling,
apologetic fashion (a trick that had come over him in the years
since he had been driven from the comfortable flat on the top
floor of the Babylon Arms). Rebecca, of course, had never heard
of Mr. Wyck, yet she noticed him now because he fidgeted with
his umbrella, and because his hands trembled violently when he
held his handkerchief to his eyes. He appeared, in his sniveling,
frightened way, to be deeply affected by the music.

He went out quickly, among the first, looking behind him as if
he stood in terror of being recognized and accused before all those
people. Once in the street, he drew his shabby overcoat close
about him, and turned his steps southward with such speed that
at times the passers-by glared at him for jostling them at the
crossings. They must have thought too, when he looked at them,
that there was a reflection of madness in the staring eyes. He
plunged south into the glare of light that pierced the darkness
above Broadway like a pillar of fire.

He had seen her again . . . the one woman whom he hated
above all persons on earth. He would have killed her. It would
have given him pleasure to see her die, but as he ran, he knew that

he had not the courage. He thought, "I could not bear to face her even for the moment before I struck. I could not bear the look in her eyes" . . . (the old look of contempt and accusation, as if she knew what it was he had told Clarence). . . .

He was gone now . . . Clarence. Perhaps one might find him on the other side.

On and on he ran past brilliant pools of light, red and purple, green and yellow; past lurid posters adorning movie palaces showing men in death cells and women being carried down ladders in the midst of flames; past billboards on which extravagantly beautiful women kicked naked legs high in the air (they were not for him, whose only knowledge of love was that feeble flicker of affection he had had for Clarence) ; past rich motors filled with furs and painted women; past restaurants and hotels glittering with light from which drifted faintly the sounds of wild music; past all this until he emerged at last from the phantasmagoria in which he had no part, into the protective murkiness of a street which led west toward the North River . . . a street which began in delicatessen and clothing shops and degenerated slowly into rows of shabby brownstone houses, down-at-the-heel and neglected, with the placards of chiropractors and midwives and beauty doctors thrust behind dusty lace curtains.

He hurried now, more rapidly than ever, with the air of a terrified animal seeking its burrow, to hide away from all that world of success and wealth and vigor that lay behind him.

She had come (he thought) out of the middle west, knowing nothing, bringing nothing, to destroy Clarence and win all that he had seen to-night. She had trampled them all beneath her feet. And what had he? Mr. Wyck? Nothing! Nothing! Only the obscenities of a boarding house into which she had driven him a second time. It was like all women. They preyed upon men. They destroyed them. And she had been vulgar and stupid and awkward. . . .

At last he turned in at a house which bore a placard "Rooms to Let." There he let himself in with a key and hurried up the gas-lit stairs pursued by a gigantic shadow cast by the flickering of a flame turned economically low.

His room lay at the end of the top floor passage beyond the antiquated bathroom with its tin tub. Once inside, he bolted the door and flung himself down on the blankets of his bed to weep. A light, brilliant but far away, cast the crooked outline of an ailanthus tree against the faded greasy paper of the room. A cat, lean and adventurous, moved across the sill, and a cat fifty times its size moved in concert across the wall at the foot of the bed. Amid the faint odors of onions and dust, Mr. Wyck wept pitifully, silently.

For a long time he lay thus, tormented by memories of what he had seen . . . the crowd cheering and applauding, the woman in crimson and diamonds (an evil creature, symbol of all the cruelties which oppressed him). There were memories too that went back to the days at the Babylon Arms before she had come out of the west to destroy everything, days when Clarence, succumbing to the glamour of a name, had treated him as if he were human . . . days which had marked the peak of happiness. Since then everything had been a decline, a slipping downward slowly into a harsh world where there was no place for him. . . .

After a time, he grew more calm and lay with the quiet of a dead man, staring at the shadows on the wall until at last he raised himself and sat on the edge of the bed, holding his head in his thin hands. It was midnight . . . (a clock somewhere in the distance among all those lights sounded the hour slowly) . . . when he again stirred and, taking up from the bed an old newspaper, set himself to tearing it slowly into strips. He worked with all the concentration of a man hypnotized, until at last the whole thing had been torn into bits. Then he went to the winddow and with great care stuffed each tiny crevice in the rattling frame. In the same fashion he sealed the cracks about the sagging door. And when he had done this he approached the jet on which he was accustomed to heat the milk which made him sleep. But to-night the bottle of milk was left in its corner, untouched. He glanced at it and, after a moment's thought, reached up and slowly turned the knob of the jet until the gas began to hiss forth into the tiny room. When he had done all this he returned to the bed and, wrapping himself in his overcoat, lay down in peace. He did not weep now. He was quite calm. He came very close to achieving dignity. He waited. . . .

Outside the adventurous cat set up an amorous wail. The shadows danced across the wall-paper in a fantastic procession, and presently as if by a miracle their place was taken by another procession quite different—a procession in which there were ladies in crinolines out of the portraits which had once known the grandeur of a house on lower Fifth Avenue, and men in trousers strapped beneath their boots and even a carriage or two drawn by bright, prancing horses . . . a dim procession out of the past. And presently the second procession faded like the first. The walls of the room melted away. There was a great oblivion, a peace, an endless space where one stood alone, very tall and very powerful. . . . A great light and through a rosy mist the sound of a tom cat's amorous wail, more and more distant, raised in an ironic hymn of love to accompany the passing of Mr. Wyck, for whom there was no place in this world.

51

THE sound of the same clock striking midnight failed to penetrate the thick old curtains muffling the library on Murray Hill. Here Thérèse and Ellen sat talking, almost, one might have said, as if nothing had happened since Ellen last passed through the bronze door on her way to the Babylon Arms. Under the long, easy flow of Thérèse's talk her irritation had dissolved until now, two hours after the concert, they faced each other much as they had done long ago. It was Ellen who had changed; Thérèse was older, a little weary, and a trifle more untidy but otherwise the same—shrewd, talkative, her brisk mind darting now here, now there, like a bright minnow, seeking always to penetrate the shiny, brittle surfaces which people held before them as their characters. She found, no doubt, that Ellen had learned the trick of the shiny, brittle surface; she understood that it was by no means as easy as it had been to probe to the depths the girl's inmost thoughts. She had learned to protect herself; nothing could hurt her now unless she chose to reveal a weakness in her armor. Thérèse understood at once that if her plan was to succeed, it must turn upon Ellen's own volition; the girl (she was no longer a girl but Thérèse still thought of her in that fashion) could not be tricked into a bargain. Beyond all doubt she understood that Richard was dangerous, that he had the power of causing pain.

As they talked, far into the night, Thérèse fancied that Ellen sat there—so handsome in the long crimson gown, so self-possessed, so protected by the shiny, brittle surface—weighing in her mind the question of ever seeing him again. They did not approach the topic openly; for a long time Thérèse chattered, in the deceptive way she had, of a thousand things which had very little to do with the case.

"You have seen Sabine now and then," she put forward, cautiously.

"Two or three times. She called on me."

Thérèse chuckled quietly. "She must admire you. It is unusual for her to make an advance of that sort."

The observation drew just the answer she had hoped for, just the answer which Ellen, thinking perhaps that the whole matter should be brought out into the light, saw fit to give.

"It was not altogether admiration," she said. "It was more fear. You see, she had imagined a wonderful story . . . a story that he had brought me to Paris, and that I was his mistress."

For a moment Ellen felt a twinge of conscience at breaking the pledge of confidence she had given Sabine. Still, she must use the weapons at hand. She understood perfectly that there was something they wanted of her; she understood that any of them (save only Callendar himself) would have sacrificed her to their own schemes. He would sacrifice her only to himself.

"She was a little out of her head, I think . . . for a long time after little Thérèse was born. She grieved too because she could never have another child. She wanted to give Dick an heir. . . . She was very much in love with him . . . then." The last word she added, as if by an afterthought.

At this Ellen thrust forward another pawn, another bit of knowledge which had come to her from Sabine. "He neglects her badly, doesn't he?"

Thérèse pursed her lips and frowned, as if for a moment the game had gotten out of hand. "I don't fancy it's a case of neglect. . . . They're simply not happy. You see, it was not . . ." She smiled with deprecation. "Shall I be quite frank? It was not a matter of love in the beginning. . . . It was a *mariage de convenance.*"

"Yes. He told me that . . . himself. Before the wedding took place."

There was a light now in Ellen's eye, a wicked gleam as if the game were amusing her tremendously, as if she found a mischievous delight in baiting this shrewd old woman with bits of knowledge which showed her how little she really knew of all that had taken place.

"Of course," Thérèse continued, "she fell in love with him after a time. . . . But for him it was impossible. . . . You see, there is only one person with whom he has ever really been in love. It was a case of fascination. . . ."

Ellen did not ask who this person was because she knew now, beyond all doubt. She had a strange sense of having lived all this scene before, and she knew that it was her sense of drama which was again giving her the advantage; once before it had saved her when her will, her conscious will, had come near to collapse. (Long ago it was . . . in the preposterous Babylon Arms which Clarence had thought so grand.)

"He gave me a dog," she said, by way of letting Mrs. Callendar know that she understood who the mysterious person was. "Just before I left for Vienna. . . . I have him here with me, at the Ritz. He is very like Richard. . . ."

Mrs. Callendar poured out more sherry. She felt the need of something to aid her. And then she emerged abruptly, after the law of tactics which she usually followed, into the open.

"I don't mind saying, my dear, that you're the one who has fascinated him . . . always."

Ellen smiled coldly. "He is not what one might call a passionate lover."

"He is faithful."

Ellen's smile expanded into a gentle laugh. "One might call it, I suppose, . . . a fidelity of the soul, . . . of the spirit, a sublimated fidelity." There crept into her voice a thin thread of mockery, roused perhaps by the memory of Sabine's confidences.

Thérèse shrugged her fat shoulders and the movement set the plastron of dirty diamonds all a-glitter. "That is that," she observed. "You know him as well as I do."

("Better," thought Ellen, "so much better, because I know how dangerous he is.") But she kept silent.

"I think he would marry you to-morrow . . . if you would have him."

For an instant Ellen came very near to betraying herself. She felt the blood rise into her face. She felt a sudden faintness that emerged dimly from the memories of him as a lover, so charming, so subtle, so given to fierce, quick waves of passion.

"Did he send you to tell me that?" she asked in a low voice.

"No. . . . But I know it just the same. I have talked to him . . . not openly, of course."

("No," thought Ellen, "not openly, but like this, like the way you are talking to me." It was dangerous, this business of insinuation.)

"It is remarkable that the feeling has lasted so long . . . so many years," Thérèse continued. "It has not been like that with any other woman. I think he is fascinated by your will, your power, your determination."

"You make me a great person," observed Ellen with irony, "but not a very seductive one."

"There are ways and ways of seduction. What seduces one man passes over the head of another."

"It is a perverse attraction. . . ."

"Perhaps. . . . But most attractions are."

Thérèse had seen the sudden change at the mention of her son's name, just as she had seen the change in her son when Ellen's name had been brought into the light. She meditated for a time in silence and then observed, "You are looking tired to-night."

There were dark circles under Ellen's eyes, pale evidences of the strain, the excitement which had not abated for an instant since they embarked for Vienna.

"I am tired," she said, "very tired."

"You should rest," pursued Thérèse. "You could go to the place on Long Island. You could be alone there, if you liked. I shouldn't bother you. I shall be busy in town until this tangle over money is settled."

Ellen stirred and sighed. "No, that's impossible. It's good of you to offer it, but I can't accept. . . . I can't stop now. You see the ball has been started rolling. One must take advantage of success while it's at hand. Never let a chance slip past. I know that . . . by experience. You see, Miss Schönberg—she's my manager—has arranged a great many engagements."

"Whenever you want a place to rest," continued Thérèse, "let me know."

It was true that she was tired, bitterly tired; and more troubling, more enduring than the mere exhaustion was the obscure feeling that she had passed from one period of her life into another, that she had left behind somewhere in these three exciting years a milestone that marked the borderland of youth, of that first, fresh, exuberant youth which, at bottom, had been the source of all her success. It had slipped away somehow, in the night, without her knowing it. She was still strong (she knew that well enough), still filled with energy, but something was gone, a faint rosy mist perhaps, which had covered all life, even in the bitterest moments, with a glow that touched everything with a glamorous unreality, which made each new turning seem a wild adventure. It was gone; life was slipping past. Here she sat, a woman little past thirty, and what had she gained in exchange? Fame, perhaps? And wealth, which lay just around the next corner? Something had escaped her; something which in her mind was associated dimly with Lily and the memory of the pavilion silvered by the moon.

She stirred suddenly. "I must go. My mother and Miss Ogilvie are waiting at the Ritz."

She rose and Thérèse pulled herself with an heroic effort from the depths of her chair. Together they walked through the bleak, shadowy hall and at the door Mrs. Callendar said, "You will come to dinner with me some night . . . yes? I will ring you up to-morrow."

And as Ellen moved away down the steps, she added, "Remember, you must not overwork. . . . You must care for yourself. You are not as young as you were once."

It was that final speech *You are not as young as you were once* which, like a barbed arrow, remained in her mind and rankled there as she drove in the Callendar motor through the streets to the Ritz where she found her mother and Miss Ogilvie sitting sleepily with an air of disapproval while Sanson and Rebecca and Uncle Raoul drank champagne and labored to be gay in celebration of the triumph.

It was about this hour that the amorous wailing of the tom-cat died forever upon the ears of Mr. Wyck.

In the morning the newspapers printed, in the column devoted to murders, suicides and crimes of violence, a single paragraph——

"Herbert Wyck, aged forty-three, single, committed suicide last
night by inhaling gas in his room in a boarding house at —— West
35th street. The only existing relative is Miss Sophronia Wyck
residing in Yonkers. It is said that the dead man's family once
played a prominent part in the life of New York in the Seventies."

But no one saw it . . . not Hattie Tolliver, nor her husband,
nor Robert, nor Ellen; they were all busy reading the triumphant
notices of the concert at which, more than one critic said, a new
Tèresa Carreño had arrived.

Thus passed Mr. Wyck whose one happiness was desolated because Lily Shane had encountered Clarence Murdock in the dining
car of a transcontinental train. "Women like that," Harvey
Seton had said. . . .

Ellen went to dine in the ugly dining room copied from the
Duc de Morny not once but many times and she met there those
people—Mrs. Mallinson, the Honorable Emma, the Apostle to
the Genteel, Mr. Wickham Chase and scores of others—who had
once sat on the opposite side of the lacquered screen waiting for
the Russian tenor, the Javanese dancer and the unknown young
American girl. She sat at dinner between bankers and bishops,
between fashionable young men and elderly millionaires. She was
a success, for she possessed an indifference bordering upon rudeness
which allowed her dinner companions to talk as much as they
pleased about themselves and led them into extraordinary efforts
to win a gleam of interest from her clear blue eyes. And she
learned that many things had changed since she last dined in the
Callendar house. She learned that Mrs. Sigourney was no longer
fashionable but merely material for the newspapers, and that Mrs.
Champion and her Virgins had sunk into a brownstone obscurity
in the face of a new age which no longer had a great interest in
virginity; and that artists, musicians and writers were becoming
the thing, that no dinner was complete without them. But it
was amazing how little the whole spectacle interested her. She
knew that it had all been arranged with a purpose; the indomitable

Thérèse, for all her fatigue and worry, was preparing for the next step. These dinners gave Lilli Barr a place in the world of the Honorable Emma and the Apostle to the Genteel; they fixed her.

52

THE first letter from Lily since Ellen had left the house in the Rue Raynouard for Vienna arrived on the eve of her departure from New York for the West. It was a sad letter, tragic and strangely subdued for one so buoyant, so happy as Lily to have written. Still, there were reasons . . . reasons which piled one upon another in a crescendo of sorrow and tragedy. It was, as Ellen remarked to Rebecca while they sat at breakfast in the bright sitting room, as if the very foundations of Lily's life had collapsed.

César was missing. "I have given up hope," wrote Lily, "of seeing him again. Something tells me that he is dead, that even if he were a prisoner I should have heard from him. I know he is gone. I saw him on the night he went into action. His troop passed through Meaux in the direction of the Germans and he stopped for five minutes . . . five precious minutes . . . at Germigny. And then he rode away into the darkness. . . . I am certain that he is dead."

Nor was this all. Madame Gigon too was dead. With Lily she had been trapped in the house at Germigny, too ill to flee. The Germans had entered the park and the château and spent a night there. Before morning they were driven out again. During that night Madame Gigon had died. She was buried now in the family grave at Trilport, nearby.

And Jean . . . the Jean (eighteen now) who was such a friend of Ellen's, who had ridden wildly through the Bois and through the fields at Germigny, was in the hospital. He had been with César's troop. César had pledged himself to look out for the boy. But César had vanished during the first skirmish with the

Uhlans. Jean had lost him, and now Jean lay in the hospital at Neuilly with his left leg amputated at the knee.

"I am back in the Rue Raynouard," wrote Lily, "but you can imagine that it is not a happy place. I am alone all day and when I go out, I see no one because all the others are busy with the war, with their own friends and relations. Many of them have gone to the country because living has become very dear in Paris. We are safe again, but I am alone. There is not much pleasure here. I too have been very ill. I know now what a stranger I have always been. I am American still, despite everything. They know it too and have left me alone."

When Rebecca had gone, bustling and rather hard, out into the streets, Ellen sat for a long time with Hansi beside her, holding the sad letter in her hands. This, then, was what had happened to Lily's world, a world which, protected by wealth, had seemed so secure, so far beyond destruction. In a single night it was gone, swept away like so much rubbish out of an open door. Only Jean was left; and Jean, who loved life and activity and movement, was crippled now forever.

Moved by an overwhelming sadness, Ellen reproached herself for having been rude to old Madame Gigon, for having quarreled with César. She had been unpleasant to them because (she considered the thing honestly now, perhaps for the first time) because the one had been of no use to her and the other had threatened to stand in her way. She knew too for the first time how much Lily had loved her César. In her letter she made no pretenses; she was quite frank, as if after what had happened it was nonsense, pitiful nonsense, any longer to pretend. They were lovers; they had loved each other for years . . . it must have been nearly twelve years of love which stood blocked by César's sickly wife. There was, Ellen owned, something admirable in such devotion, still more when there was no arbitrary tie to bind them, the one to the other.

She rose presently and began to pace up and down the sunlit room, the black dog following close at her heels, up and down, up and down, up and down. And the weariness, the strange lack of zest, which she had spoken of to Mrs. Callendar, took possession of her once more. She was, in the midst of her triumph, surrounded by the very clippings which acclaimed her, afraid with that curious fear of life which had troubled her since the beginning. It was a hostile world in which one must fight perpetually, only to be defeated in the end by some sinister thrust of circumstance . . . a thrust such as had destroyed all Lily's quiet security. It was well indeed to have humility.

She remembered too that Fergus was caught up in the torrent which had swept away so much that Lily held dear. . . . Fergus and (she halted abruptly in her restless pacing and grew thoughtful) Fergus and Callendar, the two persons in all the world whom she loved best. In the terror of the moment, she was completely honest. She loved Callendar. If there had ever been any doubt, she knew it now. She did not, even to save her own emotions, to shield her own vanity, put the thing out of her mind. She gave herself up to the idea.

In her restless pacing, she fancied that she must do something. She must save them—Callendar and Fergus—by some means; but like Thérèse in her anxiety over her fortune, like Hattie in her desperation, she found herself defeated. There was nothing to be done. This gaudy show, this spectacle, this glittering circus parade which crossed the face of Europe could not be blocked. She could not save them because they preferred the spectacle to anything in all the world. Ah, she knew them both! . . . She knew what it was in them that was captured and held fast by the spectacle. She knew that if she had been a man, she too would have been there by their side. They must be in the center of things, where there was the most going on, the one aloof, the other fairly saturated in the color, the feel, the very noise of the whole affair. It was a thirst for life, for a sense of its splendor. . . . She knew what it was because she too was possessed by it. It had nothing to do with patriotism; that sort of emotion was good enough for the French.

Like Hattie, like Thérèse, like a million other women she was helpless, and the feeling terrified her, who had never been really helpless before. This war, which she had damned for a nuisance that interrupted her own triumphant way, became a monster, overwhelming and bestial, before which she was powerless. And in her terror she was softened by a new sort of humanity. She became merely a woman whose men were at war, a woman who could do nothing, who must sit behind and suffer in terror and in doubt.

Rebecca found her there when she returned at three o'clock, still pacing up and down, up and down, the great black dog following close at her heels. She had not lunched; she had not thought of eating.

"The letter from Lily," she told Rebecca, with an air of repression, "has upset me. I don't know what I'm to do. I want to go back to Paris."

The statement so astounded Rebecca that she dropped the novels and papers she was carrying and stood staring.

"What!" she cried, "Go back now? Sacrifice everything we have worked for? Ruin everything? Give up all these engagements? You must be mad."

It was plain that Ellen had thought of all this, that the struggle which she saw taking form with Rebecca had already occurred in her own soul. She knew what she was sacrificing . . . if she returned.

"Lily is alone there, and in trouble. Some one should go to her."

So that was it! Rebecca's tiny, bright ferret's eyes grew red with anger. "Lily! Lily!" she said. "Don't worry about Lily. I'll wager by this time she has found some one to console her."

Ellen moved toward her like a thunder cloud, powerful, menacing in a kind of dignity that was strange and even terrifying to Rebecca. "You can't say that of her. I won't have you. How can you when it was Lily who has helped me more than any one in the world? I won't have it. Who are you to speak like that of Lily . . . my own cousin?"

"Lily who has helped you!" screamed Rebecca. "And what of me? What of me?" She began to beat her thin breasts in a kind of fury. Her nose became a beak, her small eyes red and furious. "Have I done nothing? Am I no one, to be cast aside like this? What of the work I have done, the slaving?"

For a moment they stood facing each other, silent and furious, close in a primitive fashion to blows. There was silence because their anger had reached a point beyond all words and here each held herself in check. It was Ellen who broke the silence. She began to laugh, softly and bitterly.

"Perhaps you're right," she said in a low voice. "I do owe you a great deal . . . as much, really, as I owe to Lily. It has given you the right to a certain hold upon me."

(But the difference, she knew, was this—that Lily would never exert her right of possession.)

"You can't go," continued Rebecca, "not now. Think of it . . . all the years of sacrifice and work, gone for nothing. Can't you see that fate has delivered triumph into your hands. If you turn your back upon it now, you'd be nothing less than a fool." She saw in a sudden flash another argument and thrust it into the conflict. "Always you have taken advantage of opportunity. . . . You told me so yourself. . . . And now when the greatest chance of all is at hand, you turn your back on it. I can't understand you. Why should you suddenly be so thoughtful of Lily?"

Ellen sat down and fell to looking out of the window. "Perhaps you're right," she said. "I'll think it out . . . more clearly perhaps."

There was, after all, nothing that she could do. The old despair swept over her, taking the place of her pessimistic anger. She could not go to the front, among the soldiers, to comfort Callendar. He would have been the last to want her there.

"Perhaps you're right," she repeated, and then, "War is a rotten thing for women."

But Rebecca had, all the same, a feeling that it was not Lily whom she was fighting but some one else—whom, she could not imagine. She could not have known of course that Thérèse Callendar had already written her son that she had seen Ellen Tolliver, that she was handsomer than ever and more fascinating and sullen, and that in a sly postscript she had remarked, "The strange thing is that I believe she is still in love with you. I watched her, out of curiosity, and I am sure of it."

And, of course, none of them knew that Callendar on reading the letter somewhere in the mud near Loos, with the throbbing of the barrage in his ears, had smiled at the trickery of women and thought, "Curiosity, indeed!"

It was in the end Rebecca who won, not a victory perhaps but at least a delay. The little Jewess was much too shrewd ever to suppose that Ellen might be conquered so easily; if she had won a temporary advantage she understood it was because Ellen chose to let her win, because Ellen had weighed the question and decided that all things considered, Rebecca was right. To turn back at this point was a folly which she could not deny. Belonging now in a sense to the whole world she was no longer absolute mistress of her own fortune; such freedom was, after all, the privilege only of the obscure. She was in truth, she thought bitterly, still a mountebank, an entertainer, who waited behind a painted screen to entertain the public. The stage was greater now and the audience had grown from the fashionable little group in the Callendar drawing-room to all the world. That was the only difference.

But stronger than any sense of duty or obligation was the old terror of a terrible poverty which forced one to keep up appearances. She had tasted the security that comes of riches and she could not turn back. There were memories which would not die, memories of the days when as a girl she had put on a bold face

before all the Town, memories, even worse, of the drab petty
economies she had known in the days at the Babylon Arms. And
even stronger than all these things was her fear of failure, a passionate fear which might easily have driven her in some circumstances to suicide. One who had been so ruthless, so arrogant,
so proud, dared not fail. That way too had been blocked.

So she found herself brought up sharply against the problem
of the Town. They wanted her there; they were, strangely
enough, proud of her. Eva Barr had written her, and Miss
Ogilvie, and even May Biggs, whom she had feared ever to see
again. She had left them all believing that she would never turn
back, believing that by stepping aboard the express for the East
she had turned her back forever upon a place which, in honest
truth, she despised. But she had not escaped; there were ties,
intangible and tenuous, which bound her to the place. There
were times when she was even betrayed by a certain nostalgia for
the sight of the roaring black furnaces, the dark empty rooms of
Shane's Castle, closed now and barren of all life; the decaying
smoke-stained houses that stood far back from the streets surrounded by green lawns and old trees.

She thought, "This again is a sign that something has gone from
me, something fierce and spirited. I am growing softer."

They had, so May Biggs wrote, built a new concert hall, and
what could be so appropriate as to have it opened by a daughter
of the Town? "A daughter of the Town," she reflected bitterly.
"Yes, I am that. It, too, claims me."

And it was true. She was a daughter of the Town. There
was in her the same fierce energy, the same ruthlessness, the
same pride. If she had been born elsewhere, in some less harsh
and vigorous community, she would herself have been softer, less
overwhelmingly successful. It was true. She *was* a daughter of
the hard, uncompromising Town.

"It happens like that . . ." Miss Ogilvie had said, *"in the most
unexpected places . . . in villages, in towns. . . . Why, even in a
dirty mill town like this."*

But in the end, it was her pride which led her back. Because, a dozen years ago, she had talked wildly and desperately, because she had boasted of what she would one day do, she must return now to let them see that she had done it. It was a triumph which in her heart she counted as more than the triumphs of London, of Paris, of New York, of all the world. For she had not yet escaped the Town. She would not be free until they saw her fabulous success.

But Hattie could not go with her. Hattie's triumph was spoiled. On the night of the concert when The Everlasting had appeared without warning, it was necessary for some one to see that the old man was returned safely to the apartment, so to Charles Tolliver the task had been assigned. Gramp, Heaven knows, could easily have found his way back; he knew more of the world than any of them, but he chose never to interfere with such plans lest he seem too active, too spry to require any attention. To guard his security, he encouraged their assumption that he was feeble and a bit childish. He had not forgotten the security which comes of being a possession.

It is impossible to have known what thoughts passed through the crafty, old mind as he walked by the side of his son through the dark streets. They did not speak; they were as strange to each other as they had always been, as remote as if there had been not the slightest bond between them. Perhaps the old man scorned his son for his gentle goodness, so misplaced in a world where there was so little use for that sort of thing. Perhaps he understood that Ellen was after all much closer to himself than to her father. Perhaps he knew that Charles Tolliver, in his heart, had been saddened by the triumph, because it stood as a seal upon his daughter's escape. Perhaps he noticed the faint weariness in the step of his son, the dark circles beneath his eyes, the listlessness of his manner, as if he had grown weary of the confused, tormented life all about him.

It was the old man . . . the father . . . whose step was light, whose eye was shining as they entered the flat. It was the old man too who sat up reading until he heard Hattie and Miss Ogilvie, returning from the Ritz, come in at three in the morning. For Charles Tolliver had gone quickly away to his bed and to the dreams that were his reality.

In the morning Hattie had called Ellen to say that her father was ill. He had been drowsy. It was almost impossible to keep him awake. The doctor had been there.

"He says," Hattie told her, "that he must have been ill for a long time without speaking of it. He has never complained. I don't understand it. And now he's too drowsy to tell me anything. The doctor says he is badly run down. He is worried because Papa seems to have no resistance."

He had grown no better with the passing of time. Indeed, the drowsiness seemed to increase, and there were times when he talked irrationally, as if he had never left the Town at all. He held long, fantastic conversations with Judge Wilkins and talked too of the Grand Circuit races and Pop Geers.

And when Ellen left for the Midlands, Hattie remained behind to sit in the rocking chair at her husband's side caring for him and for Gramp who had since the night when he ran away to the concert become troublesome again as if there were something in the air.

53

IN the Town the new concert hall of which Cousin Eva Barr and May Biggs had written with such enthusiasm and detail raised its white Greek façade a score of yards from the main street. Erected to the twin worship of the muses of Music and the Theater it supplanted the dismal opera house of an early, less sophisticated period, and so left the late U. S. Grant architecture of that shabby, moth-eaten structure in an undivided dedication to the bastard sister of Music and the Theater. a shabby, commonplace child known as the Movies, whom Sabine had once said should be christened Pomegranate. Though the new temple was barely finished and the names of Shakespeare, Wagner (who would probably be left out now that there was a war and the Germans, who were the very backbone of the Town, had become blond beasts, professionally trained ravishers, and other things), Beethoven (who would slip by the committee because he had been dead so long), Verdi (whose Aïda many supposed to be the high water mark of all opera), Molière (suggested by Eva Barr but unknown to most of the committee), Racine (likewise), Weber (who was so dead as to be a natural history specimen and therefore unlikely to ravish any one, even spiritually), Goethe and Schiller (likewise, though still under suspicion)—were not yet carven upon its limestone pediment, the building was already streaked by the soot which drifted perpetually over the city from the remote flats where the mills now worked all day and all night in making shells. Yet the handsome temple could have had no existence save for the soot; the very smudges upon its virgin face were each one a symbol of the wealth which had made it possible. The Town had known four stages in its development. In the beginning there had been but a block house set down in a wilderness. Before many years had passed this was succeeded by a square filled with farmers and lowing cattle and heavy wagons laden with grain. Then in turn a community, raw and rankly prosperous which grew with a ruthless savagery, crushing everything beneath a passion for bigness and prosperity. And now, creeping in toward its heart, stealthily and, as many solid citizens believed, suspiciously, there came a softness which some called degeneration—a liking for beauty of sound, of sight, and of color. It stole up from the rear at the most unexpected moments upon men like Judge Weissmann. The wives of leading manufacturers and wholesale grocers had traitorously admitted lecturers and musicians into a fortress dedicated hitherto to the business of making money. And then with a sudden rush, the new forces had swept out of their hiding places on every side and saddled upon the noble citizenry a concert hall, a temple erected in the very heart of the citadel to the enemy.

So it stood there, bright and new, a few hundred yards from the Elks Club—a symbol of a change that was coming slowly to pass, a sign that the women and the younger generation had grown a little weary of a world composed entirely of noise and soot and clouds of figures. Men like Judge Weissmann saw it as the beginning of the end. Judge Weissmann (himself an immigrant from Vienna) called it "a sign that the old thrifty spirit of the pioneer was passing. The old opera house was good enough for concerts and shows." And secretly he calculated how much all that white limestone and carving had cost him in taxes.

It was into this divided world that Ellen, who had known only a community that was solid in its admiration for smoke and bigness and prosperity, returned. They were good to her, despite all the things they had to say regarding her affectations. They considered her dog (Callendar's dog) ridiculous, and they disapproved of the uncompromising Miss Schönberg who demanded her cash guaranty for the concert almost as soon as she stepped from the train. In certain benighted circles (which is to say those not associated with the flamboyant Country Club set) it was even whispered that she drank and smoked. They wondered how gentle Miss Ogilvie received such behavior, for Ellen stayed with Miss Ogilvie, who watched her bird's-nest parlor grow blue with the smoke of Ellen's and Rebecca's cigarettes without ever turning a hair. Was she not entertaining a great artist? If she herself had had the courage, might not she have been smoking cigarettes and drinking champagne? Had she herself not failed because she was afraid of what people would say? None of them knew the spirit of rebellion, smoldering for so many years, that now leapt into flame beneath the mauve taffeta dress which she wore every day during Ellen's visit.

The bird's-nest parlor, with all its pampas grass and coral and curios, must have set fire to strange memories in the breast of Ellen. She sat again in the same chair where she had sat, abashed but proud, awkward yet possessed of her curious dignity, on the night of the elopement. The little room was filled with memories of Clarence. She must have seen him again as he had been on that first night (so lost now in the turmoil of all that had gone between) . . . sitting there, frightened of old Harvey Seton, ardent and excited in his choked, inarticulate fashion, a man who even then had seemed a little ridiculous and pitiful.

And once Miss Ogilvie had summoned him to life when she said to Ellen, "Poor Mr. Murdock. If only he could be here to see your success."

The little old woman had the best intentions in the world. The meager speech was born of sympathy and kindness alone. She could not have known that each word had hurt Ellen intolerably. Poor Clarence! He would not have liked it. It would have made him even more insignificant and wretched. *The husband of Ellen Tolliver. That's what I'll be!* The words echoed ironically in her ears. And Clarence had never known Lilli Barr, who was born years after he died. . . . Lilli Barr who had nothing to do with poor Clarence. So far as the world was concerned he had never existed at all.

She had her triumph. There were set floral pieces with the words "Welcome Home" worked in carnations and pansies. And there was a welcoming speech by Mrs. McGovern, president of the Sorosis Club (who had downed Cousin Eva Barr only after a fierce struggle for the honor). And they had cheered her. It was a triumph and in a poor, inadequate fashion it satisfied her. But she was not sure that it was worth all the pain.

She did not go into the empty, echoing rooms of Shane's Castle. She saw it, distantly, veiled in the smoke and flame of the Flats, from Miss Ogilvie's back window on the hill, the one monument of her family in all the Town. She could not have borne it to enter alone the door which on each Christmas Day for so many years had admitted a whole procession.

And she came to understand that it was not alone the Town which she was driven relentlessly to escape. It was the Babylon Arms, Thérèse Callendar and all her world, even her own family,

all save Fergus—she must escape forever any tie that bound her,
any bond which gave her into possession.

On the day after the concert Miss Ogilvie gave a reception.
Crowds of women and a few intimidated men thronged the tiny
parlor. They passed in and out in an endless stream, until
Rebecca, who could bear it no longer, invaded the virgin privacy
of Miss Ogilvie's bedroom and fell into a perfect orgy of smoking
while she read Holy Living and Dying, the only book at hand
to divert her. Hansi, shut in an adjoining room, howled and
howled in his solitude.

Long after the winter twilight had descended, at a moment
when Ellen thought she could endure the procession no longer,
it began to abate and as the last guest departed she saw, coming
up the neat brick walk between the lilacs and syringas, the figure
of a plump dowdy woman surrounded by a phalanx of children.
In truth there were but four in the phalanx but in the fading light
their numbers seemed doubled. As the woman came nearer there
rose about her an aura of familiarity . . . something in the way
she walked, coquettish and ridiculous in a woman so plump and
loose of figure. And then, all at once in a sudden flash, Ellen
recognized the walk. The woman was May Biggs. Years ago
May had moved thus, giggling and flirting her skirts from side
to side while she walked with her arm about Ellen's waist. Only
now (Ellen reflected) there was twice as much of her to wriggle
and the effect was not the same.

As she approached Ellen did not wait. Some memory was
stirred by the sight, something which she could no more control
than she could understand. . . . May Biggs, whom she had
scorned always, coming up Miss Ogilvie's brick walk carrying
one child and leading three others by the hand, a May Biggs
who was stout now and already middle-aged in her dowdy clothes
covered with feathers and buttons and bits of passementerie. It
was extraordinary, the feeling that overwhelmed her; it was a

sensation compounded of joy and melancholy, of guilt and a curious desire to recapture something which had escaped her forever, perhaps that first reckless youth which had slipped away in the night without her knowing it.

She stood in the doorway, crying, "May . . . May Seton!"

And then she was kissing May who blushed and held on awkwardly to the youngest of the four little Biggses.

In the little parlor they were alone, for Miss Ogilvie under the stress of the excitement and the failure of the local bakery to deliver the macaroons had retired to her chamber with her smelling salts, where she now sat in a cloud of blue smoke talking with Rebecca while the great black dog howled in the adjoining room.

Once they were seated, May put forward her offspring, one by one, in order on the descending scale. "This is Herman Junior . . . and this Marguerite . . . and this Merton . . . and the baby here is named after me."

(All in order, thought Ellen, two boys and two girls, properly alternated.)

The two boys shook hands awkwardly, Marguerite curtseyed and smirked with all the coquetry descended from her now settled mother, and the baby gurgled pleasantly and buried her head. They were all very neat and clean. Their manners were excellent. They revealed glimpses of a little world that was placid, orderly, comfortable and perhaps a little monotonous.

"I brought the children," said May. "I wanted them to meet you. This," she said, addressing the three who were able to walk, "is my girl friend I told you about. She's famous now. You can remember when you're grown up that you've met her." And then abruptly, "Marguerite, put down that cake until the lady tells you to have one."

She had not changed much. Hers was the good-natured, pleasant sort of face on which time leaves few traces, and since nothing could ever happen to May, very little could happen to her face.

It had grown more plump, and less arch, for she was content and satisfied now with a solid husband, and she showed every sign of presenting a new hostage to fortune.

"Well," she said, shyly. "A lot has happened, hasn't it, Ellen. . . . I suppose I can still call you Ellen."

There was something in May's shyness, in the awe which shone in her eyes, that struck deep into Ellen's humility. It made her feel preposterous and absurd and a little nightmarish.

"Good Heavens!" she replied. "That's my name. Of all the people in the world, you have most right to use it." And then. "But tell me the news. I've been too busy to hear any of it. It's been ten years since I went away."

She found herself blushing, perhaps at the sudden slip of the tongue that betrayed her into recognition of the one unpleasantness that stood between them. It was almost as if she had said, "since I ran away with Clarence."

May, it seemed, was no more eager to mention his name. She hastened past it. "I tried to get Herman to come, but he wouldn't go where there were so many women. He wants to see you. He said to tell you that if you would come to lunch, he'd come home from the works. You'd never know him. He's a father now," she made a sweeping gesture to include the restless troop that surrounded her, "and he has a mustache."

Ellen declined, with a genuine regret. She wanted vaguely to enter the mild, ordered world out of which these four children had come.

"I can't come because I am leaving at eight. You see, I can't do what I like any more. I have engagements . . . concerts which I must keep. But thank him. Maybe he could run over to-night."

May thought not. They were making an inventory at the Junoform factory and Herman would be there until midnight. Harvey Seton (Lily's arch enemy) was dead.

"He died last June. We found him cold in the morning in his bed in the spare room. You see he hadn't slept in the same room with Ma since Jimmy was born. She says if he had, he might be alive to-day."

So Herman was head of the factory now and he was worried. The new fashions had cut down the sale of corsets, and corsets made of rubber were putting into the discard those built upon the synthetic whalebone which old Samuel Barr had invented. Business wasn't so good. Perhaps the fashions would change. Perhaps they would put in a rubber corset department. Ellen was fresh from Paris. Did she think there was any chance of small waists coming in again?

"Of course," said May, with an echo of the old giggle, "women with my figure will always have to wear whalebone. Rubber is no good for me. And then just now, I have to wear my corsets loose. . . ." She sighed. "If only I had a figure like yours." And she swept Ellen's straight gray clad figure with an appraising and envious glance.

"And your grandfather is still alive?" asked May in astonishment. "Why, he was an old man when you left. He must be nearly ninety now."

"He's ninety-one and very spry," said Ellen. "He goes out to walk alone in the city. He hasn't changed at all."

"Well, well," echoed May, and there rose an awkward pause which neither of them seemed able to break. Now that they had gone quickly through the past there seemed to be nothing of which to speak. The sound of the black dog's howling came distantly into the little parlor. It was Merton, the third child, who saved the situation. May cried, "Merton, how many times have I told you not to touch things. Take your hand right out of that gold-fish bowl. . . . Here, come here now and wipe it on Momma's handkerchief."

While this was being done Ellen reflected, a bit grimly, that perhaps it was just as well that she could not lunch with May. If the conversation had grown sterile in half an hour, how could one hope that it could be spread over an hour? Sabine, perhaps, had been right, when she had said once that it was a bad sign when a person had a great many *old* friends. It meant that such a person had not much capacity for growth.

Here was May unchanged, exactly as she had always been, save that she had now the satisfaction of a husband and was no longer restless and coquettish. Perhaps she had been right when she said so long ago that all May wanted was a man; it did not matter what man.

"There now," May was saying. "Sit on the chair and don't swing your feet. You'll scratch Miss Ogilvie's furniture." She turned to Ellen. "Marguerite," she said, "is now taking lessons from Miss Ogilvie. Maybe some day you'll be famous too, Marguerite. Maybe you'll play for the lady. Come now . . . that's a nice girl . . . play your new piece, the one called The Jolly Farmer."

But Marguerite would not stir. She grew arch and hung her head. She threatened to sob. Her mother coaxed and argued and pleaded but nothing happened. Marguerite would have none of The Jolly Farmer. It was Rebecca who saved the situation by coming in.

"My God!" she said, on entering, but the rest of her sentence was lost forever because the sight of May and her offspring silenced her.

"Miss Schönberg," said Ellen, "this is Mrs. Biggs."

"Pleased to meet you," said May, staring at the exotic figure of Rebecca, and then after a strained silence, "I must go now. Baby wants her supper."

Ellen went with the party to the door and as she bade them farewell and the little procession got under way, she saw that May hung behind with a curious air of embarrassment until the three older children were half way down the neat brick path. With only the baby left to hear her, she turned abruptly to Ellen and with a blush, said, "There was one thing I wanted to ask you and I never had a chance until now. It's about Clarence." She hesitated and then with a supreme effort managed to say,

"There was a story that he shot himself. . . . That wasn't true, was it?"

Ellen did not answer at once. She took the hand of the baby in hers, and looking away, replied in a low voice, "No, it wasn't true. . . . You remember he had a weak heart. It was his heart that killed him."

"I'm glad," said May softly. "I always liked him. I wouldn't want to think he'd committed suicide."

She stood in the doorway, unconscious of the cold until the figure of May, swaying from side to side and surrounded by the phalanx of offspring, had disappeared among the shadows of the lilacs.

In the hallway, Rebecca was awaiting her.

"Thank God, that's over," she said with a laugh, but she must have noticed that Ellen did not respond.

"She was a friend of mine," Ellen observed gravely. "I grew up with her."

Again Rebecca laughed in that same hard, worldly fashion. "I must say she has been more abundant than you."

This time Ellen made no answer at all. She was hypnotized by the memory of the look that had come into May's eyes at the mention of Clarence. It was an embarrassed, shy look, but it glowed all the same with a fire that had never burned for Herman Biggs. And Ellen understood then for the first time that she had been wrong after all, for Clarence—poor, meek, inarticulate Clarence, who had been dead for years—was to May a romantic figure, a fascinating creature. May had thought of him always . . . perhaps in the same fashion in which she herself thought of Callendar.

It had been all wrong since the beginning. There was no longer any doubt. It was May whom he should have married. And she wondered again for the thousandth time what it was that had turned him toward herself.

But the dog was still howling in loneliness. She walked along

the tiny hall and as she opened the door he leapt at her in a
frenzy of devotion.

"Hansi, old fellow," she murmured and pressed her face against
his sleek black head.

54

IT was six years now, through the evil chance that led them
to pass each other unknowingly in mid-Atlantic, since Fergus
had seen his sister. From afar, even in the turmoil and
excitement of the war he had watched her progress, now in the
letters from his mother (which he discounted because he knew she
was inclined to exaggerate when her children were concerned)
now in the letters from Ellen, and sometimes in the newspapers which filtered through, weeks old, to his escadrille at the
front. As Ellen had guessed, he understood the ascent perfectly;
he saw her working at it doggedly with one eye always upon
the lucky chance. From afar he had admired the whole cam-
paign and developed a passionate curiosity to know this Rebecca
Schönberg who stood so cleverly in the background of the whole
affair. She too had genius.

The great distance which separated them—even the years which
had passed since he saw her, aboard the greasy old *City of Paris,*
slip away into the winter mists of the North River—had not
altered the transcendent quality of their understanding. Their
tie was not, like the love of Hattie, a thing which emotionally demanded a close and breathless contact. It was less a matter of the
senses and more a matter of the mind. Each had known always
what to expect from the other, above all else a frank and unabashed honesty. They were very like each other, save that Fergus
(and he knew it ruefully) lacked his sister's stiff, inflexible wilfulness. It was these qualities, he understood well enough, which
had given her the advantage. It had made of her a conqueror.
The lack of it had left him a charming, happy-go-lucky fellow.

But it gave him too a savor in life, a wild enjoyment, which she could never know.

The war suited him. As his mother had believed, it was to him a great show, a sort of masquerade in which he was at once a participant and a spectator; and it gave rein to impulses and inheritances which otherwise might never have been awakened— such strains as a passion for adventure that had its origin in wild cattle-thieving highland ancestors, and a love for the excitement to be found in battle high in the air above a world that lay spread out beneath him mapwise and miserably dwarfed. A little of this he managed to pin down in the eager, hurried letters he wrote to Ellen, so that she understood what it was that made him content and happy. It was a satisfaction very like her own, the satisfaction of triumph over great odds, of gambling for high stakes, of finding oneself absorbed utterly and passionately in the thing at hand. It was that queer streak again—the same queer streak which had made of Sam Barr a pauper and of Old Julia Shane a woman fabulously rich, the streak to which the clumsy perpetual motion machine rusting in a corn field of the middle-west stood as an eternal monument. It was the old fever to gobble up all of life, not alone mere stupid contentment, but danger and sorrow and even tragedy—a strange unworldly greed to get the most of a life which each of them knew in his very marrow was bitterly brief.

It was easy to see in the glowing letters of Fergus that he was wildly happy in those days. It was easy to see that the old restlessness, so long without a way to turn, at last had found its goal. The old adventurous blood had come into its own.

From a great distance he had watched his sister's triumphs but, unlike the others, he had no awe of her imperious way of riding roughshod over those who stood in her path. To him Ellen Tolliver would always exist, concealed perhaps inside the shell of Lilli Barr, but alive none the less and ready to be called forth. The core, the heart was eternal. It did not change. He saw her still, in the rare moments when he had peace enough for reflection, as he had always seen her—a wilful, smolderingly brilliant, disagreeable sister with whom he could do as he chose, no matter what her mood or temper. It did not occur to him that she had grown older, in some ways more mellow and in some ways harder than she had ever been.

It was from Ellen that he heard first of his father's death. She wrote him that the gentle man had gone to sleep on the night after her first concert in America and that afterward he had never really awakened. There had been moments when for a time he had recognized his wife and talked to her, though he did not seem quite clear and mixed the past and the present in a strange and touching confusion. And at the end she had written, in her bold, sprawling hand, "None of the doctors appeared to know what it was that killed him. But I knew what it was. He died simply of homesickness. He hated the city. He was born to hate it. But you must never say this to Ma, for it was she who forced him to leave the Town. And it was our fault in the end . . . yours and mine, because it was us whom she was pursuing. She'll never stop. She's an extraordinary woman. Time has no effect upon her, no more than it has upon The Everlasting. He is ninety-four and though he looks as old as Methuselah, he is as spry and as clear in the head as a boy. He has learned how to protect himself. Oh! So admirably! Sometimes, I fancy he will outlive us all . . . sitting in his room, rocking and chuckling! He has discovered a secret which none of us know! And he'll never tell us."

Thus Charles Tolliver had died, peacefully and without resentment, indifferent to the triumphs of his children so long as they were lost to him; for long ago he had recognized the loss, a thing his wife would never do. And he had lost not only his children but the very life he had loved. He had gone now from a sleep that had been fitful, from dreams which had been awakened harshly each morning by the noises of a hostile city, into a long unbroken sleep. Quietly and gently he had lived, a friend to all the world, serving for his part as little more than the father of

Hattie's children, passing on to them the qualities of old Gramp to unite with the qualities of Hattie and produce such offspring as Ellen and Fergus. They had never belonged to him, even for a moment. They had been Hattie's always, and old Gramp's. . . .

55

NEARLY three years passed before Ellen, having meanwhile added Australia and South America to the list of her triumphs, returned to the Paris which she had not seen since the day she left with Rebecca for the Vienna they had never reached and now never would reach; because, as Rebecca said, the old Vienna was gone now, forever. Ellen would never know it as it had been in the days when Rebecca had visited Uncle Otto who owned a sapphire mine in Cambodia.

In the end she went back to Paris over the protests of her mother and against the advice of Rebecca, who saw the return simply as a great bundle of money thrown to the winds. But she could not have done otherwise. She had to return. She was unable to explain the instinct, but she trusted it shrewdly as wise persons trust instinct for its value as accumulated experience over any mere process of logic. She had to see Lily again and the beautiful house (so saddened and changed) in the Rue Raynouard. And there were times too when she became obsessed by an inexplicable fear that if she did not go at once, she might be too late. . . . Too late for what? This she could not answer, save that vaguely it must have to do with Fergus and Callendar. Lily was in no danger; she lived quietly in the Rue Raynouard or in the white villa at Nice.

For two years she had allowed herself to be ruled by circumstance and by Rebecca Schönberg, the high priestess of opportunity. She would wait no longer now. And so, after a terrible scene with Rebecca in which they both descended to the level of fishwives, she had embarked to return to a city which could mean nothing now so far as her success was concerned, a barren city that lay dark and blue with the coming of nightfall.

The old fear possessed her now for days at a time. Life was rushing past her on and on. . . . She might be too late.

56

IT was a wet night of the early spring when Fergus got down from the Metro at Passy bound for the house in the Rue Raynouard. He had been there before, many times, for Lily, pleased perhaps to have him in a house which seemed now so empty and desolate, had given him one of the rooms opening upon the long gallery to use as he saw fit. But the visits had not been too cheerful. He had found Lily alone in the house, mourning for old Madame Gigon and her nephew, the Baron. The old beauty of the place had not faded; even Lily had not changed greatly. She was still young, amazingly so, but she appeared saddened and more quiet than in the days when, bedazzled, he had sat by her side at the family dinners in Shane's Castle. There was left of Madame Gigon's pets only Criquette, the Aberdeen, old and fat and quizzical, who followed at the heels of Augustine, the maid, and sniffed continually at Madame Gigon's chair before the fire.

He had met there Lily's son Jean, his own cousin, whom he had never seen before—a tall, red haired boy, impatient and wild over the mutilation that kept him in Paris shut up in the offices of the Ministry of War. It was strange to see one's own cousin (and Jean resembled Fergus amazingly in many ways) a Frenchman, a foreigner who spoke English with an accent. He had met there at tea a Monsieur de Cyon who seemed devoted to Lily and who was connected in some way with the government—a distinguished, white haired man recently become a widower. It was all very queer and foreign, yet when one thought of it, not so different from Shane's Castle which in the midst of the Mills had always had its own strange air of the old world. It was Lily, the sinner of the family, the one who had surrounded herself with luxury and mystery, who explained it all. Knowing her, you could understand how there could be a bond between that smoky city of the Midlands and this quiet, beautiful house in the Rue Raynouard. She belonged to both and yet in a way to neither . . . a woman of the sort which had existed since the beginning of time. Fergus knew women rather better than most men, for they were attracted easily to him, but he knew of none who approached Lily in the perfection of her rôle. He understood Lily now. . . . He was no longer a little boy sitting fascinated by her side in the gloomy dining room of Shane's Castle. He knew the world now. Experience had come his way.

He thought of all this for the hundredth time as he emerged from the Metro into the drifting mist that obscured the tall white houses of the Square Alboni. In one sense he had changed. He was a man now, though he appeared little older than on the day he bade Ellen farewell. His features were more firmly molded; he had grown more handsome. But he was young still; it was the sense of youth which always impressed people, a reckless, headlong youth, of the sort which has no value in a worldly sense but glorifies all who are sensible to its glow. And he walked with a slight swagger born not of any pomp but of an excess of animal spirits, of a great vitality.

As he stepped out into the darkness the figure of the old flower woman sitting beneath her umbrella in a mist of rain and mimosa blossoms took form in the shadows. In the faint blue light from the darkened street lamp he stooped and bought from her a great armful of golden, powdery blossoms. (The mimosa was in full blossom now in Nice, showering Lily's white villa with its scented dust.)

Touched and warmed by his youth, the old woman chuckled. "Pour votre marraine?" she asked. (She had sold him flowers before now.)

"No," he told her. "Not this time. They are for my sister."

It was Ellen whom he was to see in the Rue Raynouard, Ellen whom he had not seen in years . . . Ellen who was famous now, a great musician.

As he moved away, it struck him as luck that he had come by chance on the flower woman. For a musician, an artist, flowers were the thing . . . an enormous bunch of flowers. Ellen would appreciate the gesture. She would play up to it. She would, he fancied, even expect it.

In the blue darkness (it was an excellent night, he thought, for an air raid) he turned the corner past the Café des Tourelles and the blind, steel-shuttered magasin. The houses stood forbidding and black. The Rue Raynouard between the magasin and the tobacconist's shop gaped like the mouth of Avernus. It would be difficult to find the house, turning its deceptive, insignificant face to the street, so lost among its commonplace neighbors. From far away, on the slope that led down toward the Seine, the sound of footsteps, muffled by the damp, came to him across the cobblestones. But the solitary walker turned away and the sound died presently into silence.

A hundred paces from the square he halted before a house to search for the number. In the darkness it remained invisible; it was impossible to find it even by sense of touch. Puzzled, he stood for an instant looking up and down the street, and then through the thick stillness there rose the faint sound of music, distant and fragmentary. Listening, he found presently that the melody took form: the fragments joined into a pattern of sound. It was the Appassionata. Only the crescendos were swept toward him through the damp night air, only the moments when the music rose into a wild abandon. There could be no mistaking it . . . the music was Ellen's, more magnificent than it had ever been.

As he stood there in the thin mist upon the doorstep the sound, coming distantly from inside the house up the long paneled stairs, had upon him an amazing effect. It was a sensation bordering upon clairvoyance; he no longer stood on the dripping cobblestones before a solid door, his feet upon solid earth. It was as if he existed in space alone at a great height; rather as if he had died. There was in the feeling something of terror at the immensity which surrounded him, an emotion which he had known once or twice before when, flying at night, there had been for a time no earth below him, nothing solid in all creation—a time when, if he existed at all, it was as an atom lost in all time and space. It was, he felt dimly, like being dead . . . a reverent, humbled feeling.

And yet in a confused fashion all life had suddenly achieved an amazing clarity. He knew himself suddenly, honestly, for what he was—a man who had harmed none, who had achieved nothing, who had asked only to find pleasure in living. And the others— He saw them too with the same terrifying brilliance . . . Ellen, who for all her faults was so much more worthy, who had in her the elements of a great nobility; his mother, passionate and bursting with vitality, a little somber and tragic save that she would never recognize tragedy when it came her way; and Lily, who had lived by some plan which she had never revealed, choosing instead to hide it away among the other mysteries of her life; and Jean, whom he scarcely knew until this moment, Jean who was neither French nor American nor even an honest child. He saw Jean's life too and its queer, inarticulate tragedy. And Old Gramp, who stood outside them all, aloof and cold, uncaught by the web that bound them all together . . . Gramp hugging his secret passionately to him. But it was Ellen whom he saw more clearly than all the others, struggling, fighting with a strange unconquerable courage, using the weapons which she found at hand, weapons which were not always fair. Some day she would choose the honest ones and then . . .

Far away, somewhere in the blanket of darkness the music died away and presently he stood again before the door on the cobblestones, rubbing the sleeve of his blue greatcoat across his face with the gesture of one awaking from a profound sleep. The great bunch of mimosa lay at his feet. It was amazing. He had been for a moment dead, quite outside this world. The street was still again with a blue, dripping silence. Under each lamp there was a pool of blue light that was not light at all, but only another kind of darkness.

He gathered up the damp flowers and knocked loudly. It was too dark to find the bell and he stood there for a long time before the door was opened by Augustine who it seemed had gone to bed in the belief that no one could be out on such a night. She stood in a sort of wrapper ornamented with a gay design of Cupids, holding up her black hair with one hand. He saw with an amazing clarity each tiny detail, even the veins in her big red feet half-muffled in gigantic purple slippers.

"Ah!" she said. "It's you, M'sieu Tolliver. . . . Madame Shane is not here. She is in Nice."

And again the sense of having returned from the dead swept over him. Augustine was as astonished as if she had opened the door upon a phantom. Yet there was nothing extraordinary in calling at ten o'clock in the evening, even on a night like this.

"It is my sister I've come to see . . . Miss Tolliver."

"She is here . . . in the salon. She told me I might go to bed. There is a gentleman with her."

Clearly it was impossible for Augustine, in her state of attire, to announce him. He took off his greatcoat while the Breton girl, her eyes shining in admiration for a young aviateur, stood by holding the mimosa. He was straight and tall in his blue uniform with the silver wings glittering on his breast. He had his effect upon Augustine . . . the blue eyes, the blond curling hair, the spoiled mouth.

"I'll go in myself," he said, taking the flowers from her once more. "It's all right, I know."

And he started down the long stairs where the candles glowed dimly against the satinwood paneling. Half way down, where the gallery led off on both sides, the sound of music reached him once more. This time it was different; there were no passionate crescendos of sound, no tides of melody that swept high. The

music was low and gentle and filled with pathos. And presently
he heard a voice—Ellen's voice—begin to sing in a clear contralto
of unsuspected beauty. He went slowly, step by step, his shoulders brushing the satinwood beneath the dull flare of the candles.
Out of the depths of the warm old room the sound came to him
with the same amazing clarity which seemed to affect all his
senses. . . .

> *Nous n'avons plus de maisons,*
> *Les ennemis ont tout pris, tout pris, tout pris*
> *Jusqu'à notre petit lit.*
> *Ils ont brulé l'école et notre maître aussi.*
> *Ils ont brulé l'église et Monsieur Jésus Christ*
> *Et le vieux pauvre qui n'a pas pu s'en aller!*

She sang gently, with an infinite sadness . . . Ellen who had
damned the war, Ellen who had striven to ignore it, Ellen who had
turned her back and taken no part in all the vast parade. What
could she have known of it? What of Christmas and "les petits
enfants qui n'ont plus de maisons."

> *Les ennemis ont tout pris, tout pris, tout pris. . . .*
> *Noël! Écoutez-nous, nous n'avons plus de petits sabots.*
> *Noël! Noël! . . . Surtout pas de joujoux.*

And yet, listening, Fergus understood that she did know. This
new Ellen, the artist, knew it as she knew all things because she
was, in spite of Rebecca Schönberg, in spite of shrewd lighting
and bouquets sent by the management, in spite of all the clap-trap,
an artist. Standing there in the shadows of the stair, he knew
without having seen her that she was changed. Something had
happened to her.

> *Les ennemis ont tout pris, tout pris, tout pris . . .*
> *Jusqu'à notre petit lit. . . .*

The simple frail refrain echoed through the great rooms. It was a child who sang it—a simple naïve child. He knew for an instant what a strange, idiotic, pitiful affair this war had been. He had not known until now.

Mais donnez la victoire aux enfants de France! . . .

Fergus moved down from the last step of the long stairs. The green music of Debussy died away, and as he entered the room he saw that Ellen was not alone. She sat at the piano in the far end near the bright fire where she had sat on that first day when she had entered from the same stairway to discover Madame Gigon, little Jean and the dogs. There was only Criquette left now, lying fat and lonely before the fire, and Hansi, the great black wolf. Beside her, with his back towards the stairs, sat a man with dark hair in a uniform blue like the one Fergus himself wore; and while he stood, silent in his surprise, he saw the stranger lean forward and, taking Ellen in his arms, kiss her. He saw too that her arms were about the stranger, but it was not the embrace that astonished him; it was the sight of Ellen's strong, white hand, clenched as if in resistance, as if in pain. Yet she did not struggle. It was only the hand . . . clenched, white, as if all her will, all her resistance were centered in it.

It gave Fergus the strangest shock. He found himself turning abruptly away and hiding in the stairway with an air of having witnessed something obscene. It was all spoiled now, all the entrance he had planned, the hope of finding her alone, the mocking, teasing, grandiose speeches he had planned. The stranger had taken possession of her, placed himself there between them as a barrier. It was ridiculous. . . .

Feeling like a small boy who had been caught eavesdropping, he coughed and scuffled his feet and then made a second entrance. This time they turned and Ellen, rising to her feet, stared at him for a moment and then rushed toward him crying, "Fergus! Fergus! You should have told me you had leave!"

He knew at once that she guessed he had seen them. Her face was flushed with shame and hurt pride. He knew the fierce *pudeur* (there was no other word for it) that enveloped her. It was a part of her savage unwillingness to surrender, to reveal, anything of herself.

Her beauty astonished him. He had seen photographs of her, but in them he had seen nothing of the proud domination that gave her that look of swooping down on one. It occurred to him in a flash that old Julia Shane, Lily's mother, must have looked like this in her youth. Only she had worn crinolines and Ellen was all in black in a tight gown that made her look like (the old simile returned, the inevitable one) like a greyhound. She had changed enormously; the awkwardness had vanished. This was no girl who hurried toward him; it was a woman, superb, splendid, full of fire.

"Fergus!" she cried, and ignoring the mimosa she crushed the bright gold blossoms against his blue tunic so that the yellow pollen clung to it and dimmed the silver wings. She kissed him passionately and held him in her arms for a long time. She was excited. He had never seen her like this. The shyness, the restraint was gone, for the moment at least. He felt a quick satisfaction of vanity, almost as if he had been her husband instead of her brother. She was a creature to be proud of. No wonder this stranger . . .

The dark man had risen now and stood waiting quietly for them to join him by the fire. He was a handsome fellow of perhaps thirty-five, though he may have been older, thin perhaps from the hardships of war. And in the olive skin were set the strangest pair of gray eyes, which looked on now with an expression of mild amusement. They were eyes which fascinated you, which you were certain had the power of seeing things which other eyes had not.

"Richard," said Ellen, "this is my brother Fergus . . . Mr. Callendar."

Her voice trembled a little with excitement. It may have been that this was the moment for which she had returned. She had them together now, with her, in the very same room, the two men—indeed, the two persons—whom she cherished above all others in the world. She had not been, after all, too late.

It must have been clear to Fergus, even in the disappointment of the moment, that he had stumbled awkwardly into the midst of some queer situation. He understood now why she had sent Augustine off to bed. It explained too the excitement of her manner and the sudden falling away of the reserve which she had always held before her as a warrior his shield. She still blushed, and she lighted a cigarette with a comically obvious air of covering her confusion. It was amazing to find in this woman who was by nature so self-possessed, so cold, a sudden air of school girl coquetry. This was an Ellen whom her brother had never seen, whom perhaps no one had seen until now.

And the stranger? He still stood with his feet well apart, finishing the last of his Chartreuse, balancing himself lightly on his toes, quite calm and smiling a little in a fashion that would have been warm and friendly save for the expression in the gray eyes. In their obscure, blank depths, there lay something sinister . . . "catlike" was the word. They were eyes like those of a cat, proud, sensual, indifferent, aloof, and incapable of smiling.

They sat down and for a moment Fergus was tempted to blurt out sharply that he had spied upon them unwittingly, that he knew exactly the mood into which he had blundered so clumsily. It would perhaps have shattered the tension and cleared the air, reducing them to a common ground of meeting upon which they might laugh and talk like old friends. It did not occur to him that Callendar might be his sister's lover because, in spite even of her blushes and confusion, he knew that such a thing was impossible. Besides, their manner toward each other was not that

of lovers; it lacked the hidden intimacies which come of only
one experience. They were a little formal, a little strange. The
flame that leapt between them was not quite clear and white and
unhindered; there were obstructions, misunderstandings. It was
a complicated relationship, one could see at a glance, and a little
ridiculous. Even Callendar, so clearly a man of the world, so
clearly a man who was neither an innocent nor a yokel, was not
at his ease.

"Mr. Callendar," said Ellen, "is an old friend of mine. Until
the other day I had not seen him for years."

But for Fergus this could have been no explanation. It told
nothing of all that passed in those missing years, nothing of the
intriguing of old Thérèse, nothing of the slow passion, fed upon
absence and memories that instead of dying had, as Thérèse knew,
gained strength. It revealed nothing of all the forces, conscious or
blundering and obscure, which had been at work weaving the slow
web that was now near to its end. Fergus alone guessed how nearly
it was finished. It came to him in a return of that sudden flight
of clairvoyance which had seized him in the dark street outside the
door. He understood with an unearthly certainty that this was
the man whom fate (that nonsensical force) had marked for his
sister. This was the man destined to know all the tempestuous
sweep of her fierce energy, her vast capacity for devotion, all the
forces that until now had lain buried and dormant. This
perilous man . . . (It was strange that strong women were likely
to be unhappy in love, to make so often a choice which all the
world, even the stupidest fellow, could have told her was wrong.)

It was this current of thought which ran beneath the surface
of all their polite conversation, made so scrupulously, with such
labor in defiance of that strain which none—not even Callendar,
who perhaps chose to make no such effort—could dissipate. For
Ellen's moment had passed swiftly as such moments, awaited so
long, are likely to pass. There had been a quick flare of delight
in the possession of them both and then this confused disappointment and sense of ill-ease clouding everything.

The tension lessened a little when Fergus, seeking in his amiable way one subject after another to pierce the indifference of the stranger, stumbled upon Loos and Amiens which Callendar knew as thoroughly from the ground as Fergus knew them from the air. But this led to nothing because it was now Ellen who found herself thrust outside the pale and left to grow sulky while they talked of this sector and of that one, each discovering with a swift heightening of interest that they had taken part in the same drive.

"My battery," said Callendar, "lay just back of Hill 408, in the curve of the road beyond Jouy. . . ."

"It was at Jouy," interrupted Fergus, his good-natured face flushing with interest, "that we broke up a German escadrille . . . four of them shot down."

"Did you ever see Reymont?" asked Callendar. . . . "The general of our division? . . . A pompous ass!"

"He was at St. Pol while I was there. He reviewed the division when it came in from the east. . . . I saw him on a balcony. . . ."

And so on, talking of this spectacle which Ellen despised as much because she could have no part in it as for any other reason. She would, at that moment, have preferred the spectacle to all the success, all the triumph; but it was no good. She was, for all her strength, all her power, simply a woman, thrust outside the experience which had enkindled Callendar and her brother. They had slipped away from her into a world of which she knew nothing.

At last, turning in pique from their talk, she went out and herself fetched them whiskey and soda, and when she had interrupted them long enough to pour out a glass for each she turned to the piano and fell to playing softly, as if to draw them quietly back to her. It was a plan which proved successful, for presently their talk abated a little and finally ceased; the war was put to rout and it was Ellen once more who held the center of the stage. The two men leaned back in their chairs, scrupulously silent, listening while she played for them in a fashion she had not done in years. And for a time she recaptured a little of the joy that had escaped so quickly.

She played the things she knew would please Fergus, the music which he had loved in the days of the house in Sycamore Street and the flat in the Babylon Arms, music she had played for him alone at the moments when Clarence was not there to disturb her with the silent, unrelieved pleading of his dim eyes. She played the simple old March from The Ruins of Athens, and one or two Chopin waltzes and the Marche Funèbre, which to Hattie would always be McKinley's Funeral March and which to Fergus invoked memories of Shane's Castle and Ellen in shirtwaist and skirt wearing at her belt a jingling thing they called a chatelaine. And she wooed them with such success that, hypnotized by the spell, they did not hear the first screams of the sirens rushing through distant streets nor the faint popping of the guns far away on the summit of Montmartre.

It was not until she paused, her hands resting thoughtfully on the ivory keys, that Callendar stirred himself and murmured in French, "The Boches are here. . . . Listen. The siren!"

And from the street nearby—perhaps from the Place Passy—the shriek of a fire engine penetrated the room, even through the heavy brocade curtains that muffled the windows. There was one more scream and then another and another, and then the faint, distant popping of guns, like a barrage of tiny fire-crackers. Fergus stood up and glanced at his wrist.

"I must go," he said. "I'm late already."

"Not now," protested Ellen, turning abruptly. "Not now in the midst of a raid. You can spend the night here. . . . There is plenty of room." She trembled a little, as if in terror of losing him so soon.

Fergus smiled. "I can't," he said. "You see, I have a rendez-vous . . . with a man from my escadrille. He is waiting for me now."

"He won't be expecting you . . . not now."

"I can't help it, Ellen. He'll be waiting. Great Heavens! I've been through a hundred raids. They've tried to blow us up every night. . . ."

She had taken his hand now and was pleading anxiously. "But this is different."

Fergus laughed. "It *is* different," he said. "There's not one chance in a million here. . . ."

Callendar merely smiled, as if to confirm the statement of Fergus that it was ridiculous to suppose there were any danger. He had, of course, no reason for wanting him to remain. It was Fergus who won in the end, merely by persistence—a strange thing, for usually it was the strong-minded Ellen who had her way. To-night he was firm and certain of his purpose. She thought perhaps that it was the war, the years that had passed since she last saw him, which had so hardened him and given strength to his will.

She went with him to the door and on the stairs, when they had turned out of the big room, she said, "You are not going back to the front to-morrow?"

"No. I shall come back here. I shall be in Paris for a week. Perhaps I'll spend a night or two with you here."

In their manner there was still an air of strangeness and formality, as if Callendar had in some way followed them out of the room and walked between them up the polished stairs. She helped him into his greatcoat and kissed him affectionately.

"To-morrow," she said, "it will be better. We can be alone." And then in a low voice she added, as if in explanation, "His permission is over to-morrow."

Extinguishing the candles, Fergus opened the door and looked out. The rain had ceased and far above them beyond the roofs of the houses on the opposite side of the street, the searchlights fingered a sky that, save for one or two clouds, was blue and luminous like the street lamps.

"Look," said Fergus, softly. "They've spotted one of them." And they both stood in the open door fascinated by the sight of a

Gotha turned to a silver dragon fly by a long finger of light. Far away in another part of the city there sounded a faint crash and then another and another. The sirens still screamed, now on one side of them, now on another.

"It is magnificent," said Ellen, breathlessly.

"You see, they're not dropping them anywhere near us. They are trying to hit the bridges and the government buildings. I'm only going around the corner . . . into the Avenue Kléber."

They were speaking in hushed voices, caught again in that mood of insignificance. One might have thought that in the blackness of the empty street there were figures listening. In the eyes of Fergus there was the light of fascination . . . a bird held captive by a glittering snake.

"I must go," murmured Fergus still watching the silver dragon fly. "I'm late already."

She stood in the doorway until the darkness had swallowed him up and then, turning, slowly closed the door and went thoughtfully down the stairs. The sound of guns, the scream of the sirens and the echo of the distant, reverberating crashes grew fainter and fainter as she descended.

In the long drawing-room, standing before the fire with his glass in his hand Callendar was awaiting her. As she came toward him, she said, "I am proud of my brother," with the air of making a challenge, as if she reproached him for his indifference.

"I have heard of him," he said, quietly. "He is well known in the Division Reymont."

To this she made no reply. She drew her chair nearer to the fire and sat staring for a time silently into the bright blaze. There was no sound save for the asthmatic breathing of Criquette, the grunts of comfort from Hansi, who had flung down his great black body by her side, and the distant echoes from somewhere in the direction of the Champ de Mars.

At length he murmured, "Perhaps we had better go into the cellar. The last one was nearer."

But she refused. "No. Why should I?" For she understood well enough that to Callendar it was a matter of complete indifference. She knew his whole philosophy could be expressed in a single sentence—"If one died, one died." The thing was to live while one was alive. "No," she repeated. "Why should I be afraid? You and Fergus aren't frightened."

"It's not the same," he said softly.

"There's no reason why it shouldn't be."

For a moment it may have seemed to her that she too was playing a part in the spectacle. She too might for once undertake a little of the danger they had known, the one with indifference, the other with a kind of fierce excitement.

"It is much easier," she murmured, "to be with you both than to be here alone, not knowing what may happen to you."

Under the heavy, sensuous lids Callendar's gray eyes revealed a sudden sparkle of admiration for the fierce and sullen defiance of her mood. He must have known that she would have walked carelessly through the street, as carelessly as Fergus had done, that she would in her present mood have gone into an attack with a serene indifference; because she was angry now, angry at the war for which she had such a contempt, at circumstance, at the whole muddled business of living. She was angry and defiant with an Olympian anger, careless of cost or consequence.

There was another crash, nearer this time in the direction of the Trocadéro, and again Callendar's eyelids flickered with slow admiration. She did not move. She still sat with one hand on Hansi's head looking into the fire.

"I am not thinking about myself," she observed suddenly with the air of answering a question which he had not spoken. "It is my brother."

"He must be safe by now at his rendezvous. The Avenue Kléber is not far."

She was thinking too, in a dazed fashion, of all that had happened in the hour before Fergus blundered in upon them. Cal-

lendar had told her that at last Sabine was divorcing him. He
had not asked her to do it. She had told him that she could endure the situation no longer. For the part which Thérèse played
in the affair, he could not answer. "I don't know," he had said,
smiling. "Sabine will say nothing and my mother denies having
spoken of the matter. But if she saw fit she would not hesitate to
lie deliberately. Sometimes I think she is not clever, and then
afterward I find she has been stupid only because it suited her,
because her stupidity was dictated by a devilish shrewdness."

And then he had told her of all the tricks Thérèse had played
to bring about his remarriage, of how she had written him glowing
letters about Ellen. "All she wrote," he added, "was true, of
course. You can hardly doubt that. Still, it was not the way to
bring it about."

And Ellen too had laughed and told of her interview with
Thérèse in the library of the house at Murray Hill on the night of
her concert, and at last she had asked abruptly, "Am I to interpret
all this as a proposal?"

"My mother knew that there was no one else whom I would
think of marrying. There was no need to marry at all."

After this speech she had been silent for a time and when at last
she looked up at him it was to ask, "And you want to marry me
because it is the only way you can have me?"

"No."

Her mind wandered back to the hot afternoon in the Babylon
Arms when he had so nearly swept away all her self-possession.
He had been different then, more ardent, more overwhelming, and
yet she knew that the danger then had not been so great as it was
in this very moment when he sat beside her in the big room, quiet
and thoughtful, watching her with a fierce concentration.

"But there was a time," she said slowly, "when you would have
taken me in any way possible without marrying me."

He was sitting with his body bent forward, his elbows on his
knees, his hands clasped. The hands were tense so that the
knuckles showed through the tanned, dark skin.

"No," he said softly. "That is not true. I would have married you then. I wanted to marry you, and I was younger then and not so wise. I fancied then that I could get anything I wanted in this world for the asking. And yet it was marriage that I had in mind. I have always had . . . everything. I will be honest. I have always had women if I wanted them badly enough . . . all save you. . . . And you are the only one I ever *wanted* to marry. I swear to God that what I am saying is true."

Watching him, she could not believe that he was lying. She saw the clenched hands. She saw that the mockery had gone out of him. She saw, with a queer tragic catch of memory, the little vein in his throat throbbing as she had seen the same vein throb in the throat of Clarence. It was all so different now. There was no headlong recklessness, no wild, sudden torrent of passion. He had not seized her now and tormented her with caresses that assailed all her resistance. They talked calmly in a fashion that might have been called calculating and cold-blooded save that underneath it there lay a current which ran more deep and more powerful than any emotion they had known on that sultry afternoon in the Babylon Arms. It was all changed now. They were older, and wiser, and in some ways more understanding. And the world about them had changed . . . the shabby little flat had given way to the old, beautiful, glowing room. This calm, grave Richard was far more dangerous than the young and ardent one had been. It was more perilous now, for she was assailed through all her senses, and time was rushing on and on, past her. . . .

She did not answer him, and presently in the same low voice he continued. "'You are a woman of the world now," he said, "so you are not likely to believe what you believed then. I do not make excuses for myself. I did not love Sabine. I have never loved her. It was an arranged, a proper marriage like thousands of others, but it turned out badly. . . . I could not make myself love. No one can do that." He paused for a moment. "And she could not save herself. . . ."

This last speech he made with such a sad humility that there

was no air of conceit in it. Besides Ellen knew its truth; she had
seen Sabine with her own eyes, weeping, suffering in a fashion she
had once believed impossible, and pretending all the while that
such suffering had been caused by a sick kitten. Yet it was this
which somehow frightened her; she was afraid lest one day she
herself might be humbled in the same fashion.

"My mother," he was saying, "is as you know, a Greek, and
there is a great deal of the Greek in me. Sometimes I fancy I am
Oriental . . . utterly, completely. An eastern man admires a
woman of beauty and of spirit. He wants such a woman for the
mother of his children." He unclasped his hands and took her
hand in his. "But don't fancy that I love you in that way only.
Sabine was a fine match in a worldly sense. She was rich. She
was fashionable. But I too am that, so what could it mean to
me? It was more than that which I wanted. I still want it. I
want you to marry me as soon as it is possible."

She did not free her hand, though the touch made her faint as
it had done so many years before. She was conscious suddenly
that the old sense of conflict was gone, the old feeling of a hidden
antagonism between them. Could it be that it was because he
was humble now, asking something of her rather than coming
boldly to her to claim it?

"And still," she heard herself saying, "I am not certain that it
would work out. I don't know. . . . You must give me time."

Then he had kissed her hand and murmured, "We have not
so much time as we once had. . . . Perhaps I have even less than
I know now."

To this she had chosen to make no answer. Instead, she had
played for him until Fergus blundered in upon them.

It was in the midst of these thoughts that she heard Callendar
say, as he stood balancing himself before the fire, "We could go to
the south to-morrow, if you like. I could arrange to have my
permission extended. De Cyon could do it for me. We could
have a week together there."

He must have known that it was too late now to ask such a thing. An hour earlier, before Fergus had intruded upon them, he might have succeeded. But everything was changed now. For an instant, during the time Fergus had been there, she had caught a glimpse of the old, familiar Richard, the mocking one; and the sense of conflict had risen once more sharply between them.

"How could I do that?" she asked, and after a moment's silence, "I can't do that sort of thing. It is impossible for me. . . ."

He smiled. "But the world believes it of you already. The world will not care. The world expects it of you. It can make no difference . . . and when the divorce is finished we will be married."

Her answer was colored with a sudden bitterness. "You would not have said such a thing to me once."

It was true. There was a difference now, of a kind she had not thought of before. It was a difference which had to do with age and all the slow hardening which had come with each year that stood between them and the hot afternoon in the Babylon Arms. Something had gone from them both . . . the warmth, the gallantry, the glow that had made him then so reckless, so willing to marry her, a poor nobody, in the face of all his world. It was gone from her too. . . . She knew exactly what it was now. It was the thing which she had felt slip from her as a cloak on the night she sat talking with Thérèse in the dark library on Murray Hill. They were no longer young. They weighed chances now, cynically looking upon their problem without regard for honor. The tragedy was that they could never go back. What was gone was gone forever. And in the memory of the fierce, youthful passion, so fresh and turbulent, this new love seemed to her an obscene and middle-aged emotion.

"No," she repeated. "I can't do that. It is to myself that it matters. . . . What the world thinks does not interest me."

Long after midnight Callendar at last stirred himself and bade her good night. They had talked, long and passionately, over the same ground again and again, seeing it now in this light, now in that, arriving in the end nowhere at all; and through it all, Ellen must have caught once more the awful sense of his patience. He could wait; in the end he would have what he desired. And this she knew with an understanding that lay deeper than the mere surface of her consciousness.

Only it was all different now, even the significance of his patience, because time was rushing on and on past her. She was no longer a young girl; she was, as he had said, a woman of the world and therefore, perhaps, all the more desirable in her unchallenged, unbroken spirit.

"It is very late," said Callendar gently, as the black dog stirred himself and, yawning, rubbed his head against Ellen's hand. "And to-morrow . . ."

But she did not permit him to say, "And to-morrow I shall be back at the front." She was afraid of his saying it, because all the evening she had been fighting just this thought. She understood that it was his strongest weapon, the one thing which might demolish the wall of her resistance. It was not a fair weapon, but he would not hesitate to use it where his own desire was concerned.

"It's not late," she said, "not late for me. . . ." Yet she wanted him to go because she was afraid. She wanted to be alone, to feel her old strength return to her.

The dog followed them as they moved through the big room and up the stairs. The last of the sounds had died away—the terrifying screech of the sirens, the faint popping of the guns and the ominous shattering crash of the falling bombs. The house and the city beyond it lay in silence now, dark once more save for the showers of blue light from the street lamps.

At the top of the stairs, which lay too in darkness, he put on his greatcoat in silence, took up his cap and then faced her. He said nothing; he simply looked at her, and after a moment she murmured in a voice that was scarcely audible, "No, I cannot do it. The things which stand in the way are much stronger than we are." And bending her head, as if she had in some way been accused, she added, "I will write you."

He did not speak. Instead he simply placed his arms about her and in silence kissed her. In the same fashion, her white hand grew tense once more, just as it had done when Fergus came upon her unaware, to understand all that was happening.

As he stepped into the street, she lingered in the doorway until, in the direction of the Café des Tourelles, the darkness swallowed him. She was alone again, and when she had closed the door she did not return to the drawing-room but sat down weakly on the top step of the long stairs and presently, overcome by the terrible sense of loneliness, she began to weep in silence. She was (she thought scornfully) in spite of everything, only a poor, weak, feminine creature.

Hansi flung his heavy body against her and, whimpering a little, put his black head affectionately on her knee.

She was sitting thus when the dog leapt to his feet and barked savagely at the sound of a sharp, sudden knock upon the door. It was the knock of some one in haste. The sound, shattering the dead stillness, grew terrifying, as if the one who knocked desired in some way to communicate his terror to those inside the house.

Ellen sprang up. "Je viens! Je viens!" she cried, and to the dog, "Tais toi! Hansi." She cried "Je viens!" as if by arresting the efforts of the knocker she might also destroy the foreboding in her heart.

Opening the door, she discerned dimly in the darkness the figure of a fat, bent little old man with white mustaches that caught the faint light emerging from the staircase. "Yes," she said, in French. "What is it you want?"

A voice which trembled a little with fright and carried the ring of an accent from the Midi answered her. "You are Mees Tolliver. I come from your brother. I am sent by him to fetch you."

For a moment she stood without speaking to the queer, bent figure, regarding him with the air of utter incredulity. He could not be quite real . . . this gnome with the enormous white mustaches. And unaccountably there flashed through her mind a fragment of the letter Lily had written her long ago—*And then he rode away into the darkness. I am certain that he is dead.*

"He is hurt," said Ellen. "Something has happened to him!"

The old man answered simply. "Yes. There was an accident. He is wounded."

Without questioning him further, she wrapped herself in a fur coat and holding to the collar of Hansi she went out, after locking the door on the silent house, to follow the old man.

As they walked there were times when the darkness was so profound that she could not see him at all and was forced to call out for guidance. It was Hansi who aided her. He kept close to the heels of the old man.

She had a sense of passing through the Place Passy into the Rue Franklin.

"Who are you, mon vieux?" she asked.

The old man coughed. He went rapidly for one so old, but she fancied it was terror that gave speed to his fat legs, terror that the Gothas might return.

"I am the concierge of the building where Madame Nozières has an apartment. It was she who sent me. It is close at hand . . . in the Avenue Kléber."

Vaguely in the darkness, black against the deep blue of the sky, the ugly towers of the Trocadéro appeared a little on the right. "What is it that happened? Is he wounded . . . gravely, seriously, . . . my brother?"

The old man grunted. "I don't know. I know nothing. There was a bomb fell in the Avenue Kléber." He raised his head and sniffed like a shaggy old dog. "Smell," he commanded. "You can smell the bomb."

It was true. The faint odor of picric acid filled the damp night air. As they walked the odor grew more and more intense. In the darkness Ellen's guide pointed to the left.

"The bomb fell over there," he observed, "full in the street."

"Who is this Madame Nozières?" asked Ellen.

"I don't know," her companion repeated. "I know nothing. She has an apartment. She comes there sometimes. She is rich. She is generous. She does not live there always. She only comes now and then . . . when Monsieur has permission from the front."

"Monsieur Nozières?"

In the darkness, the old man was silent for a time. He was breathless from the effort of their haste. "No," he replied. "Monsieur . . . your brother."

This then was the rendezvous for which Fergus had left the house in the Rue Raynouard. There was some one then—some woman—who had the power of taking him from her on the very night he had returned after so many years. It must have been strong, this force, stronger than the power which Callendar himself exerted. She understood his persistence. Against such a power, she was, of course, helpless.

"It is here," said her guide abruptly. "Follow me."

He led the way through a corridor into an open court filled with summer furniture, stacked now in the corners against the empty stone urns. In the dim light that filtered through the shutters on the far side, she was able to discern the outlines of chairs and tables, piled helter-skelter, as if they too had felt the force of a bomb that hurled them into a corner.

The old man knocked on a door that led into the apartment from which the light showed itself. From inside the murmur of voices came to them, distantly. And at last the door opened.

Against the dim light, Ellen was able to discern the figure of a small woman, dressed in a trim dark suit. She wore no hat and her blonde hair, cut short, stood about her head in a halo of ringlets which caught and reflected the glow behind her. She had been weeping. Even in the emotion of the moment, Ellen saw with a feminine instinct that she had chic, and when she spoke she divined also that "Madame Nozières" was not a cocotte but a lady. She had been weeping and something of the grief carried over into her voice.

"You are Mees Tolliver," she said. "I am Madame Nozières. I have heard you play . . . many times, but I did not know until to-night that you were his sister. You do not know me, of course."

There was a quality almost comic in the formality with which the stranger went about the business of introductions. In the hallway, she continued in a low voice, "I have known your brother for a long time. We are very good friends." And then she began to weep again. As Lily had done in the letter written after César's death, the woman made no pretenses, thinking perhaps as Lily had thought, that at such a time there was place only for the truth.

To Ellen the whole affair was shot through with the light of unreality. Standing in the dark hallway, with this strange woman weeping beside her—a woman who in some vague way had been brought close to her because she too loved Fergus—she leaned back against the wall for a moment trying frantically to bring her mind back to the truth. This could not be. . . . It was unreal, fantastic. . . .

The door opened and she saw, with a clarity that stamped the scene forever on her brain, a big room furnished with luxury, and in the midst of all the feminine softness—the pillows, the gilt chairs, the mirrors and the satin—Fergus lying very white and very still upon a bed of white and gilt with gilded swans on each of its four posts. At the side of the bed stood a tall, grave man with a black beard who wore the uniform of an army surgeon. He bowed to her and Madame Nozières murmured, "Doctor Chausson."

The name struck some chord of memory in Ellen's brain, but before she could trace it to its source, Fergus opened his eyes, and grinning a little, said in a low voice, "Well, this is a pretty mess!" (This was the old Fergus. She knew it at once. All the strangeness had gone. . . .)

She asked no questions because from the look of the doctor and the tears of Madame Nozières she understood that there was only one answer. She wanted suddenly to weep, to beat her head against the wall, to cry out. But she was silent. She approached the bed and pressed his hand.

They had taken off the blue tunic with the silver wings and he lay now in his white shirt and the blue trousers with the silver braid along the seam. Around his waist he wore a woolen ceinture of brilliant yellow. The shirt was open and on his breast where the silver wings had been there was a little spot of red . . . a tiny spot, scarcely as large as a strawberry.

"I'm sorry," he murmured. "But you see I couldn't come to-morrow . . . as I promised."

She could find nothing to say. She could only press his hand more and more tightly.

"I'm glad you brought the dog," he continued. "It will be less lonely for you." And then he beckoned to the doctor and asked him and Madame Nozières to leave the room for a moment. When they had gone, he drew Ellen nearer to him and said, "You must not be hard with her. She is a lady. Madame Nozières is not her name. It is I who am to blame if any one. I wanted to marry her. . . . I'm not talking rot. We had planned it." And then for a time he was silent as if too weak to go on.

Pressing his hand more tightly, she whispered, "How could I be hard? Nothing matters . . . only one thing."

He coughed and continued. "She has done everything. She has risked the rest of her life to save me. Chausson is the great Chausson . . . the surgeon from Neuilly. She knows him and he knows her husband. They are old friends. That was why he came. He is a busy man and a great surgeon. You see, she risked everything . . . her reputation, her future . . . everything. She did not hesitate to send for him."

She knew now why the name had been familiar. She had heard

it everywhere in the journals, from her friends in Paris. If the great Chausson believed there was no hope . . .

"She is a good woman . . . a charming woman, Ellen. Madame Nozières is not her name. If she chooses to tell you who she is, be good to her, because I loved her."

"I will do what you wish."

He grinned again suddenly. "Think of it . . . to get it now, after three years . . . to get it now on the asphalt a block from the Trocadéro!" And then his face grew bitter. "It's a joke . . . that is!" And then, dimly, sleepily, he murmured, "We must hurry . . . we must hurry."

Ellen, still silent, found that she was praying idiotically for a thing which could never be. She knew now, sharply and cruelly, what the war, that grand parade, had been. Fergus who had loved life so passionately, who found pleasure and excitement everywhere! Fergus whom they had all loved so that they had spoiled him! Fergus lying there with his blond, curly head against the white pillows under the flying gilt swans! Those voluptuous, sensual swans! Eagles they should have been!

She could do nothing but wait. The minutes rushed past her, furiously. (We must hurry, he had said.) On the gilt dressing table one of the candles had begun to gutter and fade.

"Call them back," he said faintly. And she rose and opened the door. Outside Doctor Chausson had taken both Madame Nozières' small, exquisite hands and was talking to her, in a soft low voice, warm with a sort of understanding that moved Ellen queerly. They were so absorbed that they did not even notice her as she opened the door.

"Madame Nozières," she said softly, and the woman turned toward her. She was beautiful, more beautiful than Ellen had supposed, even with the tears swimming in her blue eyes. She was small and beautiful and exquisite like a bit of Dresden china. She understood the whole thing clearly; she understood perhaps even the profundity of the love which Madame Nozières had for Fergus.

Doctor Chausson refused to come in with them. "I will stay here. . . . There is nothing I can do." And so they left him, pale and hollow-eyed from work and want of sleep, to wait in the dark hallway.

Inside the room the one candle had gone out and the only light came from the single flame before the tall mirror. Fergus had closed his eyes once more, and the lids showed against the dead whiteness of the skin in a faint shade of purple. The two women sat one on each side of the gilded bed, watching in silence. Presently he opened his eyes and looking at Ellen said in English:

"This man. . . ." He had grown weaker now and spoke with difficulty. "This man . . . Callendar. Are you going to marry him?"

"I don't know."

He smiled. "I saw you when I came in. . . . That's how I knew. I saw your hand." And after a pause. "It's funny . . . I knew this was coming . . . I knew it as I stood outside your door."

Then he closed his eyes once more and when he spoke again it was to say weakly, "You must tell Ma. . . . It will be hard. . . . And you must not. . . . You must not tell her the truth. . . . She could never face the truth. She has never faced it."

He reached out weakly and took the hand, on one side of Ellen and on the other of Madame Nozières. Raising himself, he grinned again and murmured in French this time, "My life. . . . It's running away . . . inside me. You can hear it. . . . I hear it . . . now." And then for a moment there was an echo of triumph, a sudden flash of Gramp whom Fergus himself had named The Everlasting. He grinned again and said, "It was a good life. . . . I missed nothing . . . nothing at all."

And again slowly. . . . "This man Callendar . . . this man . . ."

But he never finished the sentence. He sighed and slipped back into the pillows of the bed surmounted by the four gilded swans. Madame Nozières began to weep wildly and flung herself upon him, kissing him again and again. For Ellen there was no such relief. She sat now, stark upright and tragic, bound by all the years in which she had shown a proud and scornful face to the world. No, there was no such relief for her. She knew it. She could only sit there, quietly cold and white, and all the time she wanted to scream, to cry out, to beat her head against the stone floor of the corridor where Doctor Chausson stood waiting gravely. She could only sit and watch while Madame Nozières wept out her heart.

It was the sound of weeping, wild and passionate, that summoned Doctor Chausson. The two women had forgotten him, but the good man knew well enough what the sound signified. Softly he opened the door and came into the frivolous room. There beside the gilded bed he saw the sister, a strange, silent, handsome woman, dressed in black with her fur coat slipped to the floor at her feet, a woman (he thought) *bien Anglaise,* who could not weep. He knew that she suffered more than the other, more than Colette who had flung herself on the boy to weep hysterically. Colette, the charming, the fastidious, the beautiful, flung down in utter disarray, her eyes red and swollen with weeping, her golden hair all disheveled. . . . Colette whom he had seen but two nights before flushed and radiant at the Princesse de Guermantes'. He understood now why she had been so beautiful and so happy. But the boy could not see her now, and so nothing mattered.

He stood for a moment in silence, as if in respect for the grief of the two women. All this he had seen before, many times, . . . a young man, a boy, who had loved life as this one had loved it, who could jest, as this one had jested, with his very last breath. A boy whom women loved as these two women, the one so wildly, the other so profoundly, with such an intense, secret flame. It was cruel . . . hideous. . . .

He moved forward and touched Madame Nozières on her slim shoulder. And all the while he was conscious that the eyes of the other woman were watching him, stony and cold and tragic.

"Colette," he said softly. "Colette. . . . You must not. . . . You must be quiet." With a gentle strength he lifted her from the bed. "Colette, it is nearly dawn. . . . You must be discreet. There will be questions asked."

But she paid no heed. She was sobbing now, bitterly and without shame. "You must be discreet," he repeated.

"What difference does that make now? . . . It is nothing . . . less than nothing. . . ." And she fell to weeping once more.

He mixed for her a powder and forced her to drink it, saying, "There is the necessary business. You must not be seen here . . . like this."

But she would not go. It was Ellen who at last stirred herself and succeeded in quieting Madame Nozières. "I will take him to my house," she said, quietly. "You may come there. . . . You may stay there if you like. It is a big house . . . in the Rue Raynouard. . . . No one will ever know."

She drew Doctor Chausson aside and gave him the address. "I will take care of things," she said. "I will stay here if you will arrange for the rest. I would like to stay . . . alone. It was good of you. . . . There is nothing I can say."

So at last, in care of the great Doctor Chausson, Madame Nozières, pale and with swollen eyes and disheveled hair, was led away, across the stone courtyard, gray now with the faint rising light of dawn, into the big gray motor that had followed him from Neuilly to the Avenue Kléber. Ellen watched them as they crossed the yard between the empty stone urns and summer chairs piled high in the corners.

When they had gone, she returned to the room and, locking the door, sat down to wait. Slowly, in the gray solitude, the relief of tears came to her. She wept silently. She understood now her fear of returning too late, that vague, nameless fear for which there had been no explanation until now. She had come so near to being late . . . only a matter of a few hours, of a single night. For he had escaped them all now, forever. They would never possess him again. . . .

She looked at him, lying here white and still in the gay blue trousers with the silver braid and the yellow sash, and she understood why it was that he had seemed so young. It was because he had never really belonged to any of them. He had not even had a country of his own. He had gone out into a war which was none of his concern. There was nothing which tied him down, not even the nonsense which people talked of "la gloire" and "la patrie." For she, in her aloofness, had known it for the nonsense it was, just as he in his good-nature and love for all the world had known it. She remembered what he had once written her. . . . *"A man of our generation who has missed the war will not have lived at all . . . He will be a poor thing compared to the others. It is a game in which one must take a chance. It is better to die than to have missed it."*

He had believed that to the very end. Perhaps this was the secret of Old Gramp who had roamed the world and lived in this very Paris under the Second Empire. He had lived. He had done everything, and now in his old age he had a stock of memories that would last forever, a life which none of the others ever knew. He had been certain of only one life and he had made the most of it, so that he was ready when his time came to die with satisfaction, to take his chance on what lay beyond.

And as she sat there with the black dog by her side, in the slow, gray light, it occurred to her that perhaps the end of Fergus had not been after all so tragic. He had died in the very midst of life with the woman he loved at his side. If he had lived. . . . Who could tell? There was small place in the world for men like him. He never had the strength, the fierce aloofness of Old Gramp, the savage contempt of the old man for the drones and grubbers of life.

It was all a strange business, surely. Strange and confused and without sense. In the beginning, when she had first come into this frivolous room (so cold and dead now in the gray light) she had been angry and jealous at his deception, and bitter at Madame Nozières for having caused his death. She had thought, "If he had not been going to meet her, he would not have been killed."

But she knew better now. She had been a fool. It was absurd and monstrous that any one, even herself, should fancy he could bend fate to his own ends. It was too imbecile, too senseless. No, she was wiser now. She was not the headlong fool she had once been. In the face of all that had happened in this one terrible night, she was utterly humbled. Who was she to question the behavior of this brother who lay dead under the gilded swans? Who was she, a cold, hard woman, to question a love of which she knew nothing? And what did it matter now? She was glad suddenly, with a strange, wild happiness, that he had known this Madame Nozières. Her blondeness, her beauty, her fine clothes, her spirit . . . all these things had made him happy, on how many leaves in Paris?

What did it matter now? One lived but an instant, frantically, and time rushed on and on. . . .

But he was right. Their mother must never know the truth.

She thought too of Callendar, for he was with her all the time, almost as if he had never gone away. The old foreboding returned to her—that phrase out of Lily's letter—*And then he rode away into the darkness. I am certain he is dead.* He had gone away and she did not know where. Perhaps she had been wrong to refuse him, cruel to have denied him the happiness that Madame Nozières had given to Fergus. Things mattered so little now. It seemed to her that she stood somewhere on a lofty pinnacle, looking down on the spectacle . . . a pitiful spectacle, so full of "sound and fury, signifying nothing." The old quotation came back to her out of the dim memories of the past when she had hated Shakespeare with an intense passion. "Sound and fury, signifying nothing." That was it. It was far better to be like her mother, the invincible Hattie, who never mounted to the

heights but kept her eyes always on the ground, frantically occupied with a thousand tiny things, never willing, as Fergus had
said, to face the truth. And now that he was gone, her favorite
of them all, what would she do? There remained nothing now
except the one truth which none could in the end escape.

It was daylight and the ghastly smell of picric acid had died
away before she stirred herself. The morning sun, pouring in at
the window, seemed to say, "This is another day. We must all
go on. This is not the end of everything."

(The sun, she thought bitterly, which Fergus had always
loved even as a baby.)

So she had stirred herself wearily and gone over to the little
escritoire which stood in one corner of the room. There, with the
pen of gold and mother-of-pearl that belonged to Madame
Nozières, she seated herself and wrote, one letter to Callendar and
one to her mother. To Callendar she wrote that she would marry
him as soon as it was possible. To her mother she wrote a lie.
She wrote that Fergus had died in the house in the Rue Raynouard,
alone with herself and Doctor Chausson who was a great doctor
and came only because he was a friend of hers. Everything had
been done which could be done. He would be buried not in a
grave at the front nor in a lonely Paris graveyard but at Trilport,
in the friendly cemetery where Madame Gigon lay, a little way
off from Germigny l'Evec where Lily went in the summer.

And in the end she added another lie, because she knew it was
the one thing above all else that Hattie Tolliver would want to
hear. She even framed the sentence shrewdly, sentimentally,
though it was false to her very nature. She wrote, "He died
thinking of you. Your name was the last word he said."

For Hattie had at last to face the truth, and one must make
it as easy as possible for her.

Almost the last word he had said was, "Callendar. . . . This
man . . . Callendar." . . . And she would never know now
what it was that he had meant to say.

There was a knock at the door. She knew what it was . . . the men sent by Doctor Chausson.

Ignoring it, she knelt beside the bed and pressed her cheek close to the cold face of her brother. She was alone now, more alone than she had ever been in all her life, where none could see her. Then as she stood, looking down at him, it occurred to her that this death had been in a strange way a perfect thing. . . . He had escaped in the midst of life, happier than he had ever been before. . . . There were worse things than death. It was only to those who remained that death was cruel. . . . It was cruel to understand, in that frivolous room with the bright spring sun streaming in at the window, that she had come to know him only when he was dead. There had never been time before. . . . There had been only the business of fame and glory and success.

When at last she opened the door, the men sent by Doctor Chausson saw a handsome woman hard and cold, without sympathy, who stood holding by his collar a great black dog who growled at them savagely.

In the days that followed Madame Nozières came twice to the Rue Raynouard, once on foot and once in a taxicab though it was quite clear that she was far more used to a motor of her own—a small, very expensive motor like that of Sabine. She it was who had candles placed in the room with Fergus and had masses said for him. And to all this, which old Jacob Barr would have called "popery" and denounced as rubbish, Ellen offered no resistance; for, not being sure any longer that she herself believed in anything, she saw no harm so long as it gave comfort to others. Fergus himself, she knew, would have smiled and allowed it.

Madame Nozières wept and thanked Ellen and made her ill at ease and miserable, but she did not say who she was or whence she came. Indeed, Ellen learned no more of her identity than she had discovered from Fergus himself, as he lay dying. She was a lady, a *femme du monde,* a creature of charm and (despite her grief) of gaiety. She came out of mystery and returned to it. "Madame Nozières" was a label, perhaps as good as any other. Twice, long afterward, Ellen fancied that she saw her,—once walking in the Bois and talking earnestly with Doctor Chausson and once in the establishment of Reboux, but she could not be certain because each time she turned quickly away lest Madame Nozières should recognize her. She respected the mystery; she was afraid to intrude upon it. In some way it seemed better to leave the tragedy with its proper ending—in that frivolous room by candlelight in the Avenue Kléber. It had been in its way a complete, a perfect thing. To follow it further could lead only into triviality and disillusionment. She had no desire to know too much of Madame Nozières.

But the sense of mystery fascinated her and, in the lonely days in the Rue Raynouard, it appeared to change and soften all her beliefs. She saw now that mystery had its place in the scheme of things, that it possessed a beauty of its own which lent fascination to all life. There were others, she knew, besides Callendar who were never to be understood completely, never to be pinned down and taken apart as this or that. In all her haste, she had fancied that life was thus and so, that people were easy to fathom and understand. She doubted now whether she would ever know any one—even Lily or Rebecca. There was always something which escaped knowledge, something which lay hidden deep beneath layer upon layer of caution, of shyness, of deceit, or mockery, of a thousand things . . . the something which in the end was one's own self, the same self she had guarded with savagery through so many years.

For all that people might say or think, she understood that this Fergus, the one who stood in the candlelit room in the Avenue Kléber, had been more beautiful than any other . . . as he lay there clasping with one hand his sister and with the other Madame Nozières!

57

IT is true that Ellen in life and even Fergus in death did not really know their own mother. They had said that she would not be able to face the truth; yet she had done it, bravely and with a dignity that none of them would have recognized; for they had not seen her on the day she forced Judge Weissman, her enemy, to aid her because her children were the ones at stake.

So the premonition which had troubled her for so long came now to be a reality. With Ellen in Paris, Robert joined up with his own army, and Fergus (her beloved Fergus) dead, there remained only Gramp, cold and aloof and ageless, in his chamber surrounded by books.

It was the grim old man who found her lying in the darkness of the tiny living room of the flat with Ellen's letter crushed in her hand. In his unearthly fashion he had divined the tragedy. He saw that she did not weep; she did not even moan. She lay quite still, unconscious that he stood there in the shadows watching her. It is impossible to imagine what his thoughts could have been. For a time at least the hardness which had protected him for so long must have melted a little; for Fergus had been of all the family his favorite. It was Fergus to whom he lent his precious books. It was Fergus who had seemed at times the very incarnation of his own youth—so remote now, so buried beneath all his intolerant scorn of those who were afraid to live.

For a long time he stood there watching his daughter-in-law, silently and with an intense concentration as if he were obsessed by a desire to study her sorrow with the passion of an anatomist. And then he had gone up to her and quietly taken the damp, crumpled letter with a strange gentleness out of the strong, worn hand. She did not resist; she did not even stir. She lay quite still while he held the letter close to the light and peering at it read it through, though he knew all the time what was in it.

When he had finished he laid it again by her side and said in a low voice, "The boy loved life, Hattie. And for those who die, death is not hard. There are worse things."

In thirty years it was the first time there had passed between the two any speech purified of anger or resentment.

To one of Hattie's nature there is consolation in the possession of the dead. The grim small tasks, the polite and empty phrases of condolence, the coming and going of those who care for the dead . . . all this empty hubbub and commerce serves in a fashion to conceal and break the anguish of loss. But for Hattie there were not even these things. She was left alone with Gramp in a flat which, though it had seemed empty before, now achieved a desolation beyond all belief. She (who had lived only in her children) had no friends about her; the very flat was not in the proper sense a home, such as the house in Sycamore Street had been. It was a barren, inhuman cave occupied before her by a procession of strangers which, when she left, would again close over the brief years of her tenancy. She found herself alone save for that ancient man her father-in-law, in a strange city, without even the body of her son for a bitter consolation.

So this woman, who had lived her life so richly . . . a life florid and overflowing with sentiment, a life that churned and raced along in an overwhelming current of vitality, achieved in the face of tragedy a calm and a dignity which she had never shown before. She understood, in the primitive depths of her nature, that this truth which she must face was the final one, from which there was no appeal. Always before there had been some hope ahead, some chance of turning events by a vast energy and a crude wilfulness to her own ends. There was nothing now . . . nothing save a few old clothes, some books and the Bible she had given him on his tenth birthday. To these she clung with the tenacity of a savage, and they were pitiful remnants to a woman whose love demanded the very bodies of her children.

For Hattie there were none of those shades of grief and joy which are the lot of those more completely civilized. She had no capacity for seeing herself, or, like Ellen, for finding in the death of Fergus an illumination which served in a mysterious fashion to light up the long progression of her life. In her sorrow, Hattie no longer even pitied herself; and this, of course, may have been the secret of her dignity. Hattie, the martyr, who bore her cross and flung herself before her family like the Pope before the Visigoths, no longer existed. In her place there was a strong, almost grim woman, who was silent and did not complain.

Nor had she, like the more civilized, the pleasure of books and of philosophic reflection. Her life since the very beginning had been far too active for such things; and now, when at last there was time, when she had no one to care for save the independent old man, she could not read, she could not reflect. Books were poor pale things by comparison with the ferocious activity of life itself. There were no stockings to darn, no one for whom she might make meringues, no dog to place upon his mat before locking up the house. (To the apartment there was but one door and it locked of itself. It was, properly speaking, no real home at all.) So she came to invent things for herself to do. She lingered over her work and took (though she was rich now) to such pale tasks as embroidery and knitting, only to find that the objects of her labor, having been created for no real purpose, accumulated dismally in the drawers and cupboards.

She had letters both from Ellen and Robert which she kept in the family Bible to read over and over again; and sometimes a shameful, bitter thought crept into the recesses of her active mind. It was a terrible thought, which she thrust hastily aside as impious and touched with blasphemy; but it returned nevertheless again and again to torment her. She thought, "If only it had been Robert instead of Fergus!" (Robert who was so steadfast and reliable, who already was the youngest captain of his division). She was proud of him too, but in a different way. She could not say how. . . .

The awful thought would not die. She would have given Robert to keep Fergus, though in the solitude of the empty flat she sometimes cried out, "It is not true. I could not think such a horrible thing!"

The squabbling with Gramp came quietly to an end, though neither of them ever made any allusion to the change. They lived together for the most part in silence but the old man ceased to torment and worry her. And on her side without ever knowing why, she came to treat him in a new way, almost to cherish and protect him like some brittle piece of glass, as all that remained of the old life. She even made for him little delicacies and had him to eat at the table with her. At such times they sat, awkwardly, and without conversation, each perhaps abashed by the weakness that lay in this strange truce.

In the long empty days there came to Hattie a mysterious sense of having turned a corner, of having stepped from one room into another. The door between had, she knew, closed forever, though she did not understand why. She had come now into the borders of Gramp's country. She was growing old and so she came to understand a little the old man's vast indifference.

Before he sailed, Robert, dressed in his captain's uniform, neat and spotless, every button properly arranged, came to bid farewell. She could feel certain of him. There would be no mad exploits, no wild surges of temperament ending in disaster, no idle heroics undertaken for their own selfish thrill. These things Robert would never understand.

As he sat talking to her (trying bravely in his solid, unspectacular way to take the place of Fergus) he seemed square and massive and eternal as her father, old Jacob Barr, had been. There was reassurance in the snub nose, the solid jaw and the unruly red hair. Where Fergus had not even been able to look out for himself, she knew that this other son would care for his men with a detached and efficient thoroughness. There was nothing in the death of Fergus which could be counted as a material loss, even to herself. It was Robert who had earned money when it was most needed; it was Robert who looked out for her and stood between her and the world. It was upon men like Robert that the whole world rested; he was a foundation, the beginning and end of all order and worth. And yet. . . . And yet. . . . Even while he sat there doing his clumsy best to make up for the loss of his brother, the old wicked thought kept tormenting her. . . . She wanted to tear it out by its roots, to destroy it forever; but there it was, always with her. . . . *If only it had been Robert*.

"You need not worry over me," he assured her. "I will take no chances. There's nothing romantic about war . . . at least not about this one. It's simply business. The side which is most efficient is bound to win. There won't be any nonsense. I'll look out for myself."

She said to him almost with indifference, "You're all I have left, because I don't see much of Ellen any more. She's too busy."

But she was not thinking of what she said: she was thinking that war *was* romantic. It must be so else it would not excite men as it excited Fergus. It was the romance that was the bait in the trap . . . romance and the excitement. So long as these things existed, there would be wars, for there would be men like Fergus who did not take their places efficiently but went because (she remembered one of the phrases he had used again and again in the face of her reproaches) "it was too big a show to be missed." It was not men like Robert who made war possible; it was men like Fergus. She saw it all with a vision uncluttered by talk of economics and politics; and so in her own fashion she came far nearer to the truth than this solid, logical son of hers.

But he was sure of himself, Robert. You could fancy him ordering his men about, ably and dispassionately, leading them admirably when it was necessary, as his grandfather Barr, the Citizen, had done before him in the Civil War. He would make a good job of it. You could see that he would quietly and thoroughly win distinction, not as Fergus had done, without once thinking of it, but because he had arranged it so. You could see him being decorated with medals, as his brother had been decorated, again and again; but not for the same reason. He would not wear them as Fergus had done, with a swagger. He would cherish them, in neat leather cases, and bring them out to show his children and his grandchildren, because he could not tell them what the war was like, give them the feel of it, as Fergus could have done . . . Fergus who (if he had lived) would have lost the medals or thrown them away long ago in disgust like his Grandfather Tolliver, who found the Siege of Paris more romantic than Bull Run or Gettysburg. He had, one fancied, already counted his medals. One could see that he was cut out for a good officer.

"I will see Ellen as soon as I have leave," he murmured and thought, "And I will not be walking about the streets during an air raid as if I were at a church sociable."

Yet he was not bitter because Fergus was the better loved; that fact he had come long since to accept. He was scornful only because it seemed to him an idiotic thing to be wandering carelessly into the midst of danger. There could be no reason for it . . . none on earth.

Before he left, Hattie burdened him with a great bundle of sweaters and socks, all admirably made in the hours when she had been distracted by her terror of idleness.

"You must wear them all yourself," she said. "You'll need them in time. They'll wear out and you'll lose them. I'll send you others from time to time. It's all I have to do nowadays."

And on the way past the cell occupied by The Everlasting he must have heard the squeaking of his grandfather's chair as the old man rocked and rocked, lost again in a torrent of memories; but he did not stop.

"Say good-by for me to The Everlasting," he said and then, after kissing her abruptly, he turned and disappeared quickly down the stairs, so that she could not see his tears. For Robert was, unlike the others, sentimental, though he had never once allowed his mother the joy of discovering it. It was a thing which he thought shameful.

Even he had caught a sense of her terrible desolation.

There is a rhythm in life, a certain beauty which operates by a variation of lights and shadows, happiness alternating with sorrow, content with discontent, distilling in this process of contrast a sense of satisfaction, of richness that can be captured and pinned down only by those who possess the gift of awareness. Old Gramp in his solitude knew well its workings, and Ellen, in Paris, had become, as the tempo of her own life began to lose its intensity, to understand it dimly. For Hattie, in the fretful ebb and flow of her existence there could never be such knowledge. This rhythm, this beauty, existed outside her, a thing apart, beyond the wall of her consciousness.

Gramp, in his solitude, knew too that there were in each life hills and valleys and, rising above them all, one peak which pierced the clouds. Out of the depths of his uncanny perception he came to understand that Hattie's life had passed its solitary peak. It had begun now to slip down the other side; what remained could be but a gradual falling away, a gentle decline until the end. What he knew from the summit of a monstrous detachment came to Hattie vaguely through her senses; she knew it as she knew the approach of damp weather by its effect upon her rheumatism. It was that sense of having passed from one room into another, with the door behind her closed and bolted forever.

And Ellen. . . . She too stood now on the summit, for ambition had been the beginning and end of her existence. She had accomplished; she had won. There would never be another peak so lofty, so enveloped in heady invigorating air; nor one so lonely. But there remained the things which lie always on the opposite slope of the peak—the things which the wise, like Gramp, place above all the hurry, the scramble, the headlong turmoil of the long ascent. There were the gentle pastures of reflection, of kindliness, of warmth and fine thoughts, all the rewards which succeed the terrible struggle. Ellen, he knew, had crossed the summit; and she was still a young woman.

58

ONE bright spring morning as Hattie sat looking out into the street while she sewed and thought, round and and round, over and over again, those same thoughts which stole in upon her so frequently in these days of idleness, the postman brought a letter from Ellen. It was a brief letter, written it seemed in haste, but it contained two bits of news that changed the whole face of the world.

Ellen was to be married, and she wanted Hattie to come to Paris and make her home there.

"I have talked it over with Lily," she wrote, "and she is delighted with the plan. Her house here is enormous and comfortable, and Lily is rarely in it save in the spring and autumn. You could do as you chose with no one to annoy you. And you need never think or worry about housekeeping. I am sending a cheque, and Rebecca's uncle Mr. Schönberg is arranging for tickets. It is difficult to travel nowadays, but I have talked to Mrs. Callendar and she has written to a friend of hers, Malcolm Travers, the banker, who will arrange passports for you. You will hear from him within a few days after this letter."

And about her own plans she wrote, "I am marrying Richard Callendar, the son of the same Mrs. Callendar. You remember her? You met her on the night of my first concert in America, a small, fat dark woman covered with dirty diamonds. You may have read of the family in the papers, for they are well known. They are very rich. He is four years older than me. I have known him for nearly ten years. He wanted to marry me before, years ago. (And then a sudden flash of the old Ellen who had

walked away in the sunlight to skate on Walker's Pond.)
Fancy me, marrying a millionaire!"

So, in an instant, everything was changed and Hattie's world
grew bright once more. It was all so preposterous—to have
Ellen arranging everything in this grand manner, the tickets, the
passports, as if her mother were a queen whose journey was to be
made as simple and free of trouble as possible. And the cheque
and the millionaire husband! Yet, when the sense of excitement
had abated a little, she remembered that she had always known her
children were not of ordinary flesh and blood. There had been
something extraordinary about them. Look at Ellen! Famous
and rich and now marrying a millionaire.

But her satisfaction was not free from the old doubts. Was he
—this Callendar—good enough for her? Clarence had never been.
It was a good thing, she reflected, that he had died. What could
she have done with him during all these years . . . Clarence, a
poor thing at best, always complaining of his health.

But this Callendar. Who was he and why had she never spoken
of him before? Surely she was a strange girl who kept such
secrets so passionately hidden. Where had he come from? Was
he of good healthy stock? What had his life been? For a time
she paced up and down the room in a ferment of curiosity. She
tried to imagine what sort of man Ellen would choose to marry.
(This time she must be marrying only for love; there could be no
other reason.) She tried again and again to picture him and she
found herself baffled. It was impossible to imagine. . . .

And when she had grown more calm and the sense of the dreary
flat was borne in upon her once more, she remembered The Everlasting. He was ninety-five, and yet not really an old man; his
mind had never faltered in its course. But he was feeble and
needed care. She could not desert him now. She deceived herself
into believing that it was her duty to care for him until he died;
and only the Almighty knew when that would be. No, she must
take him with her. She could not leave him, as Ellen suggested, in
some home for the aged. That would be wrong; it would be, in a

sense, indecent. He was after all the father of her husband, the grandfather of her children. One could not do a thing like that. She debated the matter with herself for hours, thinking, strangely enough, only of reasons why she *should* take him; and it never once occurred to her that she really had no desire *not* to take him. The arguments against it were simply the habit of an intermittent civil war that had endured for more than thirty years. She could not bear to leave him behind, any more than she could have borne it to leave behind the old clothes, the worn shoes, and the Bible she had given Fergus on his tenth birthday. Gramp was a fixture now, a part of the past. Without him she would feel lost and lonely.

When she told him the intoxicating news, the old man, with a wariness that placed no trust in their unreal truce, looked at her sharply and said, doubtfully, "I don't know, Hattie. I'm too old and too feeble. I think perhaps I'd better stay behind." He opposed the idea in the belief that if he opposed it she would insist upon its being carried through.

But she was firm. She would not even argue the matter. He must go with her to Paris. He would be quite as well off there as anywhere else and he would at least be where she could look after him.

"Much better off," thought Gramp, whose only desire was to see Paris again before he died. But he still maintained a resentful air as if he opposed the idea with his last breath but was far too feeble to offer any real resistance.

59

IN Paris the house in the Rue Raynouard was got ready for the arrival. It had begun again to take on a little of the old gaiety and sense of life, for it had passed through the depths of its depression in the days which first Lily and then Ellen had spent there alone in their sorrow. All things pass in time and so the grief and loneliness had begun to pass from the house. Lily, as the shrewd Rebecca predicted during her first quarrel with Ellen, found in time some one to console her for the loss of César. It was impossible that one so simple, so without complexities, should have gone on mourning; Lily lived as much in the present as Ellen lived in the future. Her consoler was the grave, dignified Monsieur de Cyon (the same white-haired gentleman connected with the government, whom Fergus had met at tea) the widower of "Tiens! Tiens!" de Cyon, whom Ellen had loathed long ago when she first came to the Rue Raynouard. He was glad no doubt to have been freed by death from the crêpe-laden "Tiens! Tiens!" and satisfied to have found so agreeable a creature as Lily—a woman whom he described to his friends as dignified, worldly, cultivated and beautiful, not omitting the fact that she was very rich and that she was an American, a factor of political importance at a moment when America was so necessary to Europe in general and to France in particular.

And Lily too was, in her casual way, content with such a marriage. In the room, smelling of scent and powder, where she had exchanged other confidences with Ellen, she said, "He is a gentleman and distinguished. Perhaps he may be in the next cabinet. I am rich. I can help him. And as for me . . ." She laughed softly, with a touch of the old abandon in her voice. "He will not bother me much. He is an old man." But she was grave too when she spoke again. "And I . . . I am no longer young. I am forty-three. I must begin to look about for something to take the place of youth. I shall make him a good wife. I shall be able to entertain and give dinners that will help him and I will have a position that I have never had before."

And then she grew thoughtful and added, "It will be good for Jean too. It is time he had a father . . . a thing he has never had. It is time that I stepped out of the picture and made way for him."

She had lived, if not a life beyond reproach, one that was at least discreet and marked by good taste, and so the other things,

since the world is as it is, did not matter. Of those who had
really known her secret only three remained . . . Ellen and
Hattie and Jean. César and Madame Gigon and Old Julia were
dead. It did not, of course, occur to her to include The Everlasting, who had known all the while.

Jean too was happier now, for he had grown used to wandering
about on crutches and had become accustomed to a new leg, made
so admirably that he could still ride as much as he liked. It
would have been impossible for him to have remained depressed;
there was too much of Lily in him and, it must not be forgotten,
he resembled Fergus greatly. The old friendship between him
and Ellen waxed stronger than ever. It seemed to her at times
that Fergus had returned or had never died at all. In the evenings while his mother sat talking quietly in the big soft drawing
room with Monsieur de Cyon, Ellen joined him at the piano in
playing with four hands the wildest songs out of the music halls.
Rebecca in rare moments of good humor added to the gaiety with
imitations of poor old Sarah Bernhardt or Mistinguette or
Spinelly.

Rebecca had long since come to make herself at home in the
big house. She was settled now in one of the rooms opening on
the long gallery and she was perpetually with them, for it never
occurred to Lily to offer objections to one more guest;.but, having
nothing to occupy her time, she grew irritable and restless. Her
occupation had gone suddenly and there remained nothing to ab-
sorb her energy. Ellen remained stubborn and mysterious. She
would not return to America where there was a fortune awaiting
her.

"I have enough," she said. "I need not work myself to death.
I am rich now. I am through with struggling. Whenever I see
fit I can return."

But to Rebecca, it must have seemed that Ellen had slipped
somehow out of her reach, beyond the control which she had once
held over her. She would not even quarrel as they had once done

so often and with such vigor. She would simply repeat, "No. When I am ready, I will tell you. I am going to rest for a time."

It was her contentment that clearly had the power of disturbing Rebecca. She seemed at times almost happy. The old wilfulness and caprice were gone, and when she sat at the piano with Jean, there were times when it even seemed that she was enveloped by a hard, bright gaiety, touched, it is true, by hysteria and bitterness. She was unmanageable in a way she had never been.

"You are deceiving me," Rebecca reproached her. "There is something that I don't know. You are keeping something from me." And she would grow tearful and descend to the rich depths of Oriental sentiment. "Me," she would repeat, beating her thin breast, "who have given my life for you . . . who have worked myself to the bone . . . given all my time. . . . For no other reason than to make you a success. It is shameful."

And Ellen, in her new wisdom, might have answered, "Because you have found the thing you were born to do. Because you were aimless till you fastened upon me. . . . Because you found happiness in taking possession of me and my life."

But she said none of these things because it seemed to her that quarreling was useless. She only laughed and replied, "And you told the most wonderful lies about me. . . . You created Lilli Barr but Lilli Barr is having a rest now. I am being myself . . . Ellen Tolliver . . . for a little time."

Still Rebecca, too wise to be put off with such answers, only looked at her with suspicion and remained sulky. She could not run off now to visit Uncle Otto and Aunt Lina in Vienna nor the aunt in Riga nor the cousins in Trieste. She could not even make a round of the watering places, for all those which were not closed or filled with wounded soldiers lay on the other side of the circus parade that had begun to draw near to the end. One could almost hear the distant toots of the steam calliope, manned and manipulated by politicians, that fetched up the rear.

July had passed and with it the last peril to Paris, but still Callendar did not return. She heard from him whenever he had time to write. They were busy now (he wrote). They were beginning to look toward the end. The arrival of the Americans had done much for the French, not that they counted for much because there were not enough of them, but because, simply, they were *there*. He had kept on the *qui vive* for her other brother—Robert—but he had not come across him. It was not strange since his own division was nowhere near the Americans. Still he might see him. . . . One could never tell. . . . They expected to be shifted soon eastward in the direction of the (here the word was deleted), quite near to the Americans. It was easy for him to make himself acquainted since he was, after all, half-American.

And he would write again and again, "Do not worry about me. I have the most incredible luck—always. There are some men who go through the thing *knowing* that nothing will ever happen to them. I *know* it. It's a feeling that is in the bones. In the worst messes, I have that feeling . . . so strong that it is physical. 'Nothing will happen to me . . . nothing whatever,' I find myself repeating over and over again."

And as she read this, it occurred to her again that such a belief belonged to the part of him which had always been strange to her—the part which escaped in some nameless fashion even the limits of her imagination. It was mystical and profound and uncanny. At the very moment that she knew he must be right in his faith, she was terrified too because he was so certain. She could not believe with such intensity save in herself. Her beliefs were related always to the power, the force which she herself had at her own command; and in all the senseless, miserable killing there was no power which lay in one's self. It was simply a monstrous game of chance with the odds all against one.

But she found a happiness in those letters of a sort which she had never imagined. It seemed to her that in some way a part of herself was there with him enduring the same hardships and dangers, and for the first time in all her life she touched the borders of the satisfaction which comes of sharing an experience. She was troubled no longer by doubts; now that she had given her word, it never occurred to her to change. There was relief in the knowledge that all the years of indecision were at an end. There was satisfaction in feeling that the thing had been settled.

But she was abashed at the bold passion with which he wrote, shamelessly, assailing the wall of her fierce reserve. She was abashed and yet triumphant, for in all the years of struggle she had forgotten at times that she was a woman and young. His letters made her know for a little time some of the joy which Lily had possessed since the beginning.

He wrote at length that Sabine's divorce was completed. "I am free now and will have a leave soon, so we can try then to make up for all the wasted years. Because they have been wasted. We should have been married long ago. We should have been courageous enough to have cut through the tangle and set things right. We were cowardly then. It is tragic that we only learn through long experience that wastes so much of joy, so much of happiness. But you are mine now . . . mine forever. I shall never lose you again. . . ."

But the letter troubled her strangely; it invoked with each line some disturbing memory of the past. The allusion to courage. . . . Who could say what had been courage and what cowardice? If the matter had rested with Callendar alone, it would have been solved because he had had what he believed was courage. He would have thrust poor Clarence aside and trampled upon him, to take ruthlessly what he himself desired. It had been a courage different from hers, whose foundations stood rooted in self-denial. Yet she had saved no one in the end, not even Clarence. Some power, in which Callendar placed such faith, had brought them together in the end, destroying Clarence despite anything she could do to save him. And it seemed to her that all the trouble, all the sorrow went back to that winter evening on the shore of

Walker's Pond when she had said "Yes" to Clarence and felt for him at the same moment a queer, inarticulate pity—a pity which she was beginning at last to understand.

She experienced again a fierce satisfaction, almost a pleasure, which Callendar, in the strangeness of his blood, would never know. It was the satisfaction in having dominated even one's own body.

But in the last lines there lay an echo of the old conflict. *You will be mine . . . mine forever. I will never lose you again.* It was an arrogant speech, so like the way he had come to her years ago in the Babylon Arms, not asking what she desired but simply taking for granted that she would do as he wished. The memory of that afternoon disturbed her again with the sense that this love of which he wrote was an obscene, middle-aged emotion worn by a too great experience. The freshness was gone and with it all the glow of their meetings in the open windows of Sherry's and the walks through the Spring in Central Park. . . . It was this knowledge perhaps more than any other, that made his passionate phrases seem shameful. All of that first youth was gone from them, yet he posed, he wrote her still in the same ardent phrases, grown threadbare and unconvincing, of a love that had once been clean and fresh and despite all that she knew, even then, virginal. There was a touch now that bordered upon the professional. . . .

He told her that Sabine was in Paris and might pay her a call, as much out of a gossip's curiosity as from her curious passion for knowing the truth, for knowing with a blazing clarity exactly how things stood.

Sabine did call, in her small, expensive motor, accompanied by little Thérèse, an awkward, sickly girl of ten, but Ellen sent word that she was out. She had no desire to see Sabine, perhaps because she feared what Sabine had to tell her. And she could not turn back now; for too many years she had followed a straight unswerving path.

60

IT was a fantastic journey for Hattie and The Everlasting. On passports arranged by Thérèse Callendar they were borne along a way made easy by all the power behind Thérèse Callendar's fortune, through all the hubbub and turmoil of the war. Their companions on shipboard were correspondents and doctors and nurses and soldiers and congressmen (bound for the front to garner out of the very graves material for new campaigns). The others aboard the ship must have found them a strange pair concerning whom it was possible to speculate endlessly—this handsome, grim woman and the old, old man in her charge. It is probable that no one ever learned precisely who they were or whither they were bound, for Hattie was a suspicious traveler who placed no trust in fellow voyagers. She warned them away by her looks; and Gramp, of course, had not the faintest desire to enter upon conversation. He read his books and once a day made a circuit, under the escort of Hattie, of the entire deck, his coonskin coat (from which he refused to be separated) blowing in and out against his skinny old body. He never spoke, even to Hattie, even in reply to such remarks as, "Now, Grandpa, you must not eat that," or "Now, Grandpa, you had best move your chair, there's a draft in that corner."

(All this to Gramp who had never denied himself anything and had a perfect digestion; who had never thought of drafts since he was born.)

Indeed, there was something touching in the spectacle of the middle-aged woman, tending so carefully the old, old man. It was as if she feared that he might by some ill chance be blown from the deck into the open sea or fall down a companionway and shatter forever the brittle old bones that had defied time itself. No one could have guessed that they were enemies, that despite the temporary truce they could never be anything but enemies by the very nature of things. Hattie treated him still as if he were some fragile piece of old glass which she must deliver safely to Lily's house in the Rue Raynouard.

It was only after she had seen him safely to bed in his cabin that she was able to give range to all her passionate energy and walk round and round the deck, her ostrich plumes blowing in the gale, her strong, buxom figure outlined against the luminous blue of the Atlantic night. At such times she was almost happy again for it seemed to her that in the winds and fogs Fergus was somewhere close at hand, just beyond reach, waiting for her.

And she was going now to take up once more the threads of life. Ellen was to be married. . . . Ellen was to be married. . . . She must have a child. . . . She must have a child. . . . These things she thought over and over again until she came at length to repeat them aloud to herself as she walked, bracing her body against the gale, through the darkness. She had joined Thérèse Callendar in this passionate desire for a grandchild, but it was not for the same reason. To Hattie a grandchild would alter everything. It would be for her like being young again, almost like bearing a child of her own.

She had never traveled before; she knew not a word of French and The Everlasting saw fit not to reveal his knowledge of the tongue; but she was undaunted. In some way, by an heroic effort touched with a profound scorn for a nation which chattered such an abominable tongue, she managed everything . . . the customs at Havre, the accommodations in hotels already crowded to the doors and, last of all, the journey from the port into the Gare du Nord. (Lily had sent a courier to meet her but the meeting never occurred.) She was indomitable and she was almost happy again in all the business of managing tickets and meals and luggage, shepherding The Everlasting and his precious books. For Hattie believed that nothing was impossible. . . .

From the corridor of the crowded train, where she stood protecting Gramp and jostling her fellow passengers, Hattie saw them standing on the platform of the smoking cave called the Gare du Nord. . . . Ellen and Lily and a dark man in a blue uniform: and as the train jolted to a halt, her own car (for she thought of it thus) stopped almost abreast of them so that she was able to see that they talked earnestly with grave faces and an air of preoccupation. Wedged between a poilu slung round with a dozen musettes and wine bottles, and a trim English colonel with white mustaches and a red face, she was held immovable, unable to signal to them though she pounded upon the glass and shouted to them through windows open by some miracle against the stifling September heat. To Hattie, nothing existed in all that echoing cavern save those three figures, standing together amid mountains of luggage.

In the resounding shed steam hissed and engines squealed in ridiculous Gallic fashion; soldiers shouted to one another and a cocotte just beneath her window cried ribald jests to a lover somewhere in the same car who joined in the shouts of laughter. They looked up and down the platform—those three. It seemed that years passed before Lily, turning languidly in the heat, caught a glimpse of Hattie's red and agitated face and Gramp's sharp nose and inscrutable eyes.

They moved toward her; the English colonel whose toes had been trampled gave way in indignation and Hattie, bearing an immense amount of luggage and followed indifferently by Gramp, descended to the platform.

Ellen kissed her and then Lily, and at last she heard Ellen saying, "This is Richard, Ma. He is on leave."

Above all the flurry and the conversation, she and Callendar regarded each other searchingly, the one with a piercing gaze of appraisal, the other with an air almost of astonishment. He had not, perhaps, pictured her as such a handsome woman, nor one, despite the grimness on which one could not put one's finger, of such immense gusto. She accounted for Ellen's strength and vitality, but there was clearly nothing subtle in her and nothing cold: the answer to all that lay elsewhere—perhaps in the ancient man who peered at them all like a spiteful mouse through his dim spectacles.

As for Hattie, her eyes asked only one thing, "Was he—this man—good enough for Ellen?" His foreign blood showed itself more plainly than she had expected. It troubled her that her daughter should be marrying a man of foreign blood; for, vaguely, all foreigners were associated in her mind with those dark, sullen, violent men who worked in the black Mills surrounding Shane's Castle.

There flashed between the two—Callendar and Hattie—no spark either of understanding or enmity. Rather it seemed that the opinions of both were colored by surprise and a touch of suspicion. In Hattie's eyes there was a fire of pride and possession, the look of one who would fight for her children, passionately; and in the gray eyes of Callendar there was only the opaque, inscrutable expression which only Ellen, of them all, had ever seen dissolve or change.

But they were grave, all of them, in a fashion that presently entered Hattie's spirit and made her feel that their welcome was lacking in enthusiasm. Perhaps (she thought) it was the war; they were so close to it and Ellen, like herself, must be thinking always of Fergus. Perhaps they did not really want her there . . . any of them. Yet they had written her with so much eagerness. It was a doubt that filled her with a sharp terror of growing old and useless and dependent.

Lily (whom she had not seen in years, Lily who was now Madame de Cyon) seemed scarcely changed at all. She could not be (Hattie, watching her, hastily calculated the years) she could not be a day less than forty-five; yet there she was, a woman who had sinned, looking young, almost fresh, scarcely a day older than Ellen who was twelve years younger . . . more plump than Ellen and, strangely enough, more soft. Still, Hattie reflected, with a grim satisfaction, she had painted her face, and her hair, it was certain, had been "touched up."

Perhaps in Paris all life was different; perhaps such a life as Lily's made not too great a difference. Looking at her cousin, so beautiful, so charming and so unnaturally young, all the deep rooted respectability of Hattie's nature rose and bristled. And as she stood on the steps of the Gare du Nord waiting for Callendar to fetch the gray blue Government motor to drive them to the Rue Raynouard, it swept over her that it was a strange and ridiculous turn of affairs which had brought her of all people "into the wickedest city in the world," to live in the house of Lily whom she had always distrusted. She had not thought of it until this moment when she stood looking out across the Place Roubaix.

The motor came abreast of them with Callendar—a stranger, a foreigner—at the wheel, driving with a cool recklessness. It was all weird and unreal, so preposterous that Hattie grew suddenly frightened. She was aware briefly of a terror at the spectacle of this new, strange city where every one spoke an ungodly language. A little while before she would not even have thought of such things. It occurred to her that she must be growing old.

"I never felt younger in my life," she repeated aloud to Lily who stood waiting for her to enter the motor.

All this time The Everlasting had said nothing. Watching the others he had kept his own silence, but he had not overlooked the Paris that lay all about him, so changed now, so different, from the Paris of his youth. He heard none of their talk, made almost laboriously against the inexplicable depression, as they drove through the Rue Lafayette. How could it have interested him who was concerned with another world . . . ? A world of gaslight and crinoline, imperials and the waltzes of Strauss and Waldteufel? To him, who had no future, this new Paris must have been less than nothing . . . this new Paris in which Lily with all her money out of the black mills in the Middle West had a house and lived as if she had been born a Parisian; this new Paris in which his own granddaughter played a brilliant part. It was a Paris. . . . How could one describe it?

Yet, as he rode over the sweltering asphalt, his eyes, his ears, his nose drank in the sights and sounds and smells . . . the sudden cry of "L'Intran! . . . L'Intran!" and "Le Petit Parisien!" the withered dying chestnut trees of the Boulevard Haussmann (he could remember when it was new), the little tables . . . Because youth was after an insidious fashion returning to him, Gramp, the bitter, the aloof, grew sentimental. It had been here, in this Paris, that he had climbed to the pinnacle of all his life, the summit from which all else had been a gentle decline. He had not died like Fergus. He had gone on and on until at last life itself had lost all its savor. . . .

They had turned now round Arc de Triomphe, and Ellen, sitting quietly by the side of Callendar, frowned. She had been silent throughout the drive, thinking, thinking, thinking bitterly with a savage secrecy because she dared not betray herself even by the flicker of an eyelid. She sat there silently, pondering how she might break the news which she herself and no other must in the end relate. It seemed to her that the whole affair was too cruel, too horrible. It was not possible that she should be forced twice to do the same terrible thing.

The sound of her mother's voice, cheerful and rich, as she talked to Lily came to her over her shoulder. . . . "And the man wouldn't open the window so in the end I opened it myself and then he began to chatter and yell at me in some ridiculous language . . . French perhaps."

"How was he dressed?" asked Lily, and Hattie described his uniform.

"Oh," replied Lily in mirth. "He was Portuguese. . . . You must never mind the Portuguese."

"Well, I don't know whether Portuguese smell worse than other nationalities but the air in that train was enough to suffocate a strong man."

. . . And now they were coming nearer and nearer to the Trocadéro. They were quite near now. Ellen turned away her eyes. They had passed the house in the Avenue Kléber. She caught a swift glimpse of the doorway which she had not seen since the bright morning she closed the door on the frivolous little room of Madame Nozières. Ah, she knew how it looked! She knew each tiny thing about it, and the gray courtyard with the summer furniture heaped into one corner. It was cruel, incredible . . . what she had to do.

Before they drew up to the door of the house in the Rue Raynouard, Hattie too had grown silent under the gray depression which claimed all the little party.

They had tea on the white terrace where they found the black dog and poor tottering old Criquette and were joined by Jean and Monsieur de Cyon, and Rebecca, whose sulkiness did nothing to raise the spirits of the party. It was, Lily remarked, as she sat behind a table laden with silver and flowers sent up from Germigny and the most delicate sandwiches of pâté and cheese and jam, like a great family reunion. The big house was full now; Lily was married, even with distinction. There were no more secrets. In some ways life had grown simple, yet in others its complexity had been increased, again and again.

Ellen, sitting there in her own pool of tragic silence, watched them all with the old knowledge that their lives were all in some way entangled and bound up together . . . all that absurd and ill assorted group, Monsieur de Cyon, gentle and white haired, Hattie, Rebecca, Jean, Lily, Callendar and herself; and even Gramp who had disappeared already into the solitude of the room which Lily had given him. Here they all were, most of them—even de Cyon, himself, a foreigner—living on the wealth poured out by the black mills of a town in the Midlands of America. And she it was who had brought them together.

Watching her mother, it occurred to her that the indomitable Hattie was no longer young. She would ask presently to be shown the room where Fergus had died, and Ellen, still lying, would show it to her, and her mother would weep and be satis-

fied in a pitiful fashion with the deception. It was better sometimes to lie, better to deceive.

But the other thing . . . She rose presently and walked away
down into the garden where she was joined after a little time by
Jean on his crutches and Hansi, panting and restless at being kept
in the summer heat of the city. And when she had gone Rebecca
drifted away with an air of resentful martyrdom. She would
have been nasty to Hattie, if she had dared, just as she had been
nasty to Callendar who was only amused by her and took pains
to show her in a thousand small ways that Ellen belonged to him
now, and that she, Rebecca, no longer counted. But Rebecca
could wait; there was the same blood in both and Rebecca understood how his game was played. She could wait, she thought
bitterly, as she went up to her own room. The game was not
yet over and she had not yielded the victory. She knew, perhaps
better than any of the others, even Ellen, what to expect of
Callendar. There was no part of him which remained a mystery
to her, for she knew the men of her own family . . . the Uncle
Ottos and Maximilians and Gustaves, all with a touch of the
Levant. But Ellen would never believe her; she would believe
only that Rebecca was jealous of him (which was true) and that
what she said was uttered only out of spite. She would not believe that he was really cruel and domineering and thought of
women as creatures who belonged in a harem. . . . Sabine could
have helped her, but Sabine whom she had never met had been
turned away from the door.

No, she had not yet lost the battle. She must save Ellen as
much because she herself needed her as on Ellen's own account.
She climbed the long stairs and left Lily and de Cyon, Hattie and
Callendar together on the terrace, talking under the guidance of
Callendar, who led them gracefully here and there, finding, it
seemed, a strange satisfaction in ignoring the terrible knowledge
which he shared only with Lily and Ellen. Lily, watching him,
must have thought him inhumanly cold. Perhaps it occurred to

her again, in the depths of her wisdom and experience, that this marriage of Ellen could end in only one way.

Meanwhile under the old plane trees Ellen, who had been walking up and down in silence with Jean and the dogs, took the departure of Monsieur de Cyon for the white pavilion (which Lily had had fitted up for him as a sort of study) as a signal to return. On the terrace she said to Callendar, "I shan't come down until dinner. If you want to see your mother before she sails, you had best go now. I'll be free later," and so dismissed him.

Then, turning to her mother, she said, "Come Ma, we'll go up and get you settled in your room," and led her away leaving the garden to Lily and Jean and fat old Criquette.

Hattie, who had noticed nothing either in the streets or in the house itself (for, as Ellen knew, she did not see its beauty but saw it only as the house which it might be said belonged to Ellen), noticed as she walked through the big drawing-room that it resembled Shane's Castle in its warm, soft beauty. The portrait of old John Shane with a white setter at his feet, and the glowing Venice of Mr. Turner which had once hung in the house among the Mills now found places against the satinwood paneling. She fancied too that she recognized the Aubusson carpet, connected dimly in her memory with the picture of old Julia, hawk-like and bitter, tracing the outlines of the extravagant flowers with her stick of ebony and silver.

"It's like the castle," she murmured to Ellen, who hurried on up the stairs without heeding her.

They turned off along the gallery and, as they passed one of the doors, the squeaking of Gramp's rocking chair (unpacked and long since placed in readiness by Lily) came to them through the paneling. Time went on. People were born and people died, but The Everlasting and his rocking chair remained the same.

"He's better now than he used to be," observed Hattie. She

did not mention him by name, for Ellen knew well enough whom she meant; together they had passed his door, together they had heard the same rhythmical squeaking a thousand times. In a sense the sound of the decrepit rocker bound them to each other in a way that nothing else could have done. It was the one thing that remained constant, unchanged, out of all the past.

Hattie's room—the room to which she had come to spend the rest of her life—was large and airy with two tall windows which opened on the garden where Lily had taken Ellen's place and was now walking up and down, up and down, with her tall red-haired son. He was a man now and it made Hattie tremble to think how little difference his improper existence had made. There in the garden, under the old trees, it seemed of no importance that he had never had, in the proper sense, a father. He belonged there, with Lily. There was a rightness about the whole thing which Hattie sensed from afar off but was unable to explain . . . a vague feeling that Lily's life had been, despite everything, a life complete and in the proper key, like a beautiful painting superbly drawn and executed with all the boldness of a sure hand. Lily perhaps had led the life for which she was born. Hattie saw that she was telling the boy something which had led her to weep, for she lifted her handkerchief to her eyes and the boy halted to face her with his brow crinkled into little furrows. He was so like Fergus. . . .

And in the next instant she knew what it was that Lily had said. Ellen put her arms about her mother and murmured in a low voice, "I have some bad news, Ma."

And Hattie, looking at her in a queer stony fashion, replied, "I know what it is. Robert too is dead."

It was true. Little by little, while her mother sat listening in the same stony silence, Ellen told the whole story. It was Callendar who had brought the news. He had come from the front on leave this very morning. There—somewhere in the Argonne—he had come across Robert's regiment and there they had become acquainted. And then on the night before Callendar left, he had been sent for by one of the Americans. He had gone to a dressing station, but Robert was dead when he arrived. He had been wounded while saving one of his own men caught among the barbed wire between the German lines and his own. The man had been saved; he would live. It was he who had told Callendar the whole story, he who in a sort of delirium had described the whole affair with a fantastic poetry . . . the fog that had settled over the lines, the swift, brilliant flare of the Veery lights, the faint, malicious, pop! pop! of the gas shells as they buried their noses so neatly in the earth. It was in this wild, unearthly setting that Robert had given up his life. Robert (thought Hattie) who had said, "There's nothing romantic about war. . . . The side which is the most efficient . . . There won't be any nonsense. . . . I'll look out for myself."

When Ellen had finished they were both silent for a time and at last, Hattie, still dry eyed, said in a firm voice, "It is a judgment . . . I love my children too well . . . better than my own God and now they have been taken from me."

(*If only it had been Robert* . . . And now it was Robert too.)

She lay down on the great bed, a strange, incongruous figure—this grim, primitive, black-clad woman—in the midst of all the luxury that Lily had provided. And presently she said, "I'd like to be alone for a time, Ellen. I'll call you . . . later on."

So Ellen left her mother in solitude, but as the door closed behind her she knew that it was herself upon whom the remnants of her family—Hattie and The Everlasting—now depended. It was she who, after all these years in which she had neglected and forgotten them, had become the rock, the foundation. And she knew too that there could no longer be any doubt about marrying Callendar. She would have to marry now . . . Now that Robert, too, was gone there were new reasons. There remained only one thing that she could do for her mother. It might as well be Callendar as any other man.

61

THEY were married a month before the armistice, quietly with only Monsieur de Cyon and Lily and Jean and Hattie at the ceremony. It was the family once more (the remnants of the vigorous family which had once filled the drawing-room at Shane's Castle) which dominated all else in fitting fashion at such events as births and deaths and weddings. Thérèse was not present, for Ellen had decided quickly and there was not time for her to return from New York. Nor was Rebecca there. A week before the wedding there had been a scene in which Rebecca played all her cards in a forlorn hope of winning the game against Callendar. She had told Ellen that she herself was a Jewess and knew what men like Callendar were like. She had told her that he was cruel and domineering and that all his patience, all his quiet aloofness only covered the steel of a will which she would come in time to know too well. She said that in the end he would do his best to destroy her, not alone as a musician but as a woman. And Ellen listened quietly, secure against it all in the knowledge of the new duty that lay before her. It was not until Rebecca in a perfect debauch of fury screamed at her, "He is marrying you only to break your will . . . to destroy you. It is that which lies behind it all. . . . A conflict. . . . I know. . . . A conflict. He has wanted it all these years," that Ellen grew white and terrifying and told her to go.

"I never want to see you again," she said. "I am grateful for what you have done, but you cannot arrange all my life for me. What you say is a lie. . . . It isn't true. You say it all because you can no longer plan my whole life."

So Rebecca had gone, her bright ferret eyes red and savage. On the long stairs she met Callendar coming in but she did not so much as glance at him. In her heart she had not yet yielded the victory. She would defeat him in the end. She would let him defeat himself, for she knew he was certain to do it.

It was de Cyon himself who arranged the transfer of Callendar to the African service, and so it happened that they went to Tunis for the honeymoon to a villa on the outskirts of the city which belonged to one of Thérèse's Greek cousins, a man who served as head of the Mediterranean banks of Leopopulos et Cie. Ellen wrote to them regularly, letters which were like all the others she had ever written her mother since that first one from the Babylon Arms, restrained, careful and filled with a host of details from which one could gather nothing, and at the end always the same comment on the weather and the beauty of their garden with a brief line to the effect that "we are well and happy."

In the Rue Raynouard, Gramp lived the same life that he had lived for thirty years. He had his books (for Hattie was rich now and expense no longer mattered) and he had his rocking chair placed absurdly among the Empire furniture of the room which Lily had given him. Nothing had changed save that his windows looked out upon a garden laid out by Le Nôtre and that he could hear the whistles of the boats on the Seine and that he went sometimes afoot on solitary expeditions through the neighboring streets, once as far as the Invalides. It was his habit to steal away secretly through the gate in the garden wall leading into the Rue de Passy. He remained inscrutable, uncommunicative and aloof, save with Jean for whom he displayed a fancy. And none of them knew that the thing he was looking for on these solitary meanderings was a youth which had returned to him now with an unearthly clarity, though there were moments when he was childish and could not remember that he was in Paris or what had happened to him only yesterday.

And Hattie, living now with Lily, began slowly to regain her interest in life. She took to inspecting the big house room by

room to see that it was properly cared for; she quarreled in a
stifled, incoherent fashion with Augustine and the other servants;
she fussed about the garden, insensible to its beauty, and interested only in its order. She even undertook after a time to do
the marketing herself when she discovered with horror that the
shopkeepers paid old Mélanie the housekeeper a commission on
what she purchased.

So Lily, for a third time, turned over the possession of her
house to another. Madame Gigon had once treated it as her
own and after her César and Ellen had quarreled over it. And
now, willingly, she delivered it into the keeping of Hattie who
had greater need of it than any of the others. She told the servants that they must not mind Madame Tolliver's eccentric behavior and she made up to old Mélanie the amount of her com-
missions. But even if she had not done these things, they would
not have left her, for Lily understood servants and had a way
with them. Old Mélanie had been with her for more than
twenty years, since Lily had come to Madame Gigon, a little
frightened but resolved, none the less, never to marry Jean's
father.

62

SABINE, in her defeat, did not complain. In all the business of the divorce, she conducted herself as she had always
done, with an amazing control; so that no one, not even
Thérèse, was able to discover whether she was willing or not to
release the pretense of a possession she had held over Callendar for
so many years. They talked it over quite calmly, arranging all the
details in the most business-like and efficient fashion, under the
guidance of that short, frumpy, powerful old woman, Thérèse,
who appeared to know the law as thoroughly as she knew the
world of banking. There was no word spoken in anger or in

haste. The withdrawal of Sabine from the position of wife was executed with as superb an air of indifference as her entrance into the rôle.

"I want no settlement and no allowance," she had said as the three of them sat about the tea table in the small sitting room of the house in the Avenue du Bois. "Whatever you care to do for little Thérèse is, of course, your own affair. She is yours as much as mine. (A lie, she thought, because they did not care for her at all.) I have all I want."

And the leave-taking had been like the departure of a woman from the office of her lawyer. There was no anger and there were no tears. Sabine rose and said, "I will go now. . . . I have taken a house in the Rue Tilsit. I shall be there in case you want me. I do not know the telephone but I will send it to you."

Thérèse bent over the table and, gathering up the papers with her fat glittering fingers, thrust them into the reticule in which she kept her important documents . . . a moldy old bag continually in a state of confusion, from which she was able by a sort of magic to produce on a moment's notice any paper she required. As she sat watching her, it occurred to Sabine that the old woman's Levantine blood had begun to claim her entirely. It was not only the diamonds and emeralds which now stood in need of cleaning; the heavy black clothes which Thérèse wore even in the hottest weather were now sometimes stained and discolored, and she had taken to carrying fragments of biscuits among the papers of her reticule, which she took out from time to time and nibbled with the furtive air of a fat squirrel. She was more near-sighted than ever and squinted up her eyes until they became mere slits through which appeared the glitter of two tiny brilliant lights. All the charm was slipping slowly away from her eccentricity; the queer abrupt manner, which in the height of her power had seemed amusing and original, was slowly turning into the queerness of an untidy old Greek woman.

Watching her, she thought, "God willing, I shall never turn

into such a grubby old woman. I shall care for myself to the very end. I shall die, handsomely dressed, with my hair in perfect order and with my corsets on. She is a Levantine after all. She might be an old woman with a fruit stand in the shadow of Brooklyn Bridge."

(Thérèse with the glitter in her dark almond eyes, poking about in a reticule that contained a vast fortune in securities.)

Callendar walked with her through the comic opera hallway and out to her motor where, with a great courtliness, he saw her step in and closed the door after her.

"Good-by," he murmured quietly. "If there is anything you want, let me know."

So although for a time it had seemed that all the cards were turning up for her, she had in the end lost her game of patience. She had lost it, she reflected, to Ellen Tolliver whom she had neglected to respect sufficiently—a crude, uncivilized mountebank brought in to amuse the guests in the house on Murray Hill. What was the secret that lay behind all the mystery?

As the motor drove away, it occurred to her that the parting had been like one between strangers. She had been to them, then, nothing at all; she might have been a clerk employed in some branch of the Leopopulos bank, a creature who had been of use to them and whom they sent away when her usefulness was ended, willing to pension her if she desired it, like an old family employee. More than twelve years she had given to them . . . years in which she tried, desperately, heart-breakingly to establish some bond that was too strong to be broken in this cold, matter-of-fact fashion. More than twelve years she had struggled against something which was stronger, far stronger, than her own will and self-possession. And now they sent her away without more than a formal good-by. . . . Thérèse had her fortune still, vaster than it had ever been. Nothing else mattered.

She took out the mirror from the side of her motor and fell to examining her face. Here at least the twelve years had not taken the toll that might have been expected. There was no gray in the brick-red hair that lay under the small, chic gray hat. The narrow intelligent eyes, set close together, were as bright as they had ever been, and the white skin, like the thick petals of a camelia, was as perfect as ever beneath the superbly disguised powder and rouge. She touched the tip of her long nose with an immaculately gloved finger, and it occurred to her that the face which looked out of the tiny rectangle of glass was a mask, really,—an admirably fashioned mask which concealed effectively a turbulence none would ever have imagined lay beneath it. They managed things better in these days: once she would have been expected to retire from the field with a broken heart, to exploit, as it were, her own suffering; to swoon and weep . . . like Lady Byron.

She looked, she felt, remarkably young; but not young enough. She could not, she thought, begin all over again; there was not time. She was past forty now. She might marry again . . . a man her own age or older, but that would not be the same. She had given what youth she possessed (beneath that hard, controlled exterior) to Callendar and Thérèse. There was not a chance of her ever being young in the way she had once been, of loving with a fierce abandon that her pride had forced her to conceal. (She fancied that they had never discovered how much and how shamefully she had loved him, yet she could not be certain. Probably he knew this too.)

She put away the mirror and, leaning back, fell to thinking, with all her cold honesty, that she would even return to him now if he so much as lifted a finger in her direction. There had been in all their life together no memory of a violent scene, no memory of blows or accusations . . . nothing about which she could build up a hatred or sense of repulsion. There had been nothing since little Thérèse was born save that aloof, courteous indifference which it had been impossible to shatter. And for a time she tried to imagine what would have happened if once—only once—

he had for a moment melted and behaved toward her as if she had been more than a mere institution, more than a wife whom one protected and to whom one was always courteous.

And old Thérèse . . . Once Sabine had fancied that they were friends. They had been, she remembered, congenial, almost alike in their point of view, in the angle from which they looked out upon the world. And then Thérèse had slipped away, slowly, imperceptibly in a fashion that it was impossible to define. There had been no quarrel, no bandying of words, yet they had come somehow to hate each other, coldly and with an ironic polish. She knew what it was that had come between them. It was that fortune and the need of an heir. And now in the end Thérèse was becoming slowly an untidy, disgusting old Levantine woman helpless in the power of her obsession.

If she had not married Callendar she might have been a friend even now, not alone of Thérèse but of Callendar himself. But that would have been unbearable . . . much worse than this. At least in this there was a sense of finality.

So she tried as she had tried many times before, to pull those twelve years apart and pick from among the ruins the elements which had been the heart of her passion for him; but she found it impossible. She could not say why she would have returned to him now if he had asked her. Over all the years there hung a faint aura of evil (an evil which she told herself was not evil at all, but simply seemed so because she had been brought up to believe that sort of love was evil). It was desire which she felt, perhaps nothing more than that; yet it was, she was certain, not such a simple and uncomplicated thing. It was sinister, perhaps entangled in all her passion for *knowing* what people were, for taking them apart (she smiled to herself) to look at the works. No, this mystery was quite beyond her. . . .

So (she thought) in the end she had not been able to compete with Ellen Tolliver. He would have her now, as he had always wanted to have her. She (Sabine) had then not been so wrong

in the instinct that led her, years before, to call at the house in
Rue Raynouard. There had been nothing to discover, and yet
everything. What was true now of Callendar and Ellen Tolliver
was true then, as they sat in the long beautiful drawing-room,
just as true as it had been in the days when the girl had come to
the house on Murray Hill. It was only that they themselves
had changed and here (she thought almost with satisfaction)
might lie the seeds of one more disaster. For Lilli Barr could
not possibly be the same as the awkward, obscure Ellen Tolliver,
and Callendar had hardened slowly in all the qualities which
made him impossible. Ellen Tolliver would not submit to the
unhappiness she herself had known; Ellen Tolliver would not
wait patiently to achieve her own desire. She was capable of
stormy scenes; she had clearly a genius for success, for having
her own way. He had, perhaps, in all his watching never discovered this. And yet, as she thought it over and over on the
drive to the Rue Tilsit, it occurred to her that it might be just
this and nothing more that was the very core of that inexplicable,
persistent attraction between them.

Lilli Barr . . . Lilli Barr . . . Lilli Barr . . . She kept repeating the name to herself. She still felt no resentment. If she
herself could not have Callendar, there was no reason why Lilli
Barr should not have him. There was, she knew, nothing more
to be done.

The voice of Amedé, the driver, roused her as he opened the
door. She stepped out, bade him wait for orders, and turning,
she saw little Thérèse standing in the window with the governess.
It reminded her that she must see Thérèse's friend Ella Nattatorini about the lease for the house at Houlgate. . . . The sea
would do little Thérèse good. And there were servants to be engaged and the packing to be done . . .

The ocean of small things which made it possible to endure
unhappiness rose and swept over her.

63

THE news of the wedding came to Sabine the following autumn while she was staying in Newport. Even the war had not crowded out of the journals an event of such interest. The bride, she read, was well known to the public as a pianist. She had described herself as Ellen Tolliver, American by birth, age thirty-four years. (It was the first time that the world knew Lilli Barr was American, for Rebecca and the forgotten Schneidermann had done their work well.) The bridegroom was prominent and the member of many clubs, the last of his family, and had not lived in America for more than ten years. He was a captain in the French army and would be stationed in Tunis where they were to spend the honeymoon.

Laying aside the *Times* and resuming her breakfast, she discovered that her only response to the news was one of shock at the haste with which the wedding had followed the divorce. It was almost as if they said that all these years she had stood between them, and now that Callendar was free, they must lose no time. Vaguely she felt that she should feel insulted. It was not until evening, when she drove over to dine with Mrs. Champion at The Cedars, that the sense of depression abated a little.

It was a gloomy place—the Cedars—built in the Seventies in the ornate style in favor at that time, and the presence of Mrs. Champion and the Virgins did nothing to raise the tone. Janey and Margaret (it seemed to her when she saw them in the dark cool rooms that she had known them always) were, as she calculated it, now forty-two and forty-five respectively and had reached the stage in which any spark that may have dwelt within their narrow-chested frames was now sublimated into an interest in garden clubs and work among the sailors. Things had changed . . . enormously, but Janey and Margaret had gone on and on, living in the gloomy Cedars with their mother, perpetually shocked and stimulated by the stories of the oil magnates and financial adventurers who had taken possession of the Casino. It was these stories which provided the opening barrage of conversation at dinner.

"There is one woman who they say gives enormous parties," Janey told her at dinner, "who was once the cook for a cousin of Mrs. Mallinson."

They assured her, although she knew it well enough, that Newport was not the same. It had lost its tone; and in losing it (thought Sabine) it had left Mrs. Champion and the Virgins far behind. Bishop Smallwood, the Apostle to the Genteel, who came sometimes to spend a week with his "wa'am friend" Mrs. Champion, shared their disgust on Sabine's right and expressed properly outraged sentiments.

If America were anything, Sabine thought, over her guinea fowl, it was change . . . change . . . change. And God help those who didn't keep up with it! All the conversation gave her a curious sense of having passed poor Janey and Margaret and the Apostle and left them far behind. They seemed very far away. She felt that she was being kind to them in having come to dine at The Cedars. And once Mrs. Champion's word had been law in that tight little world which was now exploded, leaving them stranded, remote and helpless and pitiful, pretending all the while that it was *their* world, after all, which really counted.

She knew that they would find a bitter triumph in the news that had come with the morning *Times,* for they could not have forgotten how she stole Richard Callendar (by the lucky turn of events which they would never know) from under the noses of all of them. There had been so little excitement in their lives; certainly they had not forgotten, certainly they would not miss an opportunity for which they had waited so long. Yet they seemed so remote and negligible to her that she did not even wince when at last Mrs. Champion sidled up to the subject.

She was able to tell them and Bishop Smallwood, who in the decline of the season was fairly panting for gossip, that Lilli Barr *was* the same girl who had played at that scandalous party of Thérèse Callendar's. (Did they remember the naked Javanese

—or was it Senegalese—dancer? asked Mrs. Champion. She had commanded Janey and Margaret to shield their faces with their fans). Lilli Barr *was* the same girl with whom Richard Callendar had lunched so many times in the open window at Sherry's. She saw fit to pass over the implication, thrust in slyly by Mrs. Champion, that he was making the girl, after so many years, an honest woman. Because she herself did not really know.

And speaking of the divorce, she remarked brazenly, "It was all settled without difficulty. I knew that he was planning to marry her. We talked it over and thought it the best solution."

At which Mrs. Champion shook her head and made a clucking sound to indicate, as clearly as she dared, that the cold-blooded behavior of Sabine's generation in such matters was obscene and immoral. And the Apostle to the Genteel, in obeisance to his high church opinions and his disapproval of divorce, looked gravely and silently into the depths of his sherbet, but with an air of believing that there was much to be said on both sides. (It would not be wise to offend so rich and fashionable a woman as Sabine Callendar.) Janey and Margaret only stared at her, with the round, stupid eyes of little girls.

And when she left (a little after nine when she could endure the party no longer) Mrs. Champion was able at last to deliver the blow which she had held in reserve all the evening. As they stood in the porte cochère waiting for Sabine's motor to come up, she murmured under the protection of the darkness, "I could have warned you long ago, my dear. You should never have married Richard Callendar. If you had a mother—" She sighed and continued. "I should never have allowed Janey or Margaret to accept a proposal from him."

Such a speech would have made her angry once and have aroused the sharp tongue for which she had been famous; but it made no difference to her now, save that it amused her to think of Janey or Margaret standing there, a pair of Alices in Wonderland, as the wife of Richard. And she reflected that she possessed an experience which they would never know. It was better to have been the wife of Callendar than to have dried up in the pale, shriveled fashion of Janey and Margaret (and they had been pretty once, in a silly, pink and white fashion). And she knew, with a curious pang of pity, that as they stood there in the shadow of their powerful mother, they too were thinking the same thing. They had never escaped that dowdy, stupid old woman. . . .

"Good night," she said. "I shan't see you again. I am sailing on Friday."

And then for the first time in her life, the wall of cold common sense collapsed and she exposed herself deliberately to the peril of boredom. "If you do decide to come to Paris, Janey, you must pay me a visit." For there was something unbearable to her in the thought of Janey, free for the first time from the dominion of her mother, alone in Paris. It would be like a bird set free which no longer knows how to fly. . . .

In the darkness Janey stammered and gushed like a girl of seventeen (Janey who would never see forty again), "It's kind of you, Sabine. It's wonderful. You see I've never been in Paris before without mother . . . and I wouldn't know just what to do . . . I'll come." And she subsided into a chaos of maidenly gurglings.

But as Sabine drove away from the barren shadows of the Cedars, she reproached herself for having succumbed so weakly. Something had happened to her. A year ago she would not have done such a stupid thing. . . . "Perhaps," she thought, above the distant roar of the surf, "I am growing old. . . ."

As the months passed and she returned to Paris—a Paris gay and gaudy with the excitement of the last days of the peace conference—she came to understand the satisfaction which lies of knowing that a thing is finished. She would no longer go through the torture of seeing Callendar day after day, always at hand and yet remote as the summit of a cold mountain peak. All that was over, finished; and in the sense of finality there was peace. Until now she had never known how terribly the monstrous house in the Avenue du Bois had oppressed her. It was only since she had her own house in the Rue Tilsit, a house filled with all the exquisite things she cherished and which meant so much to her, that she understood completely the torture of the house which she had called "a sort of World's Fair exhibit."

For she had never, in all the years of their life together, been able to escape from it. Always Callendar had resisted silently, quietly in the way he had, until she had come in the end to accept the place without complaint. She had been silent in the hope that he might appreciate her silence and her virtue in submitting to his will. But he had simply taken it as a matter of course. She had never been able properly to entertain because the house was so awful that one could not even forget its shame in the hollow pretense that it was bizarre and consequently chic. And she knew now beyond all doubt that he liked the house. It satisfied him in the way it satisfied his mother. And she understood that he belonged in it just as Thérèse belonged there, more than ever since her Levantine blood had come into its own.

There in the Rue Tilsit, in her own house, among the things chosen by her own fastidious taste, she began once more to take up her own life, to descend from the unreal, extravagant level of the Callendars to a plane where she might exist in her proper relation to all about her. For more than twelve years, she came to realize, her life had not been her own, even for a moment. It had been Callendar's to do with as he chose. . . . She had been his possession. It was only now that she was beginning again to be free. . . .

In the beginning, after that day when she had said good-by so formally to Richard and his mother, when all the arrangements had been completed and Thérèse had stuffed all her papers back into her reticule, she could not bring herself to reënter the house, even to return for the possessions—pictures, bits of jade and silver and silk—which she had left behind her. It was only now, long afterward, when she had come to feel the full sense of her freedom that she considered going to fetch them.

At last, after she had been in Paris for weeks, she rang up the house and learning from Victorine that it was empty and that no one was expected (Thérèse was in London, Victorine told her, and Richard and Ellen still in Tunis) she arranged to call for the things late that afternoon.

64

IT was a cold gray afternoon in the spring when the sun, breaking through the clouds, picked out for brief moments the faint green on the trees of the little park in the Avenue du Bois. Side by side the white houses stood, withdrawn a little from the street, flamboyant yet cold, ornate but barren. Sabine, watching them from the window of her tiny motor, was thankful again in a comfortable indefinite fashion that she had escaped from their insufferable pomp into the tiny, exquisite house in the Rue Tilsit.

Of late she had come at times to forget all the secret misery of the twelve years; she had been almost happy, as nearly happy as it was possible for her to be. It seemed to her now that circumstances had been cruel. She should have been born a man; and as a man, with a freedom from all the world of Mrs. Champion and her Virgins, she would have turned her mind to science. It was that sort of a mind; and it was only recently that she had come to believe it wasted . . . frittered away on tiny, nonsensical things, things which in the end only ate into her own chance for happiness. In all her life there had been nothing which had taken possession of her—nothing save the barren, futile passion for her husband. Her life, she reflected, had been a wasted one. As a man, she would have been free . . . free in the same fashion as Ellen Tolliver. She could have done as she liked, waiting upon no one. It seemed to her that her whole life had been spent in going from place to place, always in a tiny, expensive motor, arriving nowhere in the end. She was neither one thing nor the other; she had fallen somewhere between the sterility of Janey and Margaret Champion and the fierce activity of Ellen Tolliver.

Ellen Tolliver had been free, without background, without friends, alone, an adventuress (not at all in the evil sense) but one who had gone unhindered toward the thing which possessed her. Perhaps Ellen Tolliver would succeed now where she had failed. None, thought Sabine, knew the perils which lay ahead so well as herself and the old curiosity began to assail her; she wanted passionately to see Ellen Tolliver, to find out from her in any fashion possible, scrupulous or otherwise, what had happened in those months since she said good-by to Callendar and Thérèse. Perhaps Ellen saw him more clearly than herself; perhaps she had discovered his secret . . . the nature of him. She had come to respect Ellen Tolliver.

The car halted. Amedé, neat and mustachioed, stood holding the door for her. With an effort of will she wrapped her fur cloak about her and stepped on to the pavement.

"Wait for me," she said. "I may want you to carry some things. I'll send Victorine when I want you."

The big ornate house had the look of a place closed and deserted; the shutters were up and the shades drawn save in the entresol. At the door, Victorine, who had been clearly watching for her, stood waiting with a gleam in her eye which Sabine, from long association, was able to read. It was a look with which Victorine triumphantly announced household calamities. As Sabine stepped into the great hall, the housekeeper put her finger to her mustachioed lips and murmured, "Madame Callendar is here. . . ." And then, with the air of turning the morsel about, she added, "The *young* Madame Callendar." And again, when her former mistress seemed not to be sufficiently shocked, she continued, "The *new* Mrs. Callendar."

For a moment Sabine stood hesitating, as if deciding whether to turn and run; it would have been an excellent excuse for never entering the house again. But far back in her consciousness, the old, insatiable curiosity gnawed and gnawed.

"Why has she returned?" she asked. "Where is Monsieur Callendar?"

Victorine shrugged her fat shoulders. "I don't know, Madame. None of us knows anything. A cable came at noon to-day with the news that she was arriving . . . to make things ready. I telephoned you. . . . I sent messages. The word came that you did not return for lunch and no one knew where you were." With an air of drama, she said again, "The new Madame Callendar came in an hour ago."

Sabine stood biting her crimson lips. If Ellen Tolliver had returned from Tunis, it was not likely that she would be going away soon, and it would be awkward to ask her permission to enter the house. Why had she returned? Why had Callendar not come with her? She turned to Victorine.

"Where is she now?"

"Resting," replied Victorine, "in the boudoir."

(That terrible room with the bearskin rugs and the mirrors sending back and forth innumerable reflections, as if the place were filled with a host of people . . . a host of personalities all of whom were in the end contained within the flesh of the onlooker. . . . Many persons in each of us, thought Sabine. It was comic to think of Ellen Tolliver, so distinguished, so self-possessed, so cold, in the midst of all that cheap demi-mondaine splendor.)

"Are my things ready?"

"I was not sure, Madame, how many things you wished to take away with you. I got ready the things I *knew*. There may be others."

Sabine made her decision. "I will come in and get them now. Say nothing to Madame Callendar. If she's resting, I'll hurry away without her knowing that I've come."

She slipped a ten franc note into the insinuating palm of Victorine who promptly said, "It's good to see you again, Madame," in a voice which carried another meaning—"We would much prefer you to the new Mrs. Callendar."

Sabine ignored her. "And Monsieur Callendar?" she asked
again.

"He did not return, Madame. Nothing was said of him."

In the boudoir everhead Ellen lay, with her black dog by her
side, staring resentfully at the reflections. She was unable to
rest. Lying on the Egyptian chaise longue she surveyed the room
and decided that she would have the indecent mirrors taken down
to-morrow. She was certain that Sabine was not responsible
for them; she suspected, out of the knowledge that had come
to her in the past six months, that they were perhaps an idea
of Callendar. They were unhealthy, she thought; all the house,
for that matter, was unhealthy, even the hall and the glimpse of
the darkened drawing room she had been able to snatch on her
way up the marble stairs with the red plush rail. It was unhealthy to be stared at, accused day in and day out by these
innumerable stupid reflections. It was, truly, an amazing house,
and so like Thérèse. Why, she wondered, had Sabine not
changed it? Sabine, with her faultless taste, her reserve, her
ironic shell, must have hated it, always. Perhaps . . . perhaps she had not dared to oppose him. Perhaps he too, like his
mother, had been fond of the house. Perhaps he had looked
at Sabine (smiling with his mouth but not his eyes) and said,
"We will let it rest for the present. Some day . . ." and so
slipped away in that inexplicable, unconquerable fashion he had
revealed in the villa at Tunis. Perhaps . . . She began to understand a little of what Sabine's life had been. Out of her
own short, vivid experience, she was able to reconstruct bits of it,
here and there. And Sabine had endured it for more than twelve
years. . . .

The mirrors put her nerves on edge. She loathed the reflections staring back at her from every wall. They were like faces
peering in at her . . . her own face repeated over and over
again, tiresomely, for she was not vain and wasted no time over
mirrors. No, she would have them down at once. If this was

to be her home, she would not be prevented by old Thérèse or Richard himself.

Her body ached from the fatigue of the journey from Marseilles yet it was impossible to rest. Her mind was awake, nervous, irritable, now angry, now frustrated, now cold and resolute, but always in its depths uncertain and muddled in a way it had never been before. Could it be that she was losing her grip upon life? That she was being swallowed up? Always she had known exactly what it was she wanted, what it was she would do. But now . . .

At length the restlessness became unbearable and, followed by the black dog, she rose and set out to explore the rest of the house. She went from room to room and returned at length to the stairway. The rooms, each one, were associated in some way with Thérèse, with Callendar, with Sabine. In her weariness and confusion, she could not drive them from her mind. They tormented her as she turned down the marble steps. She kept thinking of the night when Sabine had allowed Callendar and herself to drive home together from the house on Murray Hill. She understood now how wise Sabine had been, how subtle. She must have known then who it was that Callendar loved; she must have thought that in the end Callendar would never marry that struggling, gauche young girl who had fascinated him. Neither of them (she thought with satisfaction) had known the strength of that raw young girl. They had thought her, perhaps, stupid and unable to protect herself against such a rich and glamorous lover. . . .

Half down the stairs, in the very midst of these thoughts, she was interrupted by the sound of voices which came from the drawing-room. The shutters had been opened and the curtains flung back and in the twilight which filtered through she saw dimly two figures bending over a little pile of bric-à-brac. The one was Victorine. The other figure was familiar—she could not say in what way. Halting for a moment she watched them and, as they became aware of her presence, the stranger turned toward her and she saw that it was Sabine, materialized, one might have said, out of her very thoughts.

She would have turned back, pretending she had seen nothing (perhaps Sabine would have hidden herself in a closet or behind a sofa, anywhere) but it was too late now. They had seen each other; they had stood for a time staring. It was impossible now to behave in any such idiotic fashion. Ellen smiled and, moving on down the stairs, was certain now of what she had suspected an hour earlier when the housekeeper greeted her—that old Victorine was devoted to the first Mrs. Callendar and looked upon herself as an intruder. Victorine, she fancied, had conspired to let Sabine into the house without announcing her.

Halting only to cuff Hansi and stop his growling, she crossed the great black and white squares of the tesselated hall and stepped into the drawing-room. She smiled and held out her hand.

"No one told me you had come in," she said. "It's pleasant to see you. . . . I arrived only an hour ago from Marseilles."

She found herself taking Sabine's hand. Their greeting was like one between two men, old friends—a symbol of the curious understanding which had existed between them since the very beginning. It seemed that they were neither friends, nor enemies, but something in between. They were always being thrown together, though neither would have said that she sought the company of the other.

Sabine laughed, with a disarming air of honesty. "I feel a fool," she said, and then explained how it was she had to come in. "I took a chance of being able to escape without your knowing it, but I am an unlucky gambler. I've never had any luck. I'm sorry." She laughed again and added, "I've no doubt (indicating Victorine) that she is enjoying it all immensely."

It was true. Victorine stood riveted to the floor, her eyes

bright with curiosity. Clearly she was confused and annoyed that they spoke English, which she could not understand.

"I'll go then," continued Sabine. "I shan't steal anything which doesn't belong to me."

At this Ellen laughed. "I've seen nothing in the house that you mightn't steal . . . gladly, for all of me."

"The boudoir . . ." murmured Sabine with understanding as she gathered up her parcels. She might have added, "Callendar and Thérèse think it a beautiful house. It suits them." But because she knew the remark would have a feline sound, she kept silent. Besides it was probable that Ellen already knew it, perfectly. She bade Victorine summon Amedé and when the housekeeper was gone, Ellen moved a little nearer and said in a low voice, "You mustn't go. You must stay for a little time. . . . Stay for a cup of tea."

But Sabine declined, protesting. "No. . . . I've a score of errands. I really must go . . . and honestly it seems to me an absurd situation."

Ellen laid one hand on her shoulder and, looking at her closely, repeated, "You *must* stay. . . . I must talk to some one. . . . There is so much to discuss."

Slowly Sabine put down her parcels, subdued once more by the old curiosity. (How could she resist the promise of such revelations?) Amedé appeared to carry away the larger bundles and she said to him, "Wait for me. I'm having tea with Mrs. Callendar."

And the eyes of Amedé grew as bright, as filled with curiosity as those of Victorine. In the hallway the housekeeper said to him with a grimace, "These Americans! What a cold blooded lot! The first wife and the second having tea in the husband's house!"

In the little sitting room where a year ago Thérèse had swept the papers from the table into her untidy reticule, Sabine and Ellen settled themselves to talk, Ellen looking worn and tired, as if a part of her tremendous spirit had been subdued or had slipped away from her, Sabine refreshed, worldly, elegant, mistress of herself . . . the Sabine who had existed in the first days of the house on Murray Hill. The odd sense of comradeship persisted. It was the same spirit that had united them on the morning, long ago, when Sabine called at the Rue Raynouard, arriving as an enemy and departing as a friend. (She had been right in the instinct that led her into that call. Ellen belonged to him now, after all those years, as much of her as any mere process of law could deliver into his hands.)

It was Victorine who broke the precedent of fifteen years by bringing the tea with her own hands. Victorine, the housekeeper, the head of the entire ménage in the Avenue du Bois, bent her dignity, stepped down from her pedestal to carry a tea tray, because she feared that some morsel of fascinating interest might escape her ears. How could she resist this spectacle? This occasion? This friendly encounter ("Figure-toi," she would say in the servants' hall) between the two wives of her master. These Americans. . . .

But she strained her ears and summoned in vain a youthful uncertain memory of English, for neither of the wives said anything of importance while she was in the room. They discussed the lateness of the spring, and even the political conditions, as if there were nothing at all extraordinary in the situation. (The cabinet, said the new Mrs. Callendar, in which M. de Cyon had served, was gone to the wall and all his gentle intrigues come to nothing.)

When Victorine, having exhausted all the possibilities of delay by poking and fussing over the tea tray, was forced by decency to quit the room, Sabine rose and said, "I know the habits of Victorine. She is at this minute standing outside the door."

To prove it she walked quickly to the door and, flinging it open, saw Victorine sidle away with a pompous air of having many duties upon her mind.

"She has listened like that before . . . many times. It is her curiosity and one can't blame her for that. If I had been born a servant I should have spent all my time at keyholes. All the same she should have been sent away long ago. One has only to shoo her off whenever there is anything important in the air."

It was her way of opening a discussion for which she hungered with a violence that made the curiosity of Victorine pale in comparison. But Ellen said nothing. She poured the tea and continued to talk of politics and the spring. It was not easy for her, who had never confided in any one. She sat behind the tea tray in the amazing, baroque room conscious that she was in the midst of a fantastic situation, yet unable to take one step in the direction she desired. She looked tall and handsome and dignified, but a little sad and weary. It was the sadness which conveyed to Sabine what was in the air.

"And Richard," she asked abruptly. "How is he?"

"I have left him," Ellen replied slowly, "for a time, at any rate."

She spoke with her eyes cast down, as if it shamed her to confess that she had not made of the marriage a complete success. She pretended to be busily engaged with the flame beneath the silver teakettle. "I do not know whether I shall go back. I am thinking it out . . . trying to decide."

Sabine, too wise to interrupt, lighted a cigarette, threw back her fur coat and waited.

"I have to decide, you see, between two things. . . . Between myself and him, you might say. Or better perhaps, whether I shall exist only in relation to him." She looked up suddenly, with an air of assurance which must have fascinated Sabine, who sat thinking of Ellen as she had been in the days of Murray Hill. "It is not only my music . . . my career. He hates that and he hates it because, in spite of anything he can do, I shall always be known to the world as Lilli Barr and not as Mrs. Callendar. I think he forgot to take that into consideration. He is very confident, very sure of himself."

Sabine still smiled faintly.

"I think you understand what it is I mean. I have been

married only six months but I realize that one of us must die . . . either Lilli Barr or Mrs. Callendar. I am trying to decide which it must be. It is hard because both of them are very much alive and neither of them is still in her first youth. That's what makes it difficult. I don't know whether it is worth while to kill Lilli Barr in order that Mrs. Callendar may live and (she made a wry face) be all that is to be expected of a lady in her position . . . the wife of Richard Callendar. I fancy you understand what I mean." She leaned forward and asked, "Will you have another cup? . . . No?"

She discussed the problem coldly, with an air of utter detachment; these two creatures—Lilli Barr and the second Mrs. Callendar—might have existed without any relation to herself. Sabine, understanding perhaps that it was only in such a fashion that she was able to discuss the affair at all, took her cue and said, "The first Mrs. Callendar is dead. She has been dying for some months, but she is dead, completely dead. And Sabine Cane is alive again, more alive than she has ever been . . . and free. My God! How free!"

For a time Ellen sat thoughtfully staring into the fire and when at length she spoke, it was to say, "Ah! I know what you mean by being free. I know perfectly. I can imagine what it must have been. . . . I've seen it myself."

And while she talked thus, calmly, with the one woman in the world who had every reason to hate her, a woman whom she had defeated but who still seemed in some outlandish fashion a friend and ally, she kept seeing the villa and the white-walled garden in Tunis. She kept seeing her husband (who had once been Sabine's husband) walking up and down in the cool of the evening, a few feet from her chair yet as remote as if he had been on the opposite side of the white desert beyond the walls. She saw him walking and smoking and ignoring her, his strong brown hands clasped behind him, absorbed always in some mystery which had nothing to do with her, and yet conscious (he must have been conscious) of a shadowy conflict that would neither vanish nor be pinned down—a man who shut her out of his existence and yet treated her as a possession. She kept seeing the handsome face, the curved red lips, the finely arched nose, the dark mustaches and above all the cold, gray, unfathomable eyes. (If only once he had given way for a moment. If only once that inhuman aloofness had melted, not into a fierce, glowing passion, but into a touching, simple affection. . . .)

"I know what it is," she repeated slowly. "I wondered some-times . . . in the long evenings, how you endured it. And I wondered too whether I should ever be able to endure it. You see, the difficulty is that I have no time now to experiment. I must decide. If I gave twelve years of my life, I should be . . ." She thought for a second. "I should be forty-seven. I dare not risk failure at that age. That would be unbearable because there would be nothing ahead." Again she was silent for a time and then murmured, "I wanted to talk with you. I should have come to you if we had not met here. . . . I could not have helped it. It was impossible to talk of him with any one who has not known him . . . who has not lived with him. Such a person could not understand what he was like. . . ."

Sabine sat on the edge of her gilt chair, hungrily, with the air of a woman whose most passionate desire was at last being satis-fied. For years she had waited. Only once before—on the morning she called at the Rue Raynouard—had she even spoken of the thing. She had said on that occasion, "You know my husband . . . a little. So you can guess perhaps a little of the story." (It was a different Sabine who sat here saying, "My God! How free!")

The cigarette had burned until it scorched her gray gloves. "But it is different with you. He is in love with you. He never loved me. It was you that he loved always. I know that." And with a pained ironic smile, she added, "Sabine Cane dares say what Mrs. Callendar could not even think."

Outside the house the twilight had come down gently over the trees in the little park. Beside Sabine's tiny motor, Amedé waited, smoking cigarette after cigarette. Belowstairs Victorine regaled the servants' hall with an embroidered description of what she had witnessed, but when pressed for details became vague and unsatisfactory.

Sabine stirred and murmured: "Besides, I don't fancy you are entirely . . . How shall I say it? I don't wish to be offensive . . . I don't fancy perhaps that you are completely in love with him. I mean that you have not lost your head. If you gave him up, it would not be the end of everything. . . ."

Ellen sat up very straight, her mouth almost hard. "No," she said. "It would not be the end of everything!" And then relaxing a bit, she continued, "No. But I am in love with him. I do love him. I can't describe it. . . . It's a kind of hypnotism."

It was impossible to be angry with Sabine. She was so calm, so obviously honest; it was impossible not to respect that incredible passion for the truth.

"I know what it is . . . I know," murmured Sabine thoughtfully.

"I think at times that I could give him up," and Ellen snapped her fingers, "like that . . . quickly, without a qualm, without so much as a backward look, and then something reaches out and takes possession of me, and in the next moment I know it is impossible. Once you are entangled, it is not easy to be free." She threw her cigarette half-smoked into the mouth of the fireplace, a monstrous, ornate affair out of all proportion to the room. "My God!" she added with a quick passion. "What is it that he does to us? . . . To women like you and me, who are intelligent women, independent . . . not fools? What is it he does to most women? I have seen them in the hotel at Tunis looking at him. I have seen that look come into his eyes. . . ."

Sabine put down her teacup, leaned forward and said, "It is an animal thing . . . what he does to us. If we are to be honest, it is that. You see, women like you and me never think of that. . . . We take it for granted there is no such thing. . . .

But there is, just the same. It is in all of us who are women at all. The power he possesses is the power of most men multiplied many times. . . . Latin women, who are more honest, can deal with it. . . . French women . . . some French women . . . are cynical and rational. . . . And they are better protected than ourselves, because they know what they are about. . . . A woman like old Thérèse could never have been hurt by him. They are protected from suffering, at least a certain kind of suffering. They would not be caught as we have been . . . stupidly."

French women! (thought Ellen). There was Madame No-zières. Had it protected her? Still, her suffering had not been of this sort. It was a different thing. What Sabine said about women like themselves was true. Somehow Sabine had cleared the air. She (Ellen) had always thought of him thus in the moments when her head had been quite clear . . . as an animal, a handsome, docile cat. It explained too why she had always had a small, secret terror of him; why she had always been shocked by the fierceness of his love. When he had come to her in the Babylon Arms the distaste had not been so strong; but he had been more fresh then, less conscious of what he was. When he returned to her, it was with the freshness gone, with the romance worn away so that only the other thing showed through, naked yet fascinating to a woman who (she was honest with herself) . . . a woman who had never known anything but the timid, pitiful love of Clarence.

And there was one thing she could not endure—that she, Ellen Tolliver, the part of her which she had guarded so jealously, should ever be destroyed by losing control over her own body.

And again she kept seeing him, dark and secret, this time as he sat across from her at the table in the small white room over-looking the Mediterranean, with the old sense of conflict rising sharply between them. She was conscious of watching him, as he watched her, of wondering how long she could go on thus, im-prisoned. She saw again the gray eyes watching her, stubbornly, as if she were a proud animal which they had set themselves to subdue. It was all confused and hateful because one could never know what he was thinking—whether behind those opaque gray eyes there were thoughts of love or of hatred. There were no intimacies of feeling, or even of taste. He was not a husband such as Fergus would have been, eager and naïvely honest, not stolid and dependable like Robert. . . . He was not like any man she could think of. He was an alien . . . an outsider. She remembered the taunt Rebecca had flung at her, "He is marrying you only to break your will . . . to destroy you. He has waited all these years."

But he had not done it! He had not done it! There were times when she hated only and felt powerful and strong, but times too when her strength oozed from her, leaving her only a poor, silly, feminine creature eager to please and fascinate him—a contemptible creature like those women in the corridors of the hotel in Tunis. No, she would not be destroyed thus!

"Sometimes," observed Sabine, in her cold, measured voice, "I think that men and women are born to be enemies, that even in the happiest of loves there is an element of conflict. One must possess and the other be possessed. There is no helping it. It seems to me that we are always fighting, fighting, to save the part of us which is ourself."

She laughed. "Why, we're doing it now, you know . . . the two of us. Richard, you may say, is the embodiment of all that part of men which we can never bring ourselves to accept . . . women like you and me."

"We quarreled," continued Ellen absorbed in her own trouble. "We had terrible scenes and terrible reconciliations. I am certain that he has already been unfaithful. In the end I came away, but until I stepped on the ship I was not certain that I had the courage. . . . Imagine that! . . . Imagine me not having the courage simply to go from one place to another. I did not tell him I was going until the morning I sailed. There was time then for a quarrel, but not time for a reconciliation, and so I got off." She looked out of the window and continued in a low voice. "And now . . . now I don't know what I'm to do. I came here to this house because I am still his wife. I wanted time to think it over . . . away from him. It would have been absurd to run away and hide like a schoolgirl."

"He will not change," observed Sabine. "I knew him for twelve years. He did not change." She flicked the ash from her cigarette and sighed. "Still, in all that time, we never quarreled. He would never have quarreled over my leaving him. . . . You see, he did not care enough."

It was quite dark now and the only light in the room came from the blaze in the huge fireplace. Sabine was drawing on her gloves. She gathered her fur cloak about her and set her small hat at exactly the right angle.

"Do you know the history of this house?" she asked. "It might interest you. You see, it was built originally by a German banker named Wolff to house his mistress. When he killed himself and she disappeared, it fell into the possession of the Callendars. Richard brought me here. . . . I followed the mistress in the possession of the boudoir . . . and now it is yours."

Ellen leaned back silently in her chair. There was something about this house which she had disliked since the moment she entered it . . . something lush and Oriental. So it had been built by a German Jew to please his mistress and after that it had sheltered first Sabine and then herself! The history seemed in some way to throw a light upon her own confusion. The house, it appeared, still carried on its traditions. She and Sabine were ladies. It was impossible to know what the mistress had been. She was dead or retired now, no doubt, in some respectable quarter of a provincial town, or perhaps become the proprietress of a café, or a bad variety actress. It was fascinating to speculate upon what had become of her. What would happen to Sabine? What would happen to herself?

Sabine interrupted her thoughts by saying, "It is ridiculous for me in my position to give you advice. Besides, even if matters were different I'm not sure that I'd do it. Advice means nothing and people seldom take it because they never tell the whole truth. There is always something which they keep concealed, and because it is concealed it is the most important element of all and influences them far more than anything an outsider can say." She stood up and walked over to the fire. "No, there's nothing I can say save that it would be a pity for the world to lose Lilli Barr. She is far more important than Mrs. Callendar, and in the end I think would be the happier of the two."

Across the room Ellen watched the back of her visitor, speculating upon what she could have meant by the long speech. Was it possible that Sabine knew there was something she had not revealed? She grew suddenly jealous and suspicious. Had Sabine been too clever for her? Had all this strange feeling of an alliance between them been simply an illusion tricked up by a shrewd adversary? Did Sabine, standing there with her foot on the fender, fancy that if Callendar were free again she might have him back?

"You see, one of the complications," she said quietly, "is that I am going to have a baby."

At the announcement Sabine turned sharply, with a queer look in her eyes. Years before in this very room, she had made the identical speech to Callendar, and he had turned and kissed her with a new sort of tenderness. But the child had been a girl . . . a poor, sickly little girl. Sabine closed her eyes, and turning, rested her head for a moment against the high mantelpiece. She had the manner of one who had been hurt suddenly.

"It is the heir they wanted," she said sardonically.

"But it may be a girl."

She smiled again, bitterly, and said, "Oh, no! I am certain it will be a boy. You have a genius for success, my dear. You were never a bad gambler. I'm certain you will not fail old Thérèse."

At the door it was Victorine (who had been waiting in the

shadows) who opened for them. The two Mrs. Callendars said good-by.

"There is only one thing . . ." said Sabine. "I wonder whether he is really worth all this trouble and anxiety. When one thinks of the matter coldly, there is nothing to commend him. He has no virtues either as a husband or a lover. Sometimes I think him merely a stupid animal with immense powers of attraction."

"But none of that makes any difference," said Ellen. "That's the queer thing! It never does."

She watched Sabine until she saw her disappear into the tiny motor whose lights made two bright sparks in the spring darkness, and when she returned to the sitting room she knew suddenly that she had left Callendar for good. There was no longer any doubt about it. If she had not, in her heart, thought of him as a part of the past, she could not have talked as she did with Sabine. And Sabine had been right in knowing that there was something which she had concealed. It was this—that in the months spent in the Tunisian villa there had been moments when she fancied that her eyes were taking on the dumb, pleading look which had always been in the near-sighted eyes of Clarence. The memory came back to her now across all the years. He had beseeched her with his eyes for all that she could not give him, pled with her not to escape forever from his life. And what was his poor, pale love in comparison with this wild, devouring emotion that sometimes took possession of her? For Clarence was not dead yet; he still had the power of returning to her. The past, which she had tried always to forget, arose again and again. She even wondered sometimes what had become of poor, forlorn Mr. Wyck and those other figures, so dim now that they seemed to belong to some earlier life. She could see Clarence once more . . . his pale, tormented eyes, his dumb adoration. It seemed to her that it was this adoration, this abasement which had been the essence of his whole existence.

No, she could not face such a thing!

Hansi, lying by the fire, watched her with his gold eyes while she paced up and down in wild agitation.

It was intolerable, loathsome, impossible that she should ever become possessed . . . possessed as Clarence had once been. She had been free always and it was too late now to change.

She had dinner alone in the same room where she had talked with Sabine, and when she had finished she sent for Victorine and told her that she was leaving the house. If there were any messages (for she knew well enough that there would be, perhaps cable after cable) they could be forwarded to the Rue Raynouard where she would be with Madame de Cyon. She was returning now to Lily, as she had done so many times before.

A little before midnight she drove away for the last time from the house in the Avenue du Bois, having spent but ten hours of her life within its flamboyant walls. And by the time the taxicab arrived at Lily's quiet, unobtrusive door her nerves were in a state of panic. She was filled with a dim sense of fleeing from some invisible, nameless thing as she had fled when a child through the dark halls of the house in Sycamore Street.

Lily and Hattie were waiting her, though she had sent no word of her coming. They were not surprised. There had been a cable from Tunis addressed to her, which they had opened and read,

"Sail tomorrow. R. C."

After she had told them, abruptly and without explanation, that she had left Callendar forever, she locked herself in her room and looked at the cable again and again to make certain that she was not out of her senses. She had told him that she would stay at the house in the Avenue du Bois. How could he have known that she would escape so soon from that opulent, fleshly house to the refuge of Lily?

No, it was unbearable. One could not live with a man like that.

65

AS the weeks passed in the quiet of the big house in the Rue Raynouard, they did not annoy her. To Hattie, Ellen's mood—her sulkiness, her silence—had a familiarity that was comforting; Ellen had been silent and sulky as a girl, she had behaved thus throughout that last happy winter before she escaped forever in company with poor Clarence. Hattie, in the midst of caring for a big house which ran much better when left to itself, went about mothering Ellen, respecting her silences, happy that for a little time her daughter seemed to have some need of her.

And Lily . . . Lily was far too wise ever to pry into the affairs of any one. In time, she knew, everything became clear, everything would stand revealed. Besides there had been for her no element of surprise in the whole trouble. She had known men like Callendar; indeed, it was men like Callendar who had always been attracted to her (save only in the case of de Cyon with whom it was not a question of love). What puzzled her was the reason why a man like Callendar—a man capable of such intense passion, a man of such fascination and elusive masculinity —should ever have loved so persistently and in the end married a creature so independent, so fierce-willed as her cousin. One might as well have expected César to love Ellen; and César had hated her always with a passion which she returned. The whole affair had been wrong since the beginning . . . perverse and unnatural. Any one could have known that they would be unhappy. And in a quiet, gentle fashion Lily found satisfaction in the spectacle of a humbled, unhappy Ellen married to a man who was a match for her, perhaps more than a match—a man who stood aside and watched her coldly in the way she had watched people all her life. It was almost as if the first poor, pale husband, whom Lily had met so long ago on the crowded train bound for the Town, was by some turn of circumstances being avenged.

Callendar, she knew, had come to the house not once but several times. He had talked with Ellen while they walked up and down the long garden beneath the mottled plane trees. She had watched them, secretly, wondering at the calm fashion in which they talked and at the inhuman hardness of Ellen. (She herself would have weakened and yielded long ago.) And each time he had gone away defeated, she knew, for the time being.

And then, slowly, bit by bit, the story came to her. She heard it even before Hattie heard it, how they had quarreled and how he had even gone so far as to strike her in a sudden gust of wild and unsuspected anger. She heard too of the women in the hotel at Tunis and of another woman, the wife of a French official living in a villa near them. Ellen had seen them walking together one night when she had stolen from the house to follow him.

"Think of it!" she cried to Lily. "I descended even to that . . . even to spying. Oh, he is a monster. You have no idea the sort of a man he is."

And yet (thought Lily) she loves him, or she would not feel so violently. And Lily *did* have an idea what sort of a man he was; she knew far more than Ellen imagined, for she was a woman of great experience, however discreet she may have been. That was perhaps the reason why every one bore their confidences to Lily first of all.

"And yet," continued Ellen as they sat late one night in the long drawing-room, "there are times when for a moment I can see how perfect a husband, how perfect a lover he could be, if he but chose to be. Once we could have been happy, for I was the stronger then and I know that I could have changed him. He is in love with me in a queer fashion. He has behaved like this with no other woman. . . . I am certain of it. . . . I could have changed him once, but it is too late now." And she, Ellen Tolliver, began to weep. "I am crying," she said, "because I have missed so much. I know that I shall never have another chance at happiness . . . of that sort."

She is crying (thought Lily) because she is a child who wants everything in the world, a child who will never be satisfied.

"None of us," she said aloud, "has everything. No one life is long enough to encompass it all. We can only try to have as much as possible."

She might have added, "You have fame and wealth. Is not that enough?" But she kept silent because she knew that Ellen had taken account of these things and would, just then, have given them all in exchange for this other happiness. For Ellen could not bear the thought of having failed.

Lily was busy too in those days with her own affairs, for in the collapse of de Cyon's party she found it necessary to entertain, to go about, to meet new people, to make new friends. She gave dinner after dinner and invited Americans who might be of importance to her husband; and because she was a woman whose life existed only in relation to the men who surrounded her, she did it all gladly, though it ran against all the indolence of her nature. It would help de Cyon and it would be good too for Jean. Lily, who no longer put up bulwarks against age—Lily, who had allowed the gray to come into her tawny hair, was stepping aside to make way for others.

In her tactful fashion she managed somehow to coördinate all the coming and going in the big house. When Ellen told her about the baby, she insisted that it be born in her house.

"It is the center of the family now and it has been my home for so long that I seem always to have lived here. It will be no trouble to any one. We will move de Cyon's books out of the pavilion and turn it over to you. Jean used it for his own when he came home from school. De Cyon will not mind. He can have a room on the second floor."

Indeed the news of the child altered the life of the entire household until the preparations took on the proportions of a royal arrival. Callendar sent flowers daily (which Ellen could not be forever sending away) and she accepted them because the child was his too. This thought saddened her and made her gentle with him when he came sometimes to call, respectfully, with a new tenderness of manner which she had never suspected. It might have weakened her will in the end and defeated her if she had not understood, as Sabine had done before her, that it was born in reality of his own vanity. He was being gentle with her now because she was the potential mother of *his* child, of *his* heir. At other times it maddened her to think that he should treat her gently and tenderly because there was the child to be considered. He had never thought of her at all. There had never been any real tenderness. She had suspicions too that it was only another way of attacking her will.

As for Hattie, the news appeared to change the whole tone and color of her life. Besides running the house she began to fuss and fidget over her Ellen. She recommended this and that; she was always advising her on the subject of prenatal influence. "You must remember," she said, "that I planned you should be a musician long before you were born. You can mold the whole life of the child."

She did not care whether the child was a girl or a boy. It was enough that she was to have a grandchild.

On the other side of the Atlantic, old Thérèse received only the calamitous news that there had been a separation. Instantly she had wound up her affairs, closed the house on Murray Hill and engaged a cabin. There was no time to be lost. Richard and Ellen must be reconciled at once. They must be brought together again. If this last chance failed, it would be the end of everything. There would be no more Callendars and no more men to care for the Callendar fortune and the ancient banking firm of Leopopulos et Cie. In an agony of uncertainty, the fat, bedizened, energetic old woman crossed the Atlantic and rushed by motor from Havre to Paris. In her heart, she had known all along that the marriage could not endure. She had played all her stakes on the chance that it would endure long enough to accomplish her purpose.

Still in ignorance of the prospects, she arrived in Paris late in the afternoon and went straight to the house in the Avenue du Bois where her son waited her in the small sitting room. Black and untidy, with her precious reticule swung over her fat arm, she closed the door behind her and faced him in a fury. She did not greet him. She did not even wait for him to speak.

"What is it you have done now? I know it is your fault. You have ruined everything." Her beady eyes glittered and she panted for breath as she flung herself down, thinking "After I work for years to accomplish this marriage."

He smiled at her. "I have done nothing," he said. "I do not know why she ran away."

But she knew he was lying. "You *do* know," she cried. "You *do* know. It is another woman. . . . Why can't you leave women alone? You," she mocked, "who thought yourself so wise, so clever with women, have ruined everything again." Her fury mounted and she began to shriek at him incoherently like a mad woman. "She will never divorce you as Sabine did. . . . Of what use are you to any one? Who would regret it if you died? You are worthless. . . . You are a waster . . . a devil." She beat her reticule with her fat bejeweled hands and gasped for breath. "I spend all my life caring for your fortune and you only waste it and run after women. . . . What sort of a man are you? You cannot even give me an heir. . . . There is a curse on you."

Callendar stood by the open window looking out, his back the picture of a cold and maddening indifference. It must have been clear to him that she cared more for her fortune than for her son. Her fortune . . . It was the one thing left her now, and what could she do with it? She could not take it into her grave. She could not even rest there knowing that it was being wasted and would in the end be broken up into small bits and distributed among obscure cousins she had never seen . . . the fortune which her family, the family of the green-eyed old banker of Pera, had built up over centuries. . . .

"Does all that mean nothing to you? Does nothing have any meaning for you?" she cried.

They were in open warfare now, the mother and the son, and after all that had been said nothing would ever again be the same between them. They stood there naked in combat, stripped of all pretense and intriguing.

Presently the old woman became more calm and in a low voice, that was strangely soft after all her harsh catalogue of accusations, murmured, as if speaking to herself, "I do not see how you can be the son of your father. . . . If I did not *know* . . . If I did not *know,* I could never believe it."

And then Callendar turned from the window and looked at her with an insolent smile.

"Where is Ellen?" she asked. "Where is she?"

"She is in the Rue Raynouard with Madame de Cyon. If you had waited," he spoke slowly now, with a tantalizing slowness. "If you had given me a moment or allowed me to speak, I should have told you. . . . Ellen is with child."

For a moment the old woman, gasping, peered at him in silence, and then she began to weep. It was the first time that any one had ever seen tears flow from those shrewd, glittering eyes. She took her reticule and pressed it against her breast as if it had been a child. "My little boy!" she said, through her tears. "My little boy . . . My Richard . . . Forgive me . . . Everything then is saved." Brightening, she continued, "And it will be a boy, *hein?* I have prayed, I have burned candles . . . I must go to Madame de Thèbes and find out for certain. I cannot wait. . . . I cannot wait. . , . She can tell everything by reading the crystal. I cannot wait."

Still clutching her reticule, she rose and, drying her tears on a dirty handkerchief of exquisite texture, she waddled to the door. As she opened it, the plump figure of Victorine vanished around a corner of the great hall. She had heard everything this time, for Thérèse and her son spoke French when they were together.

In the drawing-room at the Rue Raynouard, Ellen sat with her mother and Lily having tea when Thérèse was announced. To them she said, "If you don't mind, I'd best see her alone. . . . I don't know what it means. She has come perhaps to persuade me to return. She won't give up easily."

So Lily and Hattie left and a moment later at the foot of the stairs the figure of old Thérèse appeared, hot and untidy, peering with her eyes squinted, in search of her daughter-in-law. For a time Ellen waited in the cool shadows, watching. It was incredible (she thought) how Thérèse had changed. She was a figure of fun as she stood there, clutching her precious reticule, disheveled and bizarre, peering into the dim room. This was not the eccentric, worldly Thérèse of the house on Murray Hill. It was an old harridan, obsessed by a single idea—her fortune and what would become of it.

"Mrs. Callendar," she said softly, moving forward.

"Ah, there you are . . . My dear! My darling!" She waddled toward her daughter-in-law and embraced her.

(She has taken to oiling her hair, thought Ellen. She will be running a fruit stand soon.)

"I have heard the news. . . . I have heard the news. . . . You are to have a leetle baby."

She sat down, her fat old face all soft and beaming now, her diamonds glittering dimly as they had always glittered.

"Did Richard tell you?" asked Ellen.

"I only landed yesterday. . . . I motored all the way from Le Havre. I did not know the news then. I only knew that you had run away from him. What is it? What has happened?"

Ellen, watching her, knew that in the recesses of her Oriental mind the old woman thought her a fool for running away. Thérèse believed that any woman could make a good wife. It was a woman's duty to put up with anything, as Sabine had done until she was thrust aside as barren and useless. As Sabine had said, Thérèse could have protected herself from a man like Callendar. She had been born old and wise, expecting nothing. She could not argue with Thérèse. The old woman would have thought her crazy.

"I have left him," she said. "I shall not go back."

"Perhaps the baby . . ." And Thérèse put her head on one side in a queer foreign fashion and smirked. "Perhaps the baby will change things." Then she leaned forward and patted Ellen's hand. "Never mind, we won't speak of it now, my darling. . . . It would disturb you . . . in your condition." She kept returning again and again to the idea of the baby.

Then, settling back in her chair, she took a biscuit from the reticule and began to nibble it. "We need not worry now," she continued. "To think of it . . . a baby . . . a grandson."

Ellen could not resist the perverse temptation. It was this old woman who, after all, had forced the marriage. She said, "Perhaps it will be a granddaughter."

But Thérèse was confident. "No, I have said prayers. I have burned candles. I have done everything. . . . I have paid an astrologer . . . I have overlooked nothing. I am sure it will be a grandson. It is all arranged. You have made me happy, my child. I must arrange to reward you."

(So Ellen had made two women fantastically happy . . . her own mother and old Thérèse.)

"I will make a settlement on you. I will give you a present . . . a magnificent present." And she began to finger her reticule again as if she might draw from it a bag of great gold pieces. "I will send to-morrow for a lawyer. We will arrange it."

And then, like Hattie, she began to offer piece after piece of advice, bits of good sense and weird snatches of ancient, tribal superstition. Ellen must do thus and so to make certain the child was a boy. She must eat this and that. And she must have the proper doctors . . . the very best. They must take no risks. "I will pay for everything. . . ." she repeated. "You can charge it all to me. What is a little money to Thérèse Callendar?"

And at last she left, still excited and chattering. At the foot of the stairs, she turned, "I am going now to Madame de Thèbes to find out if it will be a boy. . . . But I am certain . . . I am sure." And she waddled up the long stairs and climbed again into the motor which drove her away on a round of fortune tellers.

The next morning she returned bringing her lawyer and with Ellen they sat for an hour in de Cyon's study arranging the settlement. It was shrewdly managed. Thérèse made a fine gift, but with many strings to it. Ellen was not to be allowed to touch the principal. The income would be hers whether the child was a boy or a girl. If it was a boy the principal would go to him on the death of his mother; if a girl it would return to the estate. The money, whatever became of it, was never to escape from the Callendar-Leopopulos fortune; but the income was large enough to support Ellen in comfort for the rest of her life. She accepted it because it made her position impregnable; it protected her, it gave her possession over the boy (for she too was certain it would be a boy) to do with as she saw fit. And she need never again know the old terror of being poor.

It was not until two days later, when she examined the settlement carefully, that she discovered a part of it was in real estate and included the flamboyant Babylon Arms, fallen now upon evil days, grown shabby and no longer respectable. The house where poor Clarence had lived until he destroyed himself was to be the property of her child . . . a child whose father was Richard Callendar.

Slowly the whole life in the big house came to revolve about Ellen and the coming child. June passed and July. The gentle de Cyon was moved with all his books and files and papers from

the pavilion into a room on the second floor. (No man save
one with the resistance of old Gramp had any chance in this
household of women.) Thérèse, untidy, her eyes brighter and
brighter with the reassurance given her by Madame de Thèbes
and a dozen other soothsayers, came daily and bore Ellen away
to a variety of doctors. Callendar came sometimes on calls which
grew more and more formal as time passed; and Sabine called
and sent baskets of fruit. Musicians, actresses, composers passed
in and out. Through it all, Hattie moved in her triumphant
way, older now but scarcely less subdued than she had been in
the days when she sat darning, surrounded by her family in the
shabby sitting room on Sycamore street. In Hattie there were
elements of the eternal which took no account of changes in the
life about her. It is possible that nothing in the whole spectacle
seemed in the least strange to her. She appeared to accept its
absurdity as a matter of course . . . the presence of Lily's French
husband, of Jean who had had no father, the glittering dinners
given in the Louis Quinze dining room which she never attended,
the comings and goings of the untidy old woman who ate biscuits
out of a handbag, the visits of the fastidious and fashionable
Sabine, and even the occasional calls of Callendar himself, a man
whom she regarded as a sinister and immoral creature, who
would have ruined the life of any one of less character than a
child of hers. She was busy. She had no time for memories.
She had no longer to invent tasks for herself, and so she was
happy. She was caught up again in the wild scurry and confusion of life.

Only Lily and old Gramp took the affair with calmness, the one
gently with the air of knowing that in all the confusion some one
must keep her head and smooth out all the little difficulties which
arose from so strange a mélange of characters, the old man with
an indifference which placed small value upon the arrival of one
more child in a world already too well filled, a world in which
there could no longer be any solitude save in one's own soul. He
came and went as he chose through the garden gate opening into

the Rue de Passy, encountering on his way now Sabine, now old
Thérèse, now de Cyon, now a doctor or two, all of whom regarded him with the air of looking upon a specter. It was impossible to believe that so old a man could still be alive. He
passed them all without so much as a glance, absorbed always in
his search for the youth which had escaped him forever. In him
too there were elements of the eternal, which nothing could alter
or change in any way. To Gramp, Sycamore Street and the Rue
Raynouard were in the end the same.

And then one morning a taxicab appeared at the door and dis-
charged into the midst of the confusion a triumphant Rebecca
Schönberg, bustling and with a new light in her ferrety eyes,
her mind full of schemes for fresh triumphs and new concert
tours; for the news of the débâcle had come to her through the
gentle and forgotten Schneidermann in Vienna where she had
gone to visit Uncle Otto and Aunt Lina. Already, before even
she had seen Ellen, she had started under way news of the return
of Lilli Barr to the concert stage. (She knew well enough that
Ellen would never return to Callendar. She knew that in the end
he had defeated himself. He had hung himself with his own
rope; but he had done it so much sooner than she expected.)

She bribed Augustine to let her know when Callendar came to
the house, and when he arrived she took care that he did not escape
without seeing her. She met him at the foot of the stairs. She
did not flaunt her triumph; she was far too subtle for that. The
same blood flowed in her veins and she understood how best to
mock him.

She said, "Ah! It's you. I hadn't expected to see *you* here."
And holding out her hand with the air of a mourner, she murmured with sad looks and a bogus sincerity, "I'm *so* sorry it
turned out badly. I had hoped you would be successful this
time. I wanted you to know that I am full of sympathy. . . .
But, of course, Ellen could not have done otherwise."

And so she left him nothing to say. She sent him away,
bedraggled and a little ridiculous, in defeat; for by the light in

her eye he could not fail to see that she was jeering him. He had not subdued Lilli Barr. She belonged once more to Rebecca and to the world. And in the end it was women who defeated him —women who had always been his obsession, the women who surrounded Ellen—Lily and Hattie and Rebecca, the subtle Sabine and even Thérèse with her gift that made Ellen unpregnably secure. He had not broken her spirit, for he had never possessed her even for a moment; it was her awareness which had baffled him, standing like a wall across his path.

The perverse experiment had failed; there had not even been much pleasure in it. Youth lay behind him. What lay ahead? As he stepped from Lily's door there were lines in the handsome, insolent face which no amount of exercise or massage could ever smooth away. . . . He was growing old. It was as if these women had banded together and, placing Ellen in their midst, now mocked him. . . . Women . . . Women . . . Women . . . One could come to hate them all in the end.

So Rebecca too, in the wholly false supposition that she had come for a brief visit, was given a room that opened off the gallery and so joined all the colony which centered about Ellen in a world founded upon dividends from the black Mills in the Midlands.

And Ellen waited, growing more and more calm as her time approached. She found pleasure in the fantastic spectacle of Lily's house. She was the center of it, and the old intoxication, so familiar to Lilli Barr, began slowly to claim her again.

66

THE thing happened on a hot breathless night in September when the shimmer of heat dying away with the fall of evening left the garden cool and dark save for the light that streamed from the windows of the long drawing room and from a single window of the white pavilion. The Eng-

lish nurse was there, waiting, and the doctor had come and
gone to return in a little while. Everything went well, save
that the patient (so the nurse explained to Hattie and Thérèse)
was not accepting the ordeal in the proper mood. She had insisted
upon playing bridge, when she should have been walking up
and down, up and down, to hasten the birth of the child. She
sat now in the drawing-room at a table with Lily, Jean and
Rebecca, angry at not being allowed to smoke, desperate that
she had no control over what was happening to her. She sat,
holding her cards stiffly before her, clad in a peignoir of coral
silk, her black hair drawn tightly back as she had worn it at her
concerts.

"Two spades," she said, and glared at Rebecca when the latter
doubled. There was a dew of perspiration on her high smooth
forehead and she bit her lips from time to time. She was magnificent and dominating (thought Lily). Really it was an amazing
kind of fierce beauty.

In one corner de Cyon, ousted from the pavilion, sat reading
his foreign newspapers—the threads which kept him in touch with
the world of foreign politics. They lay spread out before
him . . . *Le Journal de Genève, Il Seccolo* of Milan, *La Tribuna*
of Rome, the *London Post,* the *London Times,* the *New York
Times, Le Figaro, L'Echo de Paris, Le Petit Parisien, Le Matin,
L'Œuvre* . . . in a neat pile, from which he lifted them calmly
in turn, to read them through and clip now here, now there, with
the long silver scissors a bit of news, a king's remarks, a prime minister's speech or the leader of some Socialist editor. Ensconced behind the gilt table, he appeared cool and aloof, with his white hair
and his pink face. What was going on almost at his side had no
interest for him. His first wife had been barren and his second
he had married too late. He clipped and clipped, the lean scissors
snipping their way through words in Italian, Spanish, German, French and English. Snip . . . snip . . . snip . . . they
ran. . . .

A dozen feet from him and well away from the bridge table

where at the command of Ellen the others played in a disheartened fashion, Hattie and Thérèse sat side by side, the one knitting energetically at a blue and white carriage robe, the other nibbling at a biscuit. They both waited . . . they both fidgeted, not daring to risk an explosion from Ellen. She was not to be crossed at this moment.

"When Richard was born," Thérèse was saying . . . "I suffered for twenty-six hours . . . but they do things better nowadays."

And then Hattie, in a low voice lest she disturb the bridge players, "I'm not sure that nature's way isn't the best. I don't believe in hurrying things." And then in the hot silence, the click, click, click of her knitting needles.

"She ought to be walking up and down," said Thérèse anxiously. "Do you think we ought to speak to her?"

"It will do no good. . . . In a moment she won't be able to sit there playing bridge. She'll have to walk up and down. . . . I remember when my last child was born, the doctor said . . ."

And so they went on, turning over and over again incidents appropriate to the occasion, two prospective grandmothers, each of them passionately interested in what lay ahead. Thérèse, despite her swarthy skin, looked pale, and her fat hand trembled as she nibbled the biscuit. . . . Hattie only knit more and more furiously, raising her head from time to time to glance at her daughter who sat like a Spartan playing with Jean as a partner and winning steadily from Lily and Rebecca.

Snip! Snip! Snip! ran the silver scissors. Click! Click! Click! the knitting needles. Hattie halted for a moment to wipe her red, hot face. And then the cool, desperate voice of Ellen again, saying, "Five tricks and thirty-six in honors."

"It's our rubber," said Jean, white and nervous with the strain. And in his blue eyes the old light of admiration appeared. Ellen had always been like this even in the days when she had taken him, a little boy, to the Bois.

It was ten o'clock when Ellen at last pushed back her chair

and rose as the doctor entered the room. "I will walk for a time," she said and went with him out on to the terrace.

In their corner Hattie and old Thérèse grew silent and fell simply to watching for the figures of Ellen, in the coral peignoir, the doctor and the black dog, to pass and repass the tall windows. Jean smoked and quarreled in a low voice with Rebecca, and Lily going over to the side of de Cyon sat down and fell to reading the lace-like remnants of the newspapers that her husband tossed aside with the regularity of a machine. Presently, Augustine, her peasant's face beaming with the significance of the occasion, brought champagne which all save Hattie, who refused it sternly, drank against the heat.

The sounds in the distant street began to die away and the echo of the boat whistles on the Seine grew fainter and fainter. On the terrace Ellen and the doctor were joined by a second nurse, still in her cape, who had come in by the garden side.

And at half-past ten Callendar appeared at the foot of the long stairs, looking worn and old, but cool despite all the heat. At his entrance Hattie ignored him, Thérèse nodded, and the others, save de Cyon who did not notice him at all, bowed without any trace of warmth. He was an enemy; it was clear that they looked upon him thus, even old Thérèse whose only interest lay now in the child. He seated himself and fell to talking with Lily, who could not for long be disagreeable to any man, and presently Ellen appeared in one of the windows and said, "Rebecca, you and Jean play the piano . . . I can't bear to look at you all sitting like statues." And then she beckoned to Callendar who rose and went over to her.

As he left the room, Rebecca watched him with a queer expression of apprehension in her eyes. She did not trust him. He might turn the circumstances to his own advantage. He might cast a spell over Ellen at the moment when she was least able to resist. With Jean she went reluctantly to the piano where they fell to playing with four hands and with a mathematical precision they had long since perfected a variety of music hall songs. And as she played she stole a glance now and then over her shoulders at the tall windows past which Ellen and Callendar moved with a clock-like regularity. But she was not the only one who watched. There was Hattie too and even old Thérèse. Each of them desired from Ellen a different thing, and each of them was resolved to have her own will in the matter.

Outside the windows the husband and the wife with the black dog at their heels walked up and down while Ellen, looking tall and pale and desperate, talked earnestly.

"The child," she said firmly, "is to be mine. I will fight until the end for that. I have made up my mind. I will not have him go to you. . . . You are not fit."

He said nothing in reply. It was not possible to argue at such a time. She was fighting now, as he had always done, unscrupulously, to achieve what she desired. They turned at the end of the terrace and moved back once more past the windows where Rebecca and Hattie and Thérèse kept peering out. It was (thought Ellen in a peaceful moment) like bearing one's child in public . . . as the French Queens had done, with a whole crowd looking on. . . . (But she must bring her mind back to the business at hand.)

"And if anything happens to me," she said to Callendar, "if I should die and the child live . . . he is to be brought up by my mother. I have talked to my lawyers. It is possible to arrange all that. There is plenty of evidence against you . . . even a French court—" She gasped for breath and turned again. "Even a French court would uphold me in that. Besides Rebecca has promised me that she will carry on the fight. I tell you all this, because I want you to know that I am finished forever." She was walking rapidly now and made a sudden passionate gesture in the direction of the windows. "Rebecca need not look at us so anxiously. There is no question about it. . . . And I will not leave a child of mine in such an atmosphere as you and your mother are able to provide." She drew another quick, sharp breath and added, "I gave you every chance . . . and you were a rotter always. I loved you and I would love you still if I thought there was any chance of redemption . . . but there is none."

And then, before turning toward the pavilion, she said, "You did not win in the end, you see. . . . It was I who won . . . I and Sabine too. . . . And I will go on fighting, even if I should die. It has all been arranged. And now," she said, dismissing him, "will you tell my mother to come with me to the pavilion? I want none of the others . . . only her."

So it was Callendar who summonded Hattie at the moment Ellen needed her most. In the end she belonged to Hattie alone of all those people who sat waiting . . . Hattie, whose whole life had been concerned with love and birth and death.

When they had gone away, Callendar sat on the stone balustrade smoking in silence, conquered now beyond all doubt. He had been dismissed once and for all. Ellen would return now into the world out of which she had come to him . . . a world in which she belonged to Rebecca and her public. Perhaps as he sat there in the hot, still air, waiting for his child to be born, he knew the last of his adventures to which there was any savor had come to an end.

Through the windows he saw de Cyon rise presently and go up the long stairs. He saw Lily (a fascinating woman, he thought, who must have been very beautiful in her youth) talking to his mother who still nibbled at her biscuit. Jean and Rebecca had ceased their music and sat now playing double patience with a fierce, unnatural absorption.

Augustine came in presently with a message. Mrs. Cane Callendar (Sabine) would like to know if there was any news. She went away again with the message Lily gave her: Everything was going well, but there was no news yet.

They were all waiting, waiting, waiting. . . .

Callendar held tight the heavy collar of Hansi, who squirmed and moaned pitifully because he could not follow his mistress.

Rebecca found him there when at last she tired of her game and wandered out into the garden to smoke. She passed him without speaking and as he looked after her, he saw that she had taken to walking round and round the white pavilion as if she had set herself to guard it from him.

Presently he returned to the drawing-room and opening another bottle of champagne, sat silently by the side of Lily, who alone behaved with any kindliness toward him. Old Thérèse watched him, desperately, as the time drew nearer and nearer. She was pale now with terror lest Madame de Thèbes had been wrong. If the child were a girl it would be the end of everything. . . . She had even stopped nibbling her biscuits. The reticule had fallen to the floor. Her fat body rested on the edge of her chair . . . tense and strained in her passionate anxiety.

The whole room, the whole house, the whole garden stood breathless in the heat with the terrible stillness that surrounded the waiting. . . .

Somewhere in the direction of the Trocadéro a clock struck midnight, booming faintly, each stroke hanging on the hot still air to confuse the stroke which followed. The sound swam in the big room. Callendar rose and went again into the garden, into a distant corner well away from Rebecca whose progress round and round the pavilion was marked by the tiny glow at the end of her cigarette.

Thérèse, unable to bear the silence any longer, rose too and went out onto the terrace to watch the light in the pavilion. A breeze came up and the leaves of the plane trees fell to rustling. Lily and Jean talked together quietly in the corner by de Cyon's desk. From the window on the second floor which opened into Gramp's room there was a light still burning. Rebecca, looking up at it from her vigil, saw the figure of the old man show black and thin against the glow, as he leaned out and peered over the garden.

An hour passed and the distant clock struck one. A bell sounded faintly in the house and Augustine appeared. It was Mrs. Cane Callendar once more. Was there any news?

"She must have a violent curiosity," thought Lily, "to be staying up all night."

Thérèse, in the black shadow of the house, began to pray, as if it were still not too late for a miracle. She had never been religious, but like Voltaire she believed in trying everything. . . . After she had prayed for a time she grew hungry, took another biscuit from the reticule and went into the drawing-room for a glass of champagne. So it happened that before she was able to return to her watching and praying the door of the pavilion opened and the tiny lights that in the darkness marked the positions of Callendar and Rebecca moved hastily in its direction.

In the doorway stood Hattie, larger than either of them, red-faced, triumphant and with a wild light in her eyes. As first Rebecca and then Callendar emerged from the shadows, she said, "It is all over. . . . Everything is fine. . . . It is a boy!"

The news was borne by Rebecca into the drawing-room where Thérèse in her excitement put down her glass of champagne into sheer space instead of on the table, leaving it to break and spill its contents over the Aubusson carpet. On short fat legs she waddled through the window to the pavilion where Hattie, who had in the excitement of the moment forgotten her hatred, was delivering to Callendar a detailed and vivid account of the accouchement.

Thérèse forgot even her English. "Eet ees a boy," she squealed. "Eet ees a boy. God is good. He has answered my prayers . . . and what is it he weighs?"

"Seven pounds," replied Hattie. "A fine baby, though none of my children weighed less than ten."

A kind of hysteria swept them all. The waiting was over. Thérèse had an heir, Hattie had a grandchild and Callendar, at last, a son whom he would perhaps never possess as his own.

From a window above their heads, the sound of a cracked shrill voice shot at them.

"Is the child born? What is it?" . . . And then with irritation. "For Heaven's sake!"

It was Gramp. Lily answered him, and the bony head was withdrawn again, the light extinguished and the room left to silence.

They must all see the child. They must come to the very door of the pavilion where Hattie, holding them at bay like a royal nurse exhibiting the heir to the populace, thrust toward them a lusty, tomato-colored child which appeared to cry, "Ala-as! Ala-as! Ala-as!" over and over again, monotonously. She allowed no one to touch it, not even old Thérèse who, kept at bay by the threatening manner of the royal nurse, bent over it murmuring, "The darling! Isn't he beautiful? The precious darling! *Qu'il est mignon!* And he looks for all the world like Richard, the precious darling."

"You can't tell what he looks like," said Hattie with a savage indignation. "That's nonsense! You can't tell for a long time!"

Callendar, thrust aside by this regiment of women, regarded his son with a faint light in his gray eyes. He said nothing. He waited. Perhaps for an instant he wished that he might see Ellen, as a father, a husband should have done. But he was given no chance, for Hattie said, "She wants to see Lily. The doctor says she may see no one else."

Ensconced in the pavilion Hattie became a despot, a tyrant. The child at the moment it entered the world became a part of her family, swallowed up by it remorselessly.

Inside the pavilion, a pale, handsome Ellen looked up at Lily and murmured, smiling a little, "You must call Sabine. Tell her that she was right. Just tell I am a good gambler. I have been successful. Old Thérèse is satisfied."

One by one they drifted away until only Callendar was left sitting in the darkness, smoking and thinking. A little way off in the shadow where she could not be seen Rebecca waited too, watching him; and when at length he rose and went out of the gate into the Rue de Passy, she followed and stood looking after him as he climbed the slope and disappeared around a corner beneath the glare of a street lamp. He seemed not so tall and not so formidable as he had once been. The fine shoulders sagged a little; and Rebecca, looking after him, knew whither he was bound. For she had taken the trouble to find out. She had herself hunted down his infidelity. Ellen, she knew, would never forgive him and she (Rebecca) had the proof. It was the seal upon his defeat.

And as she stood there she looked not down the Rue de Passy but down the corridor of the years, and at the end she saw a defeated and bitter sensualist buying with money what had once come to him through beauty and charm and the glow of youth.

She closed the gate and turned back into the garden. The dawn had begun to filter in through the trees and to turn the pavilion from gray to white. To-morrow she must begin to work on the plans for Ellen's return. It must be triumphant, spectacular, worthy of such an artist as Lilli Barr. For Ellen belonged again to Rebecca Schönberg.

67

O N a night, five months after the breathless waiting in the garden of the house in the Rue Raynouard, Lilli Barr, under the management of the energetic and now happy Rebecca, returned in triumph. She played with the Pasdeloup Orchestra in the Theatre Champs-Elysées, a new concerto written by one of the young composers who came so often to disturb the quiet of Lily's house. From the great spaces of the dim theatre they saw her enter, making her way slowly and with a great dignity through the players of the orchestra; and as she passed them, one by one the musicians appeared to draw from her a queer inex-

plicable fire, a new, strange vitality. She was dressed as she
had been on that first night in New York—in crimson velvet and
diamonds with her black hair drawn back tightly from the pale,
handsome face.

At sight of her, a faint hush fell upon the audience and then
the slow, subdued murmur of admiration. The white faces, row
upon row, extended far back into the dim reaches of the theatre
until at length they became blurred and misty, indistinguishable.
It was all more than she had imagined in the days when she had
played savagely and sullenly in the shabby room on Sycamore
Street.

The conductor rose, a black slim figure against the lights of
the orchestra. He raised his baton and Lilli Barr touched the
first chords of the barbaric concerto. There was no doubt any
longer. She reached out in some mysterious fashion and took
possession of the great audience. She was more magnificent
than she had ever been, for in this performance there was no
longer any trickery. It was the music of a great artist.

The orchestra swept into a great crescendo, triumphant, overwhelming, above which the sound of the piano rose clear and
crystalline. . . .

Afterward in the big reception room lined with the mirrors
used by the dancers of the ballet before a performance, she waited
to receive all those who came to welcome her back into their world.
There were actresses and millionaires, demi-mondaines and composers, musicians and painters, the Duc de Guermantes and M.
de Charlus, patrons of art and adventuresses who came and went
under the brilliant, triumphant glitter of Rebecca's ferrety eyes.
And last of all there was Thérèse, untidy and covered with diamonds, and her friend, Ella Nattatorini, and Sabine who had in
tow Janey Champion whom, as one of the Virgins, Ellen had
seen so long ago through the crevice of the lacquered screen in
the Callendar drawing-room. Janey was breathless and excited

now, her hair all in disarray; for Sabine had kept her promise and Janey, for the first time in all her forty-six barren years, had escaped and was seeing life.

Ellen received them all with something of the old savor of triumph, but it was not the same. As Gramp had known, she had passed the peak of all her existence. All this array, this chatter, this confusion had begun a little to bore her.

And when they had gone she sat down to wait for Lily who had gone to the Gare de Lyon to speed a party consisting of Hattie and Old Gramp and the baby, Augustine and a gigantic Breton wet nurse with the preposterous name of Frédegonde, on their journey to the white villa in Nice where Lily had gone so many times while César was alive. For Lily, who had always followed the sun, no longer had any use for the white villa. Her place now was in damp and chilly Paris by the side of her husband.

Wrapped in her sable cloak, Ellen leaned back in her chair and closing her eyes, lost herself in this new and comfortable peace which had enveloped her since that hot terrible night in the pavilion. It seemed to her that she had never really rested before in all her life. It was over and finished. She had begun to forget a little what Callendar had been, to remember only what she desired to remember. She thought of him as dead; and it is true that the Callendar who came to her in the Babylon Arms had died long ago. She had done her duty, the one thing that she could have done, the one thing that had remained. She had borne a child and delivered it to Hattie for her own, to possess until she died or the child grew up and escaped from her. But by that time, Hattie would be so old that it would not greatly matter. She would be willing to sit by the fire in the long drawing-room as old Madame Gigon had done. And presently she rose and throwing off her cloak seated herself at the big piano in the corner of the room. She began to play softly, marvelously, and the wild savage fire which had persisted through everything began once more to shine in her

eyes. The Town, the black Mills, the Callendars, poor
Clarence and the green-eyed Mr. Wyck . . . all these were forgotten. She was freed at last of all those old bonds, possessed
now only by the beauty of the sounds she made. But, on the
high pinnacle she had built with her own hands, she was alone
. . . the woman whom Fergus had seen for a moment in a queer
flash of clairvoyance on the night of his death.

She was playing thus when Lily came in quietly to stand
listening in the shadows. . . .

The white villa, as old Madame Gigon had said, was not in
Nice proper but in Cimiez, high on the slope overlooking Villefranche and the Bay of Angels. To approach it one was forced
to descend from the carriage and climb past the statue of Queen
Victoria, carved in the manner of Thorvaldsen with an umbrella
in one hand and a reticule in the other—a reticule which Gramp
believed was the one (embroidered with a poodle-dog in gold
thread) which she had carried on the visit that was designed to
make Eugènie respectable in the eyes of royal Europe. Beyond
the Queen, there was a little flight of steps leading to a gateway
covered with bougainvillea and shaded by an ancient tree of mimosa.

It was up this exotic path that the little procession made its
way two days after Lily bade it farewell in the Gare de Lyon.
Jean went ahead and after him Hattie, with her grandson in
her arms, followed closely by The Everlasting, the gigantic,
abundant Frédegonde and her child. At the approach of evening
they were settled and under the mimosa tree Hattie sat by the
side of little Fergus, triumphant and content, singing him to sleep
as she had once done with her own Fergus. Nothing had changed,
for in Hattie there was a quality of the eternal concerned only
with love and birth and death.

While she sang thus in a low voice, The Everlasting, with a
great book under his arm, appeared in the doorway and moved
toward her. By the side of the baby he halted for a moment,

adjusted his spectacles and peered closely. He said nothing and presently his thin old lips expanded into a grin—a grin which said, "You've a lot of trouble before you, but what a good time you will have!" It was a grin, strange to say, of envy.

And as he stood there, he saw dimly the figure of a fat, untidy, bedizened old woman making her way painfully up the slope past the statue of Queen Victoria. It was Thérèse, who had altered the whole course of her journey to Trieste in order to see this precious, incomparable grandchild. Silently, lest she rouse the infant, she took her place by the side of the cradle. But little Fergus showed no signs of falling asleep. He was a fine baby. He lay looking up at them with the inscrutable gray eyes which had come from Callendar. But he had a fine pretty nose, that showed every sign of developing those handsome curves which gave Ellen and, before her, Old Julia Shane a proud look of domination. Presently in the hope of diverting him Thérèse bent down and took from her fat old fingers the carved emerald which, legend had it, had been saved during the Sack of Constantinople. The baby turned it round and round, peering at it with his wise gray eyes, until at last, letting it slip from his chubby fingers, he fell asleep under the jealous guard of the two powerful women who had called him into existence almost by the very force of will. They stood there in adoring silence, the one so primitive, the other so old and wise, that in the end they were very like each other.

Meanwhile The Everlasting, having turned his steps up the hill, sat now among the ruins of the ancient Roman arena overlooking the bay. As a substitute for his rocking chair, he had chosen an overturned stone and there he sat, his book open on his knees, peering out over the Mediterranean. After a time he took from his pocket an apple and bit into it with teeth that were still strong despite the approach of his hundredth birthday. It was a small bitter apple from Brittany, and not half so good as the apples which grew in the orchards of Ohio. Scornfully he spat the pieces from his mouth and, adjusting his spectacles once more, he bent over with a peering look and began again to read in triumph the Decline and Fall.

Ispswich, Mass.

August 6, 1923.

Cold Spring Harbor, Long Island.

May 15, 1925.